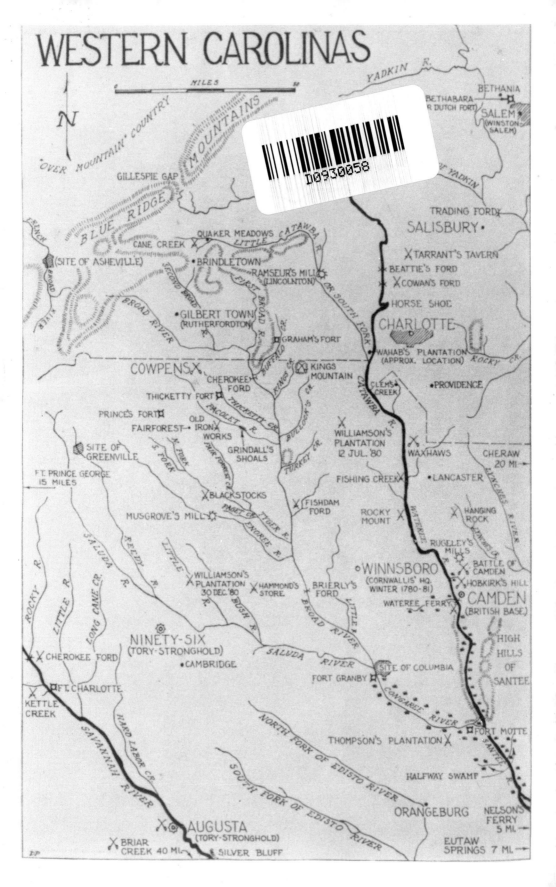

WESTERN CAROLINAS

N

MILES

YADKIN R.

"OVER MOUNTAIN" COUNTRY

MOUNTAINS

BETHANIA

BETHABARA
(OR DUTCH FORT)

SALEM
(WINSTON-SALEM)

GILLESPIE GAP

BLUE RIDGE

FRENCH BROAD RIVER

(SITE OF ASHEVILLE)

CANE CREEK ✗

QUAKER MEADOWS ✗

CATAWBA R.

LITTLE

SECOND BROAD R.

BRINDLETOWN

RAMSEUR'S MILL
(LINCOLNTON)

BROAD RIVER

GILBERT TOWN
(RUTHERFORDTON)

FIRST BROAD R.

BUFFALO CR.

GRAHAM'S FORT

YADKIN R.

TRADING FORD

SALISBURY ·

✗ TARRANT'S TAVERN

✗ BEATTIE'S FORD

✗ COWAN'S FORD

HORSE SHOE

CHARLOTTE

WAHAB'S PLANTATION
(APPROX. LOCATION)

ROCKY CR.

COWPENS ✗

CHEROKEE FORD

THICKETTY FORT

PRINCE'S FORT ⌂

FAIRFOREST ·

OLD IRON WORKS

THICKETTY CR.

KINGS CR.

KINGS MOUNTAIN

BULLOCK'S CR.

CATAWBA R.

CLEM'S CREEK

· PROVIDENCE

PACOLET R.

SITE OF GREENVILLE

FT. PRINCE GEORGE
15 MILES

N. FORK

S. FORK

FAIR FOREST CR.

GRINDALL'S SHOALS

TURKEY CR.

WILLIAMSON'S PLANTATION
12 JUL. '80

✗ WAXHAWS

CHERAW
20 MI.

✗ FISHING CREEK

· LANCASTER

LYNCHES RIVER

BLACKSTOCKS

MUSGROVE'S MILL

REEDY R.

LITTLE R.

PART OF ENOREE R.

FISHDAM FORD

ROCKY MOUNT ✗

WATEREE

HANGING ROCK

LONG OF BROAD R.

ROCKY R.

SALUDA R.

LITTLE R.

LONG CANE CR.

BUSH R.

WILLIAMSON'S PLANTATION
30 DEC. '80

HAMMOND'S STORE

BRIERLY'S FORD

BROAD RIVER

LITTLE

WINNSBORO
(CORNWALLIS' HQ.
WINTER 1780-81)

RUGELEY'S MILLS

BATTLE OF CAMDEN

HOBKIRK'S HILL

CAMDEN
(BRITISH BASE)

WATEREE FERRY

HIGH HILLS OF SANTEE

NINETY-SIX
(TORY-STRONGHOLD)

· CAMBRIDGE

SALUDA RIVER

SITE OF COLUMBIA

FORT GRANBY ⌂

CONGAREE RIVER

CHEROKEE FORD ✗

FT. CHARLOTTE ⌂

KETTLE CREEK

SAVANNAH RIVER

HARD LABOR CR.

NORTH FORK OF EDISTO RIVER

THOMPSON'S PLANTATION ✗

FORT MOTTE

SANTEE R.

HALFWAY SWAMP

ORANGEBURG

NELSON'S FERRY
5 MI. →

AUGUSTA
(TORY-STRONGHOLD)

SOUTH FORK OF EDISTO RIVER

✗ BRIAR CREEK 40 MI. →

· SILVER BLUFF

EUTAW SPRINGS 7 MI. →

EX Libris

RFAFabel
15 November 1987

Nathanael Greene (Mezzotint engraving by Valentin Greene, after C. W. Peale, Emmet Collection, Prints Division, The New York Public Library, Astor, Lenox and Tilden Foundation)

JOHN S. PANCAKE

This Destructive War

The British Campaign in the Carolinas

1780–1782

The University of Alabama Press

Copyright © 1985 by

The University of Alabama Press
University, Alabama 35486

Manufactured in the United States of America

The maps on the endpapers are reprinted
with permission from *The Encyclopedia of the American Revolution,*
by Mark Mayo Boatner III.
Copyright 1966. Published by David McKay Co., Inc.

Library of Congress Cataloging in Publication Data

Pancake, John S.
  "This destructive war."

  Bibliography: p.
  Includes index.
   1. South Carolina—History—Revolution, 1775–1783—
  Campaigns. 2. North Carolina—History—Revolution,
  1775–1783—Campaigns. I. Title.
  E263.S7P36 1985   973.3'3   83-5025
  ISBN 0-8173-0191-7

*This book is dedicated
to the memory
of the gallant men of
the Maryland and Delaware Continental Line.*

If you think ten thousand Men sufficient, send Twenty, if one Million [pounds] is thought to be enough, give two, and you will save both Blood and Treasure in the end.
　　　　—General Thomas Gage to Lord Barrington, November 2, 1774

They are now spirited up by a rage and enthousiasm as great as ever people were possessed of, and you must proceed in earnest or give the business up.
　　　　—Gage to Barrington, June 26, 1775

I have not the slightest prospect of finishing the contest this campaign.
　　　　—General William Howe to Lord George Germain,
　　　　　September 25, 1776

In the present extended situation of the King's southern army, I do not think the war can be ended during the present campaign.
　　　　—Howe to Germain, August 30, 1777

The paper delivered this day by the French ambassador must certainly overturn every plan proposed . . . for carrying on an active war in North America.
　　　　—George III to Lord North, March 23, 1778

Another year's expense of this destructive war was now being added to the four which had so unprofitably preceded without a probability of its producing a single event to . . . brighten our prospects.
　　　　—Sir Henry Clinton, *The American Rebellion* [1779]

The most threatening clouds began to gather round us on every side which not only precluded all thoughts of enterprise against the possessions of the enemy, but even excited apprehensions for the security of our own.
　　　　—Clinton, *American Rebellion* [1780]

I have the mortification to inform Your Excellency that I have been forced . . . to surrender the troops under my command.
　　　　—Lord Cornwallis to Clinton, October 20, 1781

✳ ✳ ✳ Contents ✳ ✳ ✳

✳ ✳ ✳ Illustrations ✳ ✳ ✳

Preface

In relating the history of the campaign in the Carolinas I unashamedly confess that I was drawn to the subject by the fact that it was a fascinating story. We military historians are labeled by some of our condescending colleagues as the "drum and bugle corps," and it would be less than honest to say that we are not gripped by the drama and panoply of the battlefield. But the history of warfare embraces more than battles won or lost. Social historians cannot ignore the way in which the war disrupted the lives of people in the Carolina backcountry, the effects of which were felt for years after the war. A soldier of the 1st Maryland Continentals who marched mile after weary mile from Long Island to the stifling heat of the Carolinas, and who fought alongside Wayne's Pennsylvanians and the mountain men from the Watauga settlements, surely carried these experiences and associations with him for the rest of his life. And it was no accident that men who won fame in the war traded on their military reputations to achieve positions of political leadership. I trust that these wider implications have not been completely obscured by the smoke and din of battle.

Investigation confirmed some preconceptions about the war in the South. More than in any other theater this was a civil war in which Americans fought Americans. Nevertheless, popular tradition to the contrary, the war was not won by the employment of guerrilla tactics learned from fighting the Indians on the frontier. It is true that partisan bands of Whigs and Tories fought numerous skirmishes, but, as Nathanael Greene warned Thomas Sumter, "The salvation of this Country does not depend on little strokes, nor should the great business of establishing a permanent army be neglected to insure them. . . . You may strike a hundred strokes, & reap little benefit from them, unless you have a good army to take advantage of your success. The enemy will never relinquish their plan, nor the people be firm in our favor, until they behold a better barrier in the field than a voluntary militia who are one day out, & the next at home." Not until Greene and his Continentals gave direction to the war did the strategy of victory take shape. The Americans may have been political revolutionaries, but in military practice they were orthodox European.

There were also some surprises. I was not prepared for the violence and savagery of the partisan warfare in the Carolina backcountry. The patriotic gore written by contemporaries depicting the brutish villainy of the Tories I had more or less dismissed as gross exaggerations. It was not. What was exaggerated was the purity and nobility of our patriotic ancestors. Careful scrutiny of the records demonstrated that the Whigs were every bit as vengeful as their enemies (as the most casual observer of human nature should have known). It did not require much imagination to realize that when William Bratton's Patriot militia killed thirty-five Tories at William-son's Plantation with the loss of only one man, the Americans were, to say the least, fighting under the Old Testament principle of an eye for an eye.

Another surprise was the large number of Carolinians who switched sides. This was true not only of the plain folk of the backcountry who were simply trying to survive but of the great nabobs of the lowcountry aristoc-racy. As the tide of war shifted, so did allegiances, and General Greene was led to observe in the summer of 1781 that "we fought the enemy with British soldiers; and they fought us with those of America."

The larger purpose of this study was to ask an old question in a slightly different way. Without in the least denigrating the heroic struggle of George Washington and his lieutenants, should not one ask, not why the Americans won the war but why the British lost it? I tried to view the campaign in the Carolinas in this perspective. And, as usual, I found that I raised more questions than I could answer.

A great many people helped to write this book, and space does not permit me to express adequately my appreciation nor even to list all those to whom I am indebted. The following is a partial list, not necessarily in order of importance.

The Research Grants Committee of the University of Alabama was generous in its financial support, enabling me to spend uninterrupted time in research and writing.

The American Philosophical Society awarded a grant from the Penrose Fund for travel and study in the summer of 1978.

Dean Douglas Jones of the College of Arts and Sciences and Bill Barnard, chairman of the Department of History, both conspired to ar-range reduced teaching loads and leaves of absences for me.

Ruth Kibbey typed most of the manuscript with cheerfulness and efficiency. Sara Hill, Nancy Cross, and Lena Frost also assisted in the typing.

Guy Swanson was an able and diligent research assistant, who was always available when I needed help. Many other students helped with such drudgery as checking footnotes, compiling the index, and other chores. I would be remiss if I did not thank the members of my seminar class in the spring of 1982, who were tyrannized into reading and criticizing most of the chapters.

I am also indebted to the staff members of the libraries at the University of Alabama, the University of Virginia, the South Carolina Department of Archives and History, the University of South Carolina, Washington and Lee University, Virginia Military Institute, the University of North Carolina, the William L. Clements Library at the University of Michigan, and the Library of Congress.

I am especially grateful to my friends and colleagues, who alternately encouraged and hounded me when the spirit or the flesh weakened, most notably Ruth Kibbey and Kitty Sassaman, Boyd and Beverley Childress, Guy Swanson, and Connie Weimann.

I have benefited greatly from the comments and criticisms of many people, not all of whose names appear above, but the responsibility for errors of fact and opinion are, I fear, mine alone.

JOHN PANCAKE
The University of Alabama

This Destructive War

Prologue

It was the fifth year of the war for America.

In the beginning, in the spring of 1775, suppression of the rebellion in the American colonies seemed simply a matter of smashing bands of riotous farmers who had somehow cowed royal officials and created panic among sensible, loyal Americans. By summer's end the King and his ministers had come face to face with the fact that the British army in America was besieged in Boston, not only unable to "overawe the disaffected" but totally immobilized. Under the threat of American guns on Dorchester Heights, General William Howe evacuated Boston in March 1776. From that date until the first week in July there was not a single regiment of British troops on American soil.

During this lull in hostilities the radical Whigs were not idle. In the fall of 1775 George III had issued a proclamation declaring the colonists to be in a state of rebellion and ordering that "all our Officers, civil and military, are obliged to exert their utmost endeavors to suppress such rebellion, and to bring traitors to justice." For the Whigs this marked a point of no return. Americans must either abandon their struggle for liberty and submit or take the only alternative left open to them—independence. The proclamation muted the Whig-Loyalists, who had insisted that a way could be found to secure their rights within the framework of the empire. Thomas Jefferson, the Adamses, Tom Paine, and the rest of the radicals urged the break with England by holding out the vision of a new nation no longer bound by Old World ties. All during the winter and spring of 1776 they argued and insisted until by early summer their persuasion bore fruit. On July 2, 1776, the Second Continental Congress voted for independence. The next day General Howe landed the first British regiments on Staten Island.

Lord George Germain, Secretary of State for the American Department and the minister responsible for the conduct of the war, did not stint in supporting his commanders in America. During the spring and summer of 1776 he presided over a massive troop lift that sent 16,000 additional troops to support Howe and another 10,000 men to Canada to repulse an American invasion and allow Governor-General Guy Carleton to take the offensive.

General Howe and his brother, Admiral Richard Lord Howe, in addition to their military commands, were appointed peace commissioners. But it was clear that they had little authority. Soon after Washington's disastrous defeat on Long Island in August 1776, the commissioners met with a congressional delegation. The Americans learned that although the Howes had authority to accept the submission of American rebels and to declare towns, districts, or colonies "at peace" they had no terms to offer, no concessions to negotiate. Germain had insisted that the Americans must acknowledge the supremacy of Parliament as a precondition to any settlement and that the terms of the reconciliation were to be firmly controlled at Whitehall.

The ministry's solution to the American rebellion was revealed: ". . . Lord Germain having now collected a vast force, and having a fair prospect of subduing the Colonies, he wished to subdue them before he treated at all." It was to be military conquest followed by a dictated peace.

Perhaps it was too much to expect that the King and his ministers would have enough imagination to apply the lessons of eighteenth-century diplomacy to the American war. England had just concluded a protracted period of international conflict known as the Second Hundred Years' War. From it England (and indeed all the nations of Europe) had learned the lessons of limited wars and limited victory. Wars were fought by small professional armies, and warfare was a sophisticated tool of diplomacy designed to resolve territorial disputes or dynastic settlements. A nation that went to war in the eighteenth century would never dream of having as its objective the total submission of another nation. Such an objective would drive the enemy to fight to the last ditch and would entail a drawn-out conflict that would cost the victor almost as much as the vanquished.

Although English pride would never have permitted her to recognize the existence of the new nation, British statesmen would have done well to apply the lessons of eighteenth-century diplomacy and to acknowledge, at least privately, that they were dealing with a political problem. Yet their policy demanded unconditional surrender by the Americans. The King and his ministers regarded the rebellion in much the same light as a London riot. Once order was restored and the principal rioters jailed, matters would be arranged so that such disturbances would not recur. Americans, however, were wagering lives, fortunes, and sacred honor on a last-ditch struggle for survival. Especially after July 2, 1776, the prospect of surrendering their new nationhood spurred them to a desperate fight for survival, and their tenacity and endurance exacted a price that England was finally unwilling to pay.

The initial British campaign in 1776, although haphazardly planned and conducted by fits and starts, seemed to bear out the optimism of the British high command. By the late fall of 1776 Governor-General Carleton had driven the Americans from Canada and pursued them as far as Crown Point on Lake Champlain. General Howe had smashed Washington's army on Long Island and then driven him out of New York, across New Jersey, and into Pennsylvania. More important, the American commander's army had dwindled to a scant 5,000 men. A panic-struck Congress voted Washington dictatorial powers and fled from Philadelphia to Baltimore.

It is interesting to speculate on what might have been the outcome of the American rebellion if the government in England had offered a generous settlement similar to that proffered by the Carlisle Commission a little more than a year later. Patriot spirits were at a low ebb, and Washington himself thought that "if every nerve is not strain'd . . . I think the game is pretty near up. . . ." But within a few weeks Washington had lifted sagging spirits by defeating the British garrisons at Trenton and Princeton. They were small successes, but they electrified the dying Patriot cause and forced the British to abandon New Jersey.

The British plans for 1777 were bold and wide-ranging. With nearly 35,000 troops in America and Canada, Germain and his generals prepared a campaign that called for an invasion commanded by General John Burgoyne from Canada into the Hudson Valley, which would isolate New England from the rest of the states. General Howe undertook to support Burgoyne's thrust from New York and also to invade Pennsylvania and capture Philadelphia.

In laying these plans British leaders assumed that most Americans were loyal to the crown and that once the rebel ringleaders and their henchmen were subdued royal authority could be easily restored. It was an illusion that persisted throughout the conflict and it was perhaps the most serious of many British miscalculations of the war in America. Neither in New York nor in Pennsylvania did the Loyalists appear in significant numbers to support Burgoyne and Howe.

The grandiose plans for 1777 degenerated into a confusion of mismanagement and bad judgment. Burgoyne's invasion, given only token support from the south, ran into stiff American resistance. Poor generalship by the British and hard fighting by the Patriots resulted in the surrender of Burgoyne's army at Saratoga. To the south Howe twice defeated the Americans in Pennsylvania and captured Philadelphia, but Washington's army was not seriously damaged and Howe found himself virtually besieged in the rebel capital. At the end of the year the grand offensive of 1777 was wrecked and the ministry's plan for ending the rebellion in shambles.

On the heels of the disaster in America came the realization of England's worst fears. The United States, ignoring the Carlisle Commission's generous offer of concession, concluded an alliance with France in February 1778, and it was obviously only a matter of time until Spain would join them. What had begun as a rebellion of New England farmers had burgeoned into a full-scale international war whose consequences could be as serious as any England had faced in the past century. The King was moved to consider, if only briefly, conceding independence to the Americans as the price of enlisting their aid to protect Canada and the British West Indies.

William Howe was replaced by his second in command, Sir Henry Clinton, and Germain relegated the American war to secondary importance as Britain planned a new strategy. Clinton was ordered to evacuate Philadelphia and return to New York. In Sir Henry's words, the ministry "seems to have relinquished all thoughts of reducing the rebellious colonies by force of arms, and have determined to trust the decision of the quarrel to negotiation [the Carlisle Commission], that the collected strength of the realm might be more at liberty to act against this new enemy."

Pursuant to his orders, Clinton evacuated Philadelphia in June 1778. Because large numbers of Loyalists required space aboard his transports, the British commander marched his army across New Jersey to Sandy Hook, there to be ferried across to Manhattan. General Washington, whose army had survived the agony of Valley Forge and had been to school under that redoubtable drillmaster, Baron von Steuben, decided to strike at the British column. He overtook Clinton at Monmouth Court House. In the ensuing battle the Americans fought the British on even terms—the first occasion in which they had been able to match the redcoats without benefit of either superior numbers or fortifications. But Clinton's strategic purpose was accomplished. In less than two weeks he had brought his command intact to New York.

From the summer of 1778 to the latter part of 1779 the war in America lapsed into a kind of limbo as the ministry at Whitehall struggled to meet the shift in strategic priorities necessitated by the widening of the conflict.

1. Great Britain in Adversity

Nothing so characterized the ministry of Lord Frederick North as its propensity for raising critical questions of strategy only to postpone the hard decisions needed to deal with them. Since the beginning of the rebellion in America, England had been aware of the menace of French intervention. It was no secret that France was still smarting from the defeat of 1763 and that she was eager to exploit any opportunity to weaken Great Britain and its vast colonial empire. When the gloomy news of the failure of Burgoyne and Howe reached London in December 1777, French intervention was almost certain. Yet Parliament recessed for almost six weeks, and not until mid-February 1778 was Lord North willing to discuss publicly the possibility of a war with France. This was more than a week after Benjamin Franklin and his colleagues in Paris had agreed to the terms of the Franco-American alliance.

✳ The Test of Sea Power ✳

The often-accepted version of the American victory at Yorktown is that a singular and accidental lapse on the part of the British navy gave the French admiral, the Comte de Grasse, brief control of the Chesapeake so that Lord Cornwallis' army was trapped at Yorktown between the French fleet and Washington's army. In fact, only incredible good luck and cautious French naval strategy had allowed the British to escape several such potential disasters before 1781. After 1777 Britain rarely had complete mastery of the western Atlantic, and even in European waters she faced frequent threats from the French and Spanish fleets. How was it that England, victor in the Seven Years' War and "mistress of the seas," found herself in such dire straits?

At the end of what Lawrence Gipson calls the Great War for Empire, England was burdened with a staggering national debt. It was an economic and political problem that plagued successive ministers after 1763 and led to the several abortive attempts to tax the American colonies. There had also been serious cutbacks in naval expenditures. The vast fleet that existed in 1763 included a number of old, decrepit vessels whose usefulness was at an end and others that had been hastily built of green timbers. So although it may have been the largest fleet in British history, it was certainly not the best. And as with most fleets, peacetime maintenance did not keep pace with peacetime decay. Many of the ships carried on the active list were little more than hulks, virtually useless for sea duty. When the threat of war finally stirred the Admiralty to action, it was discovered that there were also serious shortages of timber, cordage, masts, and other naval stores needed to refurbish the fleet. Building ways were crowded to capacity, and skilled labor was insufficient to meet the unusual demand.

The Earl of Sandwich, who became First Lord of the Admiralty in 1771, performed prodigious labors, and by 1779 he had brought the fleet nearly to the strength of 1759, that is, about 155,000 tons and including 100 vessels of fifty guns or more. But from the point of view of naval strategy England faced problems far more difficult than those of the earlier war.[1]

The Duc de Choiseul, Louis XV's foreign minister, who had presided over the defeat of the Seven Years' War, was determined that France would one day have its *revanche*. Even before the conclusion of the Treaty of Paris, Choiseul had begun the reformation of the French navy. His efforts and those of his successors resulted in the emergence of a French fleet superior to any in its history. Although it was not yet quite a match for the British in guns and tonnage, it was a formidable force. Presuming that Spain would shortly join France as a belligerent, the combined Bourbon fleets would have naval superiority. Moreover, for the first time in many decades neither nation had Continental quarrels to distract it and both had adequate financial resources (although Louis XVI's financial minister was deeply pessimistic about the long-range effect of an expensive war).

It should also be noted that for the first time in more than one hundred years England found herself without a single Continental ally. Prussia, the most steadfast of England's friends, felt that it had been arbitrarily deserted when Parliament cut off subsidies to Frederick the Great in 1761, two years before the end of the Seven Years' War. By 1776, moreover, Frederick was much more concerned with the partition of Poland and other problems that commanded his attention in eastern Europe.

Russia and the Baltic states were nervous about the threat to their shipping and trade routes, especially after the high-handed way Britain had enforced the Rule of 1756. Indeed, the rule itself—a nation could not trade in time of war where it was not allowed to trade in time of peace—was typical of the international hauteur with which England conducted its foreign policy. Even those nations that had not been her enemies often had their ports blockaded, their ships stopped and searched, and their commerce threatened by "the mistress of the seas." England's isolation, then, resulted partly from the fact that the interests of potential allies were focused elsewhere. But it also resulted from the colossal arrogance that characterized the conduct of British diplomacy. As Benjamin Franklin noted, "Every nation in Europe wishes to see Britain humbled, having all in turn been offended by her insolence." The only assistance that England received from abroad was the troops hired from the German princes of central Europe, and for this aid the ministry paid a stiff price. Nearly 30,000 mercenaries served with the British army during the course of the war at a cost of more than £600,000 a year.[2]

By 1779 England had committed more troops to America than at any time during the Seven Years' War, and logistical support was much more difficult. More than 40,000 mouths had to be fed and, unlike the experience of the previous war, only insignificant amounts of supplies were available from America. Between the spring of 1777 and the surrender at Yorktown, shipments to the Atlantic coast (exclusive of Canada and the West Indies) included 40,000 tons each of bread, flour and rice, 5,000 tons of beef, nearly 20,000 tons of pork, 2,000 tons of butter, 3,600 tons of oatmeal, 176,000 gallons of molasses, and 2,865,000 gallons of rum. Horses were always in short supply for the British forces because the animals were difficult to ship and because feeding them required shipment of 14,000 tons of hay and 6,000 tons of oats from England each year.[3]

Even before France entered the war the navy had had its hands full. The mobility of General William Howe's army—from Halifax to New York in 1776, from New York to Pennsylvania in 1777—depended on the transport and protection of Admiral Howe's fleet. This fleet was also expected to prevent rebel supplies from abroad from reaching America and to curb privateers from raiding Britain's supply line. In Germain's opinion, Admiral Howe failed to perform these tasks adequately, and he followed his brother into retirement in 1778. That the American Secretary may have erred in his judgment may be seen in the fact that Richard Howe became First Sea Lord before the war ended.

With the widening of the war the responsibilities of the navy seemed insuperable. There was now the burden of protecting a colonial empire that reached from India to Gibraltar to Canada to the Lesser Antilles. The foe might strike at any point on this vast perimeter, forcing British strategists to guess at the disposition of the enemy and the focus of attack.

There was also the overriding necessity of guarding the waters around the British Isles. Englishmen recalled not only the great victory over the Spanish Armada but also how swiftly the enemy fleet could assemble and descend on their coasts. In fact, the war with France was little more than a year old when her fleet appeared off the coast at Plymouth and an invasion seemed imminent. Overseas operations were always hamstrung by the necessity—or cries of alarm from the Opposition in Parliament—for the home fleet to be kept in sufficient strength to guard the Channel.

To forestall the enemy, then, required a naval administrative system that was capable of repairing and resupplying ships so that existing fleet units could be used at their maximum capability. Above all, England needed a naval command that could act with boldness and decision to overcome the disparity of forces. It was the failure of the command and support systems as much as the limitation of its size that accounted for the ultimate failure of the British navy.

The events of 1778 were a clear forewarning of England's dilemma. At the beginning of the summer, French naval power was concentrated in two forces, the main fleet at Brest on the tip of Brittany and a squadron at the Mediterranean port of Toulon. The obvious strategy seemed to be to blockade the fleet at Brest and send a squadron to Gibraltar to prevent Admiral d'Estaing and the Toulon force from leaving the Mediterranean. But this would mean weakening the home fleet guarding the Channel against invasion, especially perilous if Spain entered the war and the Cadiz fleet joined the French.

The other possibility was to wait until the enemy made a commitment of forces and then move to check it. But this called for accurate intelligence and swift, decisive movement. While the cabinet in London debated, d'Estaing sortied from Toulon early in April with nine months' provisions, clear indication that he was headed overseas. Although Germain was certain that his destination was America, Sandwich hesitated, unwilling to risk command of the Channel. Finally, over Sandwich's strenuous objection, a relief squadron under the command of Admiral John Byron was ordered to America. When he received his orders, Byron was on the point of leaving for India. His vessels had to be reprovisioned for America. Other ships from the Channel fleet were assigned to his command and had to take on additional stores for overseas service. False intelligence caused a further delay, and it was not until June that Byron finally sailed. He was directed to look for the French at Halifax, then at the Chesapeake, and finally the West Indies.

D'Estaing's destination was actually the Chesapeake. Only Clinton's decision to move the army overland to New York allowed Admiral Howe's convoy of supplies and Loyalist refugees to clear the Delaware Capes ten days before the arrival of the French fleet. Clinton's army reached Sandy Hook barely in time to be ferried across to Manhattan, allowing Howe to take a defensive position inside the anchorage.[4]

The arrival of d'Estaing led General Washington to decide to attack the British base in Rhode Island. A force commanded by John Sullivan struck at Newport while the French fleet moved in from the sea. Admiral Howe meanwhile had been joined by a few scattered units, which gave him a force strong enough to challenge the enemy. He hurried to the relief of Newport, and his arrival disrupted the allied attack. D'Estaing, anxious to bring the British to battle, followed Howe out to sea. As the two fleets maneuvered for position, a North Atlantic gale struck and dispersed both fleets. D'Estaing's force was damaged so severely that he had to retire to Boston for repairs. He then set out for his station in the West Indies, but by the time of his arrival Byron had finally made his crossing, reinforcing the British West Indian squadron sufficiently to enable it to challenge the French threat in the Caribbean. One final fillip was added to this run of British luck. As d'Estaing moved south, a British convoy carrying 5,000 reinforcements from New York to the Antilles was also sailing south on a parallel course just over the horizon to the west. For five weeks the British transports sailed undiscovered, arriving safely at their destination.

By such narrow margins was England saved from disaster in America. But there was still no resolution of the basic dilemma—how to maintain troops and ships to meet the threat of attack from Halifax to Jamaica. Except for Clinton's army in New York, dispersed garrisons were safe only if they were supported by the fleet. And the fleet was constantly hauled and pulled by conflicting demands: supplies to North America; convoys from the West Indies, India, and the Baltic; privateers raiding from the Bay of Biscay to Halifax; and always the terrifying prospect that the Bourbon fleets would join forces and sweep into the Channel. So far, good luck and frantic, makeshift strategy had dealt with the sudden new demands of an international conflict. It was now time to overhaul strategic thinking and concert plans for a new effort, including a plan to deal with the rebellion in America.[5]

✳ A New War Strategy? ✳

It was never quite clear to Sir Henry Clinton why his superiors in Whitehall continually thwarted his plans and denied him the opportunity for victory. Although he understood the importance of sea power and may even have caught glimpses of the war in its wider context, Sir Henry had a theater commander's characteristic tunnel vision of the American war. For different reasons, many military historians of the War of Independence have shared Clinton's myopia. From a purely American point of view, for example, not much happened in 1778 and 1779. The only major battle, Monmouth Court House, was inconclusive, and during the next year and a half the British commander in chief spent his time either planning operations that were never executed or carrying out minor forays that contributed little to a successful termination of the war. So at the beginning of 1779, Clinton was both gloomy and apprehensive. Calls for reinforcements from both Canada and the West Indies were making serious inroads on his troop strength, and he wondered how he was to meet the new demands that Germain and the ministry were certain to make on him.

If affairs in America appeared to be at standstill, London was the scene of frantic activity, violent political quarrels, and crises that threatened to overwhelm the King and his ministers. The return of Gentlemen Johnny Burgoyne and Sir William Howe was the signal for the Opposition to renew its attacks on Germain's conduct of the war. Little attention was paid to Burgoyne, but a parliamentary inquiry into the Howe command resulted in a bitter and inconclusive squabble that lasted until the summer of 1779.

Far more sensational was the court-martial of the commander in chief of the fleet, Admiral Augustus Keppel. The charges were brought by a subordinate officer, and the whole affair was shot through with political overtones that had little to do with whether or not Keppel was guilty of misconduct. He was exonerated, but several senior officers struck their flags, refusing to serve under him. The episode left the navy rife with internal dissension.

In the midst of these factional skirmishes, Lord Germain was trying to remedy the obvious weaknesses in Britain's military command. It was increasingly clear that the King's personal control of the army was impractical. Lord Jeffrey Amherst, who was already commander of the home forces, was induced to assume direction of the entire army and was given a seat in the cabinet. Amherst was still the sensible, competent man who had commanded in America during the Seven Years' War but, like the First Lord of the Admiralty, he tended to allow his concern for the defense of England to override considerations of global strategy.[6]

Commanders for the American theaters were in short supply. Sir Guy Carleton had resigned as governor-general of Canada in the summer of 1778, and Lord Cornwallis returned at the end of the year, pleading the illness of his wife. Of the senior generals who had commanded in America since 1775 only Clinton remained. If Germain was inclined to heed his own doubts about Sir Henry's competence or the latter's frequent requests to resign, he would find himself at a loss for a replacement. Not until March 1779 did the cabinet decide on a successor to Admiral Howe, and he did not reach America until August.

The war plans for America had not only been drastically altered by the necessity for the safety of England. There was also the alluring prospect of despoiling French overseas possessions. It should be remembered that the West Indian sugar islands were considered far more valuable than the thirteen mainland colonies. A noisy and powerful lobby of planters and merchants in Parliament was a constant reminder that the islands were the classic example of mercantilist theory in practice. One hundred thousand hogsheads of sugar and 11,000 puncheons of rum a year came into London alone. West Indian imports were estimated at £4,500,000 annually, more than twice the value of imports from the mainland colonies. Not only must these riches be protected, but there was the prospect of conquering the equally valuable French and Spanish possessions.

Such conquests would more than compensate for the mounting costs of

Sir Henry Clinton (W. L. Clements Library, University of Michigan)

the war; moreover, it could be reasoned that "having them in possession, instead of cringing to an American Congress for peace, we shall prescribe the terms and bid America be only what we please." In other words, if England could turn the tables on France and strip her of her overseas possessions, the rebellious Americans would be isolated and easily sub-dued. Yet the planners in England could not bring themselves to make a full commitment to such an audacious strategy. Supremacy in the West Indies would stretch the resources of the fleet beyond the requirements for safety at home. It would also mean that the reconquest of America would have to be virtually abandoned—and more than one-third of the entire British army was under Clinton's command in New York. It was even suggested that the army in America with its attendant naval support be shuttled between the West Indies and North America, operating to the north during the summer months, when hurricanes swept the southern Atlantic, and moving south during the winter. Such an idea was preposterous, given the practical problems of logistics, wear and tear on ships and troops, and the vagaries of wind, weather, and the French navy. That it was suggested at all indicates that desperation in Whitehall was putting a severe strain on logic.[7]

Home defense, the West Indies, and the rebellious colonies—the minis-try was unable to choose among conflicting objectives and in the end decided to pursue them all.

The ministry appeared to have a new strategy for America. After the military debacle of 1777 and the French alliance, Lord North had finally resorted to diplomacy. The Carlisle Commission had been authorized to make sweeping concessions that would have given the colonies an auton-omy not unlike the dominion status by which Great Britain in later years held together her great colonial empire. But the offer came too late. Too much blood had been spilled, and too many Americans no longer regarded themselves as Englishmen.

Germain's new strategy seemed to have abandoned the conception of sweeping military campaigns that would subdue all of America. Instead, he spoke of fending off Washington's army and establishing enclaves of loyal colonies such as New York and New Jersey. From these examples of the benefits of restoration of British rule a systematic expansion of author-ity might lead to the reclaiming of the King's empire in America. By thus concentrating on individual colonies and separating the military from the political problem, the way would be opened for American Loyalists to regain control of colonial government. "The great point to be wished for, is that the inhabitants of some considerable colony were so far reclaimed to their duty, that the revival of the British Constitution, and the free opera-tion of the laws, might without prejudice be permitted amongst them." In this way "a little political management, would with ease bring about what will never be effected by mere force."[8]

Such a strategy was based on several erroneous assumptions. One was the persisting conviction that Loyalists in America were numerous and anxious to assist in the restoration. Another was that the Patriot movement was on the wane, that despite the French alliance Congress was in disarray, and that disillusionment and war weariness would soon vitiate American resistance. Finally, although the new strategy placed more emphasis on a political settlement, the commissioners charged with the restoration of civil government were two military men, Sir Henry Clinton and his naval counterpart, neither of whom was likely to be fitted either by temperament or experience for the task of reconstruction.

Nor did the directions which Clinton received in April 1779 appear to be far removed from the older strategy that had guided British commanders in the past. Germain instructed Sir Henry to "bring Mr. Washington to a general and decisive action at the opening of the campaign," thus paving the way for restoring Loyalist government in New York. Clinton was then to conduct coastal raids along the New England coast as well as southward to the Chesapeake Bay. Finally, "it is surely not too much to expect that your force . . . [will] attack Virginia and Maryland . . ." (so much for "political management" versus "mere force"). Germain promised 6,600 reinforcements "intended to be sent out to you early in the spring." Added to his present force (including 5,500 men in Rhode Island), Clinton would have nearly 29,000 rank and file on hand. The instruction, as usual, left Clinton free "to make such alterations, either in the plan itself or in the mode pointed out for its execution."[9]

Clinton's reaction to these instructions reflected his conviction that the ministry expected him to do the impossible but that it intended to saddle him with the responsibility for failure. He was being harnessed to a detailed plan that did not allow him any discretion. "It is true . . . Your Lordship only recommends," he wrote bitterly to Germain. "But by that recommendation you secure the right of blaming me if I should adopt other measures and fail; and, should I follow that system with success, I appear to have no merit but the bare execution." His bitterness was scarcely assuaged by a subsequent dispatch from Germain that the reinforcements "intended for you early in the spring" were still in England at the end of May and that only slightly more than half of the original 6,600 men were being sent. Sir Henry gloomily noted:

. . . As my plans for the campaign had been formed under the presumption of my receiving early reinforcement, and their success-ful execution must depend upon Admiral Arbuthnot's [Howe's successor] joining me as soon as I was taught to expect him, this unexpected delay in the arrival of his fleet could not but excite in me the most serious anxiety for myself as well as the public. Another year's expense of this destructive war was now going to be added to the four which had so unprofitably preceded, without a probability of its producing a single event to better our condition or brighten our prospects. The burdens of the people were every day increasing, and their patience of course diminishing in proportion as they saw the end of their misfortunes farther removed. It was consequently a natural apprehension that the inactivity of an army on whose operations their hopes had chiefly rested might at last inflame them to a blind condemnation of the General who directed its motions. And recent history had furnished too many examples of a like injustice for me to doubt of its possibility with respect to myself, notwithstanding the utmost efforts of my zeal. The American minister's late letters had, moreover, chalked out for me expeditions and conquests much beyond anything that appears to have been expected from Sir William Howe in the zenith of his strength. . . .[10]

This quotation is one of many such lugubrious expressions of Clinton's character and state of mind. His long experience in war had surely taught him that any schedule of reinforcements or fleet movements was subject to unforeseen movements of the enemy, delays in loading troops and supplies, or the erratic weather of the North Atlantic. Yet he seemed to feel that such miscarriages were the result of malign influences that were leagued against him.

Clinton had a sound and at times brilliant military mind, but he often failed of execution. He was jealous of his authority, but in times of crisis he often failed to exert it. He was frequently torn by inner conflicts that made him hesitate at moments that called for boldness and daring. It may well be that he was fearful that failure would ruin his reputation. More probably, he was the victim of psychological conflicts buried deep within him that led him to plan far-reaching courses of action only to draw back when the time came for execution—as though his craving for heroic enterprises was overcome by a subconscious guilt that he was not deserving of such authority. This may explain the several attempts he made to resign his command. At times, both planning and execution were of a high order. But under stress, especially stress induced by quarrels with his colleagues and subordinates, his energetic planning and preparation lapsed into inactivity, which he blamed on the failure of others.

There was a good measure of justification in Clinton's condemnation of Germain's unwonted optimism and of the details that burdened his instructions. But it is unlikely that if Germain had heeded Sir Henry's querulous demand to "leave me to myself and let me adapt my effects to the hourly changes of circumstance," there would have been substantially different results. A commander who could surmount the inherent difficulties of the American war would have to be a man of energy and boldness. Henry Clinton was not such a man.[11]

Despite his resentment toward Germain, Clinton began to put together a campaign that fell generally within the framework of his instructions. But Sir Henry's plan followed a somewhat different pattern from that proposed by the American Secretary and had broader objectives. It also demonstrated that his military ideas were little altered since his days as Howe's second in command. The differences were largely those of geography and of limitations imposed by his diminished force. The latter condition was brought about partly by a detachment of 5,000 men sent to the West Indies. Before many weeks had passed, he also sent 2,000 men to reinforce General Frederick Haldimand in Canada.

Clinton's first objective was the destruction of Washington's army. Recognizing that the American forces were partially disbanded in winter and had to be strengthened by recruitment each spring, Clinton proposed a series of coastal raids on New England. He hoped thereby to induce the states to keep potential recruits at home for local defense. A raid on the Chesapeake should offer a similar distraction in Virginia and Maryland. He would then reconcentrate his forces in New York and move on the Hudson Highlands, forcing Washington to leave his fortified position in New Jersey. "My plan was consequently . . . to draw him forward before the new levies from the different states should have time to join him, and then move against him while in motion, or force him into a general and decisive action. . . ."

If Washington's army was not destroyed, at least the safety of New York would be assured. The arrival of reinforcements from England would clear the way for the final blow, an attack on South Carolina, which would be the first phase in the conquest of the entire South. "Should we be so fortunate to succeed in this . . . and no foreign interference again disturb us, I was not altogether secretly without hopes that the American war might possibly be yet finished in one campaign."[12]

✳ "Many Adverse Incidents" ✳

One of the most important factors in the conduct of British operations in America was naval support. The navy not only kept the army supplied but provided it with what Washington called "the canvass wings" that gave it mobility. During the first years of the war, cooperation between the services was assured because their command was shared by the Howe brothers. With the resignation of Admiral Lord Richard Howe in late 1778, the British lost the services of one of its ablest commanders, a fact that Clinton himself lamented. He was anxious that Howe's replacement be someone who was both able and capable of cooperating with the army. Until the successor arrived, the senior naval officer was Commodore George Collier, who had served in American waters since 1776. Thanks to

Collier, the early months of the 1779 campaign were marked by excellent interservice cooperation.

The first coastal raid was dispatched in April 1779 against the Chesapeake. A force under General Edward Mathew and supported by Commodore Collier was directed to destroy enemy supplies and, if feasible, to establish a permanent post. It was also hoped that the raid would prevent or delay Virgina troops from joining Washington. Collier put the British expedition ashore near Portsmouth on May 10, and for more than two weeks Mathew's force of 1,800 men plundered the surrounding countryside virtually unopposed. By the end of May they were back in New York, having destroyed or captured 130 vessels, confiscated 3,000 hogsheads of tobacco, and destroyed a considerable amount of military stores.[13]

Clinton was highly pleased, and he was only mildly disappointed that Mathew had not established a base on the lower Chesapeake. Clinton was aware of the vulnerability of such outposts, and he was not nearly so optimistic as Germain about the prevalence of Loyalism. Sir Henry was aware of the bitter experience suffered by Loyalists in some areas where they had demonstrated their support for the crown only to suffer savage retribution from the Patriots once British troops were withdrawn. Mathew had been cautioned against "inviting or encouraging the King's friends in that province to a junction with the army, lest they should be exposed to the resentment and malice of the disaffected by his necessary departure." Yet Sir Henry had for some time regarded the Chesapeake as an important area, and his preoccupation did not end with the foray of 1779.[14]

The next move was against the Hudson Highlands. Two years earlier, in an effort to aid Burgoyne's invasion from Canada, Clinton had made a swift ascent up the Hudson to seize American forts near Peekskill. It had been a bold and skillful operation, displaying Clinton at his best. Now, at the end of May 1779, he launched a force of 6,000 men accompanied by a covering naval force, which seized Stony Point and Verplanck's Point. This time the British occupied the forts, giving them control of King's Ferry, a link in the principal route from New Jersey to Connecticut, which forced the Americans to detour troops and supplies to and from New England almost 100 miles.

But Clinton's primary objective was to lever Washington out of his base in New Jersey by forcing him to defend West Point, which guarded the approaches to the upper Hudson. In this way he hoped to be able to maneuver the American army into a position where he could gain his "general and decisive action." Washington did interpose his force between Clinton and West Point, but his position deep in the rough hills of the Highlands was too strong for Clinton to attack with his limited force. Vainly he searched the eastern horizon for the reinforcements that Germain had promised, but only received news of more delay.

Clinton made one more attempt to lure Washington into open country.

Early in July he sent an expedition under General William Tryon, the royal governor of New York, into Connecticut with 2,600 men. Tryon's troops overran New Haven and moved on to Fairfield, looting and pillaging as they went. They put the town of Fairfield to the torch, burning almost 100 buildings, including two churches. It was one of the most savage and destructive raids yet conducted by the British. Tryon had concluded that "if a general terror and despondency can be awakened among a people already divided," Patriot resistance might be broken. Clinton was shocked. "I have been a *buccaneer* already too long; I detest that sort of war." It was an argument that the British high command never settled, neither officially condoning such terrorism nor reprimanding subordinates who engaged in it.[15]

The hope that Washington would come out of his lair in the Highlands was disappointed; in fact, the Connecticut raid produced another and unforeseen result. Clinton had reduced his forces on the Hudson to supply Tryon's detachment, and the watchful Americans were quick to take advantage. Washington was unhappy in his passive role, "mortified that the circumstances of the Army . . . oblige me to a mere defensive plan, and will not suffer me to pursue such measures as the public good may seem to require and the public expectation to demand." The commander in chief therefore proposed to General Anthony Wayne the possibility of a surprise attack on Stony Point. After careful reconnaissance and meticulous planning, "Mad Anthony" led a picked detachment of 1,200 light infantry against the British outpost. On July 16 Wayne's men stormed the works with unloaded muskets and carried the enemy position with the bayonet. The British losses were 130 killed and wounded and 543 taken prisoner. It was notable, especially in the light of Tryon's raid, that the British commander "candidly and freely acknowledges that not a drop of blood was spilt unnecessarily." The newspaper chronicler of the event added, "Oh Britain! turn thy eye inward,—behold and tremble at thyself!"

A few weeks later the Americans seized another opportunity. This time young Major "Light Horse Harry" Lee stormed the British works at Paulus Hook just across the Hudson from Manhattan. The British garrison lost more than 200 men killed, wounded, and captured.

The Americans made no attempt to hold either post. The two little victories had no strategic significance, and the British soon rebuilt and occupied both forts. But the effect could not be ignored. Coming after a period of flagging American spirits, the engagements had a tonic effect on the army. Congress voted medals for Wayne and Lee, and Patriots had news of victory to savor after a disheartening period of inactivity.[16]

The effect on Clinton was even more profound. His energy was dissipated. ". . . In truth my spirits, already pressed down by many adverse incidents, began to sink under the additional weight of new disappointments." Even the arrival late in August of the new naval commander,

Admiral Marriot Arbuthnot, with reinforcements from England did not lift his spirits. There were only 3,800 men instead of the 6,000 which had been promised, and a virulent fever had stricken hundreds of them during the long voyage across the Atlantic. When they came ashore the "bilious fever" spread like wildfire through the garrison. Soon 6,000 men were in the hospitals. With Haldimand requiring 2,000 reinforcements for Canada, Clinton was left with less than 2,000 additions to his command in New York.[17]

Although he cordially welcomed the new naval commander, Sir Henry quickly became disillusioned with Admiral Arbuthnot. Already nearly seventy years old, the admiral was querulous and unpredictable. He was alternately enthusiastic and gloomy, bold and cautious. His career until 1779 was undistinguished, and his notions on strategy at times bordered on the absurd. That such a capricious personality should have been named as a colleague of Sir Henry Clinton was disastrous for the harmony of operations between the two services.

Clinton received an early taste of what was in store for him. Admiral Arbuthnot brought with him news that French naval forces were on their way to America and it seemed likely that their objective was either New York or Rhode Island. Arbuthnot suggested that Newport be abandoned, since it had been threatened several times by attacks from both land and sea and its defense required a garrison of nearly 6,000 men. Every resource at Admiral Howe's command had been needed to defend both it and New York in 1778. Its abandonment would allow a concentration of forces at the price of a base that had been of little importance in British strategy. Clinton agreed and late in September ordered General William Prescott, commanding at Newport, to destroy his works and evacuate his troops.

Shortly afterward, news reached New York that the French were making for Halifax. Admiral Arbuthnot immediately reversed himself. Newport, he said, was essential if Halifax were to be saved. He announced that he was sailing with his entire force to meet the threat, and Clinton hurried news of these developments to Prescott with instructions to remain at Newport. He then sent his aide to the admiral's flagship off Sandy Hook to confer about the new crisis. Arbuthnot would not see him and for six days refused to communicate with Clinton. The admiral had become convinced that Clinton was conspiring to discredit him. Sir Henry was at the end of his patience and his temper. Finally, Arbuthnot abandoned his voyage to Halifax. Prescott, who had failed to receive Clinton's second order, arrived in New York with his command intact. The French fleet, as it turned out, was on its way to Savannah.[18]

Clinton's plan was now in total disarray. The raids had served no purpose. Washington refused to be drawn into battle, and the token reinforcements had left British troop strength so reduced that Clinton felt he could do little more than defend New York. A few days after his contretemps with Arbuthnot he ordered the evacuation of Stony Point and Verplanck's Point, "whose importance of course ceased the moment I gave up offensive operations on the Hudson."[19]

* * * * * * * * * *
* * * * * * * * * *
* * * * * * * * * *
* * * * * * * * * *

2. The Evolution of Southern Strategy

It was customary for eighteenth-century generals to bring their campaigns to an end in the fall of the year and go into winter quarters. But in 1779 Sir Henry Clinton was not so minded. The record of the first eighteen months of his command was not likely to redound to his credit, and "the waste of the season and the enemy's exertions . . . having rendered unsuitable to the present period that part of my plan to which the past movements of the campaign had been only prepratory, it now became necessary to . . . turn my face to the south. . . . "[1] It was not surprising that Clinton should look to the Carolinas and Georgia as a possible avenue through which British fortunes might be reversed. It was a course that had been urged upon him more than once by Lord Germain, who was seeking a new testing ground for his war strategy. Moreover, Clinton's first independent command had been an adventure to the South three years earlier.

✳ The Expedition of 1776 ✳

The early revolutionary movement in North Carolina was slow to gain support. Although it was one of the largest of England's thirteen colonies, its economy was not dominated by a large planter class such as existed in Virginia and South Carolina. Its largest port, Wilmington, could not compare with Charleston or the Chesapeake as a commercial center.

The radical Whig movement in most of the colonies was given its revolutionary impetus when the First Continental Congress created the Continental Association, a network of committees—often called associations—that were set up to enforce compliance with its resolutions designed to halt trade in English goods. In the northern colonies committees had been formed in almost every county and large town by the spring of 1775. They were often the vehicles through which the Whigs organized militia units or at least secured pledges of support for the revolutionary cause.

People were called upon to sign the "articles of association," and if they refused to do so they immediately fell under suspicion.

In North Carolina only six committees were organized by the Whigs by 1775. Five counties failed to elect delegates to the first provincial congress in 1774, and nine failed to do so when members were chosen for the second congress in 1775.[2]

This lack of enthusiasm was in part the result of the efforts of the royal governor, Josiah Martin, who worked furiously to thwart the rebels. He found support from many of the planters and merchants of the eastern counties. In the piedmont elements of discontent remained from the Regulator movement of 1770–71. The westerners nursed the usual frontier grievances: failure of the government to protect them against the Indians, underrepresentation in the colonial assembly, and tax discrimination. The Regulators had raised the cry of "no taxation without representation," not against Parliament but against the North Carolina assembly, which many of them tended to identify with the Whigs who had dominated it. It would be an oversimplification to say that the Regulator movement spawned Loyalist sentiment among the westerners, but the general unrest of the early part of the decade and the partisan feelings that were generated often determined the choice of loyalties when the revolutionary crisis came.

Perhaps the greatest ally that Governor Martin had was apathy. Many of the Carolinians were new arrivals who had moved into the central and western part of the colony. Mostly Germans and Scots, they benefited from the governor's generous land policy and had little understanding of the issues that divided Whigs and Tories to the north. They were rather inclined to till their land and keep aloof from the controversy. Both sides moved tentatively, and Whig committees were hesitant to act against even the most outspoken crown sympathizers.

The first overt move was made by Governor Martin. He concluded that a show of authority would annihilate the rebellion in North Carolina, and he so reported to the American Secretary in London, Lord Dartmouth, who was soon to be succeeded by Germain. Dartmouth immediately set about planning a response. Four regiments were detached from the reinforcements being collected for General Howe and ordered to sail for North Carolina in December 1775. Dartmouth also ordered General Howe to detach his second in command, General Clinton, who was to proceed to the mouth of the Cape Fear River and take charge of the expedition. In his letter to Howe Dartmouth warned: "In truth the whole success of the measure His Majesty had adopted depends so much upon a considerable number of the inhabitants taking up arms in support of government, that nothing that can have a tendency to promote it ought to be omitted. I hope we are not deceived in the assurances that have been given, for if we are, and there should be no appearance of a disposition of the inhabitants of the southern colonies to join the King's Army, I fear little more will be effected. . . . "[3] The admonition was one that might well have haunted Whitehall for the next six years.

Governor Martin, seemingly assured of support, sent out a call for Loyalists to rendezvous on the lower Cape Fear in mid-February. The strongest response came from the Scots, who assembled under the command of Donald McDonald, an eighty-year-old veteran of Culloden. About 1,500 Loyalists began to move eastward toward Wilmington. The Patriot forces commanded by Colonel James Caswell intercepted the Loyalists at Moore's Creek Bridge on February 27. The Americans tore up the planks of the bridge and then entrenched themselves on the far side of the creek. The Loyalists advanced headlong and attempted to cross the bridge on the stringers. A blast of fire from the Americans at a range of thirty yards shattered the attack, and the battle was over almost as soon as it was begun. Half a hundred Tories were killed, wounded, or drowned, and 850 of them were taken prisoner. Presumably Patriot Colonel James Moore was unaware of any irony when he reported to the North Carolina Congress, "Thus, sir, . . . has most happily terminated a very dangerous insurrection. . . ."

It is worth noting that most of the prisoners were sent home with only a stern warning from the Provincial Congress. The leaders were exiled to other colonies, although provision was made for the welfare of their families. The Congress noted piously that "the sad necessity which the frailties of our fellow-beings have allotted to our share; . . . we wish reformation to those who, in this unhappy contest, are severed from us. . . ." The war had not yet reached the stage at which Americans exacted reprisals on other Americans.[4]

And what of Sir Henry Clinton's supporting force? Sir Henry himself did not arrive off Cape Fear until March 12, and it was eight more weeks before the regiments from England joined him. Feeling very much like the guests who had arrived after the party was over, Clinton and his naval counterpart, Commodore Sir Peter Parker, looked about for a place to display their finery. Clinton's suggestions reveal two southern objectives that were to preoccupy his thinking for the rest of the war.

One of these was the Chesapeake Bay. Not only did its lower reaches offer attractive sites for a naval base, but the upper bay and its rivers penetrated deep into Virginia and Maryland. In the context of a strategy for dividing the colonies, the coastal plain narrowed in northern Virginia and Maryland so that, for example, Baltimore was separated from the Appalachians by only seventy miles. Clinton proposed establishing posts on the lower Chesapeake, "where the force left there would be perfectly safe . . . and might be reinforced or withdrawn at pleasure . . . and from whence the three adjoining provinces [Virginia, Maryland, and North Carolina] might be kept in constant alarm by desultory excursions . . . for the purpose of distressing the disaffected and collecting together the well affected inhabitants."

Exactly what distracted Clinton from such an attractive objective so near at hand is difficult to say. Sir Peter Parker had sent a reconnaissance vessel to Charleston, which returned and reported that the city was virtually undefended and that it could be easily taken. Probably Clinton's major consideration was that his force was ultimately intended to reinforce Howe for operations in New York. The Chesapeake plan might present complications and consume considerable time, whereas a simple foray against Charleston would allow the expedition to return to New York in a short time. In fact, Clinton seems to have had in mind an even more limited objective: "... I thought Sullivan's Island [guarding Charleston Harbor], if it could be seized without much loss of time, might prove a very important acquisition and greatly facilitate any subsequent move we should be in a condition to make in proper season against that capital." Clinton did not even contemplate capturing Charleston unless American resistance collapsed.[5]

The expedition turned south and arrived off the city early in June. After a reconnaissance of the approaches, it was decided that Clinton should attack the fort on Sullivan's Island by landing a force on Long Island, which lay to the north of Sullivan's. It was believed that the water between the two islands was shallow enough to allow his troops to reach the fort from its undefended northern approaches. Sir Peter Parker would meanwhile take his ships up the channel and bombard Fort Sullivan from the seaward side.

Although General Washington could not reinforce the threatened city, he dispatched Charles Lee, a former British colonel turned major general of the Continental Line, to command the American forces at Charleston. Colonel William Moultrie had already thrown up defense works around the city, including the fort on Sullivan's Island. Lee's principal role was to stiffen the morale of the defenders and keep them from wasting their powder. "... I must entreat and insist," he said in one of his first orders, "that you consider it as a standing order that not a [rifle] man under your command is to fire at a greater distance than 150 yards at the utmost; in short they must never fire without the utmost certainty of hitting their object. . . ." And he admonished the gunners that "four hundred yards is the greatest distance they should be allowed to fire at."

Excellent American gunnery and poor British seamanship disrupted Parker's bombardment. Three ships went aground in the treacherous waters of the channel. The fire from Fort Sullivan was "slow, but decisive indeed; [the Americans] were very cool, and took great care not to fire except when their guns were exceedingly well directed." Moultrie and his gunners richly deserved their libations of "grog in fire buckets, which we partook of very heartily."[6]

Meanwhile, General Clinton found that the water between Long Island and Sullivan's Island was too deep for his men to ford, so the land attack could not be mounted. Parker and his seamen seem to have doubted Sir

Henry's assertions, and Clinton afterward claimed that Parker should have gotten his ships and their guns closer to Fort Sullivan. The British lost one frigate, and four other ships were severely damaged. Sir Peter Parker literally had his britches blown off, and his wounds, though minor, were presumably excrutiatingly uncomfortable. The British casualties were 225 killed and wounded; the American losses totaled 37 killed and wounded. By the end of July the expedition was back in New York.

It was a bitter experience for Clinton. Germain and the King supported him in private, but the London *Royal Gazette* published accounts that were favorable to Commodore Parker and, by implication, blamed Clinton for the failure of the campaign. But there were some lessons to be learned by the British about the war in America. The response of the North Carolina Loyalists to Governor Martin's appeal to arms was highly gratifying, and the success of the Americans at Moore's Creek Bridge was the result of a combination of good luck on one side and bad judgment on the other. But it seems clear that even if the outcome had been different, the Patriots would have been able to deal with Loyalist resistance. Though not as well organized and militant as in other states, the Whigs nevertheless held the initiative, and only the timely arrival of Clinton's regulars could have afforded the Loyalists enough support to effect a successful counterrevolution and to establish crown authority. A corollary to this was the danger inherent in any kind of coordinated operation that depended on a scheduled movement of troops and ships. Dartmouth set in motion Clinton's reinforcement in the early fall of 1775, but a cumbersome bureaucracy and the capricious weather of the North Atlantic caused eight months to pass before Parker's squadron arrived off Cape Fear.

The Charleston expedition was also Clinton's introduction to the difficult business of combined land and sea operations. As he was to learn on frequent occasions thereafter, such operations required not only a clear agreement on tactics by both army and navy commanders but mutual trust and confidence that would lead each commander to cooperate generously with the other, especially when the action did not go according to plan. Such relationships were not usual, and they were certainly likely to be rare with Clinton, given his nettlesome nature and thin-skinned sensitivity to criticism. Only with Lord Howe and Commodore Collier did he ever find such kinship.

Finally, the South Carolinians were deceived into believing that they had repulsed a major attack on Charleston and that the period of relative peace which followed was the result of the stoutness of their defense. Yet Clinton's expedition was little more than a raid, and any permanent occupation would have been out of the question because British strategy for 1776 centered on New York and Canada. The British did not return to South Carolina in 1777 or 1778 simply because they were too busy elsewhere.

Almost alone among British generals and ministers Clinton was skeptical of inflated reports of the numbers of Loyalists who would flock to the support of the crown in the South. Moreover, he clearly perceived that "there does not exist in any one [colony] in America a number of friends of government sufficient to defend themselves when troops are withdrawn. The idea is chimerical, false, and if the measure is adopted . . . all the friends of government will be sacrificed *en detail*." If there was to be troop support for Loyalist uprisings, "such a disposition may be made as will give it a fair trial, but if it succeeds the troops must not be recalled." He had had no opportunity to test his ideas in 1776.[7]

✳ Germain, the Loyalists, and the Southern Strategy ✳

In every plan the ministry had adopted before 1778 an important article of faith had been that the overwhelming majority of Americans were loyal to the crown and that they needed only proper military support for putting down the rebellion and restoring constitutional government. It was true that the army in America seemed rather small for the reconquest of an area that reached from Massachusetts to Georgia, but all that was really needed was the destruction of Washington's army. Once the rebels were deprived of their principal weapon of resistance, the Loyalists would have no difficulty in restoring the King's peace.

Wishful thinking added a sort of corollary to the role of the Loyalists. As British regulars appeared, driving the rebels before them, Loyalists would presumably rise in support of the British army, and eventually the war would be "Americanized." But by the end of 1777 the British generals had discovered that Loyalists, if they existed in large numbers, were not always willing to declare themselves, much less volunteer for soldiering. Burgoyne looked for them in the Hampshire Grants, in the Mohawk Valley, and on the upper Hudson—and he looked in vain. Howe's expedition to Pennsylvania was grounded in his conviction that the presence of large numbers of Loyalists would ensure the overthrow of Whig rule once Philadelphia was taken. When he landed at the Head of the Elk in the summer of 1777, he was greeted by a handful of Loyalists and by columns of smoke on the horizon marking the fires set by Patriot farmers burning their crops.

Yet Germain's optimistic certainty that there was potential support among the Americans persisted. Part of the reason for his conviction was that he was besieged by Loyalists in England, who assured him that the evidence that confronted him was not what it seemed. Observers cited scattered and abortive risings in the Carolinas as proof that a great reservoir of the King's friends were to be found if only they could be assured of the government's support. Royal governors were not uninterested in any effort that might result in the restoration of their jobs. Governor William Campbell of South Carolina and Governor James Wright of Georgia sent a memorial to Germain urging a southern expedition: "From our particular knowledge of those Provinces, it appears very clear to us, that if a proper number of troops were in possession of Charleston . . . or if they were to possess themselves of the back country thro' Georgia, and to leave a garrison in the town of Savannah, the whole inhabitants of both Provinces would soon come in and submit."[8]

Two other sources seemed to be credible. One was Joseph Galloway of Pennsylvania, who emerged as the spokesman for the Loyalist exiles in England. Originally a member of the First Continental Congress, he had been foremost among the Whig-Loyalists advocating reconciliation with England. When the Whigs began the movement for independence, he refused to renounce his loyalty to the mother country. He had been the principal civil administrator in Philadelphia during the British occupation and had been outraged when the ministry ordered Clinton to evacuate the city in 1778. He had been successful in restoring the capital to some normalcy, which he thought demonstrated the benefits of the restoration of English rule. When he went to England, Galloway not only aired his views but wrote several pamphlets urging a more vigorous prosecution of the war and insisting that it could be won if only the Loyalists were properly supported.

Members of the Carlisle Commission returning from America after their fruitless peace mission in 1778 also attested to the strength of the Loyalists. Two of the commissioners, William Eden and George Johnstone, were emphatic in recommending the establishment of royal government in New York and exploiting similar opportunities in other colonies.

On the one hand, then, were the demonstrable instances, especially during the campaign of 1777, when expectations of Loyalist support had been almost totally without foundation. On the other hand, there was firsthand evidence given by people who were qualified (but not disinterested) judges that "good Americans" existed in formidable numbers, enough, these witnesses insisted, to enable the ministry to base its strategy on the certainty of Loyalist support. How was this conflicting evidence to be evaluated?

In the final analysis, the scales were weighted by political pressure. The Opposition in Parliament was making the most of the ministry's inept conduct of the war. Ireland was again in turmoil, doubly troublesome during wartime. The navy was being seriously challenged at sea, and two West Indian islands, Grenada and St. Vincent, had been lost to the French. Lord North seemed more helpless than ever, and the King went to the extreme length of presiding himself over a meeting of the cabinet in an effort to curb the petty feuds among his ministers. In the midst of such tumult, Germain hesitated to ask Parliament for too much. Recruiting of troops was increasingly difficult despite higher bounties and shorter enlistments. Hiring mercenaries meant adding to the annual cost the government was currently paying each year—already 25,000 Germans had been sent to America.

The Opposition had been conducting an inquiry into the command of the Howe brothers for several months. Germain had hoped that the Howes would fade from the scene, but Sir William had demanded a hearing, and it was soon evident that, in defending himself, he intended to lay the burden of failure on the American Secretary. One of the principal points of Howe's defense was that the forces furnished him had been inadequate because Germain had placed too much reliance on the Loyalists. Howe insisted that support for the government in America was negligible, and from this the Opposition drew the logical conclusion. If Loyalist support was not forthcoming only an enormous increase of troops could bring about a successful conquest of the rebel provinces. One of the Opposition's most telling blows was the testimony of Major General Charles Grey: "I think that with the present force in America there can be no expectation of ending the war by force of arms," he stated flatly. Grey then elaborated: "I do not think that from the beginning of June, when I landed in New York, in 1777, to the 20th of November, 1777, there was in that time a number of troops in America altogether adequate to the subduing of that country by force of arms." The implication was clear. In the summer of 1777 Howe and Burgoyne had had more than 30,000 troops. In 1779 Clinton's force was scarcely two-thirds that number. Millions of pounds had been expended and much blood had been spilled, and to what purpose? The rebellion was no nearer its end in 1779 than it had been in 1775.[9]

Thus success in America became increasingly important not only as an end in itself but because failure might bring about the fall of the ministry. Lord North told the King in May that "Gen. Grey's evidence and declarations . . . have made such an impression that it will be very difficult to get the better of it; . . . it is possible that some resolution may be prepared against the continuance of the War, which though not carried will be supported by so many votes as to leave it almost impossible to the present Ministry to remain in office." George III stoutly refused to consider relinquishing the thirteen colonies. "America cannot now be deserted without the loss of the Islands; therefore we must stretch every nerve to defend ourselves, and must run risks; if we are to play the cautious game ruin will inevitably ensue." So perhaps it is not too much to say that Germain accepted the evidence of Loyalist support simply because any other conclusion would have made his political position untenable.

Perforce, Germain countered the Opposition's attack with arguments and evidence of his own. Past failures were accounted for not by failure on the part of the Loyalists but by other circumstances—one of these clearly being the inadequacy of Sir William Howe. Moreover, the ministry now

Lord George Germain (W. L. Clements Library, University of Michigan)

intended to test its strategy in the South, a region much less populous and less likely to be infected by strong Whig elements such as had corrupted New England and Pennsylvania. It would be dishonorable, argued Germain, for the nation to desert His Majesty's loyal friends in America.

To counter Grey's evidence Joseph Galloway testified, but it was obvious that a civilian opinion could not outweigh the authority of one of Howe's principal commanders. But Major General James Robertson, another veteran of the American war, was as positive as Grey had been negative. Two-thirds of the Americans, he said, wanted peace and only awaited the help from England that would "enable the loyal subjects of America to get free from the tyranny of the rebels." By the end of the debate the American Loyalists had become both an end and a means. Germain had virtually admitted that the major justification for the war was that England could not honorably abandon the "loyal subjects of America." At the same time he had given assurances that the next campaign would succeed because support for the crown was widespread and, with proper assistance from Clinton's army, this support would be decisive. If the campaign failed, both means and ends would be discredited.[10]

To do Germain justice, he did not rely entirely on the evidence generated in the heat of the Howe inquiry. James Simpson, the crown's attorney general for South Carolina, was sent to Georgia in an effort to sound out the extent of Loyalist sentiment in the southern colonies. His report was too late to have any influence on the decision in London, but it did give considerable encouragement to Clinton in New York. Simpson's analysis showed a keen appreciation of the complexities of the problem, and he was careful to extend his inquiries not only to Loyalists of Savannah and the coastal area but to "several people of the Back Country" of South Carolina:

> I therefore thought it proper to represent to them that . . . altho' the Province was to be overrun, and Charles Town reduced by the King's Troops, yet unless Government was to be so firmly established as to give security to them without the protection of the Army (and which could only be effected by the Efforts of the People themselves), the Success would be far from complete. And if upon a future emergency the Troops were withdrawn, and they should suffer the party who now predominated again to prevail, their situation would probably be very deplorable. But to this they replied, "they had no apprehensions on that score, that they were numerous and able enough to protect themselves if they were once restored to an equality with their oppressors by being supplied with Arms and Ammunition, both of which they are quite destitute, and which they allege is the sole cause of their present submission. . . ."

On the whole I do not hesitate to declare to your Lordship that I am of the opinion whenever the King's Troops move to Carolina they

will be assisted by very considerable numbers of the inhabitants; that
if the respectable force proposed moves thither early in the Fall the
reduction of the country without risk or much opposition will be the
consequence. . . .[11]

All this was vastly encouraging to General Clinton although he was, as
always, skeptical about reports of Loyalist strength. Earlier in the year he
had attempted to carry out instructions from the ministry to send an
expedition to East Florida and perhaps probe the defenses of Georgia. Sir
Henry had not expected much from this foray because only about 3,000
men were involved. But, as it turned out, the results were enormously
gratifying and, coupled with Simpson's report, caused Clinton's spirits to
revive.

✳ The British Conquest of Georgia ✳

Georgia was by far the weakest of the thirteen colonies that revolted
against England. Only about 40,000 people, almost half of them Negroes,
inhabited a strip of land forty or fifty miles wide to the west and south of
the Savannah River. Indians, principally the Creeks, threatened the western frontier, and to the south East Florida provided a haven for refugee
Tories and a base from which enemy raiding parties made periodic incursions. Georgia was so obviously helpless to defend itself that Congress
passed special legislation to allow the state to recruit in other states in an
effort to fill its militia ranks and even voted a special subsidy of one million
dollars for its defense.

These inherent troubles were enhanced by squabbles among the Whig
leaders. Button Gwinnett, signer of the Declaration of Independence and
president of the new state government, also fancied himself a military
commander. The Continental Congress thought otherwise and appointed
Lachlan MacIntosh as brigadier general commanding forces in the state.
In 1777 the Georgia Provincial Congress organized a military expedition
against St. Augustine, but it was aborted when the rivalry between Gwinnett and MacIntosh forced the committee of safety to dismiss both men
from command. Their rivalry reached its climax in a duel in which
MacIntosh was wounded and Gwinnett was killed. Feeling ran so high
against MacIntosh that the Provincial Congress thought it wise to order
him to service with Washington's army. General John Armstrong, who
served with Charles Lee in South Carolina in 1776 was led to remark:

The people here [Georgia] are if possible more harum Skarum than
their sister colony. They will propose anything, and after they have
propos'd it, discover that they are incapable of performing the least.
They have propos'd securing their Frontiers by constant patrols of

horse Rangers, when the scheme is approv'd of they scratch their heads for some days, and at length inform you that there is a small difficulty in the way; that of the impossibility to procure a single horse—their next project is to keep their inland Navigation clear . . . by a numerous fleet of Guarda Costa arm'd boats, when this is agreed to, they recollect that they have not a single boat—Upon the whole, I shoul'd not be surpris'd if they were to propose mounting a body of Mermaids on Alligators. . . .[12]

At least three expeditions were proposed against St. Augustine from 1776 to 1778, but none got even as far as the Georgia-Florida border. Meanwhile, Tory raiders, especially a well-organized body called the Florida Rangers, made periodic sweeps into the region of the lower Altamaha driving off cattle, burning, and looting. Attempts to raise a militia force were only partly successful. Pay and supplies were scarce, a condition to be expected because Georgia currency was so inflated that no one outside the state would accept it. Those who joined the militia seldom served out their enlistments. They were fearful for the safety of their families, or must go tend to their crops, or were homesick. Georgia, like North Carolina, was afflicted with that most formidable enemy of the Patriot cause, apathy.

The arrival of Brigadier General Robert Howe, a North Carolinian appointed by Congress to command the Department of the South, did not improve matters. Howe was not very tactful in his efforts to bring order out of the chaotic military situation. Georgians resented high-ranking Continentals in general and North Carolinians in particular.

In the last of the attempted expeditions against Florida in 1778 the Georgia assembly ignored General Howe and granted full military authority to its thirty-year-old governor, John Houstoun. Howe had warned that the expedition was untimely and that it would strip the state of troops needed for its defense. The assembly adjudged Howe insubordinate and disrespectful and so reported to Congress. Despite the ill feeling against him, Howe agreed to join his Continentals with the motley collection of Georgia and South Carolina militia. There was also a naval force under the command of Commodore Oliver Bowen. When the various units assembled, the question of command was immediately raised. Howe claimed seniority by virtue of his position as commander of the Southern Department. Houstoun refused to take orders from Howe, and Bowen refused to take orders from either. By the time the expedition reached the St. Mary's River at the end of June, Howe and his officers decided to take their men back to Savannah. Houstoun was determined to push on to St. Augustine, but his subordinates refused. It was the last "offensive" by the Georgians.[13]

Up to this point the British in St. Augustine had acted on the defensive.

General Augustine Prevost, the commander in East Florida, had, like his American counterpart, considered that his force was not strong enough to take offensive action and had confined himself to border raids.

In New York Sir Henry Clinton had been largely preoccupied with adjusting to the defensive strategy necessitated by the entrance of France into the war. Late in 1778, he had, with considerable reluctance, detached a force of 3,000 redcoats and Hessians to reinforce St. Augustine and perhaps strike a blow at Georgia. Since he had also detached 5,000 men to the West Indies and another 2,000 to Haldimand in Canada, he was not very happy about this additional drain on his army in New York. Yet the Florida reinforcement was responsible for the first successful step in the new British effort at reconquest.

The enterprising commander of this expedition was Lieutenant Colonel Archibald Campbell, who had earned his latest rank in the 42nd Highland Regiment, the famous "Black Watch." Taking full liberties with his ambiguous orders, he headed straight for Savannah and landed his troops below the city on December 29, 1778. General Howe, who was shortly to be relieved as commander of the Southern Department, made a halfhearted effort to defend the city. As usual, there was confusion of command between Howe and Governor Houstoun, and from first to last Howe never got a firm grip on the situation. Campbell threw his troops into the attack with such force that the American defenses were overrun. With only twenty-six casualties he captured 450 of the Americans. The battle was over so quickly that the town was scarcely damaged.

Campbell and Commodore Hyde Parker immediately issued a proclamation announcing that they had come to restore the King's peace. Those who wished to demonstrate their loyalty were invited to join in suppressing the rebellion. The protection of the crown was to be extended to all who declared for the King. Clemency and protection of life and property were assured for all who took an oath of loyalty. Future conduct rather than past actions was to be the test, and pardons were assured for those who might be guilty of previous offenses.

General Prevost soon arrived from St. Augustine, and the two officers conferred. Clinton's ambivalent orders to Campbell seemed to have envisioned nothing more than the establishment of a base in Savannah. But Prevost and Campbell, encouraged by their easy success, saw the larger prospect of reclaiming the whole of Georgia. Their combined strength was now about 4,000 men, surely more than a match for any force the Americans could muster.

On January 24 Campbell started up the Savannah with 1,000 men to attack Augusta. Prevost, with the remaining troops, prepared to check the forces of General Benjamin Lincoln, now commanding the Southern Department. Lincoln's force consisted of no more than 2,500 Continentals and militia. Campbell occupied Augusta on the last day of January and was soon enlisting almost 1,400 Loyalist militia. But the ease with which the British conquest was proceeding was deceiving.

In mid-February a band of 700 Loyalists from North Carolina, encouraged by the news of Campbell's success at Augusta, had set out to join the British. By February 14 they had reached Kettle Creek, about fifty miles northwest of Augusta. Here they were surprised by a Patriot force of less than half their number led by a lean, dour partisan named Andrew Pickens. In a bloody battle that lasted almost two hours the Americans killed forty of the enemy and wounded or captured 150 more.

By this time other bands of Whig militia had taken the field, and Lincoln had sent over half of his command to join them. Campbell now faced a Patriot force of nearly 4,000 men, and his militia quickly lost their enthusiasm. "I used every argument," said Campbell, "to convince them that if they did not join the Army in defence of the frontiers, the Rebels would constantly make incursions and plunder them of their property; But they were deaf to reason, and left me to a single man." Campbell was forced to abandon Augusta, and late in February he began to withdraw toward Savannah. As a grim reminder to the Tories, sixty-five of the survivors of Kettle Creek were adjudged guilty of treason, and five were hanged.

The victory resulted in an enthusiastic turnout of Whig militia, and the Americans were emboldened to take the offensive. General Lincoln sent out three columns to gain control of the Georgia backcountry. One of these, commanded by Colonel John Ashe, attempted to cut off Campbell's column as it withdrew down the Savannah. On March 2 the British commander turned on his pursuers at Brier Creek, about halfway between Augusta and Savannah. While he demonstrated on Ashe's front, Campbell sent a flanking column upstream to circle and strike the American rear. Although Ashe was forewarned of the threat, he failed to take any precautions, and when the attack burst upon the Americans the militia panicked. Between 150 and 200 were either killed by enemy fire or were drowned attempting to escape across the river or into a nearby swamp.[14]

From a military point of view, the campaign ended in a stalemate. But in the context of controlling the Georgia backcountry, the results were disastrous for the British. Whigs in Georgia and the Carolinas were stirred into action, and the savage reprisals against the Tories taught a grim lesson. Prominent Loyalists fled to Savannah or to Florida and the rest were cowed into passive silence. The pattern was clear. A show of force by the British was useless unless it could be demonstrated that the authority of the crown was permanent. Loyalists who literally or figuratively came out of hiding found themselves abandoned to the retribution of the enemy. The sporadic offensive of Campbell and Prevost had failed to gain any territory and had thoroughly aroused the Whig partisans.

Benjamin Lincoln broke the stalemate. By now the Americans had collected 7,000 men, most of whom were militia. South Carolinians were as suspicious as Georgians of Continental commanders, and Governor John Rutledge made little effort to cooperate with Lincoln. But by late April the general felt that he was strong enough to make another attempt to extend Whig influence into the backcountry. Unfortunately, he left only a skeleton force of 1,000 men under General Moultrie to defend Charleston.

Instead of following Lincoln up the Savannah, Prevost made straight for Charleston and by May 14 was outside the city. He might have achieved complete surprise, but his march was delayed by the looting and plundering of his soldiers, who could not resist the fine plantations that lay along their route. Once arrived at the city, Prevost called on the garrison to surrender. Governor Rutledge and his council countered with the astonishing proposal that if the British would spare the city the Carolinians would remain neutral for the remainder of the war and then would pledge allegiance to the victor. But Prevost was bluffing. With Lincoln hurrying back from Augusta, his position was rapidly becoming untenable. By the time the Charlestonians recovered from their fright, Prevost had begun his withdrawal, his men staggering under mountainous loads of plunder and herding along several hundred slaves.[15]

Three months later it was the British whose foothold in the South was threatened. The French naval commander, Admiral d'Estaing, had defeated Admiral Byron and captured Grenada and St. Vincent and now offered his services for a joint expedition with the Americans against Savannah. By the middle of September 1779, the French had landed 3,500 troops below the city. Lincoln came in from Charleston with 1,500 militia and Continentals.

If d'Estaing had moved promptly, he probably could have overrun the defenses of Savannah, for Prevost was taken completely by surprise. But the French commander held a parley and attempted to induce the British to surrender. Prevost stalled and during the delay called in his scattered forces and strengthened his defenses. D'Estaing then decided to employ siege tactics, and for the next three weeks the allies laboriously advanced their lines of entrenchments in order to bring their artillery within range. By the first week in October, d'Estaing was becoming restive. His guns were ineffective against the British works, and he was worried that British naval forces or bad weather would interfere with his return to his West Indies station.

The decision was finally made to take the British position by storm. The Americans and their French allies attempted a surprise attack, but Prevost had prepared his defenses well, and the allies had to advance on a narrow front. Though outnumbered two to one, the British lines were manned by veteran troops, the Highlanders, the Hessians, and New York Loyalists from the regiments of James DeLancey and John Harris Cruger. Over half of Prevost's force was American, although almost none were Southerners.

The allied attack, although poorly planned, was pressed with great determination. The Americans and the French forced their way through the abatis and into the ditches outside the British works. Attack was met by counterattack in a vicious melee of grenadiers, French, Hessians, Continentals, and Loyalists. Men fell under an avalanche of bullets, swords, bayonets, and clubbed muskets. It may well have been the bloodiest fight since Bunker Hill. The allied force failed to penetrate the British line and finally withdrew. Their losses were fearful. Sixteen officers and 223 men were killed and 521 were wounded, a staggering 20 percent of the total number engaged. The British losses were 150 killed, wounded, and missing. D'Estaing was wounded at the head of his troops, and Colonel Casimir Pulaski, a Polish cavalryman who had volunteered for service with the Americans, was killed.

Benjamin Lincoln doggedly insisted that the siege be continued, but d'Estaing had had enough. A few days later he embarked his men and sailed for the West Indies. Savannah was saved for the British, and they gave it up only when the war ended.[16]

The defense of Savannah was virtually the only bright spot in what had been otherwise a dismal year for Sir Henry Clinton. The American Secretary continued his encouraging exhortations: "Your own determination . . . is conformable to that vigor and zeal which have distinguished your operations in every instance since you were appointed commander in chief. And His Majesty has the firmest reliance that no opportunity will be lost . . . for the speedy reduction of the rebellion by destroying the rebel force." Sir Henry's response was to request that he be relieved of his command. In full confidence that his request would be granted Clinton embarked on what he hoped was his last campaign in America.[17]

The success that HMS army has met with in this province, by penetrating without any loss of men to the very gates of Charleston, & obliging the enemy to burn its beautiful suburbs, will hardly be credited. . . . We arrived at Charlestown on the 11th in the evening after almost totally destroying or taking that famous legion of Polaski's, by 45 of our gallant dragoons under command of the brave Capt. TAWES. Among the killed of the enemy was Polaski's Lt/Col & several pris besides a gt # of prisoners [next days terms were demanded with 4 hrs for an answer] But an express having arrived in the meantime fm Gen Lincoln . . . the enemy grew more confident . . . however they proposed a neutrality for the province [Prevost refused] [Storming rejected as possible but involving too gt a loss of men, so it was resolved to keep the field supplied fm the sea] This measure is now pursued & the army is in possession of James and John's island. The enemy abandoned the v. strong Ft Johnston on James Is.

Major Graham with a party of the L.I. surprised a strong body of militia on John's Is, killed & took c. 80 men without resistance & with no loss on our side. Capts Farrel & mANSON with the Thunderer & Snake galleys, on their passage fm Beanfort to our army attacked 2 armed schooners [Eagle captured & another abandoned & burnt] Col. Prevost with a large corps under his command covers the country at Stono Ferry [Garrison of James Is removed to John Is on the night of 27/28 May over Stono R. after which a pontoon bridge was made to connect John's Is with the mainland] & over it at Stono Ferry the L.I. Lt Cavalry, rangers etc with a bn of Hessians are advanced & in a v. strong position

3. Rebels and Bloodybacks

The War of Independence was essentially representative of the first stage in the history of modern warfare. Until the end of the eighteenth century, wars were for the most part fought by small, highly trained professional armies. The civilian population was generally unaffected by these wars, although it might be affected by their outcome. Soldiers did a certain amount of stealing and looting as they passed through the countryside, but their small numbers could hardly lead to anything that could be called terrorism or "scorched earth."

But the War of Independence also marked a transition in military history in at least one respect. The Americans had no standing army so they had of necessity to create a citizen soldiery. Recognizing that their army could not match the British in training or discipline, they expected that numbers would make up for quality. This concept was later adopted by the French and especially by Napoleon, so that those accustomed to eighteenth-century warfare were astounded when Bonaparte invaded Russia in 1812 with an army of 800,000 men. So began the second stage of modern war. Civilians were still not greatly affected except—and it was an important exception—that all able-bodied males might expect to be called to military duty.

In 1790 the Secretary of War reported that a total of 396,000 names appeared on the rolls of all branches of both national and state armed services. This included a large number of men who had enlisted more than once. (There was a Joseph Pancake whose name appears on the rolls of no less than four Virginia units. Whether Joseph was a Patriot who found it necessary to go home occasionally to attend to his family and crops or whether he was a professional "bounty jumper," deponent saith not.)[1] It is a general rule of thumb that 10 percent of a nation's total population consists of adult males fit for military service. For example, the United States raised an armed force of about 14,000,000 men in World War II from a total population of 140,000,000 people. Taking into account the fact that mid-twentieth-century conscription was much more efficient than the systems used by the Continental Congress and the states in the War of Independence, one may hazard a guess that about 100,000 men bore arms at one time or another. Of these no more than about 30,000 were in the field at any one time. The largest return of the army under the immediate command of General Washington was that of October 1, 1778, which showed 18,752 men present and fit for duty.[2]

At the outbreak of the war the entire British army consisted of only about 48,000 men. Twenty thousand of these were committed to Ireland, Gibraltar, the West Indies, and other outposts of Britain's far-flung empire. To fight a war, even one against a rabble of farmers, required enormous and rapid expansion. It should be remembered that England was in the initial stages of her industrial revolution and had no desire to see skilled workers or even apprentices wasted in the ranks of the army. Steadily employed workers were therefore beyond the reach of recruiters. Their efforts were limited to enlisting the unemployed, the vagabonds, and, as the war went on, convicted criminals, who were allowed to enlist as the alternative to a jail sentence.[3]

Yet Lord George Germain, the American Secretary, was able to send General Howe a reinforcement of 26,000 men in 1776. By the end of the war England had sent nearly 60,000 men to America, a number far greater than could be recruited from "disorderly persons, . . . incorrigible rogues, . . . such recruits as a Battn. might [not] choose to take in times of profound Peace."[4]

The answer to the troop shortage was to hire foreign mercenaries. At first England hoped to get Russian troops from Empress Catherine II, but she had refused a request from Whitehall in 1775. Germain then turned to central Europe. During the course of the war nearly half of the troops sent to America, a total of 29,166 men, were from Brunswick, Hesse-Cassell, and other German states. For almost a century the German rulers had used their armies as a lucrative source of revenue. Their availability for hire was one of the reasons why nations such as England were able to maintain such small standing armies in peacetime.[5]

Recruited and trained in much the same manner as the British army, the German soldiers marched and fought well in America. British commanders were contemptuous of them and frequently blamed them for British failures, but their performance was always consistent and frequently of a very high quality. For most of the southern campaigns Cornwallis had about 100 jägers (light infantry armed with rifles) and the Regiment Bose, about 350 rank and file.

As the British faced the Americans in 1775 it seemed to be a gross mismatch. Francis Lord Rawdon was convinced that "we shall soon have done with these scoundrels, for one only dirties one's fingers by meddling with them." The army's contempt was shared by Parliament, where Richard Rigby assured members that serious colonial resistance "was an idea thrown out to frighten women and children." Five years later America was still unconquered, and Lord Rawdon himself had found that the "scoundrels" were a difficult lot to deal with.[6]

✳ The Redcoats ✳

The basic organizational unit of the British army was the regiment. But it was more than a list of names and numbers on a sheet of paper. For the enlisted man in peacetime it was his home for life. Officers who were promoted out of a regiment always regarded it with particular affection. It was no accident that the 33rd Regiment was assigned to the command of the Earl of Cornwallis in the southern campaign for it was the regiment that he had commanded as a lieutenant colonel.

In the peacetime army each regiment consisted of eight battalion companies and two flank companies. One of the latter consisted of grenadiers selected for their size and strength. Originally they were armed with grenades, primitive forefathers of the modern "pineapple." But because of their crude design the grenades often killed more friends than foes and so had long since been discarded. But the grenadiers still wore their brimless hats, souvenirs of a time when a hat brim would have interfered with their throwing motion.

The other flank company consisted of light infantry. These troops were lightly armed and equipped, quick-moving, and skilled marksmen. They were often assigned to scouting, reconnaissance, and other special duties. The best of the regiment's soldiers were assigned to the light companies (with no grenadier tradition, the American regiments had two light infantry companies).

British commanders often stripped a number of regiments of their flank companies and formed them into a single regiment if a particularly difficult assault had to be made. At Bunker (or Breed's) Hill Howe formed a regiment of light infantry and another of grenadiers to turn the flank of the American position. (Howard Pyle's famous painting of the battle shows the advance of the light infantry regiment).[7]

Regiments were combined into divisions, wings, or corps, but these were almost always temporary operational units with little or no administrative organization. General Greene referred to Daniel Morgan's command which fought the battle of the Cowpens as a corps of light infantry. A brigade of the Guards that served in America consisted of fifteen men drawn from each of the sixty-four companies of the King's Household troops. By 1777 General Washington had divided his army into three divisions, an organization he retained throughout the campaigns of 1777 and 1778.

In the peacetime British army each company consisted of thirty-eight privates, three corporals, two sergeants, two lieutenants, and a captain. In addition there was the regimental staff including chaplain, surgeon, and the colonel commanding. Reports of troop strength (and casualties) were made of "rank and file," which included privates and corporals. A regiment at full strength thus consisted of 410 rank and file.

With the coming of the war, regimental strength varied widely. Regiments newly arrived from England often had more than 600 men, but the attrition of a campaign found regimental strength sharply reduced. In Cornwallis' southern command in January 1781 the largest British regiment, the 33rd, mustered 328 rank and file "present and fit for duty," while the 7th Regiment could count only 167 men.[8]

The standard weapon of both armies was the smoothbore musket. Approximately four and one-half to five feet in length, its calibre ranged from .69 to .80. Since parts were not standardized, a musket with a broken hammer had to be turned in to the armorer, who hand made a new hammer to fit that particular arm.

A recruit was trained in loading and firing until he could deliver three rounds per minute. Since tactical doctrine dictated that firing be done in volleys, the complicated loading of the musket was done on command. Twelve separate orders were required between each fire. Powder and shot were made up in paper cartridges carried in a cartridge box of wood and leather to protect the ammunition from dampness. A heavy rain, however, could bring a battle to an abrupt halt. When a force of British and Indians ambushed Americans under Colonel Nicholas Herkimer at Oriskany in 1777, a violent rainstorm brought an immediate halt to the fighting and enabled Herkimer to reorganize his shattered command.

To load his musket the soldier extracted a cartridge and bit off the end of the paper spill. He poured a small amount of powder into a spoon-shaped pan located at the side of the breech end of the barrel. From the pan a small touchhole led to the after end of the bore. He then closed the frizzen, which covered the pan and also had a curved leaflike projection positioned so that it could be struck by the hammer. He then poured the remainder of the powder, along with the lead ball, into the muzzle using the paper as a wad. The whole was seated firmly with the ramrod. He then pointed his weapon in the general direction of the enemy (the British "Brown Bess" had no rear sight) and fired. When he pulled the trigger, the hammer containing a bit of flint struck the frizzen, simultaneously creating a shower of sparks and flipping up the lid over the pan, exposing the powder. The resultant flash penetrated the touchhole and ignited the propellant charge in the bore.[9]

These crude weapons were, of course, unreliable. A worn flint might fail to strike sparks. The touchhole might be clogged, especially after several firings. The slightest dampness could render the powder charge useless. Beyond these were human failures. Troops under fire for the first

time—and the British army had not fought for fifteen years—were notoriously inefficient. An enemy fire delivered at forty yards while a soldier was
reloading was not conducive to steady hands and calm nerves. Thus a hail
of bullets from a volley of fire might contain an admixture of flying
ramrods. And in the crash of musketry it was not easy to tell if one's own
weapon had fired, so occasionally in the aftermath of battle muskets could
be found loaded to the muzzle with unexpended charges.[10]

The maximum range of the musket was about 150 yards, but it took a
good marksman with a good musket to hit a man-sized target at half that
distance. The optimal range was thirty to forty yards. Americans then (and
some historians since) derided the close-ordered ranks of redcoats mechan-
ically parading shoulder to shoulder. But eighteenth-century generals knew
what they were about. With a weapon of such limited range and efficiency,
the only way to achieve concentrated fire was to concentrate the soldiers.
The standard method of delivering an attack was to advance to within forty
yards of the enemy, deliver a fire, and then charge with the bayonet. The
defenders would have time for only one counterfire before the bayonet
attack reached them. The combination of concentrated musket fire and
bayonet attack was extremely effective, especially against new troops. It
was not until the Americans had been trained in similar tactics that they
were able to meet the British on equal terms.

Field artillery in the British army consisted of a wide variety of weapons. In the southern campaign, however, the British were limited to only a
few choices. In the interior, where roads were bad or nonexistent, it was
simply impractical to use heavy guns. A twelve-pounder required a team of
ten to twelve horses to pull its 3,200 pounds of dead weight. Six- and three-
pounders were most often used. All guns, regardless of size, had a range of
about 2,000 yards, but the maximum effective range was 800 to 900 yards.
Guns fired several kinds of projectiles, including solid shot, grape, canister, and hot shot. Grape charges consisted of a cluster of iron balls, each
about two inches in diameter. Canister was, as the name indicates, simply a
metal container loaded with musket balls. Such charges were very inaccurate and were used at nearly point-blank range to break an enemy assault.

A six-pounder had a bore of 3.6 inches, and its gun tube was about five
feet long. The gun was trained by slewing it with a long pole called a tiller
inserted through a ring in the carriage trail. It was elevated by the use of a
screw or wedge. The gun was loaded very much like a musket except that
the charge was ignited by applying a slow match to the touchhole. Since
priming and loading could be done simultaneously, a good gun crew could
provide a fairly high rate of fire. A Hessian artillery unit that accompanied
Burgoyne from Canada gave a demonstration in which it fired twelve
rounds a minute.[11]

Mounted troops were traditionally divided into two categories, cavalry
and dragoons. The distinction was that cavalrymen fought from horseback

whereas dragoons were simply mounted infantry who rode to battle but fought on foot. In the southern campaigns mounted troops were almost always referred to as dragoons, but accounts of engagements make it clear that dragoons not only performed the tasks of scouting, breaking an enemy line by mounted charge, and pursuing a retreating enemy but also fought from horseback.[12]

Whether he was an infantryman, artilleryman, or dragoon, the life of a British redcoat was not easy. In the peacetime army, enlistment was for life, although after the war began recruits were enlisted for three years or the duration of the war. By 1779 the shortage of troops led to additional inducements such as doubling the bounty for enlistment. But national policy was geared to England's economic development, and this meant that any worker who was steadily employed was exempt from military service. Vagrants, smugglers, and those guilty of minor criminal offenses might escape imprisonment by enlisting, and by 1779 any convicted criminal could be recruited. Those who enlisted, then, were the riffraff, "incorrigible rogues," and "disorderly persons,"—in short, society's "losers." Could good soldiers be made of such grist? They could. Then as now the noncommissioned officers were the backbone of the British army. Under the rigid discipline of hard-eyed sergeants, the recruits were molded into soldiers, undoubtedly more from fear than ambition. It was not for nothing that sergeants were positioned just to the rear of the ranks as they marched into battle. A soldier who was inclined to run would be face to face with his sergeant if he turned around. No doubt he concluded that his chances of surviving in battle were better than the certain fate that awaited him at the hands of his sergeant—or a firing squad.[13]

There was another factor in the making of a redcoat. As his civilian identity merged and was finally lost in the soldiers' life, he found himself part of the Regiment. Here he found the tangibles of food, clothing, and shelter that he had not been able to acquire as a civilian "loser." There were also intangibles of which he was perhaps not fully aware: the comradeship of his fellows, status, and an order to his life. In short, the Regiment became his home. And despite the iron discipline and poor pay, the soldier's new identity led to a fierce pride, a loyalty so intense that it could explode. Men of Fraser's 71st Highlanders, mutinied upon learning that they were to be transferred to other units and could no longer wear their kilts, and some of them were killed before the mutiny could be quelled.[14]

A private's pay was officially eight pence a day, but he actually received only a fraction of this pittance. An astonishing variety of "off-reckonings," consisted of deductions "for clothing, for necessaries, for washing, for the paymaster, for the multitude of articles of useless and unmilitary fopperies (introduced by many colonels to the oppression of the soldier for what they call the appearance and credit of the regiment) . . . and as to the little enjoyment and recreation, which even the meanest rank of men can call their own in any country, the brave, the honorable veteran soldier, must not aspire to."[15]

Discipline was harsh. Petty offenses such as shirking or failure to pass inspection of uniform and equipment resulted in a week's confinement on bread and water. Striking an officer was punishable by 800 lashes. Delivered full force with a cat-o'-nine-tails, such a punishment could kill. Desertion, cowardice, or robbery meant the firing squad. Intermediate offenses were usually punished by the lash.

Yet the soldiers accepted these brutal punishments with surprising equanimity. If existence in the army was hard, so was all life among the lower classes in eighteenth-century England. Criminal codes both in England and America provided such punishments as whipping, branding, and maiming, and the tough redcoat accepted it because he could not escape it. As with soldiers in any time, he was even able to make rough jokes about it. One ranker charged with misconduct offered no defense but "to save your Honours and the Court any further trouble, you may set me down for two hundred. I'm sure you Honours will think that enough."[16]

Drinking, gambling, and women provided the only diversions in army life. Since all these required money, the soldier was a chronic thief and looter. He tended to regard all Americans as rebels and therefore fair game for his thieving instincts. The Germans were even worse because the language barrier effectively inured them to protests by Loyalists. Troop commanders recognized that looting seriously impaired their attempts to gain Loyalist support, and from time to time orders were issued threatening severe punishments for seizing civilian property. General Howe even ordered an executioner to accompany patrols in occupied Boston with orders to execute offenders on the spot, but there is no record of any executions. Indeed, junior officers and noncommissioned officers were inclined to be sympathetic toward the men, so little could be done.[17]

Women accompanied the army during every campaign, some even following their men into battle. A good many were wives, and it seems evident that many who were not married were attached to only one man. It was said that 2,000 women accompanied Burgoyne's army when the British invaded New York in 1777, and not all of them marched with the ranks. General Friedrich von Riedesel, the German commander, was accompanied by his wife and their two small children, and Lady Harriet Acland accompanied her husband, Major John Acland, even though she was pregnant. When Sir William Howe landed in New York in 1776, he authorized rations for six women per company. His army was accompanied by 2,776 women and 1,904 children.[18]

Thief, drunkard, and womanizer the redcoat might be, but he was first and foremost a soldier. He was the product of monotonous drill and stern discipline, and he performed on the battlefield with predictable precision and dispatch. Because of his discipline he was generally the superior of his

American counterpart, and only a few American formations could match his cold courage and meet him bayonet for bayonet.

Officers were almost without exception from the upper class of British society. The reasons for the class distinction were, first, that commissions in the army were obtained by purchase. An ensign's commission cost from £400 (in a regiment of foot) to £1,200 (in a Horse Guards regiment). Promotion came only when a vacancy occurred in the next highest rank. The ensign then sold his commission and, with additional funds, purchased his promotion. If he was fortunate enough to rise to colonel, the total cost was £3,500. Seniority was observed in promotions until an officer attained the rank of major. The rank of colonel usually carried with it a coveted regimental command, and this required political influence or family connection. The officer might be favored by his excellent record, but a military or political patron was also necessary.

One wonders how such a system could produce competent officers. The partial answer lies in the fact that most officers were commissioned as young as fifteen or sixteen years of age. By the time he was old enough to pursue other than military interests, the subaltern had been with the regiment for five years. Wise senior sergeants guided him through this apprenticeship so that he usually acquired a good basic training. Many officers took a genuine interest in military matters. Burgoyne, William Howe, and Clinton all produced works on military subjects, which were recognized as genuine contributions to military science.[19]

A senior officer in the peacetime establishment only occasionally did duty with his troops. More often than not he indulged in the games society played or entered politics. Both were not only preferable to the dullness of the camp but sometimes offered an opportunity to cultivate persons of influence who might facilitate his promotion. Peacetime officers seldom retired for they were entitled to only half pay. There were sometimes officers in the lower ranks who were sixty or seventy years of age. But wartime weeded out the incompetents and the infirm. Patrons who sponsored officers for promotion stood in the reflected glory of their protégés and therefore were careful to back only those with good records. The Howe brothers would not have been backed by Lord Germain if they had not proved their competence. Their failure could (and finally did) adversely affect their political sponsor.

The other factor that excluded all but gentlemen from the officer corps was historical. Eighteenth-century Britons had not forgotten England's great Civil War, when the principal factor in Oliver Cromwell's overthrow of the monarchy was his ability to seize control of the army. The military dictatorship which the "Protector" imposed on England was deeply etched in the memories of the aristocracy. What better way to protect property and prevent revolution than by putting the army under the control of the landed aristocracy? Thus the requirement that officers be drawn "from that social class the members of which are more likely to lose than to gain by military aggression."[20] Members of the officer corps also pursued political careers. In 1776 twenty-three members of Parliament held military commissions, including both Howes, Clinton, Burgoyne, and Cornwallis.

If the student of military history finds the British officer corps shot through with inefficiency and blundering stupidity, with fops who held their rank through influence rather than ability, he might recall that every system before and since has had its share of dolts and blunderers. He might also recall that rarely has a peacetime establishment developed a high command capable of fighting a war. (A survey of senior commanders in the United States armed forces in 1939 will show that only the name of George C. Marshall survived until 1943.) If Sir Henry Clinton seems weak and vacillating, if the Earl of Cornwallis blunders inexplicably, the fortunes of war cannot be expected always to produce a Wolfe or a Wellington.

✳ The Continentals ✳

Following the battles of Lexington and Concord in April 1775, a motley assemblage of soldiers appeared in the vicinity of Boston. The British commander, General Thomas Gage, found his little force of 4,000 men besieged by an "army" of between 15,000 and 20,000 men (when Washington took command in July it took him eight days to find out just how many there were). These troops were militia who had come from all over New England, and they were soon being formally enlisted by the Massachusetts Committee of Safety. But Massachusetts had no desire to assume responsibility for defending all of America and it so reported to Congress. The Second Continental Congress had assembled for the purpose of renewing colonial protest to London and asking for relief from parliamentary oppression. Before it could draw its collective breath the Congress discovered that it was being called upon to govern as well. To its everlasting credit it did not shun its burden. It adopted the New England army, and on June 18 John Hancock referred to it as the "Continental Army." By the fall of 1775 this so-called regular army was being referred to as the Continental Line.[21]

The American radicals had the traditional Whig aversion to standing armies, and some members thought they already saw the "growing thirst for power in some departments of the army." Wishful thinking also led Congress to believe that the war would soon be over so it authorized enlistments that would expire at the end of the year. This first national army thus became known as the "Eight Months' Army." George Washington took command of it a year and a day before the Declaration of Independence.

At the end of 1775, Whig fears had not abated, and Congress extended

authorization for the army only for an additional year. The Founding
Fathers were students of history, and they cited examples from Caesar to
Cromwell to show how easily armies could become vehicles of military
dictatorship. If the Fathers seem overly concerned to twentieth-century
students of history one might pause and reflect what might have happened
if George Washington had been a more successful general and a less
devoted disciple of republicanism. Attention is called to the Newburgh
affair of 1782, when Washington and the army were invited to "take
direction of affairs . . . to guide the torrent and bring order . . . out of
confusion." In other revolutions with such a pattern, civilian control is
usually regained only after the military has been overthrown by violence
(for example, Napoleon, Mussolini, and numerous revolutions in Latin
America).[22]

By the fall of 1776 Congress began to face reality. With Washington
defeated and driven from New York, his army decimated by desertion,
Congress authorized an army of 88,000 men enlisted for three years or the
duration of the war. Because there were fewer than 5,000 men in the
Continental Line and almost half failed to reenlist on January 1, it is not
too much to say that the Continental army really originated with the
recruiting of men in the spring of 1777. By this time the first flush of
patriotic ardor had faded, and those who felt an obligation to serve their
country had discovered less onerous ways to respond. Enlistment in the
state militia would mean no more than six months of active duty. If one
were reasonably intelligent and from a middle-class background, a commission in either the Continental Line or the militia was often obtainable.

When recruiting first began in 1775, the adjutant general warned
against recruiting "any deserter from the ministerial army, nor any stroller,
negro, or vagabond." By 1777 reality brought modifications, and the army
accepted not only "vagabonds" and "strollers" but free Negroes and con-
victs. A few substantial citizens, artisans, shopkeepers, and farmers may
have joined or reenlisted from a sense of duty, but at the beginning of 1777
their number was small. The army must also have contained some of the
toughest bodies and spirits in America.[23]

One of the most complete records of a private soldier is the diary and
memoir of Joseph Plumb Martin. He provides an interesting commentary
on the motives that led men to enlist. Martin was fifteen years old when the
war began, and before the year was out he decided that he wanted "to be
called a defender of my country." Rather than enlist for a year, he "wished
only to take a priming before I took on a whole coat of paint," so he joined
the state troops for six months. He received his baptism of fire at Long
Island and continued with Washington's army until his enlistment expired
in December 1776. He had, he said, "learned something of the soldiers'
life, enough . . . to keep me at home for the future." But by spring Martin
"began to think again about the army." He was soon being pressured by

friends to enlist for three years. His "most familiar associate" finally "so far overcame my resolution as to get me into a scrape again, although it was, at this time, against my inclination. . . . But I would here just inform the reader, that that little insignificant monosyllable—No—was the hardest word in the language for me to pronounce. . . ." Martin found himself "attacked front, flank and rear. I thought, as I must go I might as well get as much for my skin as I could." The inducement of a bounty tipped the scales, and Joseph Martin was a private again, "knowing that the army would bring trouble enough to counterbalance all the happiness I could procure for myself in the short time I had to tarry at home."[24]

By the spring of 1777 Congress had turned the problem of recruiting over to the states, assigning a quota to each state and paying a fee for each enlistment. By this time, Congress had resorted to the payment of bounties to encourage enlistments. By an act of 1776, men who enlisted in the Continental army were promised twenty dollars and one hundred acres of land. States, and even counties and towns, offered additional bonuses in order to meet their quotas. But the system did not work well. States were also anxious to keep their militia ranks filled and so offered competing bonuses, which often exceeded those offered by Congress.[25]

It is clear that patriotism alone did not suffice to induce men into the ranks. "We may fairly infer," wrote Washington in 1778, "that the country has been already pretty well drained of that class of men whose tempers, attachments and circumstances disposed them to enter permanently . . . into the army. . . ." In fact, toward the end of the war soldiers, many of whom had not been paid for months, deserted and then enlisted under other names and so received bounty money that they could not get from the army paymasters. And inevitably there were "bounty jumpers," men who enlisted, deserted, and reenlisted several times, receiving bounty and land certificates for each enlistment. Patriotism is the product of history and tradition, and the new nation had little of either. Loyalty was rooted in the states, and soldiers were frequently adamant in their refusal to serve under "foreign" officers. It should also be remembered that the United States has never been able to raise enough volunteers to fight a war of any consequence.[26]

For one class of soldiers circumstances were somewhat different. At the beginning of the war, both the commander in chief and Congress opposed the enlistment of Negroes, and both eventually found that necessity must overcome prejudice. By the end of 1775, Washington had issued a directive "that numbers of Free Negroes are desirous of enlisting, [and] he gives leave to recruiting officers to entertain them and promises to lay the matter before Congress, who he doubts not will approve it." By 1777 Rhode Island, New York, and Maryland had authorized the recruiting of black regiments.[27]

Once more reality and the law bore little similarity to one another.

Whites often sent slaves as substitutes, and a runaway found it was not hard to convince a recruiter struggling to meet his quota that he was a free Negro. The historian Benjamin Quarles has identified 5,000 black Americans who served in various branches of the armed forces during the Revolution. In 1778 the adjutant of Washington's army reported that 755 Negroes were serving in fourteen New York regiments. If these were typical regiments then Negroes made up 21 percent of their strength. It soon became evident that black men who served an honorable enlistment would not be returned to slavery. Attempts by Virginians to reclaim their slaves at the end of the war met with a response from Governor Benjamin Harrison, who appealed to the General Assembly, "not doubting that they will pass an act giving these unhappy creatures that liberty which they had been in some way instrumental in securing to us." The governor had his way.[28]

For the Negro, slave or free, the army offered almost everything he was denied on the outside. He was still subject to a certain degree of degradation—he was assigned the most menial jobs as teamster, cook, or orderly. But he was a soldier, subject indiscriminately to the same restrictions and privileges as white soldiers. His enlistment entitled him to land and money, things hard to come by any other way. There was little inducement for him to desert, for with honorable service there was freedom. Three years was not a long time for those who had learned that to endure was to survive.

So officers might rail at "the strangest mixture of Negroes, Indians, and whites, with old men and mere children . . . [whose] nasty lousy appearance make the most shocking spectacle," but the ranks were somehow filled, enough at least for the Americans to meet the enemy. Like his British counterpart, the recruit could be made into a good soldier. The discipline was stern and the lash frequently employed (thirty-nine lashes for menial offenses), but Americans would not have accepted the savage discipline and degrading treatment that were taken for granted by the redcoat.

Discipline and training. At times the commander in chief despaired of creating "a standing, well-disciplined Army." Part of the problem was that in the beginning there was not even a skeleton force of veterans to teach recruits the most rudimentary rules of camp life. Thus it was from the desk of the commander in chief that orders issued "to keep the men neat and clean" and for "One Man a company to be appointed Camp Colour Man for every Company in every Regiment of the Army whose particular duty it must be . . . to sweep the Street of their respective encampments, to fill up old Necessary houses and dig new ones, to bury all Offal, Filth, and Nastiness, that may poison or infect the health of the Troops." Orders had to be repeated "against the firing of small arms, it is hourly practiced."[29]

The most serious problem throughout the war was desertion. Neither Washington nor General Greene solved it to his satisfaction. They tried leniency, and harshness, and even a mixture of the two. In 1777 Washington accompanied severe punishment for one deserter with pardons for others. Greene on two occasions executed men and then marched the entire army past the dangling bodies. Yet it was difficult to be harsh for most of the desertions came from "such an unconquerable desire of returning to . . . their homes, that it not only produces . . . Desertions among themselves, but infuses a like spirit in others." It was another matter, however, when deserters were captured after serving in the ranks of the enemy. By 1781 both the British and American armies contained a generous leavening of deserters from the enemy. If captured—or perhaps recaptured—they were almost always summarily executed.[30]

Breakdown of discipline could be traced to two sources. One was the logistical support system, which rarely could keep pace with the army's demand for clothing, food, and pay. "I shall only observe," wrote General Greene on one occasion, "that an army which has received no pay for more than two years, distressed for want of clothes, often short of the usual allowances of bread and meat, will mutiny if we fail in the article of salt."

The other source of trouble was the officer corps. In most wars, for every hero there are dozens of drunkards, cowards, or incompetents. Of 900 officers who served at one time or another in seven New York regiments 135 deserted. General Adam Stephen lost his sense of direction at the battle of the Brandywine because he was drunk.

"At a time when everything is at stake," wrote the commander in chief, " . . . it will not do for the Commanding Officer of a Regiment to content himself, with barely giving orders, he should see (at least know) that they are executed. He should call his men out frequently and endeavor to impress them with a just sense of their Duty, and how much depends on subordination and discipline." Early in his career Greene had remarked, "Some captains, and many subordinate officers, neglect their duty some through fear of offending their soldiers, some through laziness, and some through obstinacy. . . . I am determined to break every one for the future who shall lay himself open to it."[31]

Washington made it clear that he preferred officers who were gentlemen. Washington was the product of the deferential social order of Virginia, and he was obviously nonplussed by the democratic New Englanders, who elected their officers. Greene had helped to raise a company at the beginning of the war, but the men refused to elect him an officer so he served in the ranks. (The Rhode Island Committee of Safety made him a brigadier general.) As it happened most of the Continental regiments that Greene commanded were southern, and so he found subordinates with names that constituted a virtual roll call of the region's aristocracy: Carrington, Lee, Washington, Howard, and Huger.[32]

The number of Continental troops who served in the Southern Department after the fall of Charleston was relatively small. After the disaster at

Camden, Gates reported that he had fewer than 1,000 Continentals at Hillsborough. At the height of the campaign, Greene may have had as many as 1,600 regulars including Colonel William Washington's dragoons and Colonel "Light Horse Harry" Lee's Legion. But Continentals were valuable far beyond their numbers. They had been trained by that redoubtable drillmaster Baron von Steuben during the winter of 1778, and they were later commanded by another German, Johann Kalb, until he fell fighting at the head of his troops at Camden.

These Continental regiments were from Virginia, Maryland, and Delaware (not until after Yorktown did any northern Continental regiments serve in the Southern Department). Two of these units, the 1st Maryland and the understrength Delaware regiment, contained as fine fighting men as could be found in either army. They were steady under fire and they could deliver a bayonet attack that often broke the best redcoat regiments. Both units had fought in every engagement from Long Island to Monmouth Court House, and despite their dwindling numbers they served Greene with an excellence that matched their reputation. Two Maryland colonels, Otho Holland Williams and John Eager Howard, were officers of superior quality.[33]

Captain Robert Kirkwood led the skeleton Delaware "regiment" whose strength was only about 100 men. Kirkwood was never promoted because it was thought that he did not command enough men. By the end of the war he had fought brilliantly in thirty-two engagements. In the southern campaign the Delaware troops frequently formed the infantry of Lee's Legion.[34]

The legion was a military formation that may have had its origin in the War of Independence. Banastre Tarleton, a dragoon officer in the British army, became commander of a force originally called Cathcart's Legion, composed almost entirely of American Loyalists. To it were attached the 16th and 17th Light Dragoons. Originally there was considerable ill feeling between the dragoons and the rest of the Legion, the former refusing to exchange their red coats for the green jackets worn by the infantry. Whether Lee's Legion in the American army was inspired by the British organization is not clear, but Lee's men also wore green jackets. They apparently welcomed the addition of the infantry of Kirkwood's Delaware troops, and on hard marches they often rode double behind the dragoons. Apparently the British dragoons of the 17th swallowed at least part of their pride because on several occasions they also carried infantry of Tarleton's Legion mounted double.[35]

In both armies the legions proved to be valuable, versatile units. Both provided "eyes" for their respective commanders, performed scouting and raiding duties, and on occasion did some hard fighting in the battle line when the two main armies engaged.

Greene was as single-minded as his commander in chief in believing

that a "regular establishment" was necessary if the war in the South was to
be won. To Governor Abner Nash of North Carolina he wrote: "Nothing
but a good regular army can save this country from ruin, and I hope the
legislature will determine on a draft to fill up their Continental battalions
on their first meeting. Don't be deceived and trust your liberties to a
precarious force [militia]; for whatever it may promise you in the first
effects, it will bring on you distress and disappointment in the issue."[36]

Like the British, the Continental army was in large measure composed
of society's losers. As John Adams observed, a regiment might possibly be
raised in New England "of the meanest, idlest, most intemperate and
worthless, but no more. . . . We must have tradesmen's sons, and farmers'
sons . . . and such men certainly would not enlist during the War, or for
long periods. . . . Was it creditable that men who could get at home better
living, more comfortable lodgings, more than double the wages, in safety,
not exposed to the sickness of the camps, would bind themselves during the
War?"[37] The "intemperate and worthless" nevertheless proved to be good
soldiers. The 1st Maryland, Kirkwood's Delaware men, and Lee's Legion
all demonstrated that they could stand up to the best the British had to offer.
There were never enough of them, but they provided a hard core around
which Washington and Greene could build a respectable force. The regulars also had a symbolic value. They constituted a national army that
epitomized the nation's resistance to England; in a word, the army *was* the
united states.

✳ The Irregulars ✳

The American colonies had a singular advantage over most revolutionary
movements. Although they had no regular military establishment, they had
since their founding been forced to rely on their own resources to defend
themselves, first against the Indians and then against the French, the
Dutch, and the Spanish. Not until the Seven Years' War did the ministry
send any considerable body of troops to defend British holdings in North
America.

In 1631 Massachusetts Bay required men aged sixteen to sixty to supply
themselves with arms and ammunition, and an officer in each township
was made responsible for seeing that the law was obeyed. In 1633 Plymouth specifically decreed that each able-bodied man must have a sword,
musket, and ammunition. Virginia had similar laws and required men to
take their muskets to church so that they could drill following the service.
By the end of the century all colonies had similar laws; and so the militia
system had been born. After the Seven Years' War militia activity declined
and drill became a sort of social occasion that enabled the men to get away
from the women folk and perhaps imbibe a few draughts of rum before (and

after) going through the motions of drilling. But what had developed over the years was a tradition that every man owed a military obligation to the defense of the colony. Almost all Americans, unlike the lower classes of England and Europe, either owned firearms or were thoroughly familiar with them. The musket was as common a "tool" on the colonial farm as the ax and the hoe, because farmers were accustomed to augmenting their crops by hunting.[38]

But few of these farmers were frontiersmen or Indian fighters. Most Americans were a generation or two removed from the frontier and had never seen a wild Indian in their lives. They might be proficient at hunting animals but not armed animals who could shoot back.

Frontiersmen armed with rifles—those remarkable weapons with an effective range of 250 yards—were small in numbers and not very well suited to the close-ordered infantry tactics in which the army was trained. The rifle took almost twice as long to load as a musket; a greased patch had to be inserted under the ball before it was rammed in order to seat it snugly enough to make the rifling of the barrel take effect. It was therefore not possible to use paper cartridges. Most rifles had an octagonal barrel and a blade sight, making them useless as bayonet handles. Riflemen were therefore particularly vulnerable to the redcoat bayonet attack.[39]

As the crisis with England approached, militia activity increased, especially in New England. Colonial governors were supposed to command the militia, but the custom of having the men elect their officers allowed the Whigs to get control of the troops and turn them into instruments of revolution.[40]

After Congress declared independence in 1776, state laws revived the colonial systems of conscription and organization. In Connecticut all males between the ages of sixteen and sixty were required to enroll with the exception of state and national officials, ministers, students and professors at Yale College, Negroes, and Indians. One could furnish a substitute or avoid service by paying a fine. North Carolina passed similar laws and added Quakers to the list of those exempted. The state was divided into five military districts, and the men were divided into classes. Those in the first class, men over fifty years of age, were not subject to call for active duty but were available as "home guards." The other four classes were to be called in rotation for a term of service not to exceed six months.[41]

The Pennsylvania militia was organized under one of the most comprehensive systems in the nation. Its conscription provisions were similar to those of the other states but spelled out a table of organization that called for each county to enlist a regiment of from 440 to 680 men. Officers were elected, but all colonels and majors had to be property-holders and all officers had to be qualified voters. County lieutenants were authorized to hire substitutes to fill the ranks, the cost to be borne by the state, presumably from fines collected from those who wanted to avoid service. This system was undoubtedly devised to deal with the problems arising from the large number of Quakers who were exempted from military service but required to pay a fine. Despite the sweeping nature of the Pennsylvania system, it did not prove to be particularly effective. In 1777, for example, Captain Thomas Askey's company from Cumberland County consisted of only forty-four men. Ten were substitutes and thirteen were hired by the county lieutenant.[42]

General Washington held a low opinion of the militia at the beginning of the war: "To place any dependence upon Militia, is assuredly, resting upon a broken reed; . . . unaccustomed to the din of Arms; totally unacquainted with every kind of Military skills, when opposed by Troops regularly train'd, disciplined and appointed, makes them timid and ready to fly at their own shadows." The state laws undermined the effectiveness of the militia. None provided for service longer than six months, and often the term was only three months. As Washington noted, "To bring men to a proper degree of Subordination, is not the work of a day, a Month, or even a year; and unhappily for us . . . the little discipline I have been laboring to establish . . . is in a manner done away with by such a mixture of Troops as have been called together within these few months." In short, by the time militia units had received even the most rudimentary training and perhaps had some experience under fire, their enlistment time had expired and they went home.[43]

Greene had similar complaints, and he added still another grievance. Militia unused to long campaigns and the necessity of husbanding supplies were extremely wasteful and therefore expensive to supply and equip: "It requires more than double the number of militia to be kept in the field, attended with infinitely more waste and expense than would be necessary to give full security to the country with a regular and permanent army." Greene had recently completed a tour of duty as quartermaster of Washington's army and he knew what he was talking about.[44]

Yet in spite of their faults the militia were necessary. Without them the American armies could not have successfully opposed the British. And there were occasions when the militia units gave a good account of themselves, especially if they were commanded by able officers. In the New Jersey campaign, General John Cadwalader proved to be such an able militia commander that Washington urged him to accept a Continental commission. Another such outstanding state officer was Edward Stevens of Virginia. Outraged and shamed that his militia would not stay beyond the term of their enlistment during a critical period in the southern campaign, he raised additional regiments and brought them into Greene's army. And on a memorable day in March 1781, the Virginia militia performed with a valor that restored Stevens' wounded pride.

These generalizations about the militia apply only in part to the troops of South Carolina and Georgia. In the latter state no Whig government existed, and most Whig sentiment was concentrated along the upper reaches of the Savannah River, where frontiersmen had only recently been exposed to Indian attacks and the most outstanding Whig leader, Elijah Clarke, had already become famous as an Indian fighter. Men of the South Carolina backcountry had ties of friendship and family with both the Georgians and the Watauga settlers of what is now East Tennessee. South Carolinians had also marched against the Indians.

What little government there was in South Carolina after the fall of Charleston was vested in Governor John Rutledge, who spent most of his time at Greene's headquarters. In neither South Carolina nor Georgia, then, was there a viable militia organization, although Rutledge issued occasional orders to his officers, who might or might not obey them. But the militia of the southern backcountry had a different history from that of most other militia. They had been tempered by almost five years of intermittent partisan warfare. They had been engaged against the Tories, who had not, as in other areas, been supported by British regulars. Thus their first experiences in combat were against other Americans who were no better disciplined and armed than themselves. They had not yet faced the disciplined ranks, the steady fire, and the bayonets of the redcoats, but they had been under fire and overcome the fear that is always present the first time one faces an enemy's bullets. They had also gained experience in two major and numerous minor expeditions against the Indians.[45]

These battle experiences had been valuable not only for men in the ranks, but they had also resulted in the emergence of commanders who had shown themselves to be capable of leading men in combat. Clarke, Thomas Sumter, and Andrew Pickens were proven officers whose charismatic leadership attracted men into the ranks. Even though the state government had vanished with the fall of Charleston, it had created an organization that had functioned effectively before 1780 and thus had conferred upon these partisan leaders the authority that enabled them to carry on. When Governor Rutledge appointed Sumter commander of all South Carolina militia, he was accepted because the militia knew he was an able commander. Rutledge subsequently appointed Francis Marion and Pickens brigadier generals, thereby confirming what their followers already knew —that they were leaders whom the men trusted.[46]

Militia from the backcountry were armed with rifles, and most of them were mounted (although they did not fight from horseback). They were designated as infantry, and from time to time both the legislatures and the regular army commanders tried to "dismount" them. The militia ignored such orders. It was just as well that they did for when Greene first took command in the Southern Department he found Continental dragoons virtually nonexistent. He therefore turned to the partisans, especially Marion and Pickens, for the scouting and reconnaissance necessary to secure information of the enemy's dispositions and movements.

By 1780, then, the backcountry militia had been successful in performing two valuable functions—suppressing the Loyalists and nullifying the
Indian threat. As the British invasion opened a new theater of operations
and Nathanael Greene began to revive the American military effort, the
partisan leaders undertook additional duties. Pickens, Sumter, and Marion
operated their units as separate forces harassing the enemy's communications and providing intelligence in cooperation with the strategic planning
of the commander of the Southern Department. Last, and perhaps least,
they comprised the reinforcements that Greene needed to augment his
Continentals and make up an effective operational force.[47]

One other contingent of irregulars needs to be examined. Early in the
war British commanders were besieged by Loyalists who were anxious to
fight for their country. Although Germain proclaimed as an article of faith
that British strategy was aimed at Americanizing the war and turning both
military and political control over to the "King's friends," Howe and
Clinton were considerably less enthusiastic. They had the usual British
contempt for Americans and especially for the notion that Americans
could be made into good soldiers. They went so far as to authorize the
raising of a number of Loyalist regiments but gave them little or no
logistical support. Of sixty-four Loyalist regiments authorized, less than a
third actually took the field. Such regiments were designated as provincial
troops, and even though they were enlisted, like the regulars, for three years
or the duration of the war, the officers were not allowed to hold regular
commissions. Some British regular officers who commanded Loyalist
troops were promoted to "provincial rank" so they could hold a title
commensurate with their function, but they were denied promotion in the
regular establishment. Banastre Tarleton, for example, was only a major
when he and his Legion won fame in the southern theater, but as commander of the Legion he held the provincial rank of colonel.

These Loyalist regiments that were raised performed with considerable
distinction. John Graves Simcoe's Queen's Rangers and Lord Rawdon's
Volunteers of Ireland had notable records. In the southern theater two
regiments of De Lancey's New York Volunteers commanded by John
Harris Cruger and George Turnbull performed as well in battle as any
redcoats. Yet English commanders stubbornly refused to accept the fact of
these fine performances and thereby neglected a valuable source of manpower.[48]

It was a bewildering array of soldiers that fought each other in the War of
Independence. If by "redcoats" is meant all who fought under the British
flag, then one must also include green-coated Legionnaires and jägers and
blue-coated Germans. Traditional art to the contrary, only a small number
of Americans were dressed in blue. Brown was the color of the uniform of
most American soldiers, if they were fortunate enough to have regulation

clothing. The predominant "uniform" of most soldiers was whatever clothes they could find. Militia were seldom in uniform, and soldiers from the frontier commonly wore long linen hunting coats. A few regiments such as Harry Lee's Legion prided themselves on the fact that they were always able somehow to appear in regular uniforms.

The background of the soldiers was almost as variegated as their uniforms. Some of the redcoats came from the slums of London or the barred cells of Newgate. German mercenaries consisted not only of recruits from classes similar to those of the British army but "a bankrupt tradesman from Vienna, a fringemaker from Hanover, a discarded secretary of the post-office from Gotha, a monk from Würzburg," all ruthlessly swept up by avaricious German recruiters.[49]

If American soldiers were not quite the dregs of humanity, it was only because poverty and pauperism were not as widespread in the colonies. But the generous bounties offered by both Congress and the states indicated that to fill the ranks it was necessary to appeal more to self-interest than to patriotism. The Continental regiments undoubtedly contained a fair number of the "miserable sharp looking Caitiffs, [and] hungry lean faced Villains" described by recruiters.[50]

Yet the history of the war tells us that these men became competent soldiers. The redcoat with his training, discipline, and equipment was the superior of his American cousin, but on occasion even the "thin red line" gave way before the onslaught of the 1st Maryland or William Washington's dragoons. For if there were many in these armies who were society's losers, in the regiment they found a home, and the stern discipline and hard training administered by capable officers and noncoms aroused their pride. The weapons carried by these soldiers were crude and unreliable, yet the British suffered 40 percent casualties at Bunker Hill and did not retreat. The 1st Maryland left nearly half its men on the field at Long Island. So both armies had tough fighters, men who were capable of moving against an enemy and killing him at close quarters. Only soldiers of hard courage perform such deeds of valor.

4. Charleston: 1780

Sir Henry Clinton's decision to open a campaign in the South was taken in spite of serious limitations that might have given pause to a man of his moody and introspective temperament. The southern campaign as originally conceived was to have been the final phase of a strategy that posited the defeat or at least serious check to Washington's army as a prerequisite. Yet the events of the spring and summer had demonstrated that the American army in the North could not be assaulted with any assurance of success. With prospects for victory in this quarter foreclosed, the southern campaign, instead of being a concluding phase of a Continental strategy, became virtually the only alternative to a static defense that could scarcely bring credit to His Majesty's American commander. "I felt, therefore," said Sir Henry, "the tottering ground on which I stood." It also meant that he could not himself remain too long in the South and that he could not spare a major part of his army to campaign there for any length of time. He must keep looking over his shoulder for any threat from George Washington.

There were other causes for concern. Clinton was separating his theaters of operations more widely than had Howe before him and with fewer troops at his command. As Clinton himself acknowledged, ". . . When I undertook this move, my army was inferior to that [of] my predecessor . . . by at least sixteen thousand men [and] the ships of war serving with me were not equal to a third the number he had. . . ." Moreover, these forces were to be dispersed between New York and South Carolina—contrasted with Howe's division between the Hudson and Pennsylvania—so that mutual support was virtually impossible should a crisis arise.[1]

Clinton's success also depended on his ability not only to hold Charleston but to control the backcountry of South Carolina, something the British had never been able to do. For this Loyalist support was essential because he did not plan to leave the entire expeditionary force in Charleston. He must return to New York by the end of the spring when the turnout of American recruits and militia would enable Washington to become active. His usual skepticism regarding Loyalists was possibly allayed by James Simpson's assurances that the British "will be assisted by very considerable numbers of the inhabitants." It is also possible that, just as the necessity for political survival had driven Germain to accept the evidence of widespread Loyalism, so Clinton's urgency to vindicate his military reputation overrode his misgivings. "This is the most important hour Britain ever knew," declared Sir Henry. "If we lose it we shall never see such another."

There was, finally, the naval problem. Clinton's father had been an admiral, and the son had always felt that "I know—without vanity I say it—more of their service, as far as it is connected with ours, than anyone of the sea service does of ours." Yet the expedition to South Carolina depended both on naval superiority during the course of the invasion and on the continuing ability to maintain lines of communication and supply. If the history of 1779 had demonstrated anything it had shown that British forces in America were not self-sustaining. The severing of these lines of support and the chance that the French fleet would descend upon a detached force and isolate it, was not just a possibility. What Clinton obviously failed to appreciate in his euphoria over the successful defense of Savannah was that d'Estaing had landed an overwhelming force on the Georgia coast without the slightest interference by the British navy. Only incredible mismanagement of the allied force and d'Estaing's impatience to return to the West Indies had allowed Prevost's stout defense to save the province.[2]

It was a lesson Sir Henry could ill afford to ignore.

✳ Clinton Moves South ✳

By November 1779, Clinton had recovered from his summer doldrums. News of the repulse of the attack on Savannah was not only a welcome note of victory but he was now assured of an advance base of operations from which to launch his attack on South Carolina. The force that Clinton assembled for the coming expedition was formidable. It consisted of two regiments of grenadiers, three regiments of light infantry, the 7th, 23rd, 33rd, 63rd, and 64th Regiments of Foot, a jäger regiment, four regiments of Hessian grenadiers, Regiment Huyn (Hessian), the British Legion, Patrick Ferguson's Rangers, detachments of artillery and engineers, and replacements for regiments in Savannah. The total was 8,708 rank and file.

Three of the officers who accompanied the expedition were to play key roles in the coming campaign. The most important was Lieutenant General Charles Earl Cornwallis. The earl was not a particularly imposing looking man. He was short and thickset, and his rather plain features were marred by a cast in one eye, the result of a boyhood accident. But he had an easy, affable manner, and "there is no saying what is not to be expected

Charles Earl Cornwallis (W. L. Clements Library, University of Michigan)

from troops under the command of a general they adore, of whose ability they have the highest opinion, and in whom they have been accustomed to place the fullest confidence."

Cornwallis had come to America with the ill-starred expedition that Clinton had led against Charleston in 1776. General Howe had from the first given him the key command in almost every battle: the column that flanked the Americans at Long Island; the landing at Kip's Bay that nearly trapped the Americans retreating from Manhattan; the flanking column again at the Brandywine; and it was Cornwallis who had averted disaster at Germantown. In these and other actions Cornwallis had demonstrated great tactical skill, and he was fearless in the field. He also possessed a characteristic that was singularly lacking in other British generals—an ability to make up his mind and then drive toward his objective.[3]

In 1778 he returned to England and resigned his commission, but after his wife's death in 1779 he was restless and unhappy. "I find this country [England] quite insupportable to me," he said, and he asked to return to active duty. Germain was loath to restore his commission, but Cornwallis took his case to the King, and shortly afterward he was ordered to America as Clinton's second in command.

Clinton seems to have welcomed this seasoned general, and in the beginning they got along well enough, especially since Clinton hoped that Cornwallis would ultimately succeed him. Sir Henry had written to Germain in August 1779 that because Cornwallis was "an officer every way so well qualified to have the interests of his country entrusted to him, I should hope I might without difficulty be relieved from a station which nobody acquainted with its conditions will suppose to have sat lightly on me." Germain's answer, denying Clinton's request, was not received until March 1780, during the siege of Charleston. In the meantime, Clinton consulted the earl and kept him fully informed of his plans, although he finally came to dislike Cornwallis intensely. Indeed, there were few officers except junior subordinates with whom Clinton had any but the most formal relations. Cornwallis would have welcomed the American command, and it must be supposed that when his hopes were disappointed his ambitions were not thereby diminished.[4]

Another officer of importance in the war in the South was Major Banastre Tarleton. Tarleton had been a law student at the outbreak of the war but had abandoned his studies to purchase a commission in the King's Dragoon Guards. By 1778 the muscular young redhead had been brevetted to lieutenant colonel of the British Legion. The Legion consisted of 300 Loyalist infantry recruited in New York and 150 dragoons of the 17th Regiment. The Legionnaires wore green coats and the scarlet-coated dragoons were at first contemptuous of the Americans. But their colonel welded them into a disciplined, hard-hitting force that seemed to reflect his own fiery spirit.[5]

Patrick Ferguson was ten years older than Tarleton and had spent twenty of his thirty-five years in the British army. Early in the war he had organized a Loyalist ranger battalion, but he was wounded severely at the Brandywine and his rangers were disbanded. He was reputed to be the best shot in the army, and he had invented a breechloading rifle (which army authorities refused to accept). He reached the rank of major in the 71st Highland Regiment, and by the time Clinton's expedition sailed he had raised another detachment of 200 rangers. Ferguson was expected to be especially valuable in recruiting Americans for the King's service.[6]

On the day after Christmas 1779, Clinton's force was finally embarked and stood southward. Arbuthnot's convoy of ninety transports and ten warships was no sooner at sea than it was being punished by the winter gales of the North Atlantic. "Snow, rain, hail, storm, foaming waves, and bitter cold," wrote German Captain Johann Hinrichs on January 13; six days later, ". . . the gale increased in violence, and our main topgallant was lowered completely. During the night the storm broke in all its fury. Never before had the wind and water raged so; never before had the ship been battered as it was last night."[7]

The fleet scattered so badly that one dismasted transport was driven all the way to the coast of Cornwall. Not until January 30 did the first ships arrive off Savannah and not until some days later did the last stragglers come in. Altogether seven ships returned to New York and two others put ashore elsewhere. Virtually all the horses were lost so that when the dragoons finally got ashore their first task was to find remounts. It was not until the second week in February that the advance to Charleston could begin.

By February 14 the British main force had occupied James Island southwest of the city and began to deploy. Cautious and thorough as always, Clinton assembled every man and gun within reach. He called on Prevost at Savannah to send reinforcements and ordered the garrison at Augusta to join him. He called for troops from as far as the Bahamas and the West Indies, and if Arbuthnot had not intervened he would have stripped the fleet of men and cannon. As it was, he pressed into service more than 1,000 sailors and forty-five guns.[8]

Clinton's zeal to leave no stone unturned in the thoroughness of his preparation for the attack on Charleston revealed a basic flaw that characterized all British commanders in America. From William Howe's total preoccupation with his own objectives in 1776 to Lord Cornwallis' fondness for the Chesapeake in 1781, every British general steadfastly refused to see beyond the range of his immediate operations. In the spring of 1780, Clinton's determination to overwhelm Charleston led him to strip Prevost's Georgia command of nearly all of his most capable troops. Sir James Wright, who had been reinstated as governor of Georgia, protested bitterly

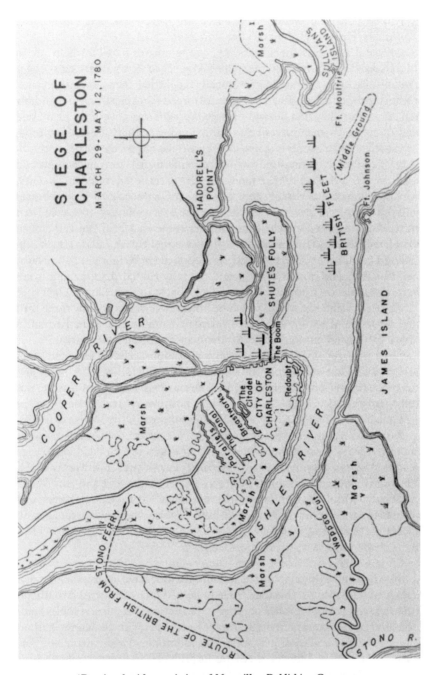

(Reprinted with permission of Macmillan Publishing Company
from The War of the Revolution, *Volume 2,*
by Christopher Ward. Copyright 1952 by Macmillan Publishing Company,
copyright renewed 1980)

to Clinton that he could no longer defend even the neighborhood of Savannah. His fears were not idle.

Prevost sent a detachment of sixty men to answer a call for help late in March from Loyalists on the upper Ogeechee River. Partisans under Andrew Pickens ambushed the Tories and killed their captain and six men. A force of King's Rangers (militia) forced the Americans to withdraw but not before they had burned the rice barns on the governor's plantation and carried off some of his slaves. Prevost reported that "it is not improbable at least some of them [Loyalists] may have joined the Rebel party on this Occasion. It is reported that they [Americans] have determined on killing such as refuse to take the Oath that is tendered to them."

Soon the rebel partisans were out again. On March 28 a detachment attacked the Loyalists in Liberty County near Sunbury and killed ten men. The appeals for help continued to come in "from the very much distressed and loyal Inhabitants . . . in St. George Parish and downwards to St. Philips, Conochee & Medway," said Governor Wright. " . . . In short, Sir, this Province is or will be broke up totally ruined if something is not speedily done." Within a week Pickens was back, this time at the Ogeechee River Ferry, where he fell upon a detachment of regulars, killing three men and wounding five. Prevost was in despair, complaining that the raiders "have baffled all our endeavors to intercept or cut off their retreat."[9]

Clinton, preoccupied with his siege operations, paid little attention to Wright and Prevost. He may have believed that the fall of Charleston and the surrounding country would end American resistance. In this he was only partly correct. What he failed to take notice of was the tendency of the Patriots to take instant advantage of any weakness in the British defenses.

More important was his seeming lack of concern for the safety of the King's friends. It was all very well to talk of grand strategy and long-range results, but the Loyalists "in St. George Parish and downwards to St. Philips, Conochee, & Medway" were interested in the here and now. When Sir Henry withdrew their protection so that rebels raided to the gates of Savannah, the Loyalists learned a bitter lesson about what the British meant by "the King's peace."

By the time Clinton was ready to begin offensive operations he had collected 10,000 rank and file. Already he had quarreled with Arbuthnot, first over the sea approaches and then over the site for putting the expedition ashore. He now urged the admiral to advance his ships into the harbor, but Arbuthnot demurred. The water was too shallow, and the guns of Fort Moultrie and Fort Johnston were too formidable. His resentment and his carping were almost constant, but once Clinton had moved his forces to the west bank of the Ashley and established his supply depots he refused to let Arbuthnot bother him. Clinton had decided to invest Charleston from the landward side so that aggressive naval support was not vital to his operation.[10]

The city of Charleston is located at the tip of a peninsula formed by the Ashley and Cooper rivers. To the seaward are a series of low, swampy islands, the most important of which are Sullivan's Island extending to the northeast of the ship channel and James Island to the south and west. In 1780 the city was bordered on three sides by the harbor and the rivers, and swampland, interspersed by slow-moving creeks and sloughs, extended for several miles on both sides. The only feasible land approach to the town was from the northwest along the Charleston Neck. Rather than make a direct attack on the seaward approaches, as he had done in 1776, Clinton decided to seize the neck, thereby closing off both any escape route and any attempt to reinforce the city.

It took Clinton five weeks to make his preparations, but on the morning of March 29 Cornwallis led a force of jägers, grenadiers, and light infantry across the Ashley about fourteen miles above the city. By noon the main body had made the crossing unopposed by the defenders. During the next two days the British extended their line across the neck and advanced to within half a mile of the American defenses, about two miles outside the city. On April 1, 1,500 workmen broke ground for the first parallel that would allow the British to bring their artillery within range of the American works.[11]

✳ Surrender! ✳

In the spring of 1779, not long after the fall of Savannah, Charles Pinckney, Jr., wrote prophetically to his mother, "In what fatal tranquility did we remain when we received the intelligence of the enemy's being in possession of Savannah, the defeat at Augusta. . . . We must surely be convinced by this time that we have been extremely remiss in suffering these encroachments upon our neighbors; that we have a restless and enterprising enemy to deal with, that all their present designs are levelled against this town, and that all opposition to them tends in some degree to the safety of the State. . . ."[12]

But the forebodings of Pinckney and others went unheeded. Perhaps it was an overconfidence bred of the repulse of the British in 1776; perhaps the ease with which they had rid themselves of Prevost in the summer of 1779. Yet their only defense force, aside from militia, which were notoriously unresponsive, was General Benjamin Lincoln, head of the Southern Department, and his slender, ill-trained force of 1,600 Continentals, with a later addition of 1,400 men from North Carolina and Virginia. Militia from both Carolinas numbered no more than 2,000 men.

When Clinton's force first appeared in mid-February, the South Carolina Provincial Congress voted dictatorial powers to Governor John Rutledge and then adjourned. General Lincoln became concerned that his Continentals, the only American force in the South, would be trapped in the city. Indeed, General Washington, perhaps mindful of his own narrow escape from Manhattan in 1776, warned that if the garrison could not defend the sea approaches, "the attempt [to defend the city] ought to have been relinquished." But as usual the commander in chief left the decision to his subordinate, and Lincoln allowed himself to be persuaded to defend Charleston by the governor and his council.

During the second week in April two developments gave certain warning that Lincoln faced impending disaster. Arbuthnot finally got several of his frigates across the outer bar, although he had to reduce their draft by removing their guns and stores. On April 7 the frigates ran past the guns of Fort Moultrie. One ship was slightly damaged and a storeship ran aground and had to be abandoned.

A few days later Clinton sent Colonel James Webster with 1,400 men, including Tarleton's Legion and Ferguson's Rangers, to the east bank of the Cooper to begin closing off the northern approaches to the city. (Governor Rutledge and four members of his council barely made their escape the day before). ". . . *To secure the capture of all the rebel corps in Charleston,*" said Clinton, "had been from the first a very principal object with me, as I saw the reduction of the rest of the province in great measure depended upon it."[13]

Lincoln had posted General Isaac Huger with some militia and 350 of Colonel William Washington's dragoons at Monck's Corner, thirty miles up the left bank of the Cooper River, to keep open the city's line of communication. Webster detached Tarleton and Ferguson to break this final link with the backcountry. Tarleton had finally obtained remounts for his dragoons—"the quality was inferior to those embarked at New York"— and on the night of April 13–14 the British took Huger's command by surprise. A bayonet charge by the Legion infantry routed the militia, and Washington's cavalry was no match for the dragoons. Thirty Americans were killed and wounded and a hundred more were captured. But most fortuitous for the British was the capture of 400 horses. The South Carolinians, Tarleton noted, "having heard of the loss of the cavalry horses at sea, had flattered themselves that they could not be speedily recruited, . . . and to prevent [the British] collecting horses in the country, some of them accoutred themselves as cavaliers. . . ." Most of the "cavaliers" fled into the swamps, and the Legion found itself superbly mounted.[14]

On the same day that Tarleton dispersed Huger's command, Clinton's parallels were close enough to allow his guns to open fire on the American fieldworks. "The cannonade and bombardment continued, with short intermissions, until midnight," wrote General Moultrie, ". . . An embrazure at redan No. 7 destroyed; a sergeant and a private of the North Carolina brigade killed . . . some women and children killed in town. The enemy's cannon were chiefly twenty-four pounders; and their mortars from five and a half, to ten inches: they threw several carcasses from eight and ten inch mortars, by which two houses were burnt."

In the grim business of war men always find an occasion for prankish humor. Into the American lines came mortar shells that did not explode. Upon examination they were found to contain molasses and flour with a message expressing the hope that this would relieve the hunger of the garrison. The shells were promptly fired back loaded with sulfur and lard—a mixture commonly prescribed as an emetic.[15]

Eight days of continuous bombardment convinced Lincoln that he should make an effort to extricate his force. He therefore proposed a parley and offered to give up the city if his Continentals were allowed to march out of the lines. Clinton dismissed it for the ridiculous proposal it was. On April 24 the Americans displayed virtually their only effort at a spirited resistance. Three hundred Virginia and South Carolina Continentals made a dawn attack on one of the British redoubts. In a savage little fight which involved bayonet work at close quarters, the Americans killed "fifteen or twenty" of the enemy and brought off twelve prisoners. The next night the Americans opened up with musket fire, and there were shouted orders to advance. Panic swept the ranks of the British in the parallel trench. "Everywhere they saw rebels. They believed the enemy had made a sortie and fired muskets for over half an hour." Seven redcoats were killed and twenty-one wounded. Not a single man had advanced from the American entrenchments.

On the 26th the Chevalier DuPortail, a French officer who was Washington's chief of engineers, made his way into the American lines. After an inspection of the defenses he not only pronounced them untenable but wondered why the British had not already taken the town. Lincoln thereupon called a council of war and proposed that the Continentals attempt to evacuate the city. The meeting was interrupted by Christopher Gadsden, the fire-eating lieutenant governor, and the remaining members of the council, who threatened to destroy Lincoln's boats and prevent his departure by force. The situation had all the elements of a comic opera—the rhetorical and bombastic Gadsden, the dejected 250-pound general, and the French engineer looking on, probably wryly amused. For Cornwallis had occupied Haddrel's Point that very day and Charleston was cordoned as tightly as a snare drum.[16]

For more than two weeks the city held out; or, more properly, Clinton continued his cautious approach, carefully restraining his gunners. He rebuked his artillery officer for not keeping his batteries in hand. "Absurd, impolitic, and inhuman," asserted Sir Henry vehemently, "to burn a town you mean to occupy!"

Finally, even Clinton's patience ran thin. On the night of May 9–10, after Lincoln had refused another surrender proposal (backed presumably by the fire-eaters of Charleston) the British opened a massive bombardment. "The fire was incessant almost the whole night," said William Moultrie, "cannon-balls whizzing and shells hissing continually amongst us; ammunition chests and temporary magazines blowing up; great guns bursting, and wounded men groaning along the lines: it was a dreadful night . . . our military ardor was much abated; we began to cool and we cooled gradually. . . ." Surveying the shambles on the morning of the tenth, the Charlestonians implored Lincoln to surrender as fervently as they had implored him to fight two weeks before. On the eleventh the American commander accepted Clinton's terms.[17]

Considering the amount of powder that had been burned, the casualties on both sides were surprisingly light. Seventy-six British were killed and 189 wounded. On the American side 89 were killed and 138 wounded, almost all of them Continentals. The German jägers, with their deadly rifle fire, had accounted for a great many of these casualties. Among the civilian population about twenty were killed and thirty or more buildings were destroyed.

There was a final episode that somewhat sobered the exhilaration of the victors. As the Continentals and militia surrendered their arms, British soldiers began storing them in a powder magazine. Although the American officers warned that some of the weapons were loaded, "they were thrown into the magazine half a dozen at a time." Suddenly the building exploded with a thunderous roar, and "carcasses, legs, and arms were seen in the air, and scattered over several parts of the town. One man was dashed with violence against the steeple of the . . . church, which was at a great distance from the explosion, and left the marks of his body there for several days." The ensuing fire destroyed several buildings, including the brothel and the city poorhouse. Probably more than 200 people were killed, including sixty or seventy British soldiers.[18]

By the terms of the capitulation the Continentals, of course, became prisoners, along with 1,200 militia who were adjudged to have been active in defense of the city, although most of these were later released. Two provisions of the surrender terms showed Clinton's disposition to be lenient, thereby inducing the inhabitants of the city to offer no further resistance. "The militia now in garrison shall be permitted to return to their respective homes as prisoners of war on parole, which parole, as long as they observe, shall secure them from being molested in their property by the British troops." The same provision was made for "civil officers and citizens who have borne arms." Finally, "such as do not choose to continue under British government" were allowed a year in which to dispose of their property and leave the province.[19]

The fall of Charleston had repercussions that echoed from Washington's headquarters to Whitehall to the Carolina backcountry. In England the news was especially welcome because the war was becoming increasingly unpopular. Twenty-five English counties had passed resolutions denouncing the corruption of Parliament and the dictatorial power of the King. Although it would be idle to attribute the troubles of the summer of 1780 entirely to the American war, the fall of Charleston, along with the surrender of Lincoln's army, was the most decisive British victory of the war, and news of it could not have come at a more propitious time. It did much to abate—though it did not silence—the protests of the Opposition.[20]

✳ Olive Branch and Sword ✳

Soon after the surrender, Clinton began taking steps to secure his victory. He issued a proclamation assuring "the King's faithful and loyal subjects" of protection and support, with further assurance that "whenever the situation of the country will permit the restoration of Civil government and peace" His Majesty's commissioners would see to "the full possession of that liberty in their persons and property which they had before experienced under the British government." And just here was the rub. His Majesty's commissioners were, of course, Clinton himself and Admiral Arbuthnot. The latter was anxious to restore civil government as quickly as possible. Whether Sir Henry's opposite view was reflex action induced by his dislike of the admiral, the fact remained that there were no instructions on which the commissioners could act, nor did they have authority to institute a permanent system of government without the consent of the ministry in England. Finally, the government in London had established no procedure for restoring crown authority. Presumably, the restoration would be under the charter by which South Carolina had been governed before 1776; but the nettlesome questions that had brought about the rebellion were still unsettled, nor was it clear that the concessions offered to Congress by the Carlisle Commission in 1778 were to apply to individual colonies.[21]

For the time being Clinton drew on the British experience in the occupation of New York and Philadelphia. A Board of Police was established headed by the former attorney general for South Carolina, James Simpson. Within a short time the board assumed broad powers extending beyond public safety (as had the boards in Philadelphia and New York). But even so its authority was sharply circumscribed by the military command. Colonel Alexander Innes, a British regular officer, was appointed to the board, and all final decisions were subject to the approval of Colonel Nisbet Balfour, the military commandant. He, in turn, was responsible to Clinton and, after his departure, to Cornwallis.

As early as July Simpson called Clinton's attention to the necessity for a more permanent arrangement:

> It affords me much pleasure to observe that the People who have been before us, appeared to have confidence in our Justice and have with Alacrity paid a prompt obedience to our decisions. But it is not yet to be expected that an Establishment so different to what the people have been used to can give permanent Satisfaction. I am indeed convinced, that this is a Critical Period in which if it is practicable it would be very expedient to restore the Criminal Jurisdiction and the Legislative Authority to this Province—the one to procure quiet Settlement and establishing the Peace of the Country—and in the Present Temper of the People, such Laws would be enacted by the other as would secure its future Tranquility.

Presumably, Clinton passed Simpson's request to London, for in November Germain gave his answer directly to Cornwallis: "As the Province is not yet restored to Peace it is not judged proper to appoint a Governor. . . ." A lieutenant governor (William Bull) was on his way to South Carolina, continued the American Secretary, and would be able to take over the conduct of civil affairs "as far as you [Cornwallis] shall judge expedient to permit the civil officer to act."[22]

Two points are of interest in Germain's letter. Obviously he was instructing Cornwallis—who was not even a peace commissioner—that he should be the judge of the extent to which Loyalists were to exercise civil authority. It is also clear that Germain did not intend that the reestablishment of civil government should be part of the overall process of reconquest. Although he had stated before Parliament that Loyalists were to wield decisive influence in restoring crown authority and had repeated his wish in his instructions to Clinton in 1779, it is evident that Germain's view now was that permanent government was to come after, not during, the reconquest. The only roles that Loyalists were to have were as provincial troop reinforcements and as minor officials who would relieve the military commanders of routine matters of civil administration. Of the reestablishment of provincial legislative bodies and courts there was no mention at all. In short, the "new" strategy had reverted to the old strategy of 1777.

In addition to the matter of civil government for Charleston, Clinton had to provide for the subjugation of the rest of South Carolina. He thought that this task would be fairly easily accomplished in view of the shocked dismay of the rebels over the fall of Charleston and Lincoln's surrender. He announced the establishment of a militia system under which men fit for military duty should "be ready to assemble when required, and serve with the King's troops for any six months of the ensuing twelve. . . ." They were allowed to elect their own officers and were assured that they would not be required to serve outside Georgia or the Carolinas. Men with families were to serve as home guards in their own districts. The organization was entrusted to Major Patrick Ferguson, who was named inspector general of militia for the province. Ferguson was instructed to restrain the militia "from offering violence to innocent and inoffensive people, and by all means in your power [to] protect the aged, infirm, the women, and the children of every denomination from insult and outrage; . . . you will promote the establishment of a domestic militia for the maintenance of peace and good order throughout the country. . . . " In other words, Ferguson was to head a provincial police force, which was to be used against the enemies of the crown, but he was also to "pay particular attention" to maintaining order. Ferguson was ill-suited to such a position by both training and temperament. His only qualification was an admitted talent for recruiting Loyalists.[23]

Within days after the fall of Charleston, Cornwallis occupied Augusta, Ninety Six, and Camden and established smaller garrisons at Rocky Mount, Cheraw, and Georgetown. The chain of posts stretched in an arc from Augusta on the Savannah to Georgetown on the lower Pee Dee. This display of force seemed to effectively discourage resistance. Patriot forces at Ninety Six and Camden as well as other militia detachments trooped in to accept the terms of surrender. Such redoubtable partisan leaders as Andrew Pickens and Andrew Williamson made their submission and went home. "I had soon . . . the satisfaction," wrote Sir Henry, ". . . to see all my measures throughout the course of this expedition crowned with the most flattering success. For, before I took my departure [June 8] for New York, Georgetown and almost the whole country . . . had submitted without opposition."[24]

Clinton was now anxious to get back to New York. There were reports that France intended to send an expeditionary force to America, and Clinton was worried about the safety of New York. Although Cornwallis was still at Camden overseeing the policing of the interior, Clinton did not wait for his return. Perhaps it was just as well. The relationship between the two, never cordial, had deteriorated completely. Sir Henry had trouble getting along with anyone, especially his senior colleagues, but Cornwallis was not blameless. Their first skirmish had taken place four years before, when Clinton had been especially vehement in one of his frequent denunciations of General Howe. Cornwallis had acted as the talebearer and carried Clinton's outburst to Howe. In the subsequent quarrels between Clinton and his chief, Cornwallis had dutifully sided with Howe.

When the earl came back from England in 1779, Clinton professed to be pleased to have so experienced a general and had hoped that Cornwallis would succeed him. As soon as Germain's refusal of Clinton's request to be relieved was received, Cornwallis dissociated himself from any consultations or conferences with Clinton, explaining that he did not want the responsibility of sharing in the decisions of the commander in chief. In short, if Cornwallis was not to have the credit he did not want to share the blame. It was not surprising, then, that Clinton did not wait for the earl's return. Cornwallis' assumption of the South Carolina command was a relief to both men, Clinton because he was rid of a high-ranking subordinate and Cornwallis because he would have a detached command without a carping superior at his elbow.

In his written instructions Clinton assumed that Cornwallis would have little trouble in securing South Carolina, and much of his dispatch was devoted to plans for a campaign on the Chesapeake. Clinton sounded many cautionary notes, especially warning that the safety of Charleston "is always to be considered as the principal object." Nevertheless, it is clear that Clinton expected Cornwallis to be available for a movement northward, which Sir Henry would be ready to support from New York.[25]

Before his departure, Clinton issued two final proclamations that did not make Cornwallis' task any easier. Clinton may have had second thoughts about the leniency displayed toward the South Carolina Patriots, a leniency that could not have endeared him to Loyalists who had been the targets of Whig abuse. He also suspected that "under the sanction of those paroles a great number of inveterate rebels might remain in the country, and by their underhand and secret counsel and other machinations prevent the return of many well disposed persons to their allegiance."

The proclamations in effect revoked the paroles and called on all citizens to "return to their allegiance," warning that those who failed to do so "will be considered as enemies and rebels . . . and treated accordingly." In short, there was no longer any room for neutrals; those who were not active supporters of the crown were its enemies.[26]

The new edicts produced a variety of reactions. Some South Carolina Whigs who had been willing to return to their homes and remain neutral now felt that they were released from all obligation because in their minds the British had violated the surrender terms. Others, especially those who were anxious to protect their property, accepted the situation and took the oath of allegiance.

In the meantime the uneasy peace was already being disturbed by news from the backcountry. At the time of the surrender, a force of 350 Virginia Continentals under Colonel Abraham Buford was on its way to reinforce the besieged city. They had gotten as far as Lenud's Ferry on the Santee when news of the fall of Charleston reached them, so Buford started back to North Carolina. Determined not to let this force escape, Cornwallis detached Tarleton's Legion and sent it in pursuit. The young dragoon drove his command 105 miles in fifty-four hours and caught up with Buford at the Waxhaws near the North Carolina border. Tarleton called on Buford to surrender, and when the American refused Tarleton launched a driving attack spearheaded by his mounted men. The Virginians gave way before the charge, "the battalion was totally broken and slaughter was commenced. . . ." Buford and his officers now tried to surrender, but the dragoons continued to cut down the Americans. Tarleton reported that his horse was shot from under him at just the time when the Americans were raising a white flag, but he was accused of refusing to give quarter and so earned for himself a notoriety that he may not have altogether deserved. One hundred and thirteen Americans were killed and 150 wounded. Reports that Tarleton's men bayoneted the wounded are hardly consistent with the fact that the British paroled the wounded and "surgeons were sent for from Camden and Charlotte town to assist them." Buford escaped with the remnant of his command. The Legion lost five killed and fourteen wounded. The Patriots were naturally anxious to overlook the fact that the British, bone-weary from their forced march, had defeated a force that outnumbered them three to two. Whatever the facts, "Tarleton's quarter" became symbolic of British barbarity, and the tough Legion commander was soon spoken of as "Bloody Ban."[27]

How much this grim little engagement and its aftermath contributed to the renewal of resistance is difficult to say. Perhaps it was too much to expect that partisans on both sides who had been clawing at each other for more than a year could now live in peace. At least two dozen clashes between Whigs and Tories had taken place since the fall of Savannah in 1778. Nor did the behavior of the British troops help matters. The regulars were the same redcoats who had plundered in New Jersey, New York, and Pennsylvania and who, from first to last, had never had much regard for Americans whether Whig or Tory. Ferguson's militia inevitably contained many who were eager to avenge the abuses they had suffered from their Whig neighbors.

It was certainly unfortunate for the British that within a few weeks raiding parties had burned out Thomas Sumter. With predictable dispatch this partisan leader took the field, but he was not the first. On the same day as the battle at the Waxhaws, Colonel William Bratton scattered Loyalist militia at Mobley's Meeting House near Winnsboro. Then in a four-day period in mid-July Whig and Tory partisans clashed at Union Court House, Williamson's Plantation, Cedar Springs, Gowen's Old Fort, and McDowell's Camp on the Pacolet River.[28]

Within six weeks after Cornwallis took command in South Carolina, there had been fifteen clashes between Tories and Whigs involving forces ranging from thirty or forty on each side to over a thousand. It is not to be supposed that men on either side limited themselves to fighting each other. Looting, plunder, and murder followed in the wake of the raiders, and undoubtedly some of the partisans cared little for the cause of either England or America. What erupted in the summer of 1780 from the

Savannah to the North Carolina border was a bloody civil war. Old feuds were settled under the banner of patriotism, and British hopes for a peaceful occupation vanished in the smoke of burning barns and houses.

Just before he took his departure for New York, Clinton wrote to Germain: "With greatest pleasure I farther report to your lordship that the inhabitants from every quarter repair. . . . to declare their allegiance to the King. . . . I may venture to assert that there are few men in South Carolina who are not either our prisoners, or in arms with us." The news of the great victory was enthusiastically received at Whitehall. "The glorious and important event of the reduction of Charleston," wrote Germain, "and the destruction or capture of the whole rebel land and naval force, that defended it, gave His Majesty the highest satisfaction. . . . I am sanguine enough to expect the recovery of the whole of the southern provinces in the course of the campaign."[29]

But the killing in the Carolinas had only begun.

5. Whigs and Tories

"... The Spirit of Plundering which prevails among the Inhabitants add not a little to our Difficulties. The whole Country is in Danger of being laid Waste by the Whigs and Tories who pursue each other with as much relentless Fury as Beasts of Prey."[1]

This observation was made by Nathanael Greene, a man already hardened by six years of war. In those six years Greene had never seen anything like the civil war that raged in the Carolinas. Nowhere in America was the fighting more bitter and savage.

✳ The War Comes to South Carolina ✳

News of the battles of Lexington and Concord and the organization of an American army in the summer of 1775 precipitated a crisis in South Carolina. The Whigs had already formed a provincial revolutionary Congress, and this body set up a provisional government. Administration was centered on three committees: a General Committee with broad executive and judicial powers; a Secret Committee primarily responsible for the collection and distribution of military supplies; and a Council of Safety that controlled the army and all military affairs. The powers of these committees were loosely defined, and there might have been some conflict of authority had it not been that members of each committee served on at least one of the others and some served on all three. The government then created a Provincial Association, which pledged subscribers to support the Provincial Congress and resist the tyranny of Great Britain. Those who did not "subscribe"—that is, sign the Articles of Association or give other evidence of support—were deemed to be enemies of the colony.[2]

The organization of the new government coincided with the arrival of the recently appointed royal governor, Lord William Campbell. He was given a perfunctory welcome. The Provincial Congress delivered an address to him declaring loyalty to the King but also listing grievances against the royal government which had necessitated the establishment of the Association government. Campbell, an amiable man who must have been appalled at his situation, made a serious effort to challenge the Whigs, but royal authority, already tenuous, declined precipitately. By the end of the summer he had taken refuge aboard a British man-of-war in the Charleston harbor.

In the meantime, the Provincial Congress had organized the military forces creating three regiments, two to operate on the coast and one ranger regiment in the interior. In doing so the Congress dissolved the colonial militia since the Whigs did not fully control it. The Council of Safety thus hoped to eliminate from the ranks of the military all who could not be trusted to support the Association. This proved to be a formidable task for it was soon evident that there was dissension within the ranks of the Whig party.[3]

The leadership was divided. The conservatives such as Rawlin Lowndes, Miles Brewton, Thomas Bee, and Thomas Heyward, Jr., wanted to proceed slowly and do nothing that might endanger reconciliation with England. William Henry Drayton, Arthur Middleton, Christopher Gadsden, and Charles Cotesworth Pinckney were much more vigorous in pressing Whig demands. They welcomed the prospect of open conflict and would have advocated independence had they not realized that such an extreme position would have been rejected by an overwhelming popular majority.[4]

News of disturbances in the interior led the Council of Safety to issue a Declaration of Alarm, which in effect called the volunteer regiments to active duty and declared them subject to military law. The soldiers of the regiments immediately protested, refusing to agree to the restrictions and severe punishments of the military code. They declined to accept the council's explanations of the need for this departure from civil law, and a crisis was averted only by rescinding the mobilization order.

That resistance to royal authority could be reconciled with protestations of loyalty to the crown was a distinction that was lost on the people at large, especially those in the backcountry. The Germans settled in Orangeburg and the surrounding Saxe-Gotha district exhibited an apathy toward the Whig cause that bordered on hostility. The controversy over stamps had no meaning for them since the colonial government had never established any courts in which the stamps were used. If Parliament taxed them without representation, so had the South Carolina assembly. And why should they go to war over tea when they seldom drank it?[5]

Further to the northwest a number of influential backcountry leaders took actions that thwarted the Whig cause: Robert Cuningham, Thomas Browne, and especially Thomas Fletchall, who was colonel of militia in the Fair Forest district. The latter's behavior had led the Council of Safety to question his conduct. In July 1775, Fletchall reported that he had mustered his regiment and had had the Association articles read to them.

To a man they had refused to sign. They had drawn up an association of their own in which they had agreed to bear arms only if royal forces were sent against them.

All this prompted the council to send a commission to attempt to persuade the backcountry to support the revolutionary cause. Five commissioners, including William Henry Drayton and Reverend William Tennant, reached the German settlements in August 1775. They sent out notices for a meeting, but no one appeared. Appeals to militia officers and local ministers fell on deaf ears. In the midst of this disappointment the commissioners learned that two companies of the ranger regiment had gone over to Fletchall and the rest were on the verge of mutiny because they had not been paid. This crisis was temporarily averted by furloughing the men home.

Drayton and Tennant continued into the backcountry and addressed several meetings, but in most cases they were confronted by Cuningham and Browne, whose local influence overshadowed that of the commissioners. Fletchall was adamant in his resolution not to bear arms against the King. When Drayton protested that it was not the King but the ministry and Parliament whose tyranny threatened America, his audiences were obviously not impressed.

Drayton decided to bring matters to a head. Interpreting his discretionary authority broadly, he called out the militia commanded by Colonel Richard Richardson and Major Andrew Williamson from the country between the Saluda and Broad rivers. They were joined by the remainder of the rangers and marched on Fletchall's men, determined to make a show of force. The two groups, each numbering about 1,000 men, camped near each other at Ninety Six. Fletchall, more temporizing than Cuningham or Browne, proposed a parley. The result was a "treaty" in which Fletchall declared that he and his followers did not intend to oppose the Provincial Congress; they refused to join the Association only out of a desire to be left alone. Drayton, for the Council, agreed that those who did not join the Association would not be molested as long as they remained neutral.

The so-called Treaty of Ninety Six did not settle the conflict because Cuningham and Browne refused to agree to it. The Council of Safety, for its part, was appalled that Drayton had called out the militia and nearly precipitated an armed conflict. Drayton was ordered to "discharge the militia as soon as he could possibly do it with safety. . . ." What followed was an uneasy truce, each side anxious to avoid bloodshed and each therefore less militant in pressing its cause. Those charged with getting signers to the Association began turning in depositions from people who agreed to the Association but declared that if there was violence they would fight "on the other side." The Council apparently found such declarations acceptable.[6]

By the late autumn of 1775 smoldering tensions in the backcountry flared again when Williamson ordered the arrest of Robert Cuningham, who was charged with seditious speech against the Provincial Congress. He was confined in Charleston although he was treated with consideration. At about the same time his brother, Patrick Cuningham, seized a supply of ammunition that the Council of Safety had dispatched to the Cherokees as a token of friendship. Cuningham charged that the Council intended to provoke the Indians into rising against the Loyalists on the frontier. He succeeded in arousing the Loyalists in the country between the Saluda and the Broad. This in turn brought out Williamson and his Whig followers. Although Williamson had only about 600 men to oppose nearly 2,000 Loyalists, he fortified himself at Ninety Six, and on November 18 Cuningham's forces attacked. The Whigs successfully withstood the besieging forces. Williamson lost one killed and eleven wounded; the Loyalists had fifty-two killed and one wounded. At the end of five days a truce was arranged by which each party was to withdraw and await further instructions, the Loyalists from Governor Campbell and the Whigs from the Council of Safety.

This was the first bloodshed of the war in South Carolina. The Loyalists were surprised at Williamson's stout resistance, and many returned home resolved to avoid further violence. The council ordered out Colonel Richardson's command, directing him to arrest the principal Tory leaders. As he marched toward Ninety Six he was joined by local militia units and 600 Whigs from North Carolina. Early in December, Richardson's force, now nearly 5,000 strong, had penetrated deep into the Cherokee country, scattering Loyalist detachments and arresting their leaders, among them Thomas Fletchall. Patrick Cuningham barely escaped. With Cuningham and Fletchall under arrest, Loyalist strength in the backcountry was dissipated, at least for the moment.[7]

The events of 1776 seemed to mark the triumph of the Whig cause. First, the British attack on Charleston was repulsed in June. A few weeks later the Cherokees attacked the frontier from the Watauga settlements (East Tennessee) to the upper Savannah. Although it was widely believed that this attack was instigated by the British Indian agent, John Stuart, to coordinate with the attack on Charleston, the fact was that Stuart opposed the use of Indians as allies of the British. He rightly supposed that the Indians could not constitute a decisive military factor and that their attacks on the frontier would only alienate the backcountry people, Loyalists and Whigs alike.

The Cherokee offensive was probably part of a general rising of the western Indians originating with the tribes of the Illinois country. Colonel Andrew Williamson marched his militia against the Cherokees in late July. He suffered an initial check when the Indians surprised him, but after a brief retreat he advanced against the Cherokee towns on the lower Keowee River. By early September he was joined by General Griffin Rutherford and his North Carolina militia. The combined force of some 2,000 men swept into the Cherokee lands, scattering pockets of resistance and destroying the Indian villages with their stores of grain. (Because of an unseasonable snowfall this was known as the "Snow Campaign.")

At the same time, an army of 2,000 Virginians and "over-the-mountain" men from Watauga under General William Christian was laying waste to the villages of the Overhill Cherokees from the valley of the Holston southwest into what is now East Tennessee. Overwhelmed all along the frontier, the Cherokees sued for peace and in a subsequent treaty ceded all their lands east of the mountains and north of the Nolichuckey River.[8]

The most important event of 1776 was, of course, the vote for independence taken by the Continental Congress on July 2. The circumstances under which the South Carolina delegation assented to this historic resolution are indicative of the ambivalence of the political moods even among the Whigs in South Carolina. Earlier in the year, when Christopher Gadsden and a few other firebrands had advocated independence, their views were expressly repudiated in the Provincial Congress. Many South Carolinians had joined in the opposition to the crown as much out of sympathy for New England as for any hardships that they themselves had suffered from British restrictions. In fact, the closed market created by the imperial system of Great Britain had been on the whole quite salutary for Charleston merchants and lowcountry planters.

When the debate in Philadelphia on the issue of independence began in June, only Edmund Rutledge represented South Carolina. He joined James Wilson of Pennsylvania and John Dickinson of Delaware in asking for a postponement. Such a momentous question, they insisted, must be decided only after the people of their provinces (or at least the revolutionary assemblies) could instruct their delegates.

By the end of June, Rutledge had been joined by Arthur Middleton, Thomas Heyward, Jr., and Thomas Lynch, Jr., all young men in their late twenties or early thirties. All brought news of the repudiation of Gadsden and the radicals, but they had no instructions from the assembly on the question of independence because news of the debate had not reached Charleston before their departure. Middleton had been among those who had advocated independence, but none knew better than he how little support separation from England had in South Carolina. Nevertheless, under pressure from members of Congress who urged the need for unanimity, the South Carolina delegation was persuaded to vote for independence on July 2. It was not until July 9 that they reported their action to the Provincial Congress, no doubt with a good deal of trepidation. It was included—indeed, nearly buried—in a report of the recent proceedings of the Continental Congress.[9]

The delegation was not aware that the timing of its report was most fortuitous, for on June 28 Patriot forces had repulsed the British attack on

Charleston, a battle in which the stout defense of Fort Sullivan had thoroughly aroused patriotic sentiment. In the euphoria of victory, the news from Philadelphia was received in South Carolina with "unspeakable joy."[10]

Thus by the end of 1776 the Whigs appeared to be firmly in control. For the next two years there was an uneasy truce between Whigs and Tories, a peace to which the moderation of the Whigs undoubtedly contributed. John Rutledge, who had emerged as by far the most popular leader among the Whigs, was elected governor under the constitution of February 1776. This document was drawn up by the revolutionary assembly and was not approved by popular referendum. It was viewed as a temporary measure and specifically avoided the question of independence.

From 1776 to 1779 the province was relatively quiet; this was partly because the fervid enthusiasms of 1776 had waned and it was evident that most South Carolinians simply wanted to be left alone. Only the abortive attempts against Florida gave evidence that a war was in progress. Few therefore expressed strong opinions on one side or the other. In fact, when a new constitution for the independent state of South Carolina was proposed by the Provincial Congress in January 1778, Governor Rutledge vetoed it. He disapproved of many of its provisions, but his primary motive seems to have been that "we still look forward to . . . an accommodation [with Great Britain], an event desirable now as it ever was. . . ." Rutledge then resigned as governor. But he did not lose his popularity, indicating that his sentiments must have struck a responsive chord among the people of the province. Rutledge was elected governor a year later, and it was obvious from his offer to Prevost to declare Charleston a neutral city that he had not abandoned his hope for reconciliation.[11]

Another indication of the weakness of the Whig cause came with the passage of a law requiring loyalty oaths of every free white male in the state. This law was enacted in response to a recommendation of the Continental Congress that the states take steps to insure internal security. Those who failed to take the oath were not only to be disenfranchised but forbidden to practice any trade or profession or to buy and sell property. The popular reaction made it clear that the law would be impossible to enforce. Its severity may have worked against it, but more probably there were simply too many people who were unwilling to commit themselves to the point of renouncing the possibility of reconciliation with England. The Council of Safety was forced to postpone the time limit for compliance. When the assembly met in the fall of 1778, it voted another postponement. The oath act had still not been enforced when the British invaded the state in 1779.

From 1776 to 1779 the internal war that had flared in the northern states had only smoldered in South Carolina because there was not enough depth of conviction on either side to move men to fight. The British conquest of

Georgia brought the war closer. An increasing number of Tories were
arrested and tried for disloyalty. Most were acquitted or pardoned, but
some were convicted and executed, most of them for such acts as murder,
arson, and conspiring with the Indians that would have been judged
criminal even if they had not been associated with disloyalty. The full
impact of the war came only when Sir Henry Clinton arrived with his
invasion force. The fall of Charleston and the British occupation forced the
issue, and it was not surprising that there was a great deal of wavering and
indecision as men groped to answer the question of where their loyalty
lay.[12]

✳ The Survivors ✳

The terms of the surrender and subsequent proclamations by General
Clinton appeared to offer a range of choices to the stunned populace of
South Carolina. Except for those who had "shed the blood of their fellow
citizens," persons who had participated in the rebellion and those who had
surrendered at Charleston (except for the Continentals) were promised full
pardon and the protection of His Majesty's government. Only those who
attempted to undermine the authority of the government were threatened
with reprisals. A Loyalist militia was to be organized to protect the lives
and property of all persons. The way seemed to be cleared for those who
wished to change allegiance regardless of past behavior.

For instance, Elias Ball was a member of a volunteer company of militia
under the revolutionary government and a member of the Provincial Congress. After the fall of Charleston, he accepted a commission in the
Loyalist militia. William Greenwood supported the revolutionary cause,
took the oath of allegiance, and was a state militiaman. With the coming of
the British, Greenwood switched sides and ultimately became a major in
the Charleston militia. John Smythe was a merchant, born and educated in
England, who held a commission in the American militia before the battle
of Charleston. He became a Loyalist officer because, he said, his refusal
would "have rendered me particularly obnoxious to the British." Scores,
perhaps even hundreds of such men were struggling for survival. Some
undoubtedly had been coerced or threatened into supporting the Whig
cause. Such, according to their testimony, were Nathaniel Wilson, John
Hamilton, Henry Siteman, and James Jones. These men welcomed the
British conquest for it allowed them to declare their true loyalty.[13]

Among the most prominent people of Charleston and the surrounding
area there were positive expressions of loyalty. More than 200 citizens
signed an address to Sir Henry Clinton congratulating him on the success
of his campaign. The addressors frankly said that they had opposed British
colonial policy, especially taxation, but that "independency" had not been

their intention and they deplored the "rash democracy" that had replaced the British constitution. Although many of the signers were Scottish merchants anxious to resume their business, there were also men of prominence, notably Paul Hamilton, John Wragg, Gideon Dupont, and Christopher Fitzsimmons. All the signers were granted pardons.[14]

Even more distinguished were the men who petitioned individually for pardons and restoration of British citizenship. Charles Pinckney, Sr., had been a member of the revolutionary Council of Safety and a colonel in the state militia. At the time of the British invasion, he was a member of Governor Rutledge's council and in fact had left the city with the governor just before the surrender. He returned and petitioned for pardon, claiming that he had been misled by "the hurry and confusion of the times." Henry Middleton had been the former president of the Continental Congress; Rawlin Lowndes had succeeded Rutledge as governor in 1778; Daniel Horry's two brothers were Francis Marion's trusted lieutenants, and he himself had been a colonel in the state militia. All these petitioned and became British subjects.[15]

This group of "addressors" and petitioners undoubtedly believed that the revolutionary cause was lost not only in South Carolina but perhaps in all America. It was even rumored that the Congress in Philadelphia intended to abandon the southern colonies, and the South Carolina representatives accused some of their fellow delegates of fostering the idea. The Frenchman, the Comte de la Luzerne, took note of the rumor and guessed that "the British will make a proposition to the ten Northern States tending to assure their independence, and their scheme will be to form into a new government the two Carolinas, Georgia, East Florida, and the Bahama Islands. . . ." Congress thought the matter serious enough to pass a resolution denying any intention of abandoning the South.[16]

So the Carolinians contemplated how best to salvage something from the ruins. Safety for their families, preservation of their considerable property holdings, and the prospect of peace and perhaps even a resumption of "business as usual"; all these must have had a powerful appeal to men who had in fact been cautious and reluctant rebels.

The terms of the surrender gave another option to those who believed that resistance was hopeless. They could accept parole and return home without having to take an oath of allegiance or be granted a pardon, thereby assuming the status of neutrals who would offer no further resistance to British authority. As the British columns made their way into the back-country one after another of the American leaders brought their commands in to accept parole. These included several of the most prominent—Isaac Hayne, Andrew Pickens, Isaac Huger, and Andrew Williamson. Colonel Williamson debated whether to retreat into North Carolina, but his choice was made when only two officers and a handful of men expressed willingness to abandon their homes.[17] Of these notable Patriot leaders only

Williamson remained inactive for the rest of the war. He returned to Charleston and thereafter retired to his home at Whitehall. Colonel Balfour interviewed him late in June and reported that he was "ready to give us every pledge in his power, for his remaining steady to the part he now takes . . . That he will immediately interest himself in gaining every man in his power, to join heartily in settling the country. And will let us know those we can depend on and what degree of trust can be put into them—" Williamson was subsequently regarded by many Whigs as the Benedict Arnold of South Carolina, but he insisted that although he had never openly opposed the British he had rendered valuable service to the American cause. The suggestion was of course that he was a secret agent working within the enemy's lines. At the end of the war, he escaped blame for his conduct largely through the influence of Governor John Mathews and General Nathanael Greene.[18]

James Simpson, the Loyalist head of the Charleston Board of Police, reported to Clinton that most of those who sought protection were either persons who professed to have been deluded into "fatal politicks" or who acknowledged that the restoration of orderly government was now the only course possible. Some still insisted that the Whig cause merited their support but agreed that further resistance was useless.[19]

By the first of June it appeared to Clinton as though the conquest of the South was virtually complete. "From every Information I receive, a number of the most violent Rebels coming in to offer their services, I have the strongest reason to believe that the general Disposition of the People to be not only friendly to Government, but forward to take up arms in its support." Colonel Balfour at Ninety Six was less certain. "Things are by no means in any sort of settled state, nor are our friends, so numerous as I expected, from Saluda to Savannah river, almost the whole district . . . are disaffected and allthow at present overawed by the presence of the troops, yet are ready to rise on the smallest change—as to their disarming it is a joke they have given in only useless arms and keep their good ones."[20]

Balfour's fears were justified. Within little more than a month after the fall of Charleston a civil war had erupted in the backcountry that forced Clinton's successor, Lord Cornwallis, to alter his plans drastically. There were several reasons for the breakdown of what was at best an uneasy peace. It was said that many Whigs who had gone home intending to mind their own affairs were outraged at Clinton's June 3 proclamation, which they regarded as a violation of the surrender terms. Yet the proclamation, which would have been difficult to enforce, could scarcely have had such pernicious effects.

More important was the increasing evidence that the military authorities could not guarantee the protection of lives and property that Clinton had promised. As early as May 28 Tarleton's Legion, on its way to overtake Buford, turned Thomas Sumter's family out of its home and burned the house. Balfour reported that he had received "many and wonderful complaints of men cloathed in *green* plundering singly every house they come across or can get at. . . ." Loyalist Robert Gray noted that "the abuses of the Army in taking peoples Horses, Cattle & Provisions without paying for them . . . disgusted the inhabitants. . . ." The clashes between the British and the partisans—at the Waxhaws, at Mobley's Meeting House, and at Ramsour's Mill just across the border in North Carolina—the single fact that emerged by the end of June 1780 was that the British conquest was not so overwhelming as it appeared.[21]

The problem of survival became more complicated than ever. In the Camden district the Loyalist militia command was given to Mathew Floyd, a former justice of the peace and captain in the state militia who had joined the British. John Lisles, a former Whig militia officer, took the oath of allegiance and was assigned to Floyd's regiment. As soon as the men were issued arms and ammunition, Lisles led a considerable body of them off to join Sumter. Two of the deserters were recaptured, and Floyd ordered them hanged as an example to the rest of the men. The effect was scarcely what Floyd expected. All but sixty of his men followed Lisles' example and joined Sumter.

William Greene was serving as a captain in the Whig militia at the time of the fall of Charleston. He was captured by Tories, but his captors were part of the force defeated at Ramsour's Mill so he escaped. Yet afterward he was recruited by Patrick Ferguson and fought with the Loyalists at King's Mountain. He was captured by the Patriots and condemned to be executed, but he managed to escape and gained refuge in western North Carolina. Surprisingly, Greene then renounced his British allegiance, rejoined the Whigs, and "battled manfully thereafter for his country."[22]

Men's loyalties could be drastically changed by the fortunes of war. The battle of King's Mountain struck terror into the ranks of the Tories in the Ninety Six district. One Loyalist partisan reported, "The militia . . . was so totally disheartened by the defeat of Ferguson, that of that whole District, we could with difficulty assemble one hundred, and even those . . . would not have made the smallest resistance if they had been attacked." Robert Cuningham, the senior Tory officer in the region, advised his relatives to leave the area.

At Cheraw Hill the British established an outpost in June 1780 manned by a small force of regulars who began organizing the Loyalist militia. At the end of July there were reports that an American army under General Horatio Gates was advancing into South Carolina. The British decided to abandon the Cheraw post because many of the garrison were sick and the regulars were needed to meet the threat of Gates' advance. The militia was ordered to escort the sick downriver to Georgetown. As soon as the regulars withdrew, the militia, escort, sick, and all, deserted to the Whigs.[23]

Loyalty can be tenuous. It rests to a certain extent upon tradition and history. The United States of America had little tradition or history for the Whigs. And even though the Loyalists "gloried in the Apellation of a British subject" they had, perhaps without knowing it, become as much American as British. But loyalty is preeminently a matter of give and take. One gives loyalty to a government in the expectation of a return—the rule of law, protection of life and property, a society that will be conducive to the "pursuit of happiness." In the chaos of revolution it is hard to determine where the path to safety and survival lies. One can sympathize with the despair and resignation of Zachariah Gibbs: ". . . The Summer has been Little Else but Merching and Countermerching never two days Calm space to mind our farm or any domestick Comfort—I had my dwelling houses burnt on two plantations my property of every kind taken even to a Spoon. . . ."

And finally there was Thomas Phepo, who tried to be all things to all men. Ordered to be banished from South Carolina in 1782 as a British adherent, he petitioned the Loyalist Claims Commission for property losses. During the war he was "persuaded to stay and endeavor to stem the tide of oppression exercised against his Majesty's friends . . . at considerable risque to his life and ruin of his fortune and did everything in his power to save the Lives and property of His Majesty's Loyal Subjects." Phepo also petitioned the South Carolina Assembly to rescind his banishment. Although he had said "some foolish things relating to the politics of that day, he was never guilty of any injurious or Oppressive Action . . . on the contrary he can prove resources and best aid of friendship employed to revive American prisoners in distress." It is not known what Thomas Phepo's fate finally was.[24]

✳ The Ravagers ✳

Perhaps it was Tarleton who started it with the slaughter of Buford's men at the Waxhaws and other depredations committed by the "men cloathed in *green*." Perhaps it was the Loyalists who were embittered by Whig suppression and anxious to avenge the recent executions. As James Simpson said, "Elated with their present triumph and resentful for their past injuries, they are Clamorous for retributive Justice, and affirm that the Province will never be settled in Peace until those People . . . shall receive the punishment their iniquities deserve." Perhaps it was the general pervasiveness of violence bred of the Indian wars and the Regulator movement. The war that blazed up in the summer of 1780 took on an aspect of vindictiveness and cruelty that at times appalled even the participants themselves.[25]

In the middle of July Captain Christian Huck, a New York Loyalist with an evil reputation, was raiding on the upper Broad River. He reputedly murdered several inoffensive people, and he had wrecked Hill's Iron

Works. A Whig party under Colonel William Bratton overtook Huck's party at Williamson's plantation. Caught in a crossfire, the Tories were overwhelmed. Huck himself was killed along with thirty-five of his men. It is said that the Whigs pursued the fugitives for nearly fifteen miles. The fact that Bratton had only one man killed and one wounded indicates that the Whigs may have been practicing "Tarleton's quarter."

Three weeks later Major William Davie, a twenty-four-year-old North Carolina cavalry commander, cut off a Loyalist detachment near Hanging Rock. Nearly all the Loyalists were killed. "As this was done under the eye of the whole British camp, no prisoners could be safely taken," noted Davie grimly, "which may apologize for the slaughter that took place on this occasion." Davie gave similar orders to his men the following September, when he attacked part of Tarleton's Legion near Charlotte. The Legion's losses were twelve killed and forty-seven wounded. Davie had one man wounded. A similar slaughter took place in mid-August at Musgrove's Mill. Elijah Clarke, Isaac Shelby, and James Williams ambushed a combined force of British regulars and Loyalists numbering about 500 men. The British lost sixty-three killed and ninety wounded. The Americans lost four killed and seven wounded.

The Tories retaliated. In the middle of September Colonel Clarke attacked the British post at Augusta commanded by one of the most prominent of the Tory partisans, Thomas Browne. Browne had incurred the displeasure of the Augusta committee of safety in 1775 and had been punished by being tarred and feathered. A year later he was again tortured by the Whigs, who burned his feet. The Georgians lived to regret it. Browne fled to Florida, where he organized a Tory regiment known as the Florida Rangers. For the next five years he terrorized the Georgia-Carolina border. By 1780 he had earned a reputation as a fearless fighter and a vindictive enemy. He repulsed Clarke's attack on Augusta, and as the Whigs retired Browne ordered thirteen Whig prisoners hanged from the staircase of the fort. Other prisoners reportedly were turned over to Browne's Indian allies to be tortured.[26]

Perhaps the most serious breach of the rules of war by the Whigs came in the aftermath of the battle of King's Mountain in October 1780. Ferguson's command, surrounded by the Americans, had difficulty surrendering. Soon after Ferguson was killed, ". . . Capt. de Peyster, who took command, ordered a white flag raised . . . but the bearer was instantly shot down. He soon had another raised and called out for quarter. Col. Shelby demanded, if they surrendered, why did they not throw down their arms? This was instantly done. But still the firing continued, until Shelby and Sevier went inside the lines, ordered the men to cease. Some who kept it up would call out, 'Give them Buford's play'—alluding to Col. Buford's defeat by Tarleton. . . ."

But the killing did not end on the battlefield. On October 11, four days after the battle, Colonel William Campbell was forced to issue an order that "officers of all ranks . . . endeavor to restrain the disorderly manner of slaughtering and disturbing the prisoners. . . . " He was also obliged to issue orders to curb the "plundering parties who issue out from the camp, and indiscriminately rob both Whig and Tory, leaving our friends in worse shape than the enemy would have done." On the 14th a drumhead court-martial tried a number of prisoners who had previously "committed cool and deliberate murder, and other enormities alike atrocious. . . . " Thirty-two were condemned to be hanged, and nine were executed before Campbell intervened and halted the killing.[27]

It was inevitable that in such an atmosphere partisan leaders conducted vengeful plundering raids whose excesses were deplored by their superiors—although there was seldom any disciplinary action. Major James Dunlap, formerly of the Queen's Rangers, who was chosen by Ferguson as one of his subordinates, had already made a reputation for himself before he came south with Clinton's army in 1780. He participated in a number of minor engagements in which he had justified his reputation as a raider and marauder. Prior to King's Mountain he was wounded in a skirmish near Gilbert Town. While he was recuperating in the home of a Loyalist, a party of avenging Whigs appeared, and one of their number shot Dunlap through the body as he lay in bed. Left for dead, Dunlap recovered and by December was again leading his dragoons in raids through the Ninety Six district. He plundered the home of James McCall, a prominent Whig partisan, and abused McCall's wife and daughter. He also made the signal mistake of burning Andrew Pickens' farm. As a result, that formidable Presbyterian elder, who had scrupulously observed his parole, notified Colonel John Harris Cruger, the commandant at Ninety Six, that he considered his parole violated. Pickens soon afterward took the field with unfortunate consequences for the British. History is replete with ironic coincidences. Within six months Dunlap was murdered by men under Pickens' command.[28]

In such chaotic circumstances it was not surprising that there were bands of freebooters claiming allegiance to one side or the other but interested primarily in looting. Perhaps the worst offender was Samuel Brown, a North Carolinian, who had earned the sobriquet of Plundering Sam. His partner in many of his ventures was his sister, uncharacteristically named Charity. When the British garrisoned the backcountry posts, Plundering Sam announced his allegiance to King George and moved into South Carolina spreading a reign of terror in what is now Laurens County. Finally, Brown overreached himself. He descended on the home of Josiah Culbertson on Fair Forest Creek and terrorized Culbertson's family. He and a companion took up Brown's trail and followed him to the home of a Loyalist. Culbertson, it is said, waited for Plundering Sam to emerge from the house and then shot him dead at a range of 200 yards.[29]

Andrew Pickens (National Portrait Gallery, Smithsonian Institution, Washington, D.C., on loan from Andrew Pickens Miller)

Colonel Hugh Ervin deserted Marion's command when the latter issued orders forbidding retaliation against Tory noncombatants. Ervin embarked on a career in which, said Marion, "he adopted the burning of houses." Maurice Murphy, another Whig partisan, became a virtual outlaw. When he was denounced by his aged uncle, Gideon Gibson, Murphy killed the old man on the doorstep of his home before the horrified eyes of Gibson's two sons, who were members of Murphy's band.[30]

The backcountry war evoked many tales in which history becomes blended with myth and legend. One of the most persistent and fascinating is the story of Nancy Hart. Mrs. Hart and her husband Benjamin settled on the upper tributaries of the Broad River in Georgia early in the 1770s. They seem to have prospered, and when the war came Hart was appointed a lieutenant in the Georgia militia. Nancy was a tall, muscular woman, red-headed and cross-eyed, "ungainly in figure and rude in speech"—in short, neither lovely nor fair. She is said to have performed a number of services for the Patriots, on one occasion entering the British post at Augusta disguised as a man in order to furnish information for Elijah Clarke.

The highlight of Nancy Hart's career occurred in 1781, when she was suspected of aiding a fugitive Whig who had escaped a Tory raiding party. Half a dozen Tories appeared at the Hart cabin and demanded food and drink. Nancy acquiesced with bad grace and worse language, but she put her enemies off guard with a combination of good food and strong drink. Meanwhile, she had dispatched her daughter to fetch her absent husband and the neighbors. Before help could arrive, however, Nancy took matters into her own hands. She seized one of the muskets which the unwary Tories had stacked and, fixing her cross-eyed gaze upon them, threatened to kill the first man who moved. One of the men attempted to disarm her, and she shot him dead. Another tried to seize her and was also shot down. Shortly afterward her husband arrived with some friends. Presumably on Nancy's insistence the rest of the Tories were hanged.[31]

Perhaps the most notorious of the Tory partisans was William Cuningham. Early in the war Cuningham had joined the Patriot militia in the Ninety Six district but resigned when his company was ordered to the Charleston area. He returned to the backcountry and in 1776 announced that he had changed his views and would no longer support the Whig cause. He was thereafter harassed and forced to become a fugitive. He finally went to Savannah and while there learned that a Whig named Ritchie had killed Cuningham's younger brother, who was a cripple and an epileptic. Cuningham returned to Ninety Six and killed Ritchie. He then raised a partisan band and began a reign of terror that earned him the nickname of "Bloody Bill." He does not appear to have served under commanders of either regulars or militia and he seems to have fought in hardly any of the engagements between American and British forces. Bloody Bill was a marauder and self-styled avenging angel.

The bloodiest episode of Cuningham's violent career came in the fall of
1781 after the British had been forced to evacuate their interior posts.
Hearing that two Whig partisans, Joseph Hayes and Sterling Turner, had
been carrying out reprisals against the families of the men under his
command, Cuningham led a party of 300 Loyalists into the backcountry.
Even though Tory resistance had largely ended in the area, he successfully
eluded the enemy's forces. Cuningham first attacked the post held by
Turner on Cloud's Creek (modern Edgefield County) and killed Turner
and his men. He then besieged Hayes Station (modern Laurens County).
Hayes and his men put up a stout defense, but the Tories set fire to the
Whig blockhouse. Upon being reassured that their lives would be spared,
the defenders surrendered. Hayes and his entire command, about thirty-
five men, were promptly sabered to death. Bloody Bill was reported to have
wielded his sword until he collapsed from exhaustion.

Cuningham's career came to an end in May 1782. He and his followers,
by this time reduced to only twenty men, were hunted down and dispersed
near Lorick's Ferry on the lower Saluda. But Cuningham managed to
escape. He took refuge first in Florida and then in England, where Parliament voted him the half-pay pension of a major.[32]

Partisans on both sides exhibited a proclivity not only for bloodshed and
vengeance but even for torture. Whipping and tarring and feathering were
common. Prisoners who escaped execution were frequently hanged until
almost dead before being released. This might be repeated several times,
especially as a means of forcing the victim to divulge information.[33]

William Gipson of North Carolina was called up for militia duty five
times between 1777 and 1781. While he was absent on his first tour of duty,
his widowed mother was whipped by Tories. During his third tour his
company captured two Tories. They were taken to Guilford Court House,
where one was condemned to death and shot. The other was sentenced to
be spicketed; "that is, he was placed with one foot upon a sharp pin drove
in a block, and was turned around . . . until the pin run through his foot."
Gipson describes his own reaction: "[I] cannot forbear to relate that as
cruel as this punishment might seem to those who never witnessed the
unrelentling cruelties of the Tories . . . yet [I] viewed the punishment with
no little satisfaction. . . ."[34]

It is perhaps a handicap to the student of history that he is committed to
viewing events of the past with detachment, that he tries to maintain a
rational and balanced perspective. It thus becomes difficult to appreciate
fully William Gipson's rage and his grim satisfaction at the gruesome
punishment inflicted on his Tory enemies. Such must have been the
reaction of the sternly honorable Elder Pickens to the wanton burning of
his home and of William Cuningham when he heard of the murder of his
crippled brother. In the absence of any government, Whig or Loyalist, that

could bring the offenders to justice the ravagers felt free to administer their own punishments.

Men were driven by lesser motives that, when viewed from a distant perspective, seem almost trivial. Those who failed to achieve military rank commensurate with their supposed abilities switched sides to satisfy petty egos. There were also the larger ambitions of those who saw a chance to achieve military distinction and thus place and status that they could not have attained in ordinary times. As Robert Gray observed, "The establishment of the King's government naturally & unavoidably occasioned an entire change of civil and military officers throughout the province, whilst their predecessors in office were stripped of their consequence and sent home. . . . The pangs of disappointed ambition soon made these men view all our transgressions with jaundiced eyes and . . . they were in general, especially the militia officers, determined to avail themselves of that opportunity to reestablish themselves in power. . . ."[35] And there was the inevitable attraction of material gain, whether from the sort of outright looting practiced by Plundering Sam Brown or from inducements such as were offered to a certain Colonel Thompson. Thompson, said British Colonel Nisbet Balfour, could be persuaded "to take the other [Loyalist] side, especially as he is fond of money. . . ."[36] Finally, there were men who simply hoped to avoid the storm of war or to take the path of least resistance. Uncertain in their political convictions, they sought only to survive.

Sir Henry Clinton first decided to inaugurate a program that would establish the King's peace by an evenhanded policy of protecting all inhabitants, allowing those who did not wish to actively support the crown a neutral status. Cornwallis strongly opposed this policy. With some justification he observed that "this means some of the most violent rebels and persecutors of the whole province are declared faithful subjects and are promised to be protected in their persons and properties." He perhaps foresaw that these neutrals were potential troublemakers "and cannot be trusted with arms, & admitted into the militia."[37]

It is difficult to argue with the earl's logic, and he may have realized the difficulties inherent in protecting former Whigs from vengeful Tories and the habitual looting of the regulars. But Clinton's change of policy on June 3 resulted in equally unfortunate consequences. According to Colonel Rawdon, "The majority of the Inhabitants of the Frontier Districts, tho' ill disposed to us were not in arms against us: They were . . . freed from the paroles [by the proclamation] . . . and nine out of ten of them are now embodied on the part of the Rebels."[38]

In attempting to pacify South Carolina the British made a major miscalculation. They overestimated the numbers of Loyalists and also their potential for assistance in the pacification of the province. In 1779, when Prevost moved against Charleston, Lord Germain noted, "The feeble

Resistance Major Prevost met with his March through so great a part of South Carolina is an indubitable Proof of the Indisposition of the Inhabitants to support the Rebel Government. . . ."[39] What Germain and his generals never understood was that failure to support the Whigs did not necessarily imply support for the crown and that Loyalist expressions of allegiance did not necessarily signify a willingness to take up arms. As the ebb and flow of American and British armies—and their partisan allies—alternately encouraged and discouraged Loyalist hopes and fears, many became convinced that lack of commitment offered the best chance for survival.

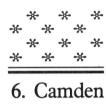

6. Camden

Lieutenant General Charles Earl Cornwallis bears the stigma of being the general who lost the campaign that lost the war. The degree to which others should share the burden of British failure is a question that has not been settled to this day. But in the spring of 1780 Cornwallis had earned the reputation of being a bold and aggressive commander, qualities difficult to find in the senior echelon of British generals who had so far directed the war for America.

✳ The Occupation ✳

Following the fall of Charleston Cornwallis had pushed into the backcountry of South Carolina and within a few weeks had established a chain of posts from Augusta to Georgetown. These posts formed a rough arc whose radius extended from 120 to 140 miles north and northwest of Charleston. For the first time in the war, the British were attempting a systematic occupation deep in the enemy's country. Its success depended on the ability of the British to contain and suppress the Whig resistance and reassure the citizenry that their lives and property were safe. Cornwallis' regular forces were thinly spread, so considerable reliance had to be placed on the vigor and good sense of his subordinates, especially Rawdon, Tarleton, and Ferguson.

The departure of Clinton made it necessary for Cornwallis to return to Charleston. He left behind him Colonel Thomas Browne and his Florida Rangers at Augusta; Colonel Nisbet Balfour with three regiments of the Loyalist Provincial Corps at Ninety Six; Lord Rawdon with his Volunteers of Ireland and two regiments of regulars at Camden; and Colonel George Turnbull with a regiment of DeLancey's New York Volunteers at Rocky Mount, only twenty-five miles south of the North Carolina border. Tarleton and his Legion seem to have been used for detached duty, hunting down bands of Patriots in the kind of operation that had led to the destruction of Buford's command.[1]

Patrick Ferguson was busily engaged in organizing the Loyalist militia. The initial problem was the difficulty of determining allegiances, especially among those who might qualify as officers. Colonel Balfour, busily recruiting in the Ninety Six area, recognized that leading citizens were the best candidates, even if their past loyalty was questionable. "Colonel Thompson of this place . . . has the greatest influence here," he wrote Cornwallis. "I certainly think he ought by no means to be allowed to remain in this part of the country, unless he has taken a very strong and active part, for if he does, by all accounts he may be trusted, but if he declines he ought to be sent on parole immediately somewhere else. If you choose to admit any of those officers into the militia who have served against us before, be so good as to let me know, that the best & most moderate may be admitted. And I own I think some might be of service, but not too many. . . ."[2]

The British soon discovered, as had Patriot leaders before them, that military service had little appeal for most South Carolinians, regardless of their loyalty. Cornwallis' recruiting instructions provided for enlistment terms of "six months of every year," and Whigs had already discovered that it was difficult to get enlistments for half of that time. The men were also liable for service "in the Provinces of Georgia, South Carolina & North Carolina. . . ." Not only did militiamen have a natural reluctance to be away from their families, but in the lawless backcountry they feared for the safety of their homes. A typical instance was that of "a Mr. Floyd," who brought thirty volunteers in to Rocky Mount. Hard on his heels came "a Couple of Expresses who apprised us that a Party of Rebels . . . had gone into the Settlement of Mr. Floyd and his Company, and was Tearing everything to Pieces." In this case Colonel Turnbull quickly dispatched a rescue party that was "Lucky enough to overtake their Rear, Killed Seven and Took Four Prisoners the rest fled to the mountains." Despite the emergency, Turnbull found time to make Floyd a colonel and his son a captain.[3]

The quality of the officers was obviously important to the success of the Loyalist militia. Nathanael Greene made an observation that Cornwallis might have heartily endorsed in the British context: "I believe the views and wishes of the great body of the people are entirely with us. But remove the personal influence of the few and they are a lifeless, inanimate mass, without direction or spirit to employ the means they possess for their own security." In England it was an inflexible rule that only gentlemen could be officers, for in a deferential society they alone possessed education and intelligence. In America such class distinctions did not always pertain, and during the Seven Years' War British officers were shocked at the American idea of allowing the men to elect their own officers. But the colonies had, of necessity, developed a system that relied on the citizen-soldier. Every man owed a military obligation to his government, but such a tradition, even when backed by laws, basically depended on local militia officers. General Washington, who also agreed that officers should be gentlemen, admitted that "a people unused to restraint must be led, they will not be drove. . . ." If a militia officer attempted to emulate the stern discipline and harsh punishments of the British army, the men simply went home, and only rarely did they feel the condemnation of their neighbors.[4]

Thus the first (if not the most important) quality of an officer was his ability to attract men to the ranks and keep them there, and this depended primarily on his ability to persuade. So both sides sought out the men of property and influence, the backcountry equivalent of the "gentry," and appealed to their patriotism or their greed, their vanity or their instinct for survival. Thomas Browne of the Florida Rangers never forgave the Whigs who tarred and feathered him and burned his feet; Richard Pearis, who was disgruntled because the Whigs had not offered him a rank commensurate with his fancied abilities; William Cuningham, a marauder whose dark deeds earned him the name "Bloody Bill"; Robert Cuningham, a judge in the Ninety Six district before he became a Loyalist general and who was as respected by both sides as his cousin "Bloody Bill" was despised; and "Plundering Sam" Brown, whose career as a thief and murderer had begun even before the war came to the Carolinas.[5]

The men they brought into the Loyalist ranks were often like their Whig counterparts, of uncertain loyalty, their courage of unknown quality even to themselves, men whose emotions were a mixture of homesickness and apathy, patriotism and avarice. It is not surprising that successful partisan leaders on both sides were a rare breed.

The British hoped to capitalize on the depressing effect that the fall of Charleston and the defeat of Buford had on Patriot morale. Adopting the tactics of the Americans, they tried to form Loyalist associations "for the purpose of watching over the peace of the country until a Militia is formed, preventing commotions of every kind and watching over the disaffected."[6] But it was an uneasy peace. "I think," wrote Balfour early in June, "the Associations will keep everything quiet in all this part of the country, but *only* for a short time."[7]

Patrick Ferguson was soon giving evidence that he was something less than the ideal inspector general of militia. "I imagine we can expect but little assistance from him further than bare inspection, . . ." Balfour noted sourly early in June. Several weeks later his doubts had changed to exasperation. "He is so extremely capricious, and violent in his whims that I doubt it will be impossible [*sic*] to keep him to any steady plan but I will keep him up to the business, as long as I can, and must prepare you for his breaking out violently." Balfour was not alone in his opinion. Rawdon thought Ferguson's ineptitude led to the premature rising of the North Carolina Tories and their subsequent defeat at Ramsour's Mill.[8]

Whether these estimates of Ferguson were expressions of the resentment that regular officers had always had for a man whose career had followed an unorthodox pattern or whether the flamboyant Scot merited the criticism, he certainly did not seem to be effective in policing the British occupation. Balfour's view was that "the disarming of the present [Whig] militia in the first place, and the new modelling of their Officers, are the first necessary steps, & a centrical place must be fixed upon . . . [where] they might be assembled and regulated with orders to meet at all times of danger when called upon, at stated times, etc."[9]

Prerequisite to the success of the British conquest was the suppression of the active Whigs accompanied by reassurances of protection for the rest of the populace. To this end, Cornwallis had published a proclamation that threatened severe punishment for those who confiscated supplies without proper authority and a promise of compensation to the owners. He had also "invested these Field Officers with Civil as well as Military power, as the most effectual means of preserving order & re-establishing the King's authority in this Country. . . ."[10]

Ferguson, on the other hand, took a much more simplistic approach. He seemed to feel that he was once again embarking on one of his military adventures, and busied himself to build an elite corps of Loyalists. Once he succeeded in "maneuvering the militia to his Whistle" he would be ready to march against the Whig banditti and scatter their forces. Ferguson, Balfour reported to Cornwallis, "seems to me to want to carry the war into N. Carolina himself at once." So Ferguson, although he was a redoubtable and fearless fighter, seems not to have possessed the peculiar talents necessary to handle a very complex task. It may well have been beyond the capacity of anyone.[11]

The British occupation was further complicated by the persistent problem of depredations committed by the troops against civilians. From 1775, when Howe occupied Boston, to the invasion of Virginia in 1781 the British were never able to cope with the pillaging and looting that was so destructive of their efforts to establish the "King's peace." The redcoats, whose poverty made them chronic gamblers and thieves, could not resist the opportunity to plunder, and they seldom recognized any distinction between "good Americans" and rebels. Although senior commanders constantly issued orders forbidding looting and threatened severe punishments, subordinate commanders seldom enforced them, partly out of sympathy for their men and partly because many believed that terrorizing the Whigs was an effective means of suppressing them. The problem is implied in Balfour's complaint, "Some stopp ought to be put *if possible* to the depredations of the cavalry who in small partys, and as expresses, commit every enormity."[12]

Loyalists who had been tyrannized by the Whigs could not be easily restrained from exacting retribution. In the Carolina backcountry, where only a few years before Regulators and Moderators had been at each others' throats, the British invasion triggered a civil war in which partisans evened old scores and outlaws and thieves plundered indiscriminately.

✳ The King's Peace ✳

Cornwallis was aware of the problems presented by his deep penetration into what was essentially enemy country. All too often in the past the appearance of the redcoats had inspired premature Loyalist risings that were doomed to failure by the inability of the regulars to give sustained support, thereby subjecting those who had declared for the king to the vengeance of their Whig neighbors. The British advance to the Ninety Six—Camden—Rocky Mount line stretched Cornwallis' resources to their limits. Therefore, "In regard to North Carolina. . . . I sent Emissaries to the leading Persons amongst our friends, recommending in the strongest terms that they should attend to their harvest, prepare provisions, & remain quiet until the King's Troops were ready to enter the Province. . . ."[13]

But the North Carolina Loyalists could not be dissuaded. Colonel John Moore had served with Cornwallis during the Charleston campaign, and the experience evidently fired him with martial ardor. He returned to North Carolina, raised a force of 1,300 Loyalists, and assembled them at Ramsour's Mill (modern Lincolnton) about twenty miles northwest of Charlotte. This threat brought a response from General Griffin Rutherford, commander of the North Carolina militia, and about 800 Patriot militia responded to his order to assemble on June 19. Colonel Francis Locke also gathered about 400 men at Mountain Creek. Since he was closer to Ramsour's Mill than Rutherford, he decided not to wait for the main body of Americans. Early on the morning of June 20 he launched a surprise attack on Moore's camp.

Locke's assault was led by mounted men who drove in the Loyalist pickets but were repulsed by the main body. More by accident than design the Americans succeeded in getting on the flank and rear of the enemy, and in the confused action that followed discipline and direction on both sides collapsed. The fighting degenerated into a desperate brawl at close quarters. Neither side got all its men into action as muskets were clubbed and steel flashed (though not bayonets). Despite the odds against them, Locke's militia managed to kill or wound about 150 of the Loyalists while losing an equal number. Locke could only muster about 110 men after the fight, but Moore's much larger force disintegrated. Moore finally reached Rawdon's post at Camden with only thirty men.[14]

Although this was a serious setback to the Loyalist cause in western North Carolina, it had little effect on the British hold in South Carolina. At the end of June conditions seemed to have stabilized enough so that

Cornwallis believed "that with the force at present under my command . . . I can leave South Carolina in security, & march about the beginning of September with a body of Troops into the back part of North Carolina, with the greatest probability of reducing that Province to its duty. . . ." Yet there were signs that the British general was being too optimistic. Tories and regulars did not abate their harassments, and Whigs were not cowed. Small marauding bands snapped at each other although it was usually hit and run on the one side followed by fruitless pursuit on the other.[15]

Then in the middle of July violence flared. Thomas Sumter had collected a patriot force of 500 men at Old Nation Ford about twenty miles south of Charlotte on the Catawba River. Colonel Turnbull at Rocky Mount ordered out Captain Christian Huck of the British Legion with 115 Tories to disrupt Sumter's recruiting and "to push the rebels as far as you may deem convenient." Huck plundered the plantation of James McClure and took McClure captive on July 11, then pushed on to Williamson's plantation only a dozen miles southwest of Sumter. After Huck's departure, McClure's wife, Mary, made her way to Sumter's camp, and by nightfall several parties set out to search for Huck.

At one time 500 Whigs commanded by no less than four colonels were on their way to Williamson's, but only about 250 arrived and deployed for a dawn attack. It is probable that Colonel William Bratton, who was rapidly gaining a reputation as a partisan leader, planned the two-pronged assault that caught Huck's command in a cross fire. Huck and thirty-five of his officers and men were killed outright, fifty were wounded, and a dozen of the rest were captured. The Americans lost one killed and one wounded.[16]

On the same day, fifty miles to the west, another encounter took place. Patrick Ferguson, who was beating for recruits north of Ninety Six, received word that a body of Whig militia had gathered at Cedar Springs (near modern Spartanburg) on their way to join Sumter. Ferguson ordered out a detachment to disperse them, but again British intentions were disrupted by a woman. Mrs. John Thomas, visiting her imprisoned husband at Ninety Six, learned of the enemy plan and was able to warn the Americans at Cedar Springs, who were commanded by her son. On the night of July 12 the Tories delivered what they thought was a surprise attack, but they charged into an ambush. About thirty of them were cut down, although they inflicted almost as many casualties on the Patriots.

As the Tory survivors withdrew from their disaster at Cedar Springs, they were again assailed by a band of Georgians under Colonel John Jones and Colonel Charles McDowell, but on the next day, July 14, the Loyalists were reinforced by Colonel Ambrose Mills' North Carolina Loyalists. The final skirmish took place on the Pacolet River just below the North Carolina border (near present Landrum, South Carolina).

Altogether three different Whig columns under no sort of coordinated command had engaged two Tory forces only a little better organized. In three days of fighting in the region north of Ninety Six the Americans had sustained about sixty casualties while killing and wounding more than ninety. Neither here nor at Williamson's plantation were any regular troops involved in the fighting.[17]

For the next two weeks there was an uneasy lull. Then, on July 30, Sumter struck directly at the British outpost at Rocky Mount. Sumter's command numbered about 600 men, outnumbering the Rocky Mount garrison more than two to one. But Turnbull's force included 150 of the tough New York Volunteers, and they held a strong position in some fortified log buildings. Sumter made three assaults against the fort but was finally forced to withdraw. The losses on each side were about fifteen killed and wounded.

On this same day, Colonel McDowell pounced on an enemy base called Thicketty Fort not far from the scene of his previous repulse on the Pacolet River. He constructed a dummy field gun out of a log and by this ruse induced ninety Tory defenders to surrender.[18]

Sumter, disappointed at his failure at Rocky Mount, turned his attention to Hanging Rock, fifteen miles to the west. The enemy force was formidable although the position was not fortified. It consisted of the Prince of Wales Loyal Americans, 150 men of the Legion, Colonel Thomas Browne's Florida Rangers, and a North Carolina regiment led by Colonel Morgan Bryan, altogether more than 500 men commanded by Colonel John Carden.

Sumter advanced on Hanging Rock on the night of August 5. He divided his force, intending to launch simultaneous dawn attacks against the separate elements of Carden's command. But in the darkness the plan went awry. The strike caught the British by surprise, but the full weight of the Americans fell on Bryan's North Carolina Loyalists, breaking them and driving them back on the Legion and Browne's Rangers. Here the Americans were checked by a bayonet charge. Carden had meanwhile pulled the Prince of Wales Regiment out of the melee and circled to strike at Sumter's flank. The American formation was broken in its turn, but the riflemen fell back only as far as the cover of an adjoining wood. From this cover they directed such a heavy fire at the Prince of Wales Regiment that it was virtually destroyed.

At this point it appeared that the Loyalists would be overwhelmed. Carden lost his nerve and turned his command over to a subordinate. Young Captain Rousselet formed his men into a hollow square and beat off Sumter's attack. The pressure was further eased by the timely arrival of the Legion dragoons from Rocky Mount. Sumter still had the advantage of numbers, but the fight had now lasted four hours and much of his command had scattered to plunder the enemy stores, especially the liquor supply. Sumter simply could not rally enough of his troops to break the British square. Reluctantly, he called off the attack, and his men withdrew, staggering under loads of plunder—and the influence of Jamaica rum.[19]

In his report to Clinton on June 30 Cornwallis had been optimistic about the prospects of the successful organization of the Loyalist militia and the establishment of the "King's peace" in South Carolina. Two weeks later he reported that "the Aspect of Affairs is not so peaceable as when I wrote last." By the first week in August his lordship's command had been attacked a dozen times by the rebels who had killed or wounded nearly 500 men. The King's peace, indeed![20]

The intensity of the partisan warfare forced Cornwallis to rethink his strategic situation. The Loyalist militia were particularly disappointing: ". . . Their want of Subordination & Confidence in themselves, will make a considerable regular Force always necessary for the defence of the Province, untill North Carolina is perfectly reduced." He had not abandoned his plan to move north, but his reasoning had altered. He now believed (or was rationalizing) that the backcountry of both Carolinas constituted a single strategic problem and that the occupation of South Carolina could succeed only if the North Carolina Piedmont was also subdued.[21]

Yet the British effort to give the widest possible support to the Loyalists forced Cornwallis to stretch his forces so thinly that the Patriots could strike at will anywhere along his line of posts or against his tenuous communication line with Charleston. The British commander, whether he realized it or not, was facing a peculiarity of South Carolina demography, namely, that the white population of the backcountry was more than three times greater than that of the lowcountry. As the British moved into the interior of South Carolina they moved into an area where not only Whig sentiment but Whig manpower was strongest. "The whole Country between Pedee & Santee has ever since been in an absolute State of Rebellion; every friend of the Government has been carried off, and his Plantation destroyed; & detachments of the enemy have appeared on the Santee, and threatened our Stores, & Convoys on that river."[22]

It was at this juncture that Cornwallis received reports that an American army was moving south. A force of Delaware and Maryland Continentals had been sent from New York to constitute the nucleus around which a new southern command could be built. All these considerations led Cornwallis to conclude that the best defense was to go over to the offensive. "If we do not Attack that Province [North Carolina], we must give up both South Carolina, and Georgia, & retire within the Walls of Charles town."[23]

✳ "Panic Upon a Multitude" ✳

At the time of the siege of Charleston in the spring of 1780, General Washington had already started a reinforcement southward. Although it was a small one it was of unusual quality and was commanded by an unusual man. The troops consisted of seven regiments of the Maryland

Continental Line and the one Continental regiment from Delaware. Two of these regiments, the 1st Maryland and the Delaware regiment, had served in every major battle that Washington's army had fought from Long Island in 1776 to Monmouth Court House. It was the sturdy counterattack of the Maryland troops that had saved the army at Long Island in 1776, and their gallantry had averted disaster again at the Brandywine. The Delaware regiment had been in the thick of every engagement; five of its commanders had been killed or wounded, and it had been reduced to two oversize companies of ninety-six men each. The whole of this force numbered 1,400 officers and men.

Their commander was General Johann de Kalb. He had earned his way to promotion and preferment partly by ability and partly by fraud. The son of Bavarian peasants, he did not warrant the aristocratic "de" in his name, but he had fought in the War of Austrian Succession and the Seven Years' War with distinction and had risen to the rank of brigadier general. He was appointed major general by Congress in 1778, but he did not receive a command until Washington ordered him south in 1780. De Kalb was over six feet tall, good-natured, intelligent, and absolutely fearless. Although he was almost sixty years old, he had tremendous powers of endurance.[24]

De Kalb had gotten his command only as far as Richmond when he learned of the disaster at Charleston. A less determined commander might have turned back; Washington had been unable to furnish him with a supply train, and Governor Thomas Jefferson was able to give only token help. But de Kalb realized that there must be a Continental force around which a new army could be created, so he pushed on southward. By June 22 he was in Hillsborough, the temporary capital of North Carolina, his army half starved and subsisting on green corn and peaches. A large, well-fed force of North Carolina militia under General Richard Caswell refused to join him, and the state government ignored his urgent pleas for food. The middle of July found the little command at Coxe's Mill, just over a hundred miles northeast of Camden.[25]

In the meantime Congress had been casting about for a replacement for the command of the Southern Department (it would not do for a foreigner to hold the position). Without seeking the advice of the commander in chief, it selected Horatio Gates. Although Gates still enjoyed the reputation that he had earned as the victor over Burgoyne in 1777, he had done little since then to merit his own high opinion of himself. His overweening ambition and vanity had involved him in that vague but unsavory affair known as the Conway Cabal, an abortive attempt to replace Washington as commander in chief. He had not improved his relations with Washington by pushing for an invasion of Canada and complaining about his assignments. He had finally asked to be relieved of duty and had gone home to Virginia.

Washington would probably have preferred Nathanael Greene for the southern command, but he was not consulted. Greene had just given up the post of commissary general for the army, and his resignation had brought on the inevitable congressional investigation of his accounts, with attendant recriminations and hard feelings. Congress was convinced by Gates' partisans, who claimed that his superior talents were just suited to the critical situation in the Carolinas. After all Gates had won the greatest victory of the war. Hero-worshiping congressmen may have been influenced by the general's visit to Philadelphia, or it may have been the spate of letters he sent to southern congressmen pontificating on military developments in the South. In any event, he was notified in mid-June that he had received what amounted to an independent command of the Southern Department. A month later he relieved de Kalb, although the baron was continued as commander of the Continentals.[26]

North Carolina seemed as oblivious to the Hero of Saratoga as it had been to de Kalb. Pleas for supplies fell on deaf ears, and Caswell at the head of 1,500 militia held aloof. Gates found himself in a difficult situation. If he stayed where he was and tried to organize and consolidate his forces, his slender supplies would soon be exhausted. If he took the offensive, he risked his few Continentals with dubious assurance of support by militia of unknown quality and quantity.

His decision was finally influenced by a report from Sumter. The partisan leader reported that British forces were still deployed from Augusta to Camden and that Cornwallis was not only absent but believed to be on his way to Savannah. If Gates could strike quickly at Lord Rawdon in Camden, the British commander could concentrate no more than a thousand men. He might be defeated or forced to retreat, leaving the Americans to occupy this most important enemy post east of the Broad.[27] Gates decided to take the offensive, and two days after he took command he issued orders to put the army on the march.

The direct route to Camden was through sparse pine barrens that had been picked clean by the armies of both sides: "The little provisions and forage which were produced on the banks of its few small streams were exhausted or taken away by the enemy, and by the hoards of banditti, (called tories) . . . who would certainly distress his army, small as it was, by removing what little might remain, out of his way."[28] Colonel Otho Holland Williams, commander of the 6th Maryland, who had been appointed Gates' assistant adjutant general, urged him to march west through Salisbury and Charlotte, a route inhabited by sympathetic Whigs who could supply his army. But this route was one-third farther than the direct march to Camden, and the delay might allow Rawdon to consolidate and reinforce his position.

Gates' decision to take the direct road was a gamble, dictated not only by the strategic situation but by a desire to do something decisive that would stir the North Carolinians out of their apathy. Certainly it would force

Caswell and the other militia commanders to join, for they could scarcely hold back if they knew he was seeking to engage the British. If Rawdon could be driven from Camden, Patriot morale would rise, and once he was established in a defensive strong point Gates could take steps to remedy his deficiencies in supply and organization. As it turned out, his knowledge of both his own forces and those of the enemy was sadly inaccurate.[29]

What Gates now styled his "Grand Army" took the road on July 27. It struggled south through the July heat, making a painful ten to fifteen miles a day with frequent halts to rest the men and gather what little food and forage could be found. Gates' orders of the day spoke of supplies that were momentarily expected, "assurances," said Colonel Williams, "that certainly were fallacious and were never verified." By August 3 the army had reached the banks of the Pee Dee, which the soldiers had been told were very fertile. "And so they were, but the preceding crop of corn . . . was exhausted and the new grain, although luxuriant and fine, was unfit for use." The men boiled it anyhow and green peaches "were substituted for bread" with unfortunate gastronomic effects. Some of the officers found better subsistence: soup made of a little lean beef thickened with hair powder.[30]

On its march the army was joined by "a gentleman of South Carolina. . . attended by a very few followers, distinguished by small black leather caps and the wretchedness of their attire; their number did not exceed twenty men and boys, some white, some black, and all mounted, but most of them miserably equipped; their appearance was in fact so burlesque that it was with much difficulty the diversion of the regular soldiery was restrained by the officers." The South Carolina gentleman was Colonel Francis Marion, and Gates "was glad of the opportunity" to detach him soon afterward.[31]

Of more significance was the general's response to an appeal from Thomas Sumter for reinforcements to attack a British detachment and cut the British supply line to Charleston. Gates, confident of his own numbers, detached 300 militia, a hundred Continentals, and two guns. Although he did not realize it at the time, he had let go 10 percent of his force and 25 percent of his artillery. But the arrival of General Caswell with his North Carolinians and 800 militia from Virginia commanded by General Edward Stevens gave Gates what he believed was 7,000 men, an overwhelming superiority of numbers over Rawdon's force at Camden. Upon his arrival at Rugeley's Mill, twelve miles north of Camden, on August 13 the American commander received a rude shock. Having overheard Gates remark several times that his force consisted of 7,000 men, Otho Holland Williams made a careful check of unit commanders. He now informed his superior that the total American force numbered just over 3,000 rank and file, less than a thousand of whom were Continentals. Concealing whatever discomfiture he may have felt, Gates remarked confidently, "These are enough for our purposes."[32] To cap his performance, on August 15

Otho Holland Williams (Independence National Historic Park Collection)

Gates decided on a night march, a difficult maneuver even for experienced troops in the presence of the enemy. On a hot, moonless night the Americans set out for Camden.

It may be that the sum of Gates' experience to this point had produced two Horatios. One was the British army veteran whose organizational and administrative abilities had done so much for the American army during its growing pains. This general thoroughly appreciated the importance of discipline, and on the march he was "much dissatisfied to see almost every good Regulation in the order of March continually violated, by Arms and Accoutrements being frequently thrown into the Waggons . . . Women frequently permitted to ride in the Waggons . . . Waggoners being sometimes suffered to halt for frivolous reasons. . . ." This Horatio's strategic sense appreciated the army's limitations in opposing British regulars. "Our Business is to Defend the main Chance; to Attack only by Detail; and when precious advantage Offers," he had said in 1776.[33]

The other Horatio was the Hero of Saratoga, anxious to regain the fame and adulation he had once enjoyed. He was once again the man of the hour, called upon to retrieve a hopeless cause, pressing forward to grip the enemy as he had in 1777 (and did he see in Sumter another John Stark, who would cripple the enemy at a southern Bennington?). The Hero would again inspire the militia to rise, take the strategic offensive, and then, having posted himself on another Bemis Heights, allow the enemy to break his army against an impregnable defense.

This time Gates had made too many mistakes. The Continentals in his army were less than one-third of his total strength (they had been 70 percent at Saratoga), and they were suffering from the enervating effects of hard marching and skimpy, indigestible rations. In his anxiety to reach his defensive position at Camden before Rawdon could consolidate, he pushed his poorly trained army into a risky night march. In addition, Sumter's information, on which Gates' entire strategy was based, was badly outdated.

Cornwallis was notified of Rawdon's danger on August 9. He hurried up from Charleston and reached Camden four days later. On the same day, August 13, four companies of light infantry arrived from Ninety Six. The British force now consisted of 1,000 regulars of the 23rd, 33rd and 71st regiments, plus the light infantry; Tarleton's Legion and a North Carolina provincial regiment, about 500 men; and 300 Loyalist militia. His total of rank and file was just over 1,900 men of whom 75 percent were either regulars or battle-tested Loyalists.[34]

Although he knew he was outnumbered, Cornwallis never seriously considered a withdrawal. He did not intend to jeopardize the large number of sick in his hospital at Camden, nor did he wish to abandon the stores he had assembled for his eventual offensive into North Carolina. Equally important was the effect that a retrograde movement would have on the morale of the inhabitants of the area, who were predominantly Loyalist. Cornwallis characteristically wasted little time. On the night of August 15 he also put his army in motion toward the enemy.

The two armies, then, moved toward each other in the summer darkness, the British force screened by the dragoons of Tarleton's Legion, the Americans covered by sixty cavalry commanded by the Frenchman Colonel Charles Armand. Neither screen performed its task very effectively, for the two armies blundered into each other, scuffled briefly, and then drew apart to wait for daylight.

Many of the Americans, who before the march had been issued a gill of molasses instead of the usual ration of rum (and "who were breaking the ranks all night"), now fell into an exhausted sleep. From prisoners taken in the skirmishing Gates learned of the presence of Cornwallis and the real strength of the enemy so he called a council of his generals (there were thirteen of them as well as a veritable cloud of colonels). When he asked them what was to be done, only General Edward Stevens spoke up, urging that they stand and fight. The rest were silent, and Gates determined to fight where he was.[35]

Daylight revealed that the position was not a bad one. Swampland on either side of the road protected the army's flanks, forcing the British to come straight in to the attack. As Gates formed his line he committed his final error; although it was inadvertent, it was probably his most costly. The British army in America usually fought "right-handed"; that is, in forming for battle the best troops were placed on the right of the line. At daylight on August 16, Gates, himself a former British officer, formed his line with the North Carolina and Virginia militia on the left, facing the British regulars of the 23rd, 33rd, and light infantry regiments. De Kalb's Continentals on the American right faced the Legion, Rawdon's Volunteers of Ireland, and the North Carolina Loyalists. (The reader should bear in mind that, as in football, one army's right opposes the other army's left.)

As the two armies made their final adjustments Colonel Williams thought he saw confusion on the British right and urged Gates to attack. Gates agreed. "Let it be done," he said, and thereby issued his first and last order of the battle. The British "confusion" was evidently nothing more than a preliminary to their advance. Recognizing the weakness of the American left, Cornwallis sent Colonel James Webster the order to attack. Webster launched regulars of the 33rd into the militia just as they began their own movement. The redcoats came on "*firing* and *huzzahing*, [and] threw the whole body of the militia into such a panic that they threw down their *loaded* arms and fled, in the utmost consternation. . . ."[36]

The Virginia militia broke first and were "almost instantly" followed by the North Carolinians. The entire American left collapsed. "He who has never seen the effect of panic upon a multitude, can have but an imperfect idea of such a thing. . . . Like electricity, it operates instantaneously—like

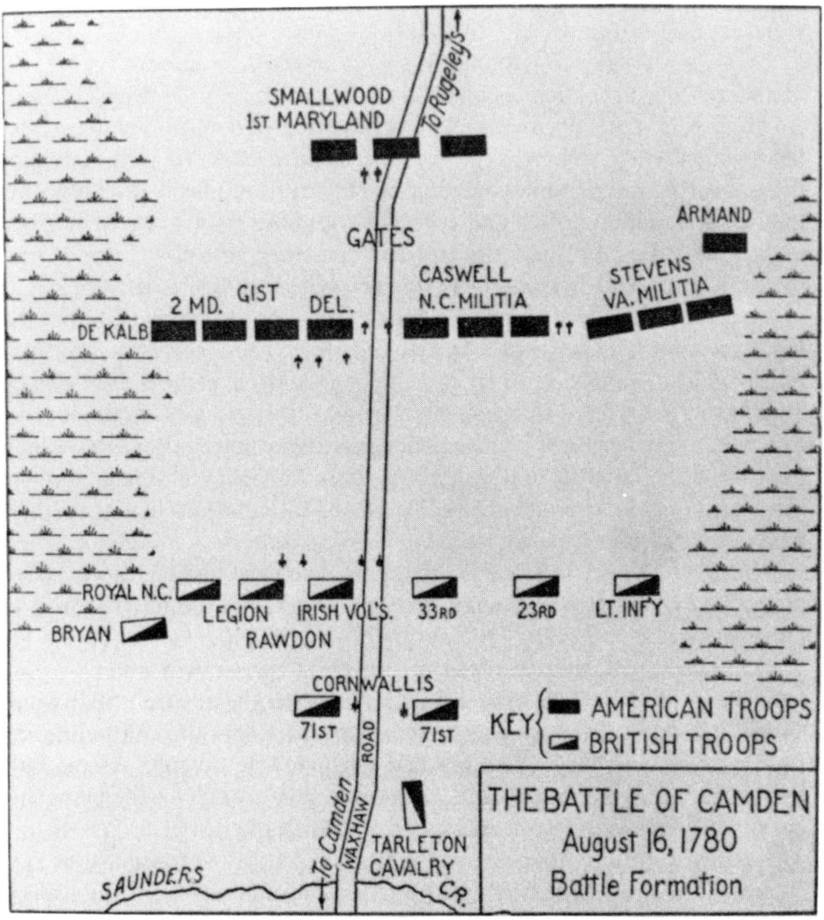
SMALLWOOD
1ST MARYLAND
To Rugeley's
GATES
ARMAND
CASWELL
N.C. MILITIA
STEVENS
VA. MILITIA
2 MD.
GIST
DEL.
DE KALB
ROYAL N.C.
LEGION
IRISH VOL'S.
33RD
23RD
LT. INF'Y
BRYAN
RAWDON
CORNWALLIS
71ST
71ST
KEY
AMERICAN TROOPS
BRITISH TROOPS
ROAD
WAXHAW
To Camden
TARLETON
CAVALRY
SAUNDERS
CR.
THE BATTLE OF CAMDEN
August 16, 1780
Battle Formation

(Reprinted with permission of Macmillan Publishing Company from The War of the Revolution, *Volume 2, by Christopher Ward. Copyright 1952 by Macmillan Publishing Company, copyright renewed 1980)*

sympathy, it is irresistable where it touches." But it did not touch the Continentals on the right.

As the left wing collapsed and was swept away, de Kalb's Maryland and Delaware troops held firm against Rawdon's attack. So did one regiment of North Carolinians commanded by Colonel Henry Dixon.[37] The 1st Maryland, which was in reserve, not only refused to be panicked by the flight of the militia but attempted to move up in support of de Kalb. The redcoats on the right, however, broke off their pursuit of the militia and wheeled in toward the center. Although the 1st Maryland twice withstood attacks from the enemy, it could not close the gap and protect de Kalb's left flank.

Meanwhile, the American right wing still stood its ground. Assailed on his flank as well as his front, sturdy old de Kalb had received no orders to retire—the smoke and dust may have hidden the flight of the militia—so he fought on. Although unhorsed and bleeding the giant Bavarian led his troops in a last desperate counterattack that momentarily drove the enemy back. Finally, de Kalb fell, wounded, it is said, eleven times, and the Continentals were overwhelmed. These hard-bitten troops had given their general the ultimate accolade: they followed him on some of the worst marching of the war, and they fought by his side until he went down. Then they scattered, and a surprising number of them finally made their way to Hillsborough.

The fugitive militia had meanwhile been driven several miles by Tarleton's Legion dragoons, who also came on Gates' supply train. Although Gates had ordered the wagons to retire toward Charlotte well before his march to Camden, the wagoners had been slow to comply. As the first soldiers fleeing from the battle reached them, they abandoned their wagons, cut the horses from their harness, and fled with the rest.

Still the fugitives' troubles were not over. As they scattered, they met "many of their insidious friends, armed, and advancing to join the American army; but, learning its fate from the refugees, they acted decidedly in concert with the victors; and, captivating some, plundering others and maltreating all the fugitives they met, returned exultantly home. . . ."[38] Loyalty in the backcountry did not run deep, and a gust of bad news could easily uproot it.

As for Gates and the other general officers, when the militia fled "they bore all before them" including the Hero and his companions. Only General Griffin Rutherford remained on the field and was captured. Gates paused briefly at Charlotte, but "reflecting that there was neither Arms . . . nor any prospect of collecting any Force at that Place . . . I proceeded with all possible Despatch hither." Indeed, Gates rode with such dispatch that he arrived "hither"—Hillsborough—in three days, 180 miles from Camden.

American casualties will probably never be known with any certainty because it was impossible even for the Continentals to muster their formations and account for their men. Cornwallis said there were 800 killed and wounded and 1,000 prisoners. There were 162 known dead from the Maryland and Delaware regiments and 63 from the North Carolina militia, most of them from Dixon's regiment. Cornwallis lost 324 of all ranks.

In the aftermath of the battle there was more bad news. Sumter's men had fallen on a British supply detachment at the Wateree Ferry on the day before Camden and captured thirty men and thirty wagons. Later in the day he took another enemy supply train of fifty wagons. Although he was soon apprised of Gates' defeat, Sumter did not take his usual precautions. When he stopped at Fishing Creek on his way to Charlotte, Tarleton and 160 of his Legion surprised the rebels—Sumter was actually asleep. Although the partisans outnumbered him by more than four to one, Tarleton's savage attack routed the Americans. They lost 150 killed and wounded and 300 captured. Sumter barely escaped.[39]

Gates' defeat was the second major disaster to American arms in the South. The defection of "sunshine patriots" in the wake of the battle at Camden boded no good for those who still declared for the Patriot cause. Ferguson began to find it easier to recruit officers and men. Congress was faced with the painful task of rebuilding still another southern army. There was, however, one result of the battle that went unmentioned in the various reports on both sides: the losses of the British regulars. Altogether Cornwallis lost 20 percent of his redcoats. The 33rd Regiment lost 36 percent of its men and half of its officers. Rawdon's Irish Volunteers lost more than 20 percent. Attrition was not yet mentioned, but Cornwallis, who already had 800 men hospitalized at Camden before the battle, must have eyed the returns grimly. Replacements for these men were to be found only in New York, and no one knew better than his lordship how niggardly Sir Henry Clinton could be in the matter of detaching men from his command. If the Carolinas were to be occupied and subdued, the strain on Cornwallis' slender forces might become severe.

7. King's Mountain

The aftermath of Camden had about it a curious air of suspended animation. It was as though the redcoats and Continentals, with their professional commanders, had stepped downstage center and demonstrated how a proper battle should—or should not—be fought. There was proper concern for lines of communication, the placing of troops in correct battle formation, even a very correct correspondence regarding the exchange of prisoners (partisans had a tendency to hang prisoners or take no prisoners at all).

Then both sides—the regulars and their generals—seemingly lapsed into inactivity. Actually, Cornwallis was busy making preparations for his planned advance into North Carolina. And Gates was furiously engaged in a letter-writing campaign pleading for troops and supplies, a campaign that brought little response.

Yet it is a fact that irregular forces on both sides fought the crucial battle of King's Mountain while Lord Cornwallis was less than thirty miles away in a haze of ignorance and General Gates was 150 miles away in a blanket of indifference.

✳ Cornwallis on the Offensive ✳

It was now time to launch what Lord Cornwallis believed would be the decisive campaign of the war. ". . . It at present appears to me that I should endeavor to get, as soon as possible, to Hillsborough," he wrote Clinton on August 23, "& there assemble, and try to arrange the friends who are inclined to our favour; and endeavor to form a very large Magazine for the Winter. . . . But all this will depend on the operations which your Excellency may think proper to pursue in the Chesapeak, which appears to me, next to the Security of New York, to be one of the most important objects of the War."[1]

In fact, an expedition to Virginia had been a recurrent theme of British planning ever since the inception of the southern campaign. In his final instruction to Cornwallis before he left Charleston, Clinton had written: "Should your Lordship so far succeed in both provinces [of the Carolinas], as to be satisfied they are safe from any attack during the approaching season, after leaving a sufficient force in garrison . . . I should wish you to assist in operations which will certainly be carried on in the Chesapeak."[2]

Cornwallis now seemed ready to conform to this strategy. On August 31 he was pressing Clinton: "I most sincerely hope that Nothing can happen to prevent your Excellency's intended Diversion in the Chesapeake. If unfortunately any unforeseen Cause should make it impossible, I should hope that you can see the absolute Necessity of adding some Force to the Carolinas. . . ."[3]

It should be noted, however, that a subtle divergence had taken place in the lines of strategic thinking pursued by Clinton and Cornwallis. In his earlier instruction Clinton had insisted that the security of the Carolinas was a precondition of Cornwallis' participation in a joint operation in Virginia.[4] But now, in August, Cornwallis viewed the Chesapeake expedition as a means of assisting him in subduing the Carolinas. In other words, Cornwallis was tacitly admitting not only that he had been unable to make the Carolinas "safe from any attack" but that he needed help to do so.

Nevertheless, on August 30 Clinton notified Germain: "By letters I have lately received from Lord Cornwallis I hold myself powerfully called upon to make a diversion in his favor in Chesapeake Bay. I have prepared for it. . . ." Six weeks later he ordered General Alexander Leslie to Virginia with a force of 2,500 regulars.[5]

For all his optimistic planning for an advance, Lord Cornwallis was uneasy. "Ferguson is to move into Tryon County [west of Charlotte] with some Militia, whom he says He is sure he can depend on for doing their Duty and fighting well; but I am sorry to say his own Experience as well as that of every other Officer is totally against him." Twice in recent weeks Tory detachments had not only deserted but gone over to the enemy; one of these had seized its own officers "and a hundred sick, & carried them all prisoners into North Carolina." Moreover, "the Disaffection . . . of the Country East of the Santee is so great, that the Account of our Victory could not penetrate into it—any person daring to speak of it being threatened with instant Death."[6]

On August 25 a detachment of regulars and Loyalists escorting prisoners from Camden to Charleston was waylaid by that odd little gentleman, Colonel Francis Marion. British Captain Jonathan Roberts, believing that the Whigs had been driven to cover, camped at Nelson's Ferry on Thomas Sumter's plantation, and his men stacked their arms. In the predawn darkness Marion sent his partisans into the attack from two directions and overwhelmed the redcoats. Twenty-five of the enemy were killed and 150 American prisoners were released. The little victory, somewhat magnified in the telling, was reported to Gates and subsequently to

Congress, a much-needed bit of good news to relieve the black aspect of affairs in the South. (It is interesting to note that Marion had told neither his officers nor his men about the defeat at Camden.)[7]

Francis Marion was a slight, muscular man whose forebears were Huguenots. In the summer of 1780 he was forty-eight years old. Unlike many of his partisan compatriots, he had earned his rank as an officer of the Continental Line and had the reputation of being a stern disciplinarian. He quickly perceived that many of his followers were less than steadfast in duty and loyalty, and he made little effort to recruit a large force. Men were inclined to wander into camp, spend a few weeks campaigning, and then drift back home. His "corps" ranged from as few as twenty men to several hundred, varying with the fortunes of war. Always suspicious of the loyalty of his transient command, Marion tended to be close-mouthed, seldom confiding his plans to any except his most faithful officers, Peter and Hugh Horry.

The "Swamp Fox" was aptly named, for he was a master strategist, and like all good strategists he relied heavily on sound intelligence, the element of surprise, and an intimate knowledge of his area of operations. Beneath his mild and courteous exterior there was a hard fighter who could kill from ambush, violate flags of truce, or court-martial a friend who failed in his duty. He was that kind of leader who attracts men, not by a convivial personality or generous nature, but because he wins, and his victories do not cost needless lives.[8]

Two days after the action at Nelson's Ferry one of Marion's officers, Major John James, clashed with Major James Wemyss' 63rd Regiment at Kingstree. The rebels were driven off after each side had sustained about thirty casualties. Cornwallis was forced to send Tarleton and his Legion down the Santee to clear his line of communication and disperse the raiders. ✳

His lordship evidently decided that it was time to pursue a hard line. Wemyss was ordered to "disarm in the most rigid Manner the Country between the Santee & Peedee, and to punish severely all those who submitted . . . and [then] have joined in this second Revolt. . . . I have myself ordered several Militia Men to be executed, who . . . had borne Arms with us and afterwards revolted to the Enemy." During his stay in Charleston he had found that many who had taken paroles "were corresponding with the enemy and encouraging the rebels." He ordered twenty of the worst offenders to be transported to St. Augustine and confiscated the property of several others. Although he was aware that it would "raise a Clamour," he felt that the time had come to deal sternly with the Whigs.[9]

It soon became evident that Draconian measures were no cure for the ills that beset the British occupation. Colonel John Cruger at Ninety Six attempted to pursue a stern but evenhanded policy, although he was said to have permitted the Indians to raid Whig settlements on the frontier. But the

Role of Light Infantry   Extract of a letter dated 29/1/81 in Royal Gazette of 28/2/81

"The provincial light infantry have not joined Ld. Cornwallis but cover the frontiers & keep the communication with Camden etc. open by taking post at Nelson's Ferry on the Santee River."

man who aroused the Whigs in the west was Thomas Browne, commander of the Florida Rangers at Augusta. Browne had been terrorizing the Georgia upcountry, especially in Wilkes County, where he encountered the resistance of Colonel Elijah Clarke, a famous Indian fighter.[10]

Instead of being intimidated, Clarke and other Georgia leaders decided that they must carry the war into South Carolina. To this purpose they had appealed for help both to Thomas Sumter and to Isaac Shelby and John Sevier, old comrades in arms from the Indian wars, who were settled in the Watauga country (now East Tennessee). The "over the mountain" men responded, and Clarke and Shelby had a brush with Ferguson at Wofford's Iron Works just before the battle of Camden.

A few days later, on August 18, Clarke and Shelby struck again. Colonel Alexander Innes, with a mixed force of Loyalist milita and New Jersey and New York Volunteers, about 500 men, was camped at Musgrove's Mill north of Ninety Six. Clarke and Shelby had a somewhat smaller force, but they managed to lure Innes into an ambush. It was a classic adaptation of Indian cunning, a small band of rebels, retreating in apparent panic before the helter-skelter pursuit of the enemy. The British blundered into a deadly cross fire of concealed Americans and the command was cut to pieces. Two hundred and twenty were killed, wounded, and captured.[11]

But as the news of Camden reached the distant settlements fewer and fewer Whigs took the field, and the Tories became bolder. After Musgrove's Mill, Shelby's men went back across the mountains, and Clarke, who was wounded in the fight, retired to his home in Georgia.

Within a month, however, Clarke had taken the field again. Tory raids had intensified, and it was reported that Browne not only was hanging Whig prisoners but had received a supply of trade goods with which to entice the Indians into raiding the frontier. Clarke believed that he could raise enough men to overrun Augusta. When he sent out the call for militia, it was obvious that Whig ardor had cooled for only 300 men assembled. Clarke was nonetheless determined to make the effort. He persuaded his followers by alternately holding out the prospect of plundering the Indian trade goods and taking vengeance on the Tories, thus protecting Patriot homes and families.

The Americans attacked on September 14 and were lucky to catch Browne with only 250 of his Rangers in Augusta. But he managed to fort up in a large building just outside the village. Although cut off from water, Browne and his men fought Clarke to a standstill for four days and inflicted sixty casualties on the Whig force. Browne himself was wounded, and his men suffered severely from the heat in the crowded building, but the Tories hung on doggedly until September 18, when Cruger arrived with a relief party from Ninety Six. As Clarke and his men retired, Browne took a grim revenge: thirteen Whig prisoners were hanged from the staircase of the Tory fortress.

It was now evident to Clarke that Wilkes County was defenseless against the incursions of Tories and Indians. As the little band returned home they were met by a congregation of 400 women, children, and old people who had banded together for protection in the absence of their men. Clarke and his officers decided to seek safety across the mountains in the valley of the Holston. Late in September the refugees started on their trek to the Watauga settlement.[12]

✳ The Advance to Charlotte ✳

During the first week of September, Cornwallis finally began his movement toward North Carolina, but the air that pervaded his advance was scarcely that of the triumphant conqueror. Many of his men were sick, and the summer heat was taking its toll. The outpost at Cheraw Hill, "a post of great consequence . . . had the appearance of being healthy, but it proved so much the Contrary, & sickness came on so rapidly that in nine days . . . two thirds of the 71st Regt. were taken ill of Fevers & Ague, & rendered unfit for Service." Under the circumstances Hillsborough seemed too ambitious an objective, but "Our Friends . . . do not seem inclined to rise untill they see our Army in Motion," so on September 7 the British main force moved to the Waxhaws, "in hopes that the change of air might be useful."

Cornwallis' immediate objective was Charlotte, but his discouragement at the slow progress of his campaign of conquest was evident. "The post at Charlotte-town will be a great security to all this frontier of South Carolina, which, even if we were possessed of the greatest part of North Carolina, would be liable to be infested by parties, who have retired with their effects over the mountains, and mean to take every opportunity of carrying on a predatory war, and it will, I hope, prevent insurrections in this country, which is very disaffected." Camden aside, there had now been twenty-five fights between Tories and rebels since the fall of Charleston. For Cornwallis the light at the end of the tunnel must have seemed very far away.[13]

At American headquarters in Hillsborough Gates was beset with difficulties. A loser's lot is not a happy one and Gates was no exception. There were polite expressions of regret and soothing assurances that he was a victim of circumstances. But Benjamin Rush, a member of Congress and longtime critic of Washington, may have made the shrewdest observation of all. "Your old friend Gates," he wrote to John Adams, "is now suffering, not for his defeat at Camden but for *taking General Burgoyne. . . .*" The mighty Hero of Saratoga had a long way to fall.

Soon embittered officers of his command were muttering, and Governor Abner Nash of North Carolina was asking Congress for his removal. A newly created state Board of War began issuing officious orders to the militia. General Gates' anger flared. He declared that he would arrest any officer "who in contempt or opposition to His orders shall dare obey an order from the Board of War." His days might be numbered, but he did not intend to relinquish his authority. He continued to press for supplies and men and announced plans to move westward to meet the advancing enemy. But help was slow in coming, and recruitment was understandably light.

There were a few bright spots. The Continentals, of whom about 800 finally made their way back to Hillsborough, showed that amazing resiliency that had characterized them during this long, hard war. There was word from Sumter that, despite the debacle at Fishing Creek, he was recruiting a new force of Patriots which numbered nearly 1,000 men.[14]

By the end of September Gates had received two additions to his little command who were to prove invaluable to his successor. The first of these was his former comrade in arms, Daniel Morgan, who had performed so brilliantly at Saratoga. A tempestuous giant who had served as a teamster for the British army in the Seven Years' War, Morgan had been with Benedict Arnold in Canada in 1775-76. He had been taken prisoner at Quebec, but Governor General Guy Carleton, in an act of mercy which he must have later regretted, released him. Morgan returned to Washington's army and organized a corps of riflemen. Although Gates had praised him extravagantly for his part in both battles at Saratoga, Congress refused to promote him to general. Wounded feelings and failing health drove him into retirement, but the desperate situation in the South and a belated promotion from Congress persuaded him to join the southern command. As it turned out, the "Old Waggoner" had one more great fight left in him.

The other addition was William Washington, a cousin of the commander in chief. He was only twenty-eight years old, but he had been fighting with considerable distinction since 1776. By 1780 this big barrel of a man had been promoted to lieutenant colonel of dragoons. His presence would do much to remedy what the southern command had conspicuously lacked—a competent cavalry commander.

Despite his shortage of troops, Gates now showed that he was still a capable organizer. Most of the reduced Continental Line was amalgamated into a single regiment and placed under Otho Holland Williams. Colonel Williams was thirty-one years old and had served with the Maryland line since 1775. He had been made colonel of the 6th Maryland when those troops were ordered south. He was a fearless fighter, and few officers could match his dexterity and skill at handling a rear-guard action.

Gates also put together a regiment of troops consisting of three companies of men especially selected from the Continentals. To these he added seventy dragoons under Washington, a company of Delaware Continentals, and sixty Virginia riflemen, the whole commanded by another young Maryland officer, Colonel John Eager Howard. Although composed of elements from various units, this command was subsequently referred to as the 2nd Maryland.[15]

William Washington (Independence National Historical Park Collection)

As Cornwallis began his movement into North Carolina, Gates ordered General Jethro Sumner and his militia to hold the Yadkin fords near Salisbury and sent Morgan with some light infantry to support him. But these movements were essentially defensive; ". . . it is in vain to think of acting Offensively," Gates wrote in mid-September. "I will not risque a Second Defeat, by marching through Famine, and encountering every distress."

Gates' orders to Sumner and the latter's movement to the Yadkin threatened to create a command problem. General Griffin Rutherford had been captured at Camden, and Caswell's conduct before and during the battle had discredited him. Sumner, whose health was chronically bad, was left as the senior militia general. He also held a Continental commission, although technically his authority was limited to the Hillsborough district. A meeting of officers at Salisbury on August 31 petitioned the legislature for the appointment of William L. Davidson to command the western militia with the rank of brigadier general. Colonel Davidson, thirty-four years old, held a Continental commission and was a veteran both of Washington's army and of the fighting in the Carolina backcountry. The petitioners included a number of the most active partisan commanders, among them Francis Locke and William Davie. Moreover, when many of the people of Mecklenburg (Charlotte) and Rowan (Salisbury) wanted to remain passive in the face of the British advance, Davidson had pugnaciously maintained his position at McAlpin's Creek, only twenty miles from Cornwallis' camp at the Waxhaws. The legislature granted the petition, and Davidson promptly ordered out the militia, although the response was small.

Sumner now ignored Gates' orders and pushed west of the Yadkin to join Davidson. The problem of command was avoided because Davidson and Sumner were old friends. Mutual respect resulted in a dual command, with Davidson technically the subordinate but often acting in command to relieve the ailing Sumner.[16]

The military situation remained gloomy for the Patriots. Militiamen were loath to stay too long in the ranks when their families might be endangered by roving bands of marauders. As Cornwallis prepared to launch his offensive, it appeared that the most that could be done was to hang on his flanks and harass the redcoats.

Late in September Cornwallis left his camp in the Waxhaws and moved toward Charlotte. With him were the regulars of the decimated 23rd and 33rd regiments, the Volunteers of Ireland, Tarleton's Legion, and Bryan's North Carolina Provincials, about 2,200 men in all. The 71st and 63rd regiments were virtually unfit for duty, the latter "so totally demolished by sickness, that it will not be fit for actual service for some months." Tarleton was also down with fever. To the west the British flank was protected by a corps of about 800 Loyalists who had been embodied by Patrick Ferguson.

His was a dual function, to act as the army's left wing controlling rebel raiders and "overawing the disaffected" and to recruit backcountry Loyalists.[17]

Sumner and Davidson made no effort to block Cornwallis' approach, withdrawing from Charlotte toward Salisbury. But Major Davie commanding a body of mounted riflemen was in close contact with the British column. At daylight on September 20 he came upon Tarleton's Legion cavalry and the 71st Regiment at Wahab's Plantation. "The enemy, being completely surprised, had no time to form and crowded in great disorder . . . when a well-reserved fire from the rifle men drove them back upon the cavalry and infantry; . . . they fluctuated some moments under the impression of terror and dismay and then bore down the fences and fled in full speed." The British left fifteen dead and forty wounded on the field. Davie coldly noted that he had "given orders to take no prisoners."

Five days later Cornwallis finally reached Charlotte, but Davie was there to harass the redcoats. With no more than 150 men hidden in the streets and buildings around the courthouse, he opened fire on the Legion as it led the British advance into the town. When Major George Hanger, commanding in Tarleton's absence, led a headlong charge against Davie's position, concealed riflemen cut down twenty of the Legion, including Hanger, and drove them back. When the infantry came up, Davie pulled his men out of the town.

Charlotte was a crossroads town which, said Tarleton, "afforded some conveniences, blended with great disadvantages. The mills in its neighbourhood were supposed of sufficient consequence to render it . . . an eligible position. . . . [But] the town and environs abounded with inveterate enemies . . . the roads narrow, and crossed in every direction; and the whole face of the country covered with close and thick woods." It was an ideal situation for General Davidson and his young cavalry commander. They invested the town so closely and harassed its outposts and patrols with such intensity that they "totally destroyed all communication between the King's troops and the loyalists in other parts of the province." Perhaps more significant, "British troops were so effectually blockaded in their present position that very few, out of a great number of messengers, could reach Charlotte town . . . to give intelligence of Ferguson's situation."[18]

✳ "Ferguson the Great Partizan Has Miscarried" ✳

Ferguson, now leading more than 1,000 men, was determined to stamp out the rebellion in the west. He was especially anxious to cut off Clarke and his refugees before they could reach the safety of the mountains. In his eagerness he pushed rapidly into western North Carolina and, according to most accounts, his men carried out savage reprisals against the Whig settlers. Spreading a reign of terror on their march north and west, the raiders reached Davidson's Old Fort by late September. Here they were deep in the foothills of the Blue Ridge Mountains, not more than fifty miles from the valley of the Holston.

Ferguson chose this moment to issue a proclamation threatening that if the rebels "did not desist from their opposition to the British Arms" he would "hang their leaders and lay their country waste with fire and sword." What effect this had on the Patriots is difficult to say, but it was probably more provocative than intimidating. But Ferguson's presence so close to their settlements thoroughly alarmed the "over the mountain" men. Hitherto they had considered themselves beyond the reach of the invaders, but the Loyalists were scarcely more than two days' march from the headwaters of the Holston. Moreover, Ferguson was now more than seventy miles from Charlotte and completely out of touch with Cornwallis. If his force constituted the army's left wing, it was dangerously extended.[19]

Shelby, John Sevier, and other Watauga leaders recognized the opportunity. They sent out a call for militia to assemble at Sycamore Shoals (near Elizabethton, Tennessee). The response was immediate and enthusiastic. From southwestern Virginia at Chiswell's Lead Mines Colonel William Campbell mustered 400 men. Charles McDowell saw to the safety of his refugees and then with 200 men set a course to rendezvous with Shelby. The "over the mountain" men crossed the Blue Ridge and came to Quaker Meadows, where General Benjamin Cleveland joined them with 350 North Carolinians. By September 29 nearly 1,300 men were on the headwaters of the Catawba. Most of them were armed with rifles and were mounted on horseback.

At about the same time, Ferguson began to worry about his exposed position. He withdrew to Gilbert Town (near Rutherfordton), and it was here that he got the first reports of the rebel force moving against him. The hunter now became the prey, although Ferguson was not seriously alarmed. He had more than 1,000 Loyalists and was confident of his ability to deal with the Patriot force. But he continued his movement eastward toward Cornwallis and on the night of October 3 crossed the Broad about forty miles west of Charlotte. A few days later he felt he was close enough to the main army to turn on his pursuers; ". . . if necessary, I should hope for success against them myself," he wrote Cornwallis, "but, numbers compared, that must be doubtful. . . . Three or four hundred good soldiers, part dragoons, would finish the business. Something must be done soon." It was Ferguson's last message, and Cornwallis never received it.[20]

The Americans meanwhile had lost track of the Loyalists. By October 2 they were in Gilbert Town, where the officers held a council of war. For one thing, there were large numbers of colonels but no generals. Gates had made no effort to keep track of Ferguson's movement or to organize a force to oppose him. The council decided to send a request that either General

Morgan or General Davidson be placed in command. In the meantime, it was decided that Colonel Campbell would serve as "Officer of the Day" to execute plans. The council also decided to make a forced march to overtake Ferguson before he could escape to Charlotte. For this operation, 910 men were chosen, taken largely from regiments that had the freshest mounts.[21]

On the morning of October 3 this force began to push rapidly eastward. "We traveled all that night and the next day through heavy rains," wrote sixteen-year-old James Collins. The men caught snatches of sleep wrapped in their wet blankets, and munched on "parched corn and . . . two or three spoonfuls of honey." Soon residents of the country though which they traveled brought word of Ferguson. He had pitched his camp on the flat crest of King's Mountain and announced that "God Almighty himself could not drive him from it."[22]

By the morning of October 7 the Americans had reached the steep hill that rises abruptly 800 feet above the low hills of the Carolina piedmont. Its mesalike crest was relatively clear and ran from northeast to southwest for about 500 yards; at the narrow southwest end it was sixty to seventy yards across, widening to nearly 200 yards at the northward end, where Ferguson's men were camped. The steep flanks of the mountain were heavily wooded, offering good cover but somewhat heavy going for an advancing force.

The mountain men tethered their horses and began to form around the base of the ridge. There were a considerable number of officers, but the force was divided into nine "regiments." Benjamin Cleveland and Isaac Shelby directed the men on the northern slope while John Sevier and William Campbell led the men on the south side. The regiments almost entirely circled the mountain, for the rebels intended not just to defeat Ferguson but to destroy him.

Ferguson's men were all Loyalists, of whom about 100 were provincials of the New York Volunteers and the Queen's Rangers. The rest, like their opponents, were from the backcountry. Ferguson was the only regular of either army on the field. His position seemed extremely strong.

About three o'clock the Americans began their advance through the dense woods and undergrowth on the flanks of the mountain. The Loyalists soon found that it was difficult to check the long, irregular line of the attackers. The descending angle of fire was very sharp, and it is probable that the Loyalists' aim was high. Several times Ferguson sent parts of his line down the slope in bayonet charges to check the Patriots, but their ranks merely sagged back down the hill and then came on again. Campbell and Shelby probably gained the summit first at the narrow end of the ridge. They began to attack up the length of the crest as the rest of the ring closed. Although the American advance had been fairly orderly in the first stages,

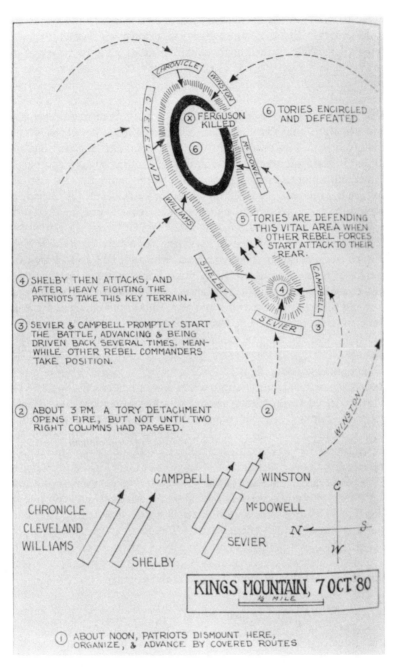

KINGS MOUNTAIN, 7 OCT '80

(Reprinted with permission from
The Encyclopedia of the American Revolution,
by Mark Mayo Boatner III. Copyright 1966.
Published by David McKay Co., Inc.)

the battle soon developed into a desperate melee as more and more Patriots reached the top. Ferguson was seen to ride from point to point, furiously rallying his men and trying to hold them in formation. Then horse and man went down, and with the fall of their leader the Loyalists also fell into disorder.

At the end of forty-five minutes it was clear that the British were beaten. White flags began to appear, but as fast as they did their bearers were shot down. "It was some time," Isaac Shelby recalled, "before a complete cessation of the firing on our part could be effected. Our men had been scattered in the woods and were continually coming up and continued to fire, without comprehending in the heat of the moment what had happened; and some who had heard that at Buford's defeat the British had refused quarters . . . were willing to follow that bad example."[23]

Finally, the firing ceased. One hundred and fifty-seven Loyalists were killed, and 163 were wounded so badly they could not be moved. Nearly 700 were taken prisoner. The Americans lost 28 killed and 62 wounded.

Patrick Ferguson's body, shot in the chest and face, was wrapped in a raw cowhide and buried on the field. The rest of the Tories "were thrown into convenient piles and covered with old logs, the bark of old trees and rocks, yet not so as to secure them from becoming prey to the beasts of the forests. . . . Also the hogs in the neighborhood gathered into the place to devour the flesh. . . . In the evening there was a distribution of the plunder, and we were dismissed."[24]

And what of Cornwallis, only twenty-five miles away? Davidson and Davie had drawn a tight cordon around Charlotte, so much so that Rawdon reported to Clinton: "By the enemy having secured all the passes on the Catawba, Lord Cornwallis . . . received but confused accounts of the affair for some time: but at length the truth reached him. . . ." Not until the morning of the battle did British headquarters know of Ferguson's presence in the area. By then it was too late.

But the news spread like wildfire among the backcountry Whigs, who sensed that this was a turning point in their battle against Loyalist raiders. General Davidson notified Sumner that "Ferguson, the great Partizan, has miscarried." James Collins, a veteran at age sixteen, wrote, "It seemed like a calm after a heavy storm . . . and for a short time every man could visit his home, or his neighbor without being afraid."[25]

Usually it is the lot of the historian, with the perspective of hindsight, to point out the significant battles of history. No such perspective was necessary for Lord Cornwallis. Rawdon's report to Sir Henry Clinton in October revealed the full measure of British miscalculations (to add to all his other troubles, Cornwallis was down with "a severe fever"):

Orders were therefore dispatched [after Camden] to our friends, stating that the hour, [for] which they had so long pressed, was arrived; and exhorting them to stand forth immediately, and prevent the re-union of the scattered enemy. Instant support . . . was promised. In the fullest confidence that this event would take place, Lord Cornwallis ventured to press your Excellency for co-operation in the Chesapeak, hoping that the assistance of the North Carolinians might eventually furnish a force for yet farther efforts. Not a single man, however, attempted to improve the favourable moment, or obeyed that summons for which they had been so impatient. It was hoped that our approach might get the better of their timidity; yet during a long period, whilst we were waiting at Charlotteburgh for our stores and convalescents, they did not even furnish us with the least information respecting the force collecting against us. In short, Sir, we may have a powerful body of friends in North Carolina—and indeed we have cause to be convinced that many of the inhabitants may wish well to his Majesty's arms; but they have not given evidence enough either of their number or their activity, to justify the stake of this province, for the uncertain advantages that might attend immediate junction with them. . . .

Whilst this army lay at Charlotteburgh, Georgetown was taken from the militia by the rebels; and the whole country east of the Santee, gave such proofs of general defection, that even the militia of the High Hills could not be prevailed on to . . . protect our boats upon the river. The defeat of Major Ferguson had so dispirited this part of the country, and indeed the loyal subjects were so wearied by the long continuance of the campaign, that Lieutenant Colonel Cruger (commanding at Ninety-six) sent information to Lord Cornwallis, that the whole district had determined to submit as soon as the rebels should enter it. From these circumstances, from the consideration that delay does not extinguish our hopes in North Carolina . . . [he] has resolved to remain for the present in a position which may secure the frontiers without separating his force. . . . Lord Cornwallis foresees all the difficulties of a defensive war. Yet his Lordship thinks they cannot be weighed against the dangers which must have attended an obstinate adherence to his former plan.

By the first week in November Cornwallis had evacuated Charlotte and withdrawn to Winnsboro, between Camden and Ninety Six.[26]

8. Greene Takes Command: The Cowpens

The practice of war has always abounded with principles. These represent the collective experience of centuries of combat and are formulated to guide the untutored and the ignorant. The principles of warfare are given special authenticity if they are enunciated by famous commanders such as Caesar or Napoleon. These principles or rules also tend to become institutionalized until they are called laws and are preceded by such imperatives as "always" and "never": when fighting on the defensive always protect the flanks; never leave an enemy post in the rear; never divide forces in the face of an enemy of equal or superior strength.

Such rules are invaluable for young and inexperienced captains, and a senior commander, if he observes them carefully, will seldom be overtaken by disaster. If he fails, he can always justify his conduct and escape censure. Armies are shot through with generals who are so preoccupied with avoiding failure and maintaining reputation that they never grasp the opportunity for dazzling success. Possessed of a thorough knowledge of the laws to which they assiduously adhere, such commanders become mere mechanics working at a fairly simple trade.

But what if there is a context of time and place in which the rules do not apply? Then warfare becomes not a trade but an art. Two of the most creative practitioners of the art of war were Nathanael Greene and Daniel Morgan.

✳ After King's Mountain ✳

The Santee River splits the wedge of South Carolina almost in the middle. It is the principal of several streams that meander out of the low hills of the Carolina piedmont and find their way through the coastal plain to the sea. The mouth of the Santee offers no suitable harbor for ships. In fact, the only two ports, Charleston and Georgetown, have no navigable rivers leading inland. In 1780, the Santee was navigable by boats, and the British used it as a supply route, but to get troops and supplies to the interior it was necessary to use both roads and rivers, both wagons and boats. One of the factors in Cornwallis' decision to drop back from Charlotte to Winnsboro was his increasing concern for the security of his communications with Charleston. The upland between the Santee and the Pee Dee was dotted with farms, many of which were called plantations, but which were neither as large nor as productive as the great holdings of the Carolina nabobs of the lowcountry. It was mainly a land of forest and swamp traversed by a few bad roads that crossed and recrossed numerous creeks and rivers at fords and ferries. In the summer it was incredibly hot, humid, and fever-ridden. This was the stamping ground of Francis Marion, the Swamp Fox.

A week before King's Mountain, Marion had surprised and routed a Loyalist force under Colonel John Ball at Shepherd's Ferry, inflicting twenty casualties. Shepherd's Ferry was only twenty miles from George-town, the post that anchored the British line on the coast northeast of Charleston. Marion seems to have considered driving toward Georgetown itself since "the Toreys are so affrighted with my Little Excursions that many is moving off to Georgia with their Effects others are rund into Swamps." But his own forces (which British Major Wemyss reported at 400 men) had dwindled to less than a hundred as his men began to drift homeward to look after their families.[1]

Marion confessed that he could not hold his men in the ranks, nor did he blame them, for the internecine war was becoming so savage that no one was safe. Bands of outlaws took advantage of the chaos of war to rob and plunder. They professed nominal allegiance to one side or the other, but their principal loyalty was to booty.

After Ferguson's defeat, Marion felt that the time had come to mount a sweeping campaign east of the Santee. It took him some weeks to recruit his men, for Tory partisans were busy, but by the middle of October he was on the move. He first made a thrust at Georgetown. He had no difficulty driving in the British pickets and occupying the town, but the small garrison fortified itself in a strong redoubt around the brick jail. Unable to prize them out, Marion was forced to abandon the town.[2]

On October 24 his scouts brought information that the Loyalists were out in force led by Colonel Samuel Tynes. They had drawn equipment at Camden and were camped at Tearcoat Swamp between the Black River and the High Hills of the Santee. On October 26 Marion led 150 men in a dawn attack on the Loyalists. They were scattered leaving six dead and fourteen wounded. Twenty-three were captured, and Marion was not surprised when most of the captives asked to join the Whigs. Such shifting loyalties occurred frequently and the partisan leader welcomed these men to the ranks, although he kept a wary eye on them. Marion also sent a detachment under Captain William Snipes to run down Tynes. Snipes

*Francis Marion (Emmet Collection, Engraving by T. B. Welch,
after T. Stothard, Prints Division, The New York Public Library,
Astor, Lenox and Tilden Foundations)*

returned a few days later with the Loyalist colonel and several of his officers in tow.[3]

Marion next undertook a campaign of harassment along the British line of communication between Winnsboro and Charleston. Gates, now in the last weeks of his command of the Southern Department, paid no attention to Marion's movements. (When General Henry Harrington moved down from North Carolina and began to issue orders, Marion paid no attention to *him* because, in his view, North Carolina militia generals had no authority over a Continental officer in South Carolina.)

Cornwallis was obviously vexed by his increasing inability to control his own supply line and the surrounding countryside. "If [the Loyalists] will allow themselves to be plundered and their families ruined, by a banditti not one third their numbers, there is no possibility of our protecting them," he remarked petulantly. By early November he was aroused sufficiently to order Tarleton and the British Legion to "get at Mr. Marion."[4]

Although his force had increased to several hundred men, Marion knew that he was no match for the Legion. He set an ambush for Tarleton but came up empty when the British took another route. Tarleton in his turn laid a snare for the Swamp Fox, but Marion was warned and slipped away. This cat and mouse game finally gave way to an all-out pursuit by Tarleton, but the partisans led him a merry run of forty miles across creeks and through trackless swamps until Tarleton, his horses and men exhausted, gave up the chase. After laying waste to a number of farms and plantations the Legion commander reported to Cornwallis that Marion's force had been disbanded.[5] On December 3 Cornwallis confidently wrote to Clinton in New York that "Tarleton ... pursued Marion for several days, obliged his Corps to take to the Swamps, and by convincing the Inhabitants that there was a power superior to Marion who could likewise reward & Punish, so far checked the Insurrection, that the greatest part of them have not dared openly to appear in Arms against us since his expedition."

Just ten days after Cornwallis wrote this dispatch Marion, with 700 men at his back, fell upon part of the 64th Regiment under Colonel Francis McElroth and drove it into the swamps at Singleton's Mill. The next day he waylaid a British supply boat at Nelson's Ferry and burned it.

A few days later Marion received his first dispatch from the new commander of the Southern Department. It was clear that Nathanael Greene did not intend to ignore the Swamp Fox. It was also clear that, for better or for worse, the days of independent command were at an end.[6]

Meanwhile, on the upper reaches of the Broad and the Saluda Thomas Sumter was again in the field, now commissioned by Governor Rutledge as commander of militia in South Carolina. By early November he was scouring the country from Fishing Creek southeast of King's Mountain to the upper Saluda, scattering bands of Tories and gathering recruits. Major Wemyss, commander of the 63rd Regiment, who had been terrorizing the Santee country (and vainly pursuing the Swamp Fox) got Cornwallis' permission to go after Sumter.

With the 63rd and forty dragoons, numbering 250 men, Wemyss surprised Sumter at Fishdam Ford on the Broad River on November 9. Although he was outnumbered, Wemyss made a night attack that might have badly damaged Sumter. But the British commander himself was cut down as the redcoats stormed the partisan camp. The Americans recovered, but they were also leaderless. Wemyss had sent a small party to find Sumter's headquarters and kill him. Sumter barely escaped and was forced to flee into the night. The battle raged in the confusion of darkness, and when dawn came the field was deserted except for the killed and wounded. The Americans had dispersed into the forest, and the British had retreated. Sumter and a handful of his men returned to the battlefield at midday, recovered their wounded, and paroled the enemy wounded. In the pocket of the wounded commander of the 63rd Sumter found a list of the men Wemyss had hanged. Sumter burned the list and kept its contents from his men.[7]

With Wemyss out of action, Cornwallis ordered Tarleton to try his hand against Sumter. With the Legion, the 63rd Regiment, a battalion of the 71st, and two guns, Tarleton took up Sumter's trail. Unable to catch up with the swiftly moving Americans, Tarleton divided his force and pressed forward with the Legion cavalry and part of the 63rd mounted as dragoons. At Blackstock's plantation on the Tyger River he found Sumter drawn up in a formidable defensive position. Two log buildings and a heavy rail fence covered his front. His flanks were protected by heavy woods and the river.

Tarleton halted to wait for his infantry to come up, but Sumter refused to postpone the action. His force of about 400 men was slightly superior to the British advance party, and he did not wait for the odds to change. He ordered an attack on the dismounted infantry of the 63rd while a flanking party was directed against the Legion dragoons. The 63rd counterattacked and, as Sumter had hoped, pressed forward until it came under fire from the main American line. Tarleton was then forced to extricate the infantry by attacking with his dragoons. The attack was beaten off, and the British were driven back until they reached the support of the infantry and its guns.

Tarleton claimed a victory because the Americans, faced with a superior force, withdrew, allowing the British to "claim the field." Sumter was badly wounded and put out of action for several weeks. But Tarleton's losses were serious, more than ninety killed and seventy-five wounded. The 63rd Regiment, which had suffered so severely in previous months from sickness as well as casualties, lost one-half its men. The Americans reported three killed and three wounded.[8]

Although he could not take the field, Sumter was determined to continue his command. He was now aware that as head of all of South Carolina's militia forces his responsibilities included more than calling up militia volunteers who could live off the countryside and harass small enemy detachments. His colonels were required to report all their movements, and he began to collect supplies at Hill's Iron Works. His patrols watched every move of the enemy, and he even sent a spy to Charleston to report on the arrival of General Leslie and his reinforcements from New York.

It was therefore with some chagrin that Sumter discovered that he was, in a sense, being superseded. General Greene had sent Daniel Morgan west in command of a corps of light infantry with "entire command in that quarter, and [I] do hereby require all officers and soldiers engaged in the American cause to be subject to your orders and command." It must have been a bitter pill for Sumter, veteran of a dozen battles and six months of hard fighting against the British. But Morgan was a brigadier general of the Continental Line. Moreover, General Greene had an altogether different view of Sumter's way of fighting.[9]

✳ "New Lords New Laws" ✳

Perhaps Congress had finally learned its lesson. It had appointed Robert Howe to the southern command in 1777, and Howe had lost Savannah and Georgia. Benjamin Lincoln had been the next to go, and he had lost his army and Charleston. Congress' latest choice had been Horatio Gates, who had also lost an army and most of the Carolinas. Not even the victory at King's Mountain could retrieve Gates' reputation, for he had contributed nothing to the victory, nor did he attempt to claim credit for it. So in the fall of 1780 Congress did what it probably should have done in the first place—and asked Washington to name a southern general.[10]

The commander in chief did not hesitate in his choice. Nathanael Greene had already emerged as Washington's ablest lieutenant. Greene was a Rhode Islander, the son of Quaker parents, but he was disavowed by the Friends' Meeting when he raised a company of militia in 1774. His men elected another captain, for they were not impressed by Greene, perhaps because a stiff knee caused by a childhood accident gave him an unsoldierly appearance. So the unassuming Quaker served as a private in the ranks. Six months later, when the state raised three regiments to send to Boston, it named the gimpy private a brigadier general. A month later Congress confirmed him in rank in the Continental Line. Before the year

was out he had become Washington's most reliable commander. He fought
in every major engagement from White Plains to Monmouth Court House,
and at the time of his appointment to the Southern Department he had just
completed a tour of duty as the army's quartermaster general. The settlement of his accounts had inevitably brought him in conflict with the
pettifogging bureaucrats in Congress, who made a career of denouncing
high-ranking officers, especially those who were not sufficiently impressed
with the dignity of that august body.[11]

Greene had just settled down to the relative serenity of the command of
West Point when he was summoned to his new duties. His progress south
was slow but deliberate. Washington professed to be unable to furnish him
any reinforcements although 6,000 French troops had arrived in July 1780
and Washington had not fought a major battle in two years. So Greene
from the outset had to drum up his own men and supplies. He visited
Philadelphia and lobbied for clothing, money, and additional troops. In
Maryland he pleaded with state officials and merchants for help for the
state's Continentals. In Virginia Governor Thomas Jefferson heard his
appeals for horses, wagons, and men. Everywhere he was welcomed
effusively, and everywhere the story was the same. Money was either
exhausted or consisted of worthless paper. Men and supplies must be
retained to protect the states from invasion. All of which led General
Greene to remark caustically, "It is much easier to oppose the Enemy in
those States while the tide of Sentiment is in our favour, than it will be to
secure *Virginia* after they are over run."[12]

The new commander reached Charlotte on December 2. He was taking
command of an area that was totally strange to him, for Greene had never
been south of Pennsylvania. His appetite for information became insatia-
ble, and even before he reached Charlotte he was starting to gather it.
General Edward Stevens, a Virginia militia officer, and Colonel Edward
Carrington were sent off to explore the Carolina river system. To Stevens
he wrote:

> Lieutenant-Colonel Carrington is exploring the Dan River, in order
> to perform transportation up the Roanoke ... and I want you to
> appoint a good & intelligent officer with 3 privates to go up the
> Yadkin ... to explore carefully the River, the Depth of the Water, the
> Current, & the Rocks, & every other Obstruction that will impede
> the Business of Transportation. ... When the Officer gets up to
> Hughes Creek, I wish him to take a Horse & ride across the Country
> ... to the upper Saura Town, and report the Distance & Condition of
> the Roads. At the upper Saura I expect the officer will meet the Party
> exploring the Dan River. I wish him to get the Report of that
> party ... [and] to make inquiry respecting Transportation that may
> be had from the Yadkin to the Catawba River. ... [13]

Greene relieved Gates on December 2. The ceremony was brief. Greene brushed aside that part of Washington's orders that had directed a court of inquiry for the retiring commander on the ground that there were not enough senior officers available. He spent most of the first night in conversation with Colonel Thomas Polk, who had been Gates' commissary officer. When Greene finally allowed the elderly colonel to stagger off to bed, the latter was convinced that Greene "better understood [the supply problem] than Gates had done in the whole period of his command."

The next day an order went out to detachment commanders requesting troop returns, including "Time of Service, how posted and where employed . . . and as Militia is fluctuating, a weekly Report will be necessary, specifying the Number, Condition, and Time of Service of the Troops under your Command." A request was sent to the state quartermaster "for every kind of Smith and Carpenter's Tools. . . . Files & Crosscut Saws are very much wanted; and if you could forward us a Quantity of both, it would relieve us from great Distress."[14]

Young Colonel Carrington was named quartermaster general for the Southern Department and Greene scarcely gave him time to catch his breath after completing the river surveys. ". . . I have sent a Letter of Credit on Mr. Hunter, that you may draw upon him, and I wish to have forwarded from his Manufactory 500 felling Axes, 5000 pairs of Horse Shoes, . . . half a Ton of Boat Nails for constructing Batteaus. . . . It will be well for you to consult with a good Shipwright, the Tools that will be necessary for Building about 100 large Batteaus. . . ." The pilfering of supplies en route to the army must cease forthwith. "Forward all stores coming from Philadelphia, and allow none of them to be stopped in Virginia, unless it is for corps that are to march immediately to the Southward. . . ." Once this was done, "The Six Tons of Iron I mentioned to you at Hillsborough you will order on without loss of Time."[15]

Colonel Polk confessed that his advanced years and health were not up to the demands of his office as commissary general. Greene at once selected young Major Davie, the fiery cavalry commander. When Davie demurred, Greene must have thought of his own remark when Washington had asked him to give up his troop command: "Nobody ever heard of a quarter master, in history." Davie insisted that he knew nothing of bookkeeping or accounting, but Greene dryly pointed out that this was unlikely to be a problem because there was no money to account for. It was much more important that "you are a single man, and have health, education, and activity to manage the business. . . ." Although Greene realized that he was losing a splendid troop commander, Davie's reputation would give him "an extensive influence among the inhabitants" and at the same time would make him "much respected in the army."[16]

To Marion, Sumter, and Pickens he wrote urging that they continue to harass the enemy but also "to fix Plans for procuring . . . Information and conveying it to me with all possible Dispatch. The Spy should be taught to be particular in his Enquiries, and to get the Names of the Corps, Strength, and Commanding Officers' name, Place whence they came and where they are going." The new commander missed no details, and he expected his subordinates to be equally particular.[17]

The army that Greene commanded was a ragtag body. The returns showed 2,300 men of whom somewhat less than 1,500 were present and fit for duty. There were 950 Continentals. The biggest problems were uniforms and equipment, for the "whole force fit for duty that [were] properly equipt" came to fewer than 800 men. In addition to the army's physical state, morale and discipline had suffered. "The Officers have got such a habit of negligence, and soldiers so loose and disorderly that it is next to impossible to give it a military complexion." The problem with the officers was a delicate one and Greene solved it by tact and indirection. He invited the officers to his tent for meals where the food was spartan but the conversation easy and informal. Greene was well-read and intelligent, and he was a good listener. As the officers learned to know their commander, they soon came to trust him, and this was the essence of leadership. Few officers who worked for Greene found themselves with time on their hands.[18]

The matter of troop discipline was different. The men were soon given to understand that orders were to be obeyed, camps were to be policed, and uniforms and equipment, however shabby, were to be neat and clean. Greene announced that desertions must cease and that he was prepared to make an example of the first offender. In the second week of December a deserter was tried, convicted, and hanged, and the entire army was paraded to witness the execution. The men discovered that Greene meant business, and the word among the troops was, "It is new lords new laws."[19]

Greene decided that it would be impossible to remain very long at Charlotte. Having been occupied for some time by both armies, Mecklenburg and Rowan counties were nearly swept clean of food and forage. In his own words, Greene needed "a camp of repose," where he could pull his little army together, feed it, and train it. Thaddeus Kosciuszko, the faithful Polish engineer who had served so many American generals so well, was sent to locate a site that met Greene's requirements. It must support the army, but it must not appear to indicate a withdrawal because it was necessary to keep up the high spirits occasioned by the victory at King's Mountain. It should afford a line of retreat in the event that Cornwallis took the offensive. Kosciuszko decided on a location near Cheraw, and on the day after Christmas the army settled down at its new base. Although, as Greene remarked, "It is no Egypt," food and forage were more easily obtained, and he could take time to organize his command.[20]

✳ Hannah's Cowpens ✳

In making his move to the upper Pee Dee, Greene decided to pose a problem for his opponent. Cornwallis had based his army at Winnsboro, fifty-five miles east of Ninety Six and thirty miles west of Camden. As the British commander noted, "Wynns-borough is . . . well situated to protect the greatest part of the Northern Frontier, and to assist Camden and Ninety Six. . . . I determined to remain at this place until an Answer arrived from Genl. Leslie, on which my Plan for the winter was to depend."

When Greene moved to Cheraw, he left Morgan behind with 320 of the Maryland and Delaware Continentals, 100 dragoons of William Washington's cavalry, and 200 Virginia riflemen (many of the Virginia militia were veterans of the Continental regiments whose enlistments had expired and who were reenlisting as three-months men). Morgan expected that this force would be increased by militia, and he was not disappointed. Andrew Pickens, the dour Presbyterian elder, brought in 350 mounted South Carolinians. General William Davidson added 120 North Carolinians, and with this force Morgan moved south across the Broad to the Pacolet.[21] So Cornwallis, to his amazement, found that his weaker opponent had divided his army. But Greene knew precisely what he was doing.

> It makes the most of my inferior force, for it compels my adversary to divide his, and holds him in doubt as to his line of conduct. He cannot leave Morgan behind him to come at me, or his posts at Ninety- Six and Augusta would be exposed. And he cannot chase Morgan far, or prosecute his views upon Virginia while I can have the whole country open before me. I am as near to Charleston as he is, and as near Hillsborough as I was at Charlotte; so that I am in no danger of being cut off from my reinforcements.[22]

One immediate result of Greene's strategy was to cut General Leslie's reinforcement by 1,000 men. When Leslie disembarked at Charleston, he found orders from Cornwallis to leave a detachment with the city's garrison in case the rebels attacked.

Greene did not intend to remain entirely passive. Light Horse Harry Lee arrived from the North with 300 men of his Legion, half of them cavalry, and all well equipped and armed. Greene at once sent Lee down the Pee Dee to find Marion and harass the British supply line. They made a foray against Georgetown on December 28, but once more the fortified garrison withstood the assault, although the Americans captured the British commandant. Lee and Marion now turned up the Santee and attacked Fort Watson above Nelson's Ferry, but again they were foiled. By this time momentous events called Lee back to Greene's headquarters.[23]

In the west Morgan sent Colonel William Washington's dragoons and some militia to harass the Tories between Winnsboro and Ninety Six. The first opportunity came with a report that 250 Georgia Loyalists were raiding along Fair Forest Creek just north of Ninety Six. On December 30 they were overtaken by the Americans at Hammond's Store. Washington's attack was as ruthless as Tarleton's. One hundred and fifty Loyalists were killed or wounded and forty were taken prisoner. Washington had no casualties. The raiders swept on to attack a "fort" at Williamson's Plantation, but the defenders had fled to Ninety Six, only fifteen miles away.[24]

Washington's success and the addition of militia to his force emboldened Morgan to consider moving on Augusta. He envisioned his force as a relatively small, fast-moving corps—indeed, Greene had referred to Morgan's wing as light infantry. But except for the Continentals, Morgan's men lacked the training or discipline to qualify them as an elite corps. Nonetheless, under the driving force of the "Old Waggoner" they might have been capable of penetrating deep into the enemy country. But Morgan did not lose sight of Greene's overall strategy and the necessity of maintaining position on Cornwallis' front. So he made his proposal and awaited Greene's judgment.

Meanwhile, there was trouble with Thomas Sumter, still recovering from his battle wounds but contracting a severe case of wounded feelings. When Morgan sent to Sumter for men and supplies, the latter coldly informed Morgan's aide that the chain of command ran from Greene to Sumter to Morgan. Morgan curbed his temper and bucked the problem to headquarters. It was a touchy business, for if Sumter were recalcitrant the badly needed militia support might collapse. Moreover, Governor John Rutledge, still at American headquarters, had been unsuccessful in trying to persuade the "Gamecock" to serve under Morgan. There was some feeling that the South Carolina Achilles was sulking, so Greene tried to be tactful. But he did not conceal the firmness of his purpose: "Partisan strokes in war are like the garnish on the table; . . . but they afford no substantial national security. . . . The enemy will never relinquish their plan, nor the people be firm in our favour until they behold a better barrier in the field than a Volunteer Militia who are one day out and next at home."[25]

Questions of strategy were soon resolved, not at Cheraw but at Winnsboro. Cornwallis had word that Leslie was on his way up the Santee and so, with a reinforcement of 1,500 regulars near at hand, Cornwallis decided to counter Greene's gambit with a division of his own. Tarleton's Legion was reinforced with 200 men of the 7th Regiment, a battalion of the 71st Highlanders, 50 men of the 17th Light Dragoons, and two guns, giving him a total of 1,100 men. He was directed to swing to the west "to endeavor to strike a blow at General Morgan, & at all events to oblige him to repass the Broad." Cornwallis himself would push up the east side of the Broad, cutting between Morgan and Greene, thus assuring the destruction of the American right wing. The success of the plan depended on three assumptions: that Tarleton could defeat or drive Morgan; that Cornwallis could get between Morgan and Greene; and that Leslie and his reinforcements could come up in time to support Cornwallis if he were forced to deal with the combined American forces.[26]

Almost immediately the timing of the plan began to go awry. Heavy rains swelled the rivers and filled the swamps, bringing Leslie's advance almost to a standstill along the lower reaches of the Santee. Cornwallis, also hampered by the weather, paused to wait for Leslie to come up. Morgan, now aware that he must go from the offensive to the defensive in the face of Tarleton's threat, also found the going heavy as he recrossed the Pacolet toward North Carolina.[27]

Tarleton started after Morgan on January 6, 1781, but it was almost a week before he could get across the Enoree and the Tyger. By the 14th he was hurrying toward the Pacolet as the Americans retreated toward the Broad. Morgan hoped to make his crossing about twenty miles west of Charlotte and, if Tarleton was in close pursuit, take a strong defensive position at Thicketty Mountain. On January 16 he was pushing his men hard, with Washington screening his rear. By nightfall he was still six miles from the crossing of the Broad, and his scouts brought word that the river was swollen from recent rains. Washington reported that Tarleton was less than ten miles in his rear. Morgan decided to fight the British where he was.[28]

Much has been said about why Morgan chose this battleground. It was an area of open wood in a loop of the Broad River frequently used by herdsmen to graze their cattle. It was known in the neighborhood as Hannah's Cowpens. The ground rose in a long slope toward the river, dipped in a shallow swale, and then rose again to a low hill before it dropped off again. The reason Morgan fought there was simply that he had little choice. To gamble that he could escape was to risk being caught at the river crossing in a disorderly and confused battle that would certainly panic his militia. By halting where he was, he could feed his men, give them a night's rest, and make leisurely preparations for his battle. Morgan must have talked with officers and men who had fought the Legion. Its greatest successes had come when the enemy was surprised and disorganized. In such circumstances the sudden charge, the cut and thrust of the Legion dragoons, had overwhelmed the rebels. But Tarleton, tireless and utterly fearless, was no tactician. The Legion knew only one maneuver, the head-on, slam-bang assault. It had seldom been successful against troops who were battle-tested and well led. Hanging Rock, Wahab's Plantation, and Blackstocks had thrown the harsh light of reality on the myth of the Legion's invincibility. ". . . I knew my adversary," said Morgan, "and was perfectly sure I should have nothing but downright fighting."[29]

So as the men cooked their supper and prepared for the night, Morgan called his officers together, not to ask advice but to give instruction. To

Daniel Morgan (Independence National Historical Park Collection)

Andrew Pickens he gave command of the militia, who would be divided into two groups. As the British moved up the gradual slope of the Cowpens, they would first encounter a skirmish line of riflemen acting as sharpshooters. These would fall back to the main line of militia. This line was to hold its fire until the enemy was within fifty yards. The men were to deliver two fires and then file off to the left rear and act as a reserve. The main American line would be 150 yards to the rear of the militia at the crest of the slope. Here the Continentals and the Virginia militia commanded by John Eager Howard would form, and here Morgan intended to make his stand. William Washington's dragoons would be in the swale behind the Continentals to act as a reserve. Morgan would muster just under 1,000 men.

Morgan's preparations were not over. After the officers' conference Morgan went through the camp detailing his plans to the rank and file. The militia, he explained, *were expected to retreat.* Only give two fires, the big general exhorted, and "Ben" Tarleton was finished. Don't run away, Washington will protect your backs. To the Continentals he explained that the militia would be retreating—they were supposed to. Tarleton's line would have some holes in it when it got up that hill. All through the night Morgan stalked among the campfires, exhorting and cajoling—men rest before a battle, but they seldom sleep. They were the finest troops in the world, he told them, "and when you return to your homes how the old folks will bless you, and how the girls will kiss you for your gallant conduct." Thomas Young, one of Washington's dragoons, had never seen a general like this one. "I don't believe he slept a wink that night," he recalled.

Tarleton's men also camped, but they were astir at three o'clock. They still had five miles to go before they met the enemy. Tarleton was in a hurry for he assumed that Morgan would be trying to escape. The road was muddy, cut by deep ruts and small streams. Wagons had to be manhandled through mudholes, and the march was halting and confused. Finally, Tarleton left the wagons behind and pushed on with the men and the guns. By seven o'clock they had reached the Cowpens.

Tarleton noted that "an open wood was certainly as proper a place for action as [I] could desire; America does not produce many more suitable. . . ." He shook out his line with three companies of light infantry and the Legion infantry on the right. The 7th Regiment formed on the left. Fifty mounted dragoons were assigned to each flank, with the 71st in reserve behind the 7th. The Legion cavalry was also held in reserve. The troops were ordered to "disencumber themselves of every thing, except their arms and ammunition." Then Tarleton gave the order to go forward.

The eighteenth century was the age of picture-book wars, and Thomas Young remembered the long rank of green jackets and red coats that formed the advance. "It was the most beautiful line I ever saw." The British raised a shout, and Morgan, riding his lines and haranguing his men,

ordered, "Give them an Indian halloo, by G[od]!" Pickens and his officers
along with the militia line shouted to their men to hold their fire. The
British first met the fire of the skirmishers. Then as they came within range
of Pickens' line; "first . . . pop, pop, pop, and then a whole volley; but when
the [British] regulars fired, it seemed like one sheet of flame from right to
left. Oh! it was beautiful." After delivering their volleys, the militia moved
off, but their orderly withdrawal was interrupted by the flanking Legion
dragoons. They burst upon the retreating men, and James Collins, that
seventeen-year-old veteran of King's Mountain, "thought . . . 'my hide is in
the loft.'" But Washington's cavalry came thundering up "like a whirlwind," and the militia were safe.

The British advance now reached Howard's line of Continentals on the
crest of the slope and was stopped cold by the steady fire of the Maryland
and Delaware veterans. Tarleton now extended the 71st Regiment to
overlap the American right flank. Howard "attempted to change the front of
Wallace's company, . . . in doing it some confusion ensued. . . . The officers
along the line . . . supposing orders had been given for a retreat, faced their
men about and moved off." There was no disorder in the movement.
Kirkwood's Delaware troops beat off the flank attack as the American line
disappeared down the reverse slope of the hill. The British, however,
assumed that the line had been broken, and their own line lost formation as
they charged forward.

In the swale behind the hill Morgan appeared and "rode forward to fix
on the most proper place for us to halt and face about." As the British came
over the rise, they met the Continentals where Howard had "made a perfect
line. . . . Our men commenced a very destructive fire, which they little
expected, and a few rounds occasioned great disorder in their ranks. While
in this confusion I ordered a charge with the bayonet. . . ." Washington
simultaneously drove his cavalry against the British right flank. As
Thomas Young recalled, "At this moment the bugle sounded; we made a
half circuit at full speed and came upon the rear of the British line,
shouting and charging like madmen. . . . The British line broke—" On the
far side of the field the militia under Pickens, "being relieved from the
pursuit of the enemy, began to rally and prepare to redeem our credit, when
Morgan rode up in front and, waving his sword, cried out, 'Form my brave
fellows. . . . Old Morgan was never beaten.' We then advanced and gained
the flank of the enemy. . . ."

The steady Continentals and the swarming militia had performed a
classic battle maneuver, a double envelopment. With both flanks caved in
and their center assailed by Howard's bayonets, Tarleton's Legion and the
regulars collapsed; "many of them laid down their arms and surrendered,
while the rest took to the wagon road and did their prettiest kind of running
away."

In an effort to stem the panic, Tarleton galloped back to bring up the

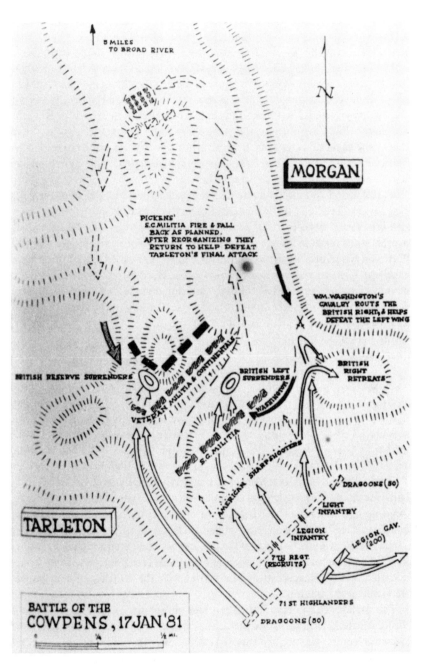

BATTLE OF THE
COWPENS, 17 JAN '81

*(Reprinted with permission from
The Encyclopedia of the American Revolution,
by Mark Mayo Boatner III. Copyright 1966.
Published by David McKay Co., Inc.)*

Legion dragoons that had remained in reserve. To his chagrin, the Legion refused to attack. "Above two hundred dragoons forsook their leader, and left the field of battle." By this time the British had also lost their guns. Tarleton rounded up about sixty officers and men and recklessly charged his pursuers. Washington's cavalry broke them, and the two commanders almost engaged in hand-to-hand combat before the Englishman broke off the battle and fled. The final irony came when Tarleton reached his wagons and found his Tory followers looting them. The enraged dragoons drove them off and set the wagons afire before they resumed their flight.[30]

The battle destroyed Tarleton's Legion and wrecked two of Cornwallis' regiments, the 7th and the first batallion of the 71st. The British lost more than 100 killed and 200 wounded with 525 taken prisoner. The Americans had about 75 killed and wounded.[31]

The British disaster can be traced to several causes. Tarleton's tactics were not seriously at fault, although he failed to control his men at critical points in his battle. Tarleton himself put his finger on an important point: "the loose manner of forming which had always been practiced by the King's troops in America." He is referring here to the open formation recently adopted for light infantry and thought to be particularly suited to the American war.

> The extreme attention of the files always exposed the British regiments and corps, and would before this unfortunate affair, have been attended with detrimental effect, had not the multiplicity of lines with which they generally fought rescued them from imminent danger. If infantry who are formed very open, and only two deep, meet with opposition, they can have no stability . . . when they experience an unexpected shock, confusion will ensue, and flight, without immediate support, must be the inevitable consequence.

Colonel Howard reported another British view, rendered by Major Archibald McArthur, the grizzled commander of the 71st Highlanders, who "said that he was an officer before Tarleton was born, [and] that the best troops in the service had been put under '*that boy*' to be sacrificed. . . ."[32]

The battle was, as much as anything, the personal achievement of Daniel Morgan. His tactics aside, Morgan had instilled in the militia a confidence and elan that they had never felt before. He was the "Old Waggoner," larger than life, his giant frame prowling the campfires, his brawling voice praising their courage and hurling threats at "Benny" Tarleton. No one but Morgan could have made such a performance believable—not John Howard the Baltimore aristocrat, nor the scion of the famous Virginia Washingtons.

But such emotional binges were no substitute for discipline over the long haul. It was the tough veterans of Maryland and Delaware that took the shock of the British attack and blew it back with their disciplined fire. And when Morgan set his army in motion again to slog through the mud and rain to join Greene, much of the militia's enthusiasm ebbed, and its ranks began to melt away.

Through most of 1780 the American cause in the Carolinas had been largely sustained by the partisan forces. From the advent of Robert Howe in 1777 to the disintegration of Gates' army at Camden, the Continental forces had done little except provide a symbolic force around which Patriots could rally—and the failures had resulted in deep discouragement among the Whigs.

The successes had been scored, instead, in the numerous small but damaging fights waged by the Whig militia. These had hamstrung the British effort to control the Carolina backcountry and inflicted a corrosive attrition on Cornwallis' forces. King's Mountain was not only a sort of climax to the partisan effort, lifting Patriot spirits, but it bit deeply into the British effort to organize a counter revolution. Although Cornwallis still hoped that the King's friends could defray some of his manpower shortage, he could no longer entertain much hope that they could occupy the countryside and "overawe the disaffected," leaving him free to resume his offensive northward. In fact, it was this realization that forced upon him the "domino strategy" that was beginning to pervade his thinking—that is, that the conquest of South Carolina depended on a successful invasion of North Carolina and, at last, that both Carolinas would fall if Virginia were conquered.

The danger for the Americans was that they would fall into the same strategic trap that had ensnared Germain and the ministry and place too much reliance on "the armed yeomanry of America." To a Maryland writer, "a respectable and well-regulated militia is the safest palladium of the liberties of the state. . . . Deprived of their property, banished from their domestic engagements, and fired with the remembrance of repeated injuries, aggravated by repeated insult, a noble spirit of revenge conspired with love of country to impel them to the field."[33] It was the beginning of the myth of the Invincible Patriot Volunteer, a myth that was to be the despair of military leaders from George Washington to George Marshall.

Nathanael Greene knew better. "It requires more than double the number of militia to be kept in the field, attended with infinitely more waste and expense than would be necessary to give full security to the country with a regular and permanent army." He did not wholly discount the value of the short-term troops, and he was well aware that they often constituted the only forces available to supplement the Continental Line.

It affords me great satisfaction to see the enterprise and spirit with which the militia have turned out lately in all quarters, and this great bulwark of civil liberty promises security and independence if they are not depended upon as a principal, but employed only as an auxiliary; but if you depend upon them as a principal, the very nature of the war must become so ruinous to the country, that though numbers for a time may give security, yet the difficulty of keeping this order of men in the field, and the accumulated expenses attending it, must soon put it out of your power to make further opposition, and the enemy will have only to delay their operations a few months to give success to their measures. It must be extreme folly to hazard our liberty upon such a precarious tenure when we have it so much in our power to fix them upon a more solid basis.[34]

9. Doubt, Discord, and Despair

Sir Henry Clinton in New York found himself "at the close of the year 1780, without my having received the smallest reinforcement to the army under my immediate command . . . or any definite promise upon which I could venture to form an operative plan for the ensuing campaign. . . ."

Lord George Germain still spoke optimistically. "Indeed, so very contemptible is the Rebel Force now in all Parts, and so vast is Our Superiority every where, that no resistance on their Part . . . can materially obstruct . . . the Speedy Suppression of the Rebellion. . . ." But Lord George's words had a hollow ring. Harried by a timid and indecisive ministry, the growing Opposition in Parliament, and an enemy that gnawed at the flanks of Britain's vast empire, the American Secretary found that his conduct of the war was inextricably interwoven with his struggle for political survival.

At American headquarters on the Hudson, George Washington wrote to a friend, "It is . . . certain that our Troops are approaching fast to nakedness . . . That our Hospitals are without medicines, . . . That all our public works are at a stand . . . but why need I run into the detail, when it may be declared in a word, that we are at the end of our tether."[1]

So although the battle of the Cowpens had not altered either British or American strategy in the Carolinas, in a wider context the events of the past year had changed the character of the war and blurred strategic objectives. And after six years the weight of war was imposing a severe strain on the nerve and judgment of those who planned and fought it.

✳ New York ✳

Before Sir Henry Clinton set sail from Charleston in June 1780 to return to New York, he characteristically settled an old score. Undoubtedly his quarrel with old Admiral Arbuthnot had recalled his bouts with Sir Peter Parker in these same waters four years before. Parker had enraged Clinton by refusing to bombard Fort Moultrie at close range, contending that the waters of the channel were too shallow for his capital ships. Now, in 1780, Sir Henry commandeered a ship's boat and had himself rowed to the waters off the fort. He took soundings and found that the depth was ample for the passage of ships of the line. The spectacle of a lieutenant general taking soundings from a small boat must have evoked colorful comments from the seamen who toiled at the oars, but they are not recorded. Sir Henry, however, noted with satisfaction, "What say you now, S. P. Parker?"[2]

Back in New York Clinton found himself confronted with two problems. The first was the obvious danger from the French. This might take the form of a thrust by the French navy at Charleston or New York. There was also good reason to believe that France was at last about to send troops to the support of Washington's army.

The second claim on his attention was the Chesapeake, an objective that was the subject of discussion by almost everyone: the King, Clinton himself, and especially Lord George Germain. Virtually every dispatch from the American Secretary referred to some scheme involving a lodgment on the great bay. Such a project had much to commend it. The Chesapeake had an ample anchorage at Hampton Roads from which naval forces could operate, and it was centrally located to support Charleston and the West Indies as well as to interdict any reinforcement that Washington might send to the Carolinas. The Chesapeake was also the gateway to Virginia, largest and richest of the colonies. Virginia had been, along with Massachusetts, the center of the rebellion, but it was also thought that there were large numbers of Loyalists among its people. Given a permanent British post as a rallying point, the conquest of the Old Dominion might be a feasible project that would not require a prohibitive number of regular troops. The bay and the great rivers that emptied into it would provide easy access to the interior so that logistical support would not be the problem that had hamstrung the British in the Carolinas.[3]

The French threat claimed Clinton's immediate attention when he returned to New York, for he had definite word early in July that a fleet under the Chevalier de Ternay had left Brest carrying 6,000 French troops to America. It was logical to assume that de Ternay's destination was Rhode Island. Two possibilities offered. One was to intercept the French admiral at sea, where he would be hampered by his transports. Admiral Arbuthnot at once rejected this proposal because he was not sure that his force was sufficiently superior to the French. The second possibility was to attack during or immediately after the French made their landing and before they had time to fortify their position. A naval reinforcement under Admiral Samuel Graves was on its way from England, so there was a good chance that the British would have decided superiority.[4]

Perhaps emboldened by his success at Charleston, Clinton readied 6,000 men, and within days after his return he notified Arbuthnot that he was prepared for a joint operation. The admiral replied that he was convinced that the French were bound for the Chesapeake (relations between the two had deteriorated to the point where they did not confer personally but communicated by notes carried by aides). Clinton was wild with impatience. Graves had indeed arrived with reinforcements, thereby establishing naval superiority. The idea that the French would land troops in Virginia when Washington's army was on the Hudson appeared ridiculous. Clearly, the French must be attacked the moment they landed at Newport if the British were to use their opportunity to the fullest. But Arbuthnot would not budge.

The full measure of the old admiral's dereliction was revealed by the fact that his reconnaissance was so laggard that he could not find the French. At last, army scouts from the eastern end of Long Island reported that de Ternay had put in at Newport and had been there for more than a week. The opportunity for surprise was lost. Clinton now proposed an alternative. If the French had not yet fortified, troops could be landed east of Newport and the enemy could be attacked from the rear or landward side of their position. If the French were well along in the construction of their works, the British fleet and transports could sail through Narragansett passage and land a force north of Newport. Clinton, who had led the expedition against Rhode Island in 1776, knew the area like the palm of his hand.

He was convinced that a crushing defeat of the French would not only be a signal victory but would deal a devastating blow to the Franco-American alliance. This was the first contingent of troops committed to the American cause since the conclusion of the treaty of 1778. If it could be defeated or destroyed, the French government, its finances already strained to the limit, would be extremely reluctant to send additional reinforcements and might even sue for peace. Sir Henry appears to be eminently correct in regarding this as a "very critical and important moment in the war."[5]

On July 19, Arbuthnot and Graves sailed for Rhode Island. Arbuthnot assured Clinton that "if it is possible to put your plan into execution, you shall hear from me immediately." Clinton at once prepared to embark his regiments—and found that the fresh water in the transports had been used to replenish Arbuthnot's ships. It was not until the 28th that he brought his troops into Long Island Sound to wait for word from the admiral. He also sent his own reconnaissance officer to get information on the French dispositions.[6]

As Admiral de Ternay and General Rochambeau, the French army commander, waited fearfully for the blow they were sure would destroy them, Arbuthnot sent word that the enemy had been reinforced by American militia and was too strong to be attacked. "I never was here before, and am totally ignorant of the situation of this place," he complained, although he confessed, "It is sixteen days since I have been about this place." One is constrained to wonder what he had been doing for sixteen days. The final

absurdity was that the captain of the frigate carrying Clinton's own reconnoitering party refused to put it ashore. He had orders, he said, not to risk
his ship. Clinton reluctantly brought his transports back to New York.[7]

(During this sortie, Clinton became convinced that someone had attempted to poison him. He and two of his aides became violently ill, and
Sir Henry hid a suspect bottle of wine under his pillow for several days. He
afterward said that his physician found that the wine contained arsenic,
although it is extremely unlikely that the chemical analysis could have
been performed by an army doctor.)[8]

On August 10 Arbuthnot, still patrolling off Rhode Island, proposed a
conference. Clinton eagerly gathered an escort and rode the length of
Long Island, 120 miles, to Gardiner's Bay. To his surprise and chagrin,
when he arrived the sea was empty. Arbuthnot had literally left him high
and dry. Not even a dispatch boat remained to give word that the admiral
had sailed that very morning to pursue a rumor that de Ternay was about to
sortie. Clinton's fury was evident in his barely courteous dispatch: "I . . . at
least expected to learn the cause which had induced you to leave me in
disappointment at the extremity of this island. . . ." As for the attack on
Newport, Arbuthnot gave it as his opinion that there was never "any
prospect of it unless Sir Henry Clinton had an army of eighteen or twenty
thousand men to form a regular siege."[9]

Relations between the two commanders were now in a shambles. Both
sent recriminating letters to London, Arbuthnot complaining of "Sir
Henry Clinton's amusing me . . . with his troops in transports and aide-de-
camps dancing backwards and forwards with reports . . . till time slipped
from under my feet and obliged me at last to retire. . . ." Clinton was more
forthright. He wrote home that unless there was a new naval commander
he would resign.[10]

The British were given one more chance. On September 14 Admiral Sir
George Rodney, commander of the West Indian fleet, surprised both the
French and the British by appearing in New York with ten sail of the line.
Rodney was the very antithesis of Arbuthnot, energetic and daring. Although he was abrasive and quarrelsome, he and Clinton got along well
together. Moreover, he was senior to Arbuthnot and gave every evidence of
being willing to assert his authority if an attack was in prospect. The
British, with eighteen capital ships, now outnumbered de Ternay by more
than two to one. The French at Newport were sure they were doomed. But
Clinton had lost either his enthusiasm or his nerve. He told Rodney that he
could now furnish only 3,000 men and, curiously enough, used Arbuthnot's own reports and arguments to convince Rodney that Rhode
Island could no longer be attacked.[11]

The missed opportunity seems incredible, especially with Rodney's
aggressive presence to bolster Sir Henry's confidence. A partial explana-

tion was that Clinton was about to try to capitalize on the treason of Benedict Arnold and seize West Point, although the plans had not progressed so far that they could not have been postponed. Also Clinton was about to send General Alexander Leslie's expedition to the Chesapeake, and Rodney's return to the West Indies would assure their safe passage. But his failure to seize the Rhode Island prize was disastrous. Even as the opportunity faded, Louis XVI was considering a negotiated peace, and only the most powerful arguments by Vergennes finally dissuaded him.[12]

Clinton's concern with the Chesapeake reflected Germain's insistence on its strategic importance. In May 1779, Clinton's probe toward Virginia had been tentative and halfhearted. In the fall of 1780 Clinton dispatched 2,500 troops under General Alexander Leslie with orders to "make a diversion in favor of Lieutenant General Earl Cornwallis. . . . I should judge it best to proceed up the James River . . . in order to seize or destroy any magazines the enemy may have . . . and finally to establish a post on Elizabeth River." Clinton explained to Cornwallis that he hoped the expedition would "call forth our friends and support them" and that Leslie would be able to prevent American supplies and reinforcements from moving southward from Virginia to Greene. But he warned Leslie that he was to be guided by circumstances and reminded him that when he landed his force in Virginia he would pass from Clinton's command to that of Cornwallis. He was also cautioned against enrolling Loyalists or organizing their militia "without you determine to Establish a [permanent] Post."[13]

It should be remembered that when he issued these instructions Clinton's last word from Cornwallis was that the earl was about to move into North Carolina by way of Charlotte and Salisbury. Clinton had heard of rumors of the battle of King's Mountain but believed that Ferguson had encountered "a little Cheque." He did not learn of the full extent of the defeat until the second week in November.[14]

How Leslie's troops wound up as part of Cornwallis' army is a lesson in the way a resourceful commander can "steal" from another even when the latter is his superior officer. Leslie had landed at Hampton Roads on October 20. He had established his post at Portsmouth but found that the Virginians had known in advance of his coming and had fortified the James River below Richmond. The people of the coast seemed either frightened or indifferent although a few Loyalists turned out ready to fight (to Leslie's discomfiture because he did not wish to encourage them). Within days after his arrival he was bombarded with conflicting orders. Clinton's additional instructions suggested a move to the Cape Fear River at Wilmington. A dispatch from Cornwallis informed him of the setback to his plans for moving into North Carolina. An almost hysterical note from Colonel Balfour, commanding at Charleston, urged that "the Safety of this Province *now*, is concerned in your getting as fast as possible near us. . . .

Gates is advancing as we are told towards this Province & already near it."
Leslie conferred with his officers, and "we all agree to go to Cape Fear as
soon as possible, very sorry it is necessary. . . ."

Leslie tried to keep his withdrawal a secret until the last moment, but
one of his vessels went aground and a gale held the fleet in Hampton
Roads. Finally, on November 18 his command was under way. It was
obviously an embarrassing leave-taking. Leslie admitted that his men had
plundered so outrageously that he had left 100 guineas to be distributed "to
the poorer Sort who had lossed *their all.*" Although he had been careful not
to encourage the Loyalists to take up arms, obviously some of them did, and
"many blame me for it." English pride was mollified in some small degree
for "not a Shot has been fired, so that they can't say we are drove from their
Shore." And he noted sourly, "I am sorry to observe the Women don't Smile
upon us—"[15]

Meanwhile, Cornwallis had notified Leslie that as soon as he heard of
the latter's arrival at the Cape Fear River he intended "to join you at Cross
Creek [now Fayetteville]. We will then give our Friends in N. Carolina a
fair Trial. If they behave like Men it may be the greatest Advantage to the
Affairs of Great Britain. If they are as dastardly & pusillanimous as our
Friends to the Southward we must leave them to their fate. . . ."

There is a curious afterthought to this dispatch. "If," said his lordship,
"you find it difficult from contrary Winds to get into Cape Fear [River] . . .
it will be very little out of your way to look into Charles Town." Charleston
was nearly 200 miles from Cape Fear, and it is extraordinary that Cornwallis should be so vague about Leslie's movement if he did indeed expect
to move to Cross Creek, ninety miles up the Cape Fear River.

The cat was out of the bag in Cornwallis' next dispatch. By the first of
December he had sent ships to Cape Fear to bring Leslie directly to
Charleston. It seems clear that Cornwallis had made up his mind to add
Leslie's command to his own in order to resume his offensive. After King's
Mountain he had retired to Winnsboro and had spoken to Clinton of "the
little prospect that the Expedition on its original plan should compass any
service adequate to its force, & to your Excellency's expectations." (Cornwallis had been seriously ill in October and this may well have sapped his
will as well as his energy.)[16] But he must have realized that unless he could
carry the war to the enemy he would find his reputation tarnished by
passive and timid conduct such as had stigmatized Howe and Clinton.

Perhaps Captain Alexander Ross, who had taken the news of Camden to
London, sent him word of Germain's enthusiasm for the offensive. Certainly he knew it when Germain wrote him early in November, "I impa-
tiently expect to hear of your further Progress, and that Sir Henry Clinton
and Vice Admiral Arbuthnot have found Means of sending a Force into the
Chesapeak, to cooperate with you: for if that be done, I have not the least

doubt, from Your Lordship's vigorous and alert Movements, the whole Country South of the Delaware will be restored to the King's Obedience in the Course of the Campaign."[17]

Leslie's junction with Cornwallis in January, then, was undoubtedly what Cornwallis intended all along. And it was not without significance that part of Leslie's command was detached to strengthen the garrison at Charleston and another force was sent to secure a base at Wilmington. Cornwallis thereby took additional precautions for the safety of Charleston and prepared the way for a movement to Wilmington where he could be reinforced by sea on his way to Virginia. As for Clinton, he resigned himself to the loss of Leslie's command; the troops "will be gone out of my reach and will be more than he can want."

But Clinton did not abandon the Chesapeake project, well aware that this was consistent with Germain's thinking. The American Secretary seldom missed the opportunity to press the point. When he learned that Leslie's expedition had been aborted he wrote, ". . . I am commanded to acquaint you that it is the King's pleasure you do carry it into execution whenever the King's service will admit of it. My Opinion of the Importance of the Measure . . . makes me repeatedly press its Execution. . . ."[18]

By the middle of December Clinton had another force ready, this one of 2,000 men commanded by Benedict Arnold, now a brigadier general in the British army. There was to be no question of the destination and purpose of this expedition: ". . . You are as soon as possible to establish a post at Portsmouth . . . make known your intention of remaining there . . . and assemble and arm such of those people [of Princess Ann and Norfolk counties] as you shall have reason to believe are well-affected. . . ." Arnold was to cooperate with Cornwallis only if he "should positively direct. . . ." It thus became clear that although Clinton conceded the importance of a base in Virginia he did not regard it as a point of departure for a sweeping campaign of conquest.[19]

Arnold landed on December 30 and made a lightning but devastating raid on Richmond. He then retired to establish the post at Portsmouth. He became increasingly concerned with the difficulty of locating a base that would protect him from attack from both land and sea. The complex geography of the lower Chesapeake, where the James, the Nansemond, and the Elizabeth rivers empty into Hampton Roads, posed problems for effective defensive works that would have baffled even the great Vauban. Arnold confessed that he saw no satisfactory solution. Before another year had passed Cornwallis would be faced with the same problem.[20]

✳ London ✳

For a brief time in the summer of 1780 Sir Henry Clinton was England's hero. The news of the fall of Charleston and the conquest of South Carolina reached London at a most fortuitous moment for the American Secretary and the ministry. Earlier in the summer, twenty-five English counties had passed resolutions denouncing the corruption of Parliament and the dictatorial power of the King. In June the Gordon riots broke out in London, and for three days the city was in chaos. Diplomatic relations with Holland were reaching a crisis, and Catherine the Great was organizing the League of Armed Neutrality. In this atmosphere of anxiety and gloom, with the Opposition more strident than ever in its denunciation of the war, the good news from America was a godsend to the government. Lord Elphinstone swore that the "Administration owe in great degree their present existence to you [Clinton]," but he was wise enough to warn him, ". . . So long as you continue to be victorious, so long will they be grateful—and no longer."[21]

Both Clinton and Arbuthnot had sent personal emissaries to London, ostensibly to convey the news of victory but actually to make sure their interests were protected. "If the navy talk nonsense about their exploits here," Clinton instructed, "tell the truth. If they are silent, be so too. . . ." Clinton used the opportunity to press his demands: that Arbuthnot be replaced; that reinforcements be sent; and that transports and supply ships be placed under the control of the army. He accompanied these with his oft-repeated assertion that if the ministry could not demonstrate its confidence in him by meeting his requests he stood ready to resign.[22]

Lord Cornwallis had begun making reports directly to Germain soon after the victory at Camden. Although this violated the chain of command, Clinton later said that he was aware of it and sanctioned it, but he must have realized that Cornwallis would use this conduit to promote his own exploits to Germain. His first dispatch to the American Secretary was a report of his victory over Gates, and it was sent to London by Cornwallis' aide, Captain Ross. This second major victory of British arms in the South presented the ministry with an attractive alternative both of command and of strategy. There were those who thought that the war might be won in the Carolinas rather than in New York. And certainly Clinton's threats to resign could be taken lightly with a man of Cornwallis' rank and achievements available as a replacement.[23]

All these factors, then, hamstrung Clinton's efforts to coerce the ministry. Germain was not yet ready to take the drastic step of asking Clinton to resign, but he was perfectly willing to accept a resignation if the initiative came from Sir Henry.

All during the late summer and fall, the cabinet considered the situation in America. It finally came up with answers that were becoming increasingly characteristic of the North administration. By mid-October it had decided to relieve Arbuthnot, but no replacement was designated, although Clinton had suggested six admirals with whom he would be pleased to work. The cabinet also decided that Clinton should receive "such reinforcements as can be spared." His other requests were ignored, and he was plainly told that if he wished to resign the King would not refuse him.[24]

Germain meanwhile had admonished Clinton privately "either to remain in a good humor, in full confidence to be supported as much as the nature of the service will admit of, or to avail himself of the leave of coming home, as no good can arise to the service if there is not a full confidence between the General and the Ministers."[25] One cannot help feeling sympathy for Clinton. He was being asked to have confidence in a ministry that had promised him an unknown number of troops to be sent at some unspecified time in the future. Arbuthnot had been relieved, but no successor was named. In fact, the old admiral did not go home until July, 1781—more than nine months after the decision was taken to replace him!

What was happening was that under the pressure of events, a cabinet composed of mediocrities had become fearful of making decisions; or, if a decision was made, it was subsequently revised and amended in the face of threats and uncertainties until its purpose was vitiated. For example, the decision was taken in March 1780 to send Admiral Graves with eight ships of the line to intercept the French squadron which was sailing from Brest (and whose arrival at Newport caused the fiasco between Clinton and Arbuthnot). Having made its decision, the cabinet then engaged in a long and time-consuming argument about where de Ternay was bound. Next, fears that Rodney in the West Indies was not strong enough led to the detachment of two of Graves' ships. Finally, Graves was ordered to delay his departure in order to escort Commodore Walsingham's West Indian convoy clear of possible interference from the enemy. Altogether it was more than ten weeks from the time the decision was made to send Graves to America and his actual departure in the middle of May. By that time de Ternay had been at sea for two weeks.[26]

Thus instead of boldness there was timidity. Instead of grasping at opportunities for victory the cabinet sought to avoid failure, lest the Opposition seize upon it and drive the members from office. Even Germain, who had once been the driving force behind the war in America, seemed to have lost his nerve. He was full of strategic suggestions for Clinton, but he would not arbitrarily order them. Ever since Burgoyne had claimed (without justification) that he had been committed by his orders to march to Albany in 1777, Lord George had avoided binding a commander in the field. Clinton had bitterly protested, "For God's sake, My Lord, if you wish me to do anything, leave me to myself. . . . If not, tie me down to a certain point, and take the risk of my want of success." But Germain was too wary to be caught in that trap.[27]

Part of the problem was that under increasing pressure from the Opposition, Germain and his colleagues tended to hear only what they wanted to believe. One of Clinton's aides reported an interview with Germain in which he prefaced each remark with, "'Is not such a thing so and so?' And, as these *previous* answers were frequently wrong, they laid me under the unpleasing necessity of beginning mine with a contradiction."[28] Thus Sir Henry's army became 25 percent greater than it actually was; all serious resistance in the Carolinas had ended; Virginia, Maryland, and Delaware fairly teemed with Loyalists. These misrepresentations were not altogether Germain's fault for omnipresent "authorites" such as General Robertson and Joseph Galloway were always ready to paint the American picture in tones that were pleasing to the ministerial eye. Even Cornwallis tended to tell one story to Germain and another to Clinton. The American Secretary's view of the war was also badly out of date. Until the end of April 1781, Germain knew little or nothing that had happened in the South since the beginning of the year.

The situation in the Carolinas in the middle of January 1781 is a proper point of departure from which to consider the strategic planning of the British high command for 1781. On January 6 Cornwallis wrote to Clinton, "I shall begin my march tomorrow [from Winnsboro] . . . and propose keeping on the West of the Catawba for a considerable distance. I shall then proceed to pass that River, and the Yadkin [that is, turn to the northeast]. Events alone can decide future Steps. I shall take every Opportunity of communicating with Brg^r- Genl Arnold." (Greene had sent Morgan to the westward, Tarleton had been sent in pursuit of Morgan, and Leslie's reinforcement was on its way to join Cornwallis.) Twelve days later, despite the fact that Tarleton had lost the Legion at the Cowpens, Cornwallis reassured Clinton that "nothing but the most absolute necessity shall induce me to give up the important object of the Winter's Campaign." Cornwallis, writing after the event, explained that he had proceeded by the upper fords of the North Carolina rivers because heavy rains had made them impassable to the east: ". . . I hoped in my way, to destroy, or drive out of South Carolina, the Corps of the Enemy, commanded by General Morgan . . . and . . . by rapid marches, to get between General Greene and Virginia, and by that means, force him to fight . . . or . . . to oblige him to quit North Carolina with precipitation, and thereby encourage our friends, to make good their promises of a general rising. . . ."

His ultimate objective was undoubtedly the Cape Fear River from which he could be supplied and then consider the best means of cooperating with the British on the Chesapeake. The January 18 letter was the last word that Clinton had from Cornwallis for three months (it reached Germain via

Clinton on April 25). The earl might as well have vanished off the map of North America. Arnold reported hearing that Cornwallis was in southside Virginia in February with Greene "retiring before him," a rumor that was wildly incorrect.[29]

Clinton, who was completely in the dark as to Cornwallis' movements except for the meager clues of the January dispatches. He was torn between his own fears for the safety of the Chesapeake garrison and what he conceived to be his own reduced forces in New York. He finally decided early in March to reinforce Arnold, but he had long since abandoned the idea of a major offensive in Virginia. To General William Phillips, who commanded the expedition and who was to succeed Arnold in command on the Chesapeake, he spoke of raids up the James River, ensuring the security of the base at Portsmouth, and the desirability of fortifications that would guard a naval anchorage either at Hampton Roads or on the York River. But his disillusionment with the Chesapeake was clear in the concluding paragraph of his orders: "It is probable, whenever the objects of this expedition are fulfilled, . . . that you may return to this place [New York]—. In which case, you must bring with you Brigadier-general Arnold, the Light Infantry, Colonel Robinson's corps, or the seventy-sixth, and, if it should be possible, the Queen's Rangers."[30]

When Germain learned of these intentions in late April, he was dismayed. In his mind Clinton's reinforcement of the Chesapeake would enable "Lord Cornwallis to effect a Junction with General Phillips, and . . . by convincing the Loyalists that the Recovery of the Southern Provinces is the unalterable Object of the King's Measures, excite them to exert themselves. . . ." Convinced that the Carolinas were subjugated and clinging obstinately to the conviction that thousands of Loyalists were at hand to assist the King's arms, he now viewed the withdrawal of Phillips and Arnold with "great Mortification."

Then came the most explicit instructions that Clinton had received in many months: "I am commanded by His Majesty to acquaint you, that the Recovery of the Southern Provinces, and the Prosecution of the War by pushing Our Conquests *from South to North,* is to be considered as the Chief and principal Object for the Employment of all the Forces under your Command, which can be spared from the Defence of the Places in His Majesty's Possession, until it is accomplished. . . ."

There followed what those familiar with military humbug will recognize as "paper foxholes" designed to furnish cover for the American Secretary if the plan went awry. Clinton was warned against endangering his troops by campaigning to the south during unseasonable weather; he was to miss no opportunity to strike Washington; favorable openings might present themselves in New England. But the intention was clear. ". . . His Majesty's Purpose," Germain reiterated, "[is] that the War should be conducted upon a permanent and settled Plan of Conquest . . . and not by desultory

Enterprizes, taking Possession of Places at one time, and abandoning them at another, which can never bring the War to a Conclusion, or encourage the People to avow their Loyalty and exert their Endeavors to relieve themselves of the Tyranny of the Rebel Rulers. . . ."[31]

Whatever may be the judgment of Cornwallis' later decision to go to Virginia, one thing is clear. He was doing what Lord George Germain wanted him to do. In the middle of April, Cornwallis wrote, "I cannot help expressing my wishes that the Chesapeak may become the Seat of the War, even (if necessary) at the expense of abandoning New York. . . ." The American Secretary, when he read these words, must have beamed with pleasure.[32]

❋ New Windsor ❋

It had been the most discouraging year of the war for George Washington. Both Congress and the states were bankrupt. Continental paper was worthless. Besides shortages of food, clothing, and supplies, the men had not been paid for months. Money from France had barely eased the crisis, and the Comte de Vergennes was constantly reminding Benjamin Franklin in Paris that the treasury was virtually empty. The alliance with the United States and the attendant war with England had been denounced by virtually every financial expert in Louis XVI's kingdom as a prelude to disaster for the economy of France. At one point Vergennes had notified Franklin that his government would no longer pay bills of exchange drawn by the United States, although the threat was never carried out.[33]

It was not just the shortage of money and goods. After six years of war, Congress was still trying to run its affairs through committees whose recommendations were subject to approval by Congress—often only after tedious debate and acrimonious nitpicking. The administrative system, if such it could be called, was a shambles. Not until 1781 would Congress create quasi-executive departments for the conduct of the war and for foreign affairs.

Congressmen were thoroughly imbued with republican principles, including an inordinate fear of standing armies. There were those who saw in the commander in chief a dictator and were anxious to curb his power. One of the miracles of the war was that a man of Washington's temperament tolerated the officiousness and paranoia of some of the members. Not until 1780 did Congress even consult Washington about the appointment of theater commanders. Under the Articles of Confederation a congressman could serve no more than three years in any six-year period, so the national legislature resembled the army in that by the time a member became experienced and expert in his job, his term expired and his services were lost. Others who were able and conscientious wore themselves out by their exertions and retired to avoid a breakdown.

The authority of Congress depended, in the final analysis, on the goodwill of the states. If the latter chose to ignore requisitions for supplies or men there was little that Congress could do about it. And the jealousy with which the states guarded their prerogatives and their reluctance to do more than the barest minimum led Washington to remark, ". . . The contest among different states *now*, is not which shall do the most for the common cause, but which shall do the least."

By 1780 Congress had, in desperation, turned over to the states the responsibility for recruiting men for the Continental Line and furnishing the army with supplies, tasks for which the states proved totally inadequate. "There are two things (as I have often declared) which in my opinion, are indispensably necessary to the well being and good Government of our public Affairs," wrote Washington from his headquarters at New Windsor on the Hudson; "these are, greater powers of Congress, and more responsibility and permanency in the executive bodies. If individual States conceive themselves at liberty to reject, or alter any act of Congress, which . . . has been solemnly debated and decided on; it will be madness in us to think of prosecuting the War. And if Congress suppose, that Boards composed of their own body, and always fluctuating, are competent to the great business of War . . . they will most assuredly deceive themselves."[34]

There had been one great hour in the otherwise gloomy summer of 1780. France had at last sent an army and a fleet to America. In July 6,000 well-fed, well-armed French troops had landed in Rhode Island, and Washington was immediately full of plans for an attack on New York. But the high expectations were soon deflated. Admiral de Ternay informed the American commander in no uncertain terms that his fleet was not strong enough to risk an attack on New York. Washington, who had raised his Continental force to more than 6,000 men and had added nearly 4,000 militia, was anxious to strike a blow. He sent Lafayette to Newport, but the young marquis, who was an American major general but only a captain in the French army, made little headway with the French commander. Major General Rochambeau, although ordered to place himself under Washington's command, was obviously under certain restrictions. Among these were his orders to keep the French contingent separate from the American army until an actual campaign was begun.

Washington finally went to Hartford himself to confer with his allies. The meeting was not altogether happy, although generals and admirals were carefully courteous. De Ternay pointed out that naval superiority was necessary before a major campaign could be launched. Rochambeau raised objections to an attack on a place as well fortified as New York. Washington was wise enough not to press his prerogative as commander in chief. It was decided to ask for additional forces, military and naval, from France. In the meantime the Americans must wait. "It is impossible," wrote Washington to Lafayette in October, ". . . to desire more ardently than I to terminate this campaign by some happy stroke; but we must consult our means rather than our wishes; and not endeavor to better our affairs by attempting things, which for want of success, may make them worse."[35]

It was on his return trip from Hartford that Washington received the most shocking blow of this disastrous year. What was intended as a courtesy call on General Benedict Arnold at the fort at West Point became a nightmare revelation of Arnold's treason. The plot was revealed by the capture of Clinton's emissary, Major John André, who had been sent up the Hudson to complete the details of a plan that entailed Arnold's surrender of West Point to the British. Arnold fled to an enemy man-of-war in the river only moments before the commander in chief arrived. "Whom can we trust now?" was Washington's anguished reaction.

Young André was tried by a court-martial and hanged, much to the regret of many in both armies. But Washington resisted appeals for clemency. In response to a plea from Sir Henry Clinton, he grimly replied that only the handing over of the traitor could save André from the gallows. This the British commander could not do.[36]

As winter approached, Washington resigned himself to the usual reduction of his army. Those whose enlistments expired on January 1 he allowed to go home at different times in small numbers so that the enemy might not guess at the slender force that would remain at the beginning of the year.

Then on New Year's Day came the crisis that Washington and his officers had long dreaded—mutiny. General Anthony Wayne sent word to headquarters that most of the Pennsylvania line, including noncommissioned officers, had evicted their commanders from the camp at Morristown. They had shouldered their muskets and taken the road to Philadelphia. Their object was clear. They intended to ask Congress for back pay and clothing at the point of the bayonet.

From the outset it was obvious that the immediate provocation was the cash bounties that were being given to enlist recruits while the veterans went unpaid or were paid in worthless Continental currency. Numbers of soldiers announced that they intended to leave the army so that they could reenlist and receive bonuses. It was clear that the men had no intention of going over to the enemy. When British agents appeared among them, the soldiers arrested them and delivered them to General Wayne, announcing indignantly that the army had no idea of "turning Arnolds."

Washington made no effort to intervene directly to stop the mutineers because he believed that "an attempt to reduce them by force will either drive them to the Enemy, or dissipate them in such a manner that they will never be recovered." But he hurried aides to Philadelphia to urge Congress "to stay and hear what propositions the Soldiers have to make."

Ultimately, the mutiny was quelled but at a price. In addition to back pay, the mutineers were allowed to be permanently discharged, and half were furloughed until April. The Pennsylvania line had, for the moment, been wiped out more thoroughly than if it had been overwhelmed by redcoats.

The mutiny had a tragicomic aftermath. Two hundred troops of the New Jersey line also mutinied after overindulging in rum. This time the commander in chief was ready. The mutineers were quickly surrounded by a special force that had been organized for just such a contingency. The ringleaders were arrested and tried by drumhead court-martial. Three were executed by a firing squad composed of their own comrades.[37]

A pusillanimous Congress, treason, and an army wracked by mutiny and depleted by expiring enlistments—surely these were burdens too great for the most stout-hearted commander. Yet scarcely were his troops settled in their winter quarters when Washington turned his attention to the desperate situation of his southern commander and began to consider how he could be succored.

When Greene had gone southward in December there was little that Washington could offer him save encouragement. He had asked Governor Jefferson to divert supplies requisitioned from Virginia by Congress to the Southern Department. He had also dispatched Light Horse Harry Lee and his Legion to Greene's command. These troops were well equipped and mounted on fine animals, but they numbered only about 300 men. But amidst all his other troubles there seemed little else that the commander in chief could do to ease Greene's precarious position. Washington was alarmed by the news that Cornwallis had been reinforced by Leslie, and Arnold's expedition to the Chesapeake was cause for further concern.[38]

As Washington saw it, Cornwallis would soon "recommence the offensive; and we have to apprehend, with too much success, as General Greene's accounts of his situation are far from flattering." Arnold's force in Virginia was in a position to interdict the flow of men and supplies to the southward. Indeed, any augmentation of the Chesapeake force would find the tiny southern army caught between the two British forces and destroyed.[39]

Yet it was characteristic of Washington that in the looming disaster he saw an opportunity to strike the enemy. Toward the end of January 1781, news came from Rhode Island that a violent North Atlantic gale had struck and badly damaged the exposed British fleet at the eastern end of Long Island. Washington grasped at this opening. Might not it be possible for the French to send ships and men to the Chesapeake? If even a small naval force and 1,000 French troops could be spared, Washington could send a like number, commanded by Lafayette, to assure cooperation. The combined force could trap Arnold and destroy his force (perhaps the arch-traitor himself might be captured). Hastily the American commander forwarded his plan to Rhode Island.

The French responded but not with the audacity for which Washington had hoped. A ship of the line and two frigates were sent to the Chesapeake, but Rochambeau would not risk troops aboard slow transports. Storm damage to the British turned out to be less severe than had been supposed. The French squadron struck at the British in the Chesapeake and inflicted some damage but was forced to withdraw.[40]

Perhaps the opportunity was not as great as Washington supposed. In any event, by early February he had word from Greene of the unexpected victory at the Cowpens, but the southern commander was still not strong enough to force a showdown with Cornwallis. Reluctantly Greene reported that he must reunite his divided force and withdraw into Virginia to escape destruction. But for Washington, as for others, the Chesapeake held an ambiguous fascination—it posed both a grave threat and a tempting opportunity.[41]

As the new year came in, British southern strategy had degenerated into a shambles of contradictory and confused objectives. Whatever vague intentions the ministry may have had for establishing civil government in South Carolina had long since been abandoned. As to the military recon-quest, Sir Henry Clinton was virtually immobilized by the intransigence of his naval counterpart. He had managed to satisfy Germain's insistence on an expedition to the Chesapeake, but its mission was unclear. The American Secretary was issuing instructions based on information that was badly out of date and assumptions that had little basis in fact.

In the South, Cornwallis was doggedly pursuing Greene in North Carolina, ignoring Clinton's injunction that the first priority was the security of South Carolina. He expected that success against Greene would justify his conduct to Germain if not to Clinton. Of the earl's decision Sir Henry commented sourly that "with less means & less hopes than you ever had before . . . you move into N. Carolina for no other purpose I am convinced than to receive the Command from me."[42]

10. Retreat

Daniel Morgan did not delude himself into believing that the victory over Tarleton had changed the balance of forces in the Carolinas. Eight hours after the victory at Hannah's Cowpens he had assembled his corps with its weapons, prisoners, and booty and crossed the Broad, continuing the retreat he had begun on the Pacolet.[1]

In the lexicon of popular history, armies that retreat do not appear to be heroic. Yet the professional soldier knows that an orderly and skillful retreat is one of the most difficult of all military maneuvers. This was especially true in the army of the Southern Department for its experienced soldiers, the Continentals of Maryland and Delaware, comprised only about half of the total strength of Greene's army. Retreat not only tests physical endurance; it tests the nerve of an army. And militia, as Greene and Morgan well knew, were notoriously nervous.

Despite the setback to Tarleton, Cornwallis' strategy was still sound. If he could keep Morgan and Greene separated, his veteran regulars and provincials could destroy the two wings of the rebel army with ease. Even if they were able to join, the British still possessed the superior force.[2]

Greene's problem, then, was twofold. He must reunite with Morgan and then take the combined force to safety. In retreat, the pursuer can afford to move despite laggard troops or slow-moving baggage. The pursued must adapt his pace to the slowest of his elements, and he must husband his supplies. The art of retreat requires the nicest kind of calculation. It requires an intimate knowledge of roads and rivers and fords by which rivers can be passed. It is a commentary on Nathanael Greene's quality of mind that, although he had been south of Maryland for only eight weeks, his grasp of the geography of the region was superior to that of his opponent, who had been on the ground for almost a year.

✳ The Pursuit Begins ✳

It is something over a hundred miles as the crow flies from the Cowpens to the site of Greene's camp at Hicks Creek on the Pee Dee. But not until the sixth day after the battle did a courier from Morgan traverse the muddy roads and streams swollen by rain to bring the news of victory to headquarters. (The courier was Major Edward Giles, and his travels had only begun. Greene sent him on to Philadelphia and to Washington's headquarters in New York.)

Morgan's victory was an enormous tonic to the southern commander and his men. "We have had a *feu de joie*," wrote Colonel Williams to Morgan, "drunk all your healths, swore you were the finest fellows on earth, and love you, if possible, more than ever." Such fervid language from the dignified adjutant suggests that Williams may have had more than a few drafts of cherry bounce.[3]

When Congress heard the news, it voted a gold medal for Morgan and silver ones for Howard and William Washington. The commander in chief in New York hailed the victory as "decisive and glorious" and predicted that it "must have an important influence on the affairs of the South." Perhaps. But Greene, writing to his "darling Kitty," viewed his situation realistically: "I am of Spanish disposition, always most serious when there is a great run of good fortune, for fear of some ill-fated stroke."[4]

He sent word to Light Horse Harry Lee and Francis Marion to abandon their raids on British communications and to gather horses and wagons for the march. As soon as the army was ready to move, Lee was to join while Marion returned to his harassing tactics on the lower Santee. Above all, Marion was to keep Greene informed of enemy movements. "Get good information before you attempt anything" was a maxim that Greene urged upon his subordinates, especially those on detached duty. The orders and dispatches continued to stream from headquarters. Carrington was to have boats ready on the Dan if the retreat moved as far as Virginia. Greene asked Steuben in Virginia to send reinforcements and urged William Davidson, the North Carolina militia commander, to summon the Whigs of the piedmont to his support. He ordered General Edward Stevens, the tough Virginia militia general, to escort prisoners northward and to see to it that foragers and quartermasters gathered supplies along the probable line of march. Calls went out to Governor Abner Nash for men and supplies, especially for muskets to equip the numerous unarmed militia who appeared in the camps.[5]

This meticulous planning, however, would be useless unless the two separated corps could make a successful junction in the face of Cornwallis' determined advance. To coordinate the movements of the main army with those of Morgan required not only sound judgment but flexibility in the face of changing circumstances. Above all, Greene required precise information of the location and movement of both Morgan and the enemy. It was typical of Greene that he did not remain at headquarters and rely on scouts and couriers to furnish him with this vital intelligence. On January 28, as the army prepared to move, he turned over command to General Isaac Huger of South Carolina. Then, accompanied by a squad of cavalry, he set off through the rain-swept North Carolina piedmont to find Morgan.[6]

Lord Cornwallis was an angry man. Stragglers from Cowpens had brought the first confused reports of the disaster on the night of the battle. The next day the shattered remnants of Tarleton's troops came into the British camp on Turkey Creek, twenty-five miles southwest of Charlotte. Now the earl stood with his dress sword thrust into the ground, his hands resting on the pommel, as he listened to the report of the Legion commander. By the time Tarleton had concluded, Cornwallis was leaning forward, his suppressed fury thrusting his weight down on the light blade until it snapped. He swore he would retake Morgan's prisoners no matter what the cost. The outburst did nothing to assuage Tarleton's humiliation.[7]

Several days later, Tarleton asked Cornwallis either to give his "approbation of his proceedings [in the battle], or his leave to retire till an inquiry could be instituted, to investigate his conduct." Whether or not his lordship's anger had cooled, Cornwallis could not afford to lose Tarleton. "You have forfeited no part of my esteem as an officer by the unfortunate event of the action of the 17th," he said. He praised Tarleton's pursuit of Morgan, but of the battle itself he would say only that "the total misbehavior of the troops" had led to the defeat (and was not a commander responsible for the behavior of his troops, especially veteran Legionnaires?). Tarleton was ordered back into the field to reorganize the Legion.[8]

Cornwallis now undertook to make good his threat to crush Morgan. Leslie's command was now up: a crack regiment of the Brigade of the Guards commanded by General Charles O'Hara; the German Regiment Bose; a detachment of jägers, and one of dragoons. The total of this reinforcement was 1,530 men. The earl was now ready to resume his invasion of North Carolina. A cold appreciation of his situation told him that he could deal with almost any combination of American forces then in the field. But his task would be much easier if he could overtake and destroy Morgan, thus giving Greene a lesson on the error of division of forces. "It is impossible to foresee all the consequences, that this unexpected, & extraordinary event [the Cowpens battle] may produce," he wrote to Clinton, "but . . . be assured, that nothing but the most absolute necessity shall induce me to give up the important object of the Winter's Campaign."[9]

One of the "consequences" of the "extraordinary event" immediately manifested itself. With the Legion out of action, Cornwallis had to guess at

Morgan's movements. Since the British were closer to Morgan by half than Greene's main army it was natural to suppose that the American light corps would withdraw westward toward the refuge of the mountains. On January 21 Cornwallis resumed his march, his troops slogging along muddy roads northwest toward Gilbert Town. It was two days before Tarleton was able to scout ahead and discover Morgan's whereabouts—to the northeast. The Old Waggoner had indeed marched to Gilbert Town, but he had turned due east, heading for the fords of the Catawba north of Charlotte. Belatedly the British turned on the track of the Americans and on January 23 made camp at Ramsour's Mill. Morgan had already crossed the river at Sherrald's Ford. He had considered either retiring to the mountains or making a raid on Ninety Six. But both ventures risked too much, and he did not want to lose the booty and the prisoners taken at the Cowpens. Most of all, he knew Greene was anxious to reunite the army. He had therefore divided his force, sending the prisoners northward under the guard of the Virginia militia, whose terms had expired and who could perform this chore on their way home. Then he led his troops in an arc that took him clear of the blundering British column, and on January 22 he crossed the swollen Catawba. His swing around the enemy had taken him nearly 100 miles across two rivers in six days. It was not for nothing that he was called the Old Waggoner.[10]

For almost a week the bad weather, the flooded river, and exhaustion held the two armies motionless on opposite sides of the Catawba less than twenty miles apart. On January 30, General Greene and his little party, tired and begrimed with mud, splashed into Morgan's camp. The commanding general had ridden a little over a hundred miles in three days.

The Rhode Island scholar and Virginia frontiersman debated their position. It was apparent to them that the call for militia had brought disappointing results. Cowpens had effects both positive and negative. Tories were cowed into inactivity so that the British army found itself passing through a hostile countryside. The fact that American forces were in retreat before the British invasion was scarcely encouraging to the Whigs. And Greene undoubtedly realized that the Carolinians, Tory or Whig, were not eager to go campaigning in the rain and cold of winter. It was a tribute to the North Carolina militia commander, William Davidson, that under such conditions he was able to bring 700 men into Morgan's camp on the Catawba. But it did not help matters that more Virginia militiamen announced that their time had expired. The day after Greene's arrival they left camp for home. The Virginia militia with Huger also departed, to the disgust of their commander, General Stevens.[11]

As the two generals discussed the discouraging situation, Morgan once again suggested retreat to the mountains. Greene emphatically vetoed the idea, whereupon Morgan heatedly announced that he would not be responsible for the consequences. Of course not, the commanding general replied calmly. ". . . I shall take the measure upon myself." It was a gentle rebuke to the old man, reminding him that Nathanael Greene commanded and Nathanael Greene took complete responsibility. The retreat would be to the north and east, all the way to Virginia if necessary, where supplies and men could be found to restore the army so that it could fight again. Orders were dispatched: stores to go by way of Salisbury to Guilford Court House; Huger to impress horses and wagons to get the stores out of reach of the enemy; Marion to go west of the Santee once more and harass Cornwallis' line of communication with Charleston. Morgan would assign Davidson and his militia to dispute the crossings of the Catawba. Another call went out for militia to rally, and a rendezvous was set between the river and Salisbury. Morgan's corps would take the road immediately to join with Huger.

And outside of Greene's tent the rain stopped. It was as if an alarm bell had sounded. In a matter of hours the floodwaters would drop and the fords be passable for the pursuing enemy.[12]

It was time to move.

❋ M' Cowan's Ford ❋

Lord Cornwallis used the delay caused by the rain to prepare for a daring gamble. British officers had always contended that when their army was outmarched it was because the Americans carried so little equipment and baggage. Determined that the rebels would not again elude him, the British commander decided to beat the Americans at their own game. He ordered the army to strip itself to the bare essentials. This included "destroying superfluous Baggage, and all of my Waggons, except those loaded with Hospital Stores, Salt, and Ammunition. . . ." Four wagons were designated as ambulances, but the rest went up in flames, and with them "all prospect of Rum, and even a regular supply of provisions to the Soldiers. . . ." According to the earl, the army reacted with "the most general and chearfull acquiescence." If so, it was probably the only time in history that regulars were "chearfull" at the disappearance of their rum.[13]

Cornwallis approached the Catawba fords cautiously. Although he was uncertain whether Morgan would dispute the passage, he had the choice of any of five fords in the vicinity. The best were Beattie's Ford, which lay directly on his route, and Tuckaseegee Ford some miles downstream. In between these were several others more difficult to cross. Cornwallis decided to make a feint at Beattie's Ford and then make a dawn crossing at M' Cowan's Ford, six miles downstream. He would then be on the flank of any force guarding the main road to Salisbury.

The Americans had already decided not to risk Morgan's command in a fight for the crossings. But Morgan intended to be as troublesome as

possible with the minimum of risk. His huge frame was racked by sciatica
and rheumatism occasioned by the strenuous march and the rain and cold.
Yet he was out of his bed to inspect the fords and determine the best means
of harassing the enemy. When the Old Waggoner came into Davidson's
camp at Beattie's Ford, the militiamen raised a cheer. Davidson's Scotch-
Irish Carolinians, many of them Presbyterians recruited by their ministers,
had responded to his call. When the Reverend James Hall at the Fourth
Creek Church was interrupted in the midst of a sermon by a courier from
Davidson, the parson immediately switched from preaching to recruiting.
But many more in the neighborhood had either stayed at home to protect
their families or joined the stream of refugees moving northwest.[14]

Davidson was thirty-five years old. Already a veteran Indian fighter in
1776, he had joined Washington's army as a militia officer. His conduct had
earned him a commission in the Continental Line, and his gallantry at
Germantown had brought him promotion to lieutenant colonel and command of a regiment. When the North Carolina Continentals were sent
south to reinforce Lincoln in Charleston, Davidson had stopped off to visit
his family in Rowan County. Before he could rejoin, Charleston had fallen
and he found himself without a command. He then accepted service with
the North Carolina militia under General Rutherford's command. He was
severely wounded at Colson's Mill in July 1780 and was out of action for
two months. Upon his return to duty, he was made commander of militia
for the Salisbury district with the rank of brigadier general. A proven
soldier and a natural leader, Davidson was unusually successful at recruiting militia. He was said to have persuaded some of his men to turn out by
promising to credit them with three months of service if they would serve
for six weeks.[15]

Now Morgan gave Davidson the task of making the Catawba crossing as
difficult as possible for the redcoats. Then he returned to his command and
put it on the road to Salisbury and to the next river crossing at the Yadkin.

Davidson stationed 500 of his men at the obvious danger point at
Beattie's Ford. Two hundred more were placed at Tuckaseegee Ford on
the main road from Charlotte to Salisbury. This left under 100 men to
guard the fords in between, 70 at Tool's Ford and 25 at M'Cowan's. On the
last day of January, Greene himself made a final inspection of Davidson's
dispositions. The militia commander noted that "General Greene had
never been on the Catawba before, but he appeared to know more about it
than men who've been raised on its banks." Greene suggested that Davidson put 200 of his men on horseback to provide a mobile reserve to prevent
surprise at the lightly guarded crossings. Greene also arranged a rendezvous point about fifteen miles from the river, where he expected additional militia to gather. Nobody could remember when the commanding
general had had a night's sleep. He had been on the road for three days and
then had found time to issue a stream of orders: to Huger; to militia

General John Lillington at Rocky Mount; to Marion; to Quartermaster General Carrington. Now he left the river and splashed off to see Morgan on his way and then to wait for Davidson's militia at the rendezvous.[16]

As darkness fell on January 31 Cornwallis made his dispositions. Colonel Webster commanded the force that threatened Beattie's Ford. The flanking party, consisting of the Guards, the 23rd Regiment, Regiment Bose, 200 cavalry, and two guns, made its tortuous way downstream to M'Cowan's Ford. "The morning being very dark and rainy, & part of our way through a wood, where there was no road, one of the three pounders ... overset in a swamp, and occasioned those Corps to lose the Line of March...." In the confusion some artillerists stayed to assist in the recovery of the mired gun while others went ahead with the remaining piece. One who stayed behind had the only slow match with which the guns were fired. When the column reached the river, the gun they had managed to drag through the swamp and mud was useless.[17]

Shortly before first light, the command reached the crossing. Its appearance was formidable. M'Cowan's was really two fords, a wagon ford that led directly to the opposite bank and a horse ford that angled upstream. The latter, although longer, was much more shallow. The river had fallen somewhat, but it was still far above its normal level, and the horse ford was obviously the best route, especially for the infantry. The British column paused as the men gazed at the "ford"—fully 500 yards wide with the water running in a swift, heavy current. Forbidding as the crossing appeared, delay would only widen the gap between Cornwallis and the Americans. It had begun raining again, ending whatever hope there might be that the river would continue to fall. Cornwallis gave the order. The brigade of the Guards led the way, and all three generals urged their horses into the stream.

Whether the Tory guide did not know about the horse ford or whether he deliberately misled the redcoats, the soldiers headed directly across, "up to their breasts in a rapid stream, their knapsacks on their backs and sixty or seventy rounds of powder and ball in each pouch tied at the pole of their necks, their firelocks with bayonets, fixed on their shoulders." General Leslie's horse was carried downstream, and O'Hara's mount was bowled over by the current. Cornwallis' horse was shot, but all three generals continued the crossing.[18]

On the American side of the river the darkness and the roar of the water concealed both sight and sound of the British approach until the redcoats had nearly reached the northern bank. Robert Henry, a schoolboy who had taken a bayonet wound at King's Mountain, was on picket duty. He was awakened by a companion, who had spied the enemy. Henry had previously picked out a vantage point from which he intended to fire at the British as they crossed. "By the time I was ready to fire, the rest of the guard had fired.... I fired and continued to fire, until I saw that one on horseback had passed my [marker] rock. . . ." As he turned to run, Henry was halted by the sight of his lame schoolmaster still calmly firing from his post. "I thought I could stand it as long as he could and commenced loading. Beatty fired, and then I fired, the heads and shoulders of the British being just above the bank. They made no return fire. . . . I observed Beatty loading again. I ran down another load. When he fired, he cried, 'It's time to run, Bob.'"

General Davidson had been holding a mounted reserve upstream at the horse ford. At the sound of firing, he brought his men downstream and was placing them on a ridge above the bank to check the British advance when it emerged from the river. As he directed his men into their positions, the British delivered their first fire. Davidson was shot in the chest. He fell from his horse, dead before he hit the ground. Without his leadership, his militia command disintegrated.[19]

Cornwallis assembled the rest of his troops and turned upstream, driving the force that opposed Webster's crossing at Beattie's Ford. Militia and refugees now crowded the road to Salisbury, pursued by Tarleton and the Legion. He scattered a small militia force on its way to rendezvous with Greene, which had made the mistake of stopping for refreshment at Tarrant's Tavern. (Had Tarleton only known it, the commander of the Southern Department was only a few miles away, virtually unescorted, where he waited for the expected reinforcements until midnight.) Tarleton's pursuit harried refugees and militia alike for several miles, making little distinction between soldiers and civilians.

Cornwallis reported that the crossing at M'Cowan's had cost him three killed and thirty-six wounded, but Robert Henry remembered: "A great number of the British dead were found on Thompson's fish dam [below the fords], and in his trap, and numbers lodged on brush. . . . The river stunk with dead carcasses, the British could not have lost less than one hundred men." But the bitterest loss was time. Cornwallis' deliberate preparations and the delay caused by the militia gave Morgan the time he needed. When the British resumed their march, Morgan was thirty miles away, headed for the crossings of the Yadkin.[20]

Greene was also on the move. His wait at the militia rendezvous had placed him in the dangerous no-man's-land between the two armies, but he made his way safely to Salisbury, where new disappointments awaited him. Here Greene found the long-awaited requisition of arms from the North Carolina government—1,700 muskets rusted and useless from improper storage. Morgan continued ailing, a bad case of the piles adding its acute discomfort to the rheumatism. "This is the first time that I ever experienced this disorder," he told Greene, "and from the idea I had of it, sincerely, prayed that I might never know what it was." He had reached the conclusion that he could not continue much longer in the field.[21]

And it continued to rain. Privates and generals slogged through the mud and cold. Greene and Morgan rode together until they reached the Yadkin seven miles beyond Salisbury. The river was impossible to ford and looked dangerous even for the boats Greene had arranged for. Should the Americans make a stand here against the enemy or risk the crossing? Probably the commanders did not debate the question at length. Cornwallis could easily overpower Morgan's slender force even if it was reinforced by militia— whom their own commander, General Stevens, denounced as willing only "to Rub through their Tower of Duty with whole Bones." The boats were brought up. Some had been collected along the river, others hauled from the Catawba by wagons. Men and equipment were embarked on the swollen, roiling Yadkin. Miraculously, the crossing was made without the loss of a single man. Greene crossed with the rest.[22]

Cornwallis was close on their heels. The British army had marched twenty miles that day, a performance that would have been creditable in fair weather. Extra horses, no longer needed to pull abandoned wagons, were used to double mount some of the soldiers. Despite their headlong pace, the British still found time to loot and burn. In vain, orders were issued to put a stop to the raiding for Cornwallis correctly perceived that "this licentiousness . . . must inevitably bring disgrace on His Majesty's service. . . ." But the tavern at Tarrant's was burned as was the home of the prominent Brevard family. Orders were issued to "find out the persons who set fires to houses this day." But such orders availed little.

The British column entered Salisbury on February 3 after a hard march through the rain. With the river running out of its banks, Cornwallis was certain that he had Morgan pinned against the Yadkin. Told that the Americans still had not crossed the river, the British commander sent General O'Hara's Guards in the direction of Trading Ford to engage the enemy until the main column could be brought up. O'Hara's men stumbled through the darkness and mud, arriving at the ford at midnight. Scattered firing broke out, and the Guards formed in line of battle, but their advance disclosed that they were opposed only by a few videttes left behind to cover the last boats. Morgan was east of the Yadkin and the boats with him.[23]

The next morning Cornwallis brought up the rest of his command and had a full view of the American camp across the river. But they were as safe as if they had been miles away. The British spitefully unlimbered their guns and sent several salvos into the rebel encampment. The only visible target was a cabin where Greene had set up his headquarters. Soon round shot splintered the shingles and ricocheted off nearby rocks, but the light three-pounders could do little damage. Dr. William Read, who must have been carefully watching the general who never slept, noticed that Greene refused to allow the din to distract him. "His pen never rested, but when a new visitor arrived . . . answer was given with calmness and precision, and the pen immediately resumed." One of these orders was to Huger, whose army had also been held up by the rains. It was obvious that he could not reach Salisbury so he was directed to a new junction with Morgan's command at Guilford Court House. Appeals went out to Virginia for militia reinforcements, and Steuben was warned to be ready to cooperate if an opportunity offered to lure Cornwallis to Virginia.[24]

It should be noted that Greene was now no longer entirely committed to retreat. If that had been his sole purpose, why had he waited at the Catawba, and why was he now encamped on the Yadkin? The Americans had crossed the river on February 3, yet Greene seemed in no hurry to seek safety in Virginia. When the river finally receded enough for Cornwallis to make a crossing on February 8, Morgan's force was little more than a day's march ahead of him. Greene was careful to instruct Colonel Carrington to have boats ready for crossing the Dan, but he was equally careful to watch for an opportunity to catch the British napping. And when he learned that Cornwallis had stripped his army of his excess baggage and equipment at Ramsour's Mill, he was reported to have exclaimed, "Then he is ours!" An enemy short of supplies and low on ammunition, especially if he was far from the base of supplies, was highly vulnerable. It was a delicate game: stay away from an enemy who had the superior force but maintain contact so as to take advantage of a lucky chance that might favor the inferior Americans.

A clue to Greene's thoughts may be found in the fact that when the two wings of his army finally were reunited at Guilford Court House the American commander spent almost half a day reconnoitering the ground as a possible battle site.[25]

✳ Hare and Hounds ✳

On February 6 Cornwallis turned up the Yadkin toward Shallow Ford, twenty-five mile above Trading Ford. The British column was under way only a short distance when Tarleton's vanguard received a check. A small force of Whig militia under Colonel Francis Locke was defending a bridge over Grant's Creek so stubbornly that Tarleton was delayed more than three hours while his troops flanked the Americans and finally drove them off. Locke and his men destroyed the bridge, forcing another delay while the British rebuilt it. Ironically, Tarleton had reported that his raiders had killed Locke at Tarrant's Tavern.

The crossing at Shallow Ford was not as much of a detour as might appear from the map, given Cornwallis' strategy. It was known that the lower reaches of the Dan were deep and swift, especially after the incessant rain, which showed little sign of abating. Greene's army, more than double its numbers after his junction with Huger, could not possibly find enough boats to ferry it across the lower Dan. He would, therefore, so Cornwallis reasoned, be forced to turn northwest to the upper fords of the river. Once across the Yadkin, then, Cornwallis took a route that would keep him well to the west of the Americans but would enable him to reach the upper fords by the shortest, most direct route. Sure of his adversary's objective, the British commander paused only long enough to acquire some bread and meal at the Moravian village of Salem.[26]

The British found the Moravians mild and inoffensive folk. But as the army moved on, its backwash of camp followers looted the village, this despite the peremptory orders of Cornwallis admonishing his officers "that if their duty to their King and their country and their feelings of humanity were not sufficient to enforce obedience [to orders against plundering] . . . he must make use of such power as military law placed in his hands." For the poor Moravians there was worse to come. Hard on the heels of the British came a voracious band of Whig guerrillas, who stripped Salem clean of what little was left, including, it is said, the very clothes from the backs of the inhabitants.[27]

Meanwhile, Greene had reached Guilford Court House. On the same day that Cornwallis crossed the Yadkin, Huger reached the rendezvous and the two divisions of the army were finally reunited after a separation of two months. The gratification at having successfully united his army aroused Greene's fighting blood. He now had more than 2,000 men of all arms, making his force about equal to the British. The ground around the courthouse was well suited for a defensive position, and the commander called a council of his officers to discuss the possibility of making a stand. All of his officers were present: Huger, Morgan, Light Horse Harry Lee, William Washington, Otho Williams, and John Eager Howard. To them he presented his case: perhaps never again would they find the enemy with so reduced a force, so low on supplies, and so far from his base of operations. To continue the retreat to the Dan would be to abandon the North Carolina Whigs to the British and their Tory allies.

His officers were emphatic in their opposition to a fight. The army was in a pitiful condition, lacking such basic necessities as clothing and shoes. The only tents were those used to cover the ammunition. The men had just completed an arduous march on slender rations. Of his 2,000 men only 1,400 were combat veterans. Militia from the piedmont had been slow to respond. Only 200 had gathered at Guilford Court House, with perhaps another 200 coming in under General Lillington. Even the mountain men from the west had not been heard from. The army needed the essentials of rest, good food, and reinforcements. These could be had only in the friendly country north of the Dan in Virginia.[28]

It is doubtful if Greene argued his position very strongly. His good sense obviously told him that his officers were right. Instead he proposed to give Cornwallis another lesson in strategy. He had learned that the British were still to the west, evidently making for the fords of the upper Dan. Greene had already planned for the contingency of retreat: he would go to Irwin's

Ferry, more than fifty miles below the upper fords. The tireless Carrington had for some time been collecting boats on the lower Dan River; and Colonel Thaddeus Kosciuszko was sent to Irwin's to make preparation for the defenses of the crossing.

Meanwhile, Cornwallis must be kept in ignorance of the direction of the American movement. For this purpose Greene organized a screening force to operate to the west of the main army, staying as close to the British as possible to give the impression that Greene's march was closely parallel to that of the enemy. In short, Cornwallis was to be gulled into thinking that Greene's objective was also the upper fords and that he was in a desperate race to win the crossings ahead of the British.

The screen to which this delicate task was entrusted consisted entirely of veterans: 250 cavalry under William Washington; 280 Maryland and Delaware Continentals under John Eager Howard; 60 riflemen under Colonel William Campbell; and about 100 men of Lee's Legion. These 700 men formed a corps that was not unlike the regimental combat team of World War II. It was a force exactly suited to the talents of the Old Waggoner, Daniel Morgan.

But Morgan demurred. He was worn out. His body racked by pain and fever, he insisted that he must quit the army. Even exhortations from his fellow Virginian, Light Horse Harry Lee, would not move him. Soon he was on his way home to the Shenandoah Valley and out of the war. Said Nathanael Greene sorrowfully, "Great generals are scarce. There are few Morgans to be found."[29]

The command of the screen was given to Otho Holland Williams, next to Morgan Greene's most trusted officer. On February 10 the American army broke camp. The main column took the road to Irwin's Ferry seventy miles away. Williams' little command swung westward, sniffing out the enemy. Cornwallis left Salem the same day. The rain continued to fall, and the February chill penetrated the scanty clothing of the troops.

Williams made straight for the British and found them before the day was out at Reedy Fork. The British vanguard, composed of Tarleton's Legion and a contingenet of jägers, was brought up short by a roadblock. A few shots were exchanged, and Tarleton halted until the main column came up. It seemed obvious to Cornwallis that this was more than a scouting party because he discerned infantry in addition to cavalry. Apprehensive that he was confronted by Greene's army, the British commander closed up his column and advanced cautiously. There was intermittent firing, and the Americans destroyed the bridge across Reedy Fork. After several hours' delay, the British resumed their march. Cornwallis continued to move toward the fords of the upper Dan. Williams' screening movement effectively denied the British commander exact knowledge of Greene's army, but he probably concluded that a force as large as Williams' command must be a rear guard within supporting distance of the main American column.[30]

Now both forces pushed hard. It required all of Williams' quick eye and sharp intelligence to avoid being overtaken and at the same time keep his light troops between Cornwallis and Greene. A hard day's march did not end with darkness. The redcoats marched on into the night before they camped. Williams finally halted about nine o'clock in the evening, allowing only half his men to sleep. The rest were needed for strong picket forces thrown out to prevent a surprise night attack. Camp was broken at three in the morning, and the troops took the road for several hours, thereby gaining enough time to stop and cook breakfast, the only meal of the day. The next night those who had been on duty the night before were allowed to sleep—six hours of sleep per man in every forty-eight. This march punished the men so severely that when the late camp was finally made, the soldiers not on duty dropped in their tracks, too desperate for sleep to think of eating. "Notwithstanding this privation, the troops were in fine spirits, and good health," remembered Harry Lee, "delighted with their task and determined to prove themselves worthy of the distinction with which they had been honored."[31]

The redcoats matched the pace of the Americans. The British advance guard, commanded by General O'Hara, had brief clashes with Lee and Washington, who acted as the American rear guard. The test became sterner, the pressure greater. The Americans were constantly on the move, snapping at the British van and then dashing out of harm's way. The Americans were better off than the British in at least one respect: their cavalry mounts seized in Virginia were greatly superior to the British horses. (Precisely how Lee and Washington were always able to mount their men so superbly is something of a mystery, one which the commanding general never seemed to question too closely.) Under the skilled direction of the two cavalry commanders the Americans displayed an endurance and agility for which Tarleton's Legion was no match.[32]

On the evening of February 12 Cornwallis finally realized that he had misjudged Greene's destination and turned eastward. Determined that his enemy should not escape, the Englishman issued orders that he expected the army to march twenty-five miles the next day. The redcoats broke camp soon after midnight, and scouts discovered a road that would shorten their route.

There were two crossings on the lower Dan, one at Dix's Ferry and one at Irwin's five or six miles downstream. Williams had been marching toward Dix's to divert Cornwallis from Greene's crossing at Irwin's. Early on the 13th word came from Greene that the main army was approaching the lower ferry. Williams must march straight for the crossing. Williams forwarded this order to Lee, guarding the rear, and the latter decided to reach his position on the army's new line of march, by taking a short cut— along the same road that the British scouts had discovered.

The doughty Virginian was enjoying a leisurely breakfast when a farmer

Henry "Light Horse Harry" Lee
(Independence National Historical Park Collection)

of the neighborhood came hurrying into the American camp. The British, he said, were only four miles away. Lee hastily turned out his troops and advanced in the direction of the enemy, pushing forward a section of his men as scouts. They soon came in contact with Tarleton's dragoons, one troop of which charged the small American detachment. As pursuers and pursued approached, Lee pulled his men off the road, allowing Tarleton's men to pass. Then he snapped the trap shut, falling on the British rear. When Tarleton's command reached the scene, eighteen bodies lay in the roadway.

Lee then resumed his rear-guard station. "More than once the Legion of Lee and the van of O'Hara were within musket shot. . . ." But by now the men were too exhausted to indulge in useless skirmishing; "the demeanor of the hostile troops became so pacific in appearance that a spectator would have been led to consider them members of the same army."[33]

That evening as the light corps continued to march through the darkness they perceived campfires ahead. At first the troops were convinced that they were approaching Greene's camp and that their comrades had lost the race. But as they came nearer they found the camp deserted, the fires attended by friends who knew that Williams' tired men would welcome a resting place. But within hours the enemy was driving in the pickets and the weary men took up their muddy march again. As they paused on the morning of the 14th to cook breakfast a dispatch rider came into the camp. Greene was across the Dan.

Williams took his men on a quick march to Irwin's Ferry. Washington and Lee covered this last retreat, and when they reached the ferry they found that the light corps had crossed and the boats had returned for the cavalry. They boarded the boats and swam their horses alongside as they crossed to the safety of Virginia.[34]

The long march was over.

On the face of it Greene's masterful retreat had resulted in a narrow escape from the enemy. But his strategy involved a far more subtle purpose than eluding Cornwallis' pursuing army. After Morgan crossed the Catawba and Greene joined him, the American commander seemed almost to be waiting for the river to fall and for Cornwallis to finish his preparations for the pursuit. When the British resumed their march, Morgan's men had little more than a day's start. Again after crossing the Yadkin Greene paused as if he wanted to be sure that Cornwallis was ready to resume the game. He delayed again when Huger joined him at Guilford Court House. The whole episode resembled nothing so much as a child's game of hare and hounds.

11. Guilford Court House

North of the Dan, Nathanael Greene paused to consider his strategic situation. He had skillfully extricated his command from great danger and now found himself in hospitable country, where he might expect supplies and reinforcements to rebuild his tatterdemalion army. But retreat, however masterful, was still retreat. The fact remained that Cornwallis had driven him out of North Carolina, therby giving vast encouragement to the Loyalists. There could be no rest for the American commander if he meant to retrieve the situation and rob the British of their advantage. He must go over to the offensive, and he must do so without delay.

Cornwallis withdrew to Hillsborough and rested his army after its strenuous march. The surrounding countryside had been thoroughly scoured by friend and foe alike, and the British had great difficulty finding enough food and forage. Having stripped his force of its supplies and provisions in his headlong pursuit of Greene, the British commander now found himself with an army that was almost as footsore and ragged as that of his opponent.

Moreover, his march had carried him into a position that was strategically precarious. He was nearly 200 miles from Rawdon's garrison at Camden, and 150 miles from his nearest sure source of supplies and reinforcements at Wilmington. The one cause for optimism was that the British were at last among friends. The country between the Haw River and the Deep had been a stronghold of Loyalism, and when Cornwallis raised the King's standard at Hillsborough "many hundred inhabitants of the surrounding districts rode into the British camp, to . . . inquire the news of the day and take a view of the King's troops." Unfortunately, the visitors were not enthusiastic when the talk turned to enlisting for service, rather, expressing "the dread of violence and persecution. . . ."[1]

As it happened, the Loyalists had reason for their fears.

⁂ General Greene Returns ⁂

Dr. John Pyle was a Loyalist resident of the country east of the Haw River. The arrival of the British at Hillsborough was the first appearance of any considerable royalist force in central North Carolina, and the good doctor, commissioned a colonel of militia, rallied some 300 to 400 of his neighbors to join His Majesty's forces. Colonel Pyle notified Cornwallis that he was on his way. The British commander thought it possible that Greene had recrossed the Dan and was south of the river, so Tarleton was dispatched to escort the Loyalists to Hillsborough. Tarleton had a skirmish with Patriot militia and learned from prisoners that a force of Continentals was in the vicinity. He immediately sent a message to Pyle urging him to hurry his march.

The Loyalist colonel and his men were caught up in the adventure of going to war and so "thought fit to pay visits to their kindred and acquaintances before they repaired to the British camp. Inspired by whiskey and the novelty of their situation, they unfortunately prolonged their excursions."[2] At last on the road to Hillsborough on February 25, Pyle sent out scouts to locate the British Legion. His men returned and reported that they had met Tarleton's command. Pyle was requested to draw up his troops to one side of the road to allow the Legion column to pass. The Loyalist colonel complied, and soon a column of green-coated cavalry was passing the militia, its commander in the lead. As the two forces reached a parallel position and the dragoon commander met Colonel Pyle, firing broke out at the rear of the column. To their consternation, the Loyalists found that they were facing Light Horse Harry Lee's dragoons—whose short green jackets were similar to those worn by Tarleton's troops. Lee's men, supported by South Carolina militia under Pickens, fell upon the hapless Loyalists. Sabers flashed and rifles fired at point-blank range. The onslaught was sudden and the surprise complete. "The conflict was quickly decided and bloody on one side only. Ninety of the royalists were killed and most of the survivors wounded. . . . in some parts of the line the cry for mercy was heard . . . but no expostulation could be admitted in a conjuncture so critical." The Americans did not lose a single man. It was a massacre to match Tarleton's slaughter of Buford's men at the Waxhaws nine months before. Lee justified his action on the ground that the first rule of war "is to take care of your own safety, and our safety was not compatible with that of the supplicants, until disabled to offend."[3]

Light Horse Harry may have hoped to preserve for posterity a reputation for chivalry, but such notions had little place in the grim reality of the war that was being waged in the Carolinas. "Massacre" it may have been but it was devastating to Cornwallis' hopes for assistance from Loyalist militia. Nathanael Greene thought Pyle's disaster "so happily timed, and in all probability will be productive of such happy consequences, that I cannot help congratulating you on your success."[4]

A few days later Tarleton's men ran into a body of militiamen who failed to respond to a challenge. Assuming that they were rebels, the British dragoons charged and scattered them—and found out too late that they were Loyalists. Undoubtedly they had remembered Pyle's experience and had hesitated to identify themselves. These episodes, together with the British insistence on enlisting men for eighteen months, effectively killed any chance that Cornwallis might strengthen his command with Loyalist reinforcements. The news that Greene had recrossed the Dan added to the doubts that the King's friends already had of the ability of the army to protect them. "The report of his [Greene's] advance soon made the luke-warm friends abandon the British camp. . . ."[5]

Greene had made good use of his brief sojourn in Virginia. His first need was for men to fill his ranks and for supplies. Only slightly less important was the need for remounts for his cavalry. The skill with which Lee's Legion and William Washington's dragoons had covered the retreat to the Dan confirmed Greene's conviction that cavalry was essential to the gathering of intelligence as well as screening his own movements from the enemy. He therefore importuned Governor Thomas Jefferson to allow him to requisition horses from the farms and plantations surrounding his head-quarters at Halifax Court House. Jefferson gave his approval, and Greene set William Washington to work rounding up horses. Although Washington was enjoined to treat the Virginians with courtesy and considera-tion, the howls from the countrymen were soon reverberating in the ears of the governor. Jefferson protested to Greene that "the harsh act of taking their valuable Horses by Force . . . has been frequently accompanied by defiances of civil Power . . . free People think they have a right to an Explanation of the Circumstances which give rise to the necessity under which they suffer." Greene tartly reminded the governor that "Superior Cavalry is of the greatest importance to the salvation of this Country and without them you would soon hear of detachments being cut to pieces in every quarter."

When the time came to return to North Carolina, the dragoons of Washington and Lee were superbly mounted. Said Lee of his cavalry, "Lieutenant Colonel Tarleton was obliged to use such horses as he could get. . . . The consequence was, the British dragoons were mounted upon small, weak horses: those of the Legion on stout, active horses, and kept in the highest condition. When they met, the momentum of the one must crush the other; and if the latter fled, he could not escape from his enemy, so excellently mounted."[6]

In addition to improving his cavalry force, Greene found supplies plenti-ful and even a limited amount of clothing for his ragged men. But best of all, recruits began to come into the camp at Halifax. The quality of these

Virginia units was better than the usual run of militia for several reasons. Nearly 400 of the reinforcements consisted of mountain riflemen commanded by Colonel William Campbell, the veteran of King's Mountain. General Edward Stevens, who brought in a regiment of 700 militia, was that rarity—a militia general with combat experience. He had been outraged when his first command had fled from the battlefield at Camden. He had returned to serve under Greene and had the further discomfiture to watch his second command go home when the troops' enlistment expired at the critical juncture of the retreat to the Dan. It was this group that had escorted prisoners to Virginia after Cowpens, and Stevens had gone with them. He was now back again at the head of another brigade, which, however, had a generous leavening of former Continentals. They had gone home at the expiration of their enlistments but were now turning out as militiamen to have another round with the redcoats. With Greene's 1,000 Continentals, Lee's Legion, and William Washington's cavalry, the total American force counted about 2,600 men.[7]

The reorganization of Greene's army was accomplished in an amazingly short time, once again attesting to the administrative genius of the Rhode Islander. Within four days after his precipitous crossing of the Dan, the American commander had put a scouting force south of the river. It consisted of Lee's Legion and the two companies of Maryland Continentals, plus a newly arrived regiment of South Carolina militia commanded by Andrew Pickens. Its mission was to gather intelligence and to discourage the rising of the Loyalists. How well it performed the latter assignment has already been noted.

On February 22 Greene crossed with his main army and once more organized a screening force under Colonel Otho Williams, combining the Legion with a corps of light infantry, William Washington's cavalry, and Pickens' riflemen. The army now began to shift from one encampment to another, never remaining in the same place for more than forty-eight hours. Greene and his staff were taxed to the utmost, for the movement of the troops was not revealed even to the regimental officers. Colonel William Davie, the indefatigable commissary, did not know until he was called to the commander's tent late at night where he would have to establish his depot of supplies for the next day's destination. Yet he must have the new bivouac ready by the time the army arrived at the next encampment. Brigade and regimental officers must be alert to put their troops on the road at a moment's notice.[8]

All this was in turn dependent on a constant and accurate flow of information from Williams and his scouts. To acquire intelligence meant keeping in close contact with the enemy, and clashes were frequent. Lee laid an ambush for Tarleton near Clapp's Mill on Alamance Creek on March 2, killing and wounding twenty of the British Legion before pulling his men out of danger.

Thus the two armies sparred with each other in the country around Guilford Court House. Greene's evasive action had two almost contradictory purposes. His force was not yet strong enough to risk a pitched battle with the British regulars. Yet it was necessary to keep his army in the field in order to discourage Loyalists who might turn out to assist Cornwallis. The constant marching and countermarching gave the Tories the impression that the countryside was swarming with Americans, while Greene's careful planning and skillful maneuvering kept them just out of Cornwallis' reach.[9]

✳ "We Marched . . . to Look for Lord Cornwallis" ✳

The British commander was having his troubles. His army was in severe straits for want of supplies. It was not surprising that the redcoats in their desperate search for food and forage made little effort to distinguish friend from foe. ". . . The most infamous looters" were the women accompanying his army. In an effort to control them, Cornwallis ordered them to muster with the troops, had their belongings searched for loot, and forced them to witness punishments. It was all to little purpose.[10]

Tarleton was busy trying to keep track of the rebel army in order to discover a way to bring it to battle. Time was against Cornwallis, for the longer he stayed far from a reliable source of supplies the more his army deteriorated. He was anxious to challenge the enemy, convinced that he could do so because of his faith in the quality of his veterans even if faced by superior numbers.

In the first week of March he thought he saw an opportunity. Tarleton reported that Williams had split his force and that the militia and light infantry were camped some distance apart. Cornwallis launched a sudden thrust with his main army, hoping at best to cut off Williams' command. At worst he would catch Williams napping and drive the American back on Greene's force, thereby bringing on a general engagement. He came close to success. Campbell's riflemen were surprised and driven against the banks of Reedy Fork at Wetzell's Mill. Williams recovered nimbly and with the aid of some reckless demonstrations by Lee's dragoons escaped with his command across the river with the redcoats nipping at his heels. On the north bank Williams posted a defensive line to check the pursuit, but the British formed a storming party led by Colonel James Webster's tough 23rd Regiment. As Webster led his men across the creek Harry Lee ordered some riflemen stationed in a nearby log cabin to shoot down the British commander. At musketshot range the mountain marksmen "discharged their rifles at him, one by one, each man sure of knocking him over . . . eight or nine of them emptied their guns a second time. Strange to tell . . . himself and horse were untouched. . . ."

The British drove Williams back for several miles, but this was a game at which Williams was too skilled for the enemy. It became obvious that the Americans could not be dispersed and that any chance of pinning Greene had been lost. The losses on each side were twenty-five to thirty killed and wounded.[11]

Four days later the first of the expected reinforcements began to come into Greene's camp. Two brigades of North Carolina militia and a regiment of eighteen-month troops, all commanded by Generals John Butler and Thomas Eaton and amounting to almost 1,000 men, arrived on March 10. Campbell now had about 400 mountain riflemen. One thousand Virginia militia under General Robert Lawson swelled Stevens' command to 1,700. Finally, on March 11, 550 Virginia Continentals arrived from Steuben's command in Southside Virginia. Greene now commanded between 4,600 and 5,000 troops of whom about 30 percent were Continentals. Several other units such as Campbell's men had had combat experience so that nearly 2,000 of the Americans were battle-tested. "Hitherto," said Greene, "I have been obliged to practice that by finesse, which I dare not attempt by force." But it was time to alter strategy. He was now strong enough to challenge the British. "The great advantages which would result from the action if we were victorious, and the little injury if we were otherwise, determined me to bring on an action. . . ." The army sensed that the game of hide and seek was over. Major St. George Tucker wrote his wife on March 13, "We marched yesterday to look for Lord Cornwallis. . . . We are now strong enough, I hope, to cope with him to advantage."[12]

The earl needed no encouragement from Greene. For once the British army was in almost as dire straits as the Americans. Their uniforms were in tatters, and the shortage of provisions had become serious. But the British commander had the utmost confidence in his regulars and, as the event proved, his faith was justified.

On March 14 the British were in motion. Tarleton's Legion composed the advance guard and almost immediately there was desultory skirmishing between the outriders of the two armies. It was quickly apparent that the Americans were no longer trying to stay out of the way of their enemy.

Early on the morning of the 15th Tarleton made solid contact with Lee's Legion. The American cavalry charged the British van and forced it back on the main column. Campbell's riflemen came up in support and opened fire on the brigade of the Guards. Cornwallis sent in the Welsh Fusiliers (the 33rd) and drove the rebels off. British casualties were between twenty and thirty, and Tarleton received a painful wound in his hand. By midmorning Lee's party had rejoined the main American army, which was deploying near Guilford Court House. This ground was thoroughly familiar to Greene, for he had contemplated fighting the British here several weeks before and had personally scouted the ground.[13]

The courthouse stood in a clearing on high ground at the junction of the main Salisbury road and the road that led northwest to the upper fords of the Dan River. The ground sloped gently southward in the direction from which the British would approach. There was a stretch of woodland several hundred yards to the south, then another clearing.

Shortly before the battle, Greene received a letter from Daniel Morgan. The Old Waggoner was still with Greene in spirit, and he did not hesitate to offer advice. If the militia did their duty, he said, "You will beat Cornwallis; if not he will beat you and perhaps cut your regulars to pieces. . . ." He further advised Greene to adopt the three-line tactics that had been so effective at the Cowpens, and the American commander heeded the suggestion. On the crest of the hill near the courthouse he deployed his best troops, the 4th and 5th Virginia Continentals on the right, commanded by General Huger, and the 1st and 2nd Maryland under Colonel Williams on the left. Altogether this line consisted of just over 1,400 men. Three hundred yards down the hill beyond the first clearing and straddling the road was a second line containing the Virginia militia. Lawson commanded the left wing and Stevens the right. General Stevens, determined that his Virginians should not again disgrace themselves, posted forty sharpshooters in the rear of his line with instructions to shoot any man who left his post without orders. This line contained about 1,300 men.[14]

On the far side of the wood, facing the second clearing, was the forward line made up of North Carolina militia commanded by Generals Butler and Eaton. There were few veterans in this line, and Greene informed them that they had only to deliver two fires before retreating from their position. He had also strengthened this position by posting William Washington's cavalry and Kirkwood's Delaware veterans on the right flank supported by 200 Virginia riflemen under Colonel Thomas Lynch. On the North Carolina left was Lee's Legion, about 150 cavalry and infantry, and 200 riflemen under William Campbell. This forward line was a full 500 yards in front of the second line, and the whole distance from the North Carolinians to the courthouse was almost half a mile. Thus Greene had followed Morgan's suggestion to the extent of organizing his force in successive lines of resistance. But in order to take full advantage of the terrain and ground cover he had to separate his lines so that they were too far apart to support each other.[15]

✳ "Now I Am Perfectly Easy" ✳

About noon on the 15th the British van appeared, marching up the Salisbury road. If Cornwallis had doubts about Greene making a stand they were soon dispelled by a salvo from Captain Anthony Singleton's six-pounders, which were stationed in the middle of the first line of militia.

Their fire did not disturb the British as they deliberately deployed from line of march into battle formation. To the left were the veteran redcoats of the 33rd and the 23rd with the light infantry and the jägers on the flank. Their commander was Colonel James Webster, who was the most experienced combat officer in Cornwallis' command. The left was supported by the Grenadiers and the second battalion of the Guards. The British right wing consisted of the 71st Highlanders and the German Regiment Bose, with the first battalion of the Guards in reserve. On the road between the two wings of the British line were two three-pounder guns commanded by Captain Alexander McLeod, and behind him Tarleton's Legion dragoons prepared to pursue if the enemy broke and retreated. It was a splendid sight: the red coats of the regulars intermixed with the green of the jägers on the left, Tarleton's green dragoons, the tartan kilts of the Highlanders, and the blue-coated Regiment Bose. And over all was the gleam of the bayonets with the light here and there flashing on the gorgets of the officers and an occasional saber which commanders used to direct the movement of the men. But this redoubtable line was bone weary. The men "had no provisions of any kind that day" and had marched almost twelve miles to reach the battlefield. Yet on perhaps no field of the war did the British better display their discipline and courage than at Guilford Court House.[16]

On order from Cornwallis the advance began. As the British line approached within about 150 yards of the North Carolinians they met the first militia fire—the range was too great for muskets but effective for those militiamen who had rifles. As the British advance shortened the range, at least some of the militia delivered a second fire. Sergeant Roger Lamb of the 23rd observed that "within forty yards of the enemy's line, it was perceived that their whole force had their arms presented and resting on a fence rail. . . . They were taking aim with the nicest kind of precision." The British line wavered momentarily, but Colonel Webster was immediately at their front, urging them on. The redcoats charged with the bayonet and the American line broke—but not before it had exacted a price. Captain Dugald Stuart of the 71st said that "one half of the Highlanders dropped on that spot," undoubtedly an exaggeration, but another observer noted that "the part of the British line at which they aimed looked like the scattering stalks in a wheatfield when the harvest man had passed over it with his cradle."[17]

Both Greene and Lee thought that the North Carolinians had behaved ignominiously and had fled without firing a shot, but the former was too far from the scene to see what happened and the latter did not know that Greene had ordered them to retreat after they had delivered their first fires. There is no question, however, that the men of Butler and Eaton kept going once they withdrew and that they failed to halt at the second line. In fact their losses were 3 killed, 9 wounded, and 549 missing.[18]

On the left flank of the first line Lee's Legion infantry and Campbell's

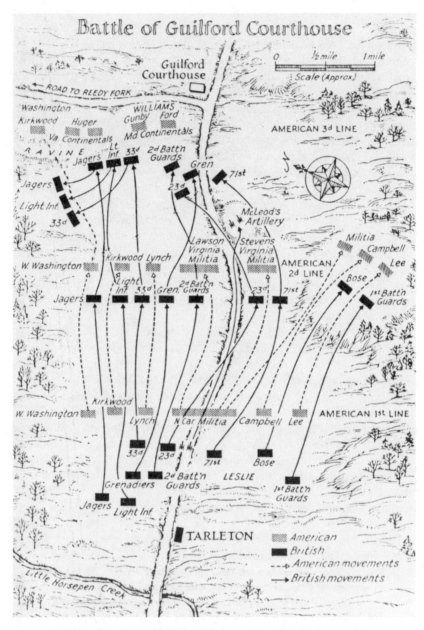

Battle of Guilford Courthouse

(*From Cornwallis,* The American Adventure *by Franklin and Mary Wickwire. Copyright 1980 by Franklin B. and Mary B. Wickwire. Reprinted by permission of Houghton Mifflin Company*)

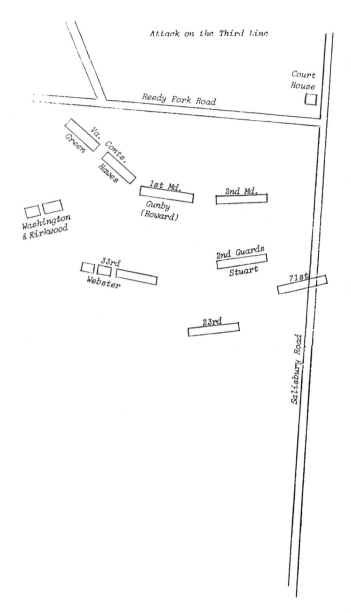

Attack on the Third Line

Court House

Reedy Fork Road

Green
Va. Conts.
Hawes

1st Md.
Gunby
(Howard)

2nd Md.

Washington
& Kirkwood

2nd Guards
Stuart

71st

33rd
Webster

23rd

Salisbury Road

Almost all accounts of the battle place the Maryland troops on the left of the
American third line, as shown in the map, with the Virginia Continentals
aligned with them to the right. If this formation is correct, the standard
accounts (Wickwire, Ward, and others) have Webster, Cornwallis' ablest
lieutenant, advancing across the front of the Virginians to attack the 1st
Maryland, thereby exposing his flank. A more likely arrangement is
suggested in the sketch above. Although Greene nowhere states exactly the
dispositions of the third line, it is logical to suppose that this formation of the
Virginia Continentals would refuse the American right to protect the flank
and also cover the line of retreat along the Reedy Fork road.

men stood firm. As the 71st Highlanders and the Regiment Bose pursued the retreating militia, they found their flank enfiladed by the deadly fire of the mountain riflemen. The Highlanders and the Germans were forced to refuse their flank on the right and drive at an oblique angle to the east. General O'Hara brought up the 1st Guards in support. There was hard fighting as this part of the British line forced the Americans back but failed to break them. The 71st resumed the advance with the rest of the British line. But the Regiment Bose and the 1st Guards on the one side and Lee's Legion and the riflemen on the other fought their way clear of the main engagement and drifted off, absorbed in a private battle all their own.[19]

This brought about a gap in the British right. Similarly, the British left had trouble with Colonel Washington's cavalry and Kirkwood's Delawares. Washington and Kirkwood fell back to the right flank of the second line of Americans. As the British continued their advance, their precise formations fell into some confusion, since the approach to the Virginians was through the woodland. To rectify the formation and strengthen the line, General Leslie sent in his reserves, the 2nd Guards and the Grenadiers, filling the gap between Webster on the left and the 71st on the right. As the British advanced toward the second line, then, Cornwallis had committed his entire reserve; his line consisted of, from left to right, the jägers, the light infantry, the 33rd, the 23rd, the Grenadiers, the 2nd Guards, and the Highlanders of the 71st. The 1st Guards and the Regiment Bose had moved off to the right of the main battle, stubbornly resisted by Lee and Campbell.[20]

At the second American line, located in the cover of the wood, the British met stiffer resistance. Stevens and Lawson took a heavy toll of the redcoats, but the right of the Virginians was gradually pushed back toward the center, although the line did not break immediately. The 33rd, the light infantry, and the jägers made no attempt to press the Virginians but moved on toward the third line at the courthouse. Once again, Washington and Kirkwood fell back to take a position on the right flank of the main line of the Continentals. Most of the fighting was now taking place between the two clearings, as Stevens and the militia still stubbornly resisted in the center. Webster and the British left suddenly found themselves clear of the woods ahead of the rest of the British line. Without waiting for support, Webster straightened his line and charged.

The Continentals waited until the British were within thirty or forty yards. Then they delivered a fire and counterattacked. The British were stunned. This was their first encounter since Camden with the Continentals—including the crack 1st Maryland—men who were not only armed with bayonets but knew how to use them. The British attack was broken, and the redcoats reeled back in confusion.[21]

This was the point at which Greene might have won the battle. If he had attacked as Webster fell back, he might have cracked Cornwallis' line wide open at the moment the rest of the British line was still engaged with the Virginia militia in the woods. But Greene had few reserves, and he was keeping in mind strategy as well as tactics. The strategy was to punish the enemy without risking the existence of the Southern Army.

By now the battle had lasted more than an hour. As Stevens finally gave way in the center—and was himself carried from the field with a bullet in his thigh—the full weight of the British attack was thrown against the Continentals of the third line. Lieutenant McLeod had moved his guns up the road to support the final drive. The attack in the center was headed by Colonel Duncan Stuart and his 2nd Guards battalion. Like Webster, he did not wait for support. But unlike Webster, he did not meet with resistance. The 2nd Maryland, composed mostly of recruits, was a green outfit containing few veterans. Scarcely firing a shot, they turned and ran. Stuart and the Guards drove at the gap in the Maryland line as the Grenadiers and the 71st began to emerge from the woods.[22]

Now an accident of position presented the Americans with a fine opportunity. Colonel John Gunby, who had led the charge against Webster, was withdrawing his 1st Maryland and Delaware troops to their original position on the hill. With the headlong advance of the Guards Gunby found himself on the flank of the advancing British. As he swung his men around into position, his horse was shot down, pinning its rider, and Colonel Howard assumed command. At about this time William Washington saw the same opportunity. Sabers flashed as his dragoons stormed into the British ranks. As the Grenadiers and the Guards staggered from this blow, Howard slammed the 1st Maryland in after them. Most of the British right was now engaged, and the Maryland and Virginia Continentals steadily pushed them back. In the midst of the melee Colonel Stuart was cut down, and with his fall the redcoats faltered.

Cornwallis, observing this critical action from a point near McLeod's guns, ordered the battery to open fire with grape. General O'Hara, who had been wounded and was nearby, remonstrated—McLeod would be firing into his own men. The grim British commander was not moved. The blasts of grape tore into the ranks of the Guards where they struggled with the 1st Maryland, and the American attack was broken. By this time the laggard Highlanders were up, and Webster had pulled together the scattered ranks of the 33rd on the left. As the reordered British line advanced to renew the attack, Greene ordered a retreat.[23]

In the meantime the fight on the extreme left of the American line had continued as the British pressed Campbell and Lee's Legion. When the 1st battalion of the Guards broke off to rejoin the main British line, Lee also pulled out his force, concerned because he had no contact with the American line to his right. This left Campbell alone to deal with the Germans. Light Horse Harry said only that "every obstacle now removed, Lee pressed forward, followed by Campbell, and joined his horse close to

John Eager Howard (Independence National Historical Park Collection)

Guilford Court House." But William Campbell was furious. He insisted that Lee had pulled out prematurely. Toward the end of the battle, Tarleton led his Legion to the assistance of the Germans, and according to the dragoon commander, "The enemy gave way on all sides, and were routed with confusion and loss." Tarleton undoubtedly exaggerated, for it was about this time that Greene ordered a general retreat. But Colonel Campbell was so offended by what he regarded as Lee's defection that he left the army a few days later.[24]

Greene's withdrawal was orderly. Although Cornwallis ordered a pursuit, he admitted that the Continentals "went off by the Reedy Fork [road], beyond which it was not in my power to follow them." Indeed, Greene halted his movement only three miles from the battlefield to rest his men and collect stragglers. Then the exhausted troops resumed their march to one of their old camps at Speedwell's Iron Works on Troublesome Creek.[25] The American losses had been severe: 261 killed and wounded from the ranks of the Continentals; 361 killed, wounded, and missing from the Virginia militia; and 562 from the North Carolina militia. Of the militia casualties 846, or about 91 percent, were missing.[26]

Cornwallis was in no position to pursue. His men had marched all morning with little or nothing to eat and had fought a long and wearing battle which had ranged over a distance of half a mile. Most serious was the fact that of 2,000 regulars who had faced the enemy that day 515, or more than one-quarter, were killed or wounded on the field at Guilford Court House. Almost as serious was the loss of 27 officers and 28 noncommissioned officers. Two of his finest combat officers were gone—Duncan Stuart dead on the field and James Webster mortally wounded.[27]

Lord Cornwallis had paid an exorbitant price for his victory.

Nathanael Greene had not had his clothes off for six weeks. Since the night when he had set off in the mud and rain for Morgan's camp on the Catawba, he had rarely slept more than a few hours at a time. He had frequently shared the mean rations of the troops, even sending his aides among the campfires to beg food for the commanding general. A story that became a legend in the army related that Greene came upon one of his officers asleep and gently reprimanded him. The officer replied, "Why, general, I knew that you were awake." There is little evidence that he possessed the charisma of a Morgan or a Lee. The few times that he attempted to impress the troops with speeches were not notably successful. Greene, in short, was not beloved by his men. But they had marched long marches for him and they had done hard fighting. So he had earned what a good general must earn from his men—their respect and trust.[28]

On the night following the battle at Guilford Court House he collapsed from exhaustion. Or perhaps the iron will had at last relaxed, for he had achieved his purpose.

Greene had damaged Cornwallis so severely that the British command was no longer capable of acting offensively. The battle at Guilford Court House was decisive in determining the ultimate outcome of the war in the Carolinas, and Greene knew it. "I have never felt an easy moment since the enemy crossed the Catawba until the defeat of the 15th," he wrote three days after the battle. "But now I am perfectly easy, persuaded that it is out of the enemy's power to do us any great injury. Indeed, I think they will retire. . . ."[29]

Just as perceptive as Greene, apparently, were the Loyalists. Cornwallis might report a great victory to his superiors in New York and London—he persistently credited Greene with having more than 7,000 men—but unwittingly or not his own words revealed how hollow his victory had been.

> The principal reason for undertaking the Winter's campaign were, the difficulty of a defensive War in South Carolina, and the hopes that our friends in North Carolina, who were said to be very numerous, would make good their promises of assembling and taking an Active part with us, in endeavoring to re-establish His Majesty's government. Our experience has shown that their numbers were not so great as had been represented and that their friendship was only passive. For we have received little assistance from them since our arrival in this province, and altho' I gave the strongest and most publick assurance that after refitting and depositing our Sick and Wounded, I should return to the upper country, not above two hundred have been prevailed upon to follow us either as Provincials or Militia.[30]

Thus ended the critical phase of the southern campaign. Cornwallis' vision of the strategy necessary to restore the colonies to the empire was almost as limited as that of Sir Henry Clinton and Lord George Germain. He had harried his opponent from one end of the Carolinas to the other, and, except for Tarleton's gaffe at the Cowpens, he had driven every American force he had faced from the field. His strenuous offensive had surpassed any effort previously conducted by the British command. Yet he had completely underestimated Nathanael Greene. British victories in the field had meant nothing in the face of the American's clever maneuvering and the stubborn resistance of the partisans.

So Cornwallis turned his back on the Carolinas and started on another march, a march that would finally take him to a village on the Chesapeake Bay called Yorktown.

✳ ✳ ✳ ✳ ✳ ✳ ✳ ✳ ✳ ✳
✳ ✳ ✳ ✳ ✳ ✳ ✳ ✳ ✳ ✳
✳ ✳ ✳ ✳ ✳ ✳ ✳ ✳ ✳ ✳
✳ ✳ ✳ ✳ ✳ ✳ ✳ ✳ ✳ ✳

12. The Reconquest: Hobkirk's Hill

It has been said that all great generals owe their success in some degree to good luck. The genius of Nathanael Greene lay in the fact that his strategic objectives relied less on good fortune than on planning that could be adapted to any contingency.

Six weeks before the battle of Guilford Court House, when he had joined Morgan's command and learned that Cornwallis was stripping his army to bare necessities, he remarked simply, "Then he is ours." To General Huger he was only a little more explicit: ". . . I am not without hopes of ruining Lord Cornwallis, if he persists in his mad scheme of pushing through the country."[1] Certainly Greene would have liked to defeat the Englishman in battle and destroy his army. But a calculated appraisal told him that he had only to exploit the basic logistical problem that any enemy force encountered when it ventured too far into the interior of North America. Guilford Court House was indeed a devastating blow to Cornwallis, but even before the battle his men had not eaten for twenty-four hours, and they did not get their next meal until the following day. His Lordship's own words attest to the condition of his command: "With a third of my Army sick and wounded . . . the remainder without Shoes, and worn down with fatigue, I thought it was time to look for some place of rest and refitment. . . ." He was almost 200 miles from Wilmington on the coast and nearly 150 miles from Camden. Small wonder that Greene felt "perfectly easy" for he had indeed "ruined" Cornwallis' army as an effective striking force.[2]

Perhaps the Englishman did not fully realize that the initiative had now passed to the Americans. As he had done so often in the past, Cornwallis made assumptions about what Greene *would* do instead of what he *could* do.

✳ Greene Takes the Offensive ✳

Lord Cornwallis was now faced with a decision as to where his next move would take him. There were two sets of considerations, one purely military and the other having to do with how he was to retrieve his reputation and bring about a successful conclusion to his performance as an independent commander.

Strategically the earl was in the worst situation he had been in since the beginning of the campaign. His army was "without tents or covering against the climate, and often without provisions. . . . This whole Country is so totally destitute of subsistence, that forage is not nearer than nine miles, and the Soldiers have been two days without bread." Now it was Cornwallis who was anxious to avoid another pitched battle and Greene who entertained thoughts of seeking out the enemy. (In the American camp a story circulated that the general was ready to sell "another field at the same price.")³

For Cornwallis to reunite with Rawdon at Camden meant a march that involved a series of river crossings during the continuing spring rains. Intelligence reports indicated that Marion and Sumter were active in the country beyond the Pee Dee so that with Greene pressing his pursuit the British would be assailed front and rear. The alternative would be a retreat down the Cape Fear River to Wilmington, where he could dispose of his sick and wounded and refit his ragged army. To do so would not only be disastrous to the Loyalist cause in North Carolina but would leave the entire burden of the defense of the Carolinas upon the force at Camden under Lord Rawdon and the scattered posts of the backcountry.

Could he thus abandon Rawdon? He could: "The immense distance from hence to Camden, the difficulty of subsistence on the road and the impracticability of the passage of the Pee Dee against an opposing enemy would render a direct movement totally useless to Lord Rawdon, and this Corps might be lost in the attempt." He professed to believe that Greene would follow him to the southeast down the Cape Fear and that even if he moved north into Virginia his move would draw Greene away from South Carolina and prevent him from threatening Rawdon.⁴

When the British finally moved from the battlefield at Guilford Court House on March 18, they left seventy of their wounded to be taken care of by the Americans. Cornwallis moved toward Cross Creek (modern Fayetteville), where he hoped that Colonel Balfour, the commandant at Charleston, had provided a store of supplies from Wilmington. His ragged, hungry army looted indiscriminately, killing whatever enthusiasm the appearance of the redcoats might have inspired. "The whole country was struck with terror; almost every man quit his habitation leaving his family and property to the mercy of the merciless enemies."[5]

As the British moved down the Haw toward the Cape Fear, Greene followed as fast as the debilitated state of his army permitted. He hoped perhaps to catch Cornwallis as he crossed to the south bank of the Cape Fear, but in addition to the exhaustion of the Continentals other obstacles plagued him. The Virginia militia had served out their time and were about to go home. It had been expected that they would be replaced by new levies that Steuben was raising in Virginia. But the descent of Arnold and Phillips on the Chesapeake caused Governor Jefferson and the state council to withhold these precious replacements. Although Steuben protested mightily and Greene himself remonstrated, the politicians had their way. The logic of long-range strategy that would result in the reconquest of the Carolinas failed to impress the Virginia authorities, who must cope with the present threat of an enemy invader.[6]

Cornwallis reached Cross Creek only to find that supplies had not been sent up the river to meet him. His hungry army moved on downriver toward the coast, sweeping up everything in its path. Despite the efforts of the British commander and his officers, the soldiers seized horses, cattle, forage, and even the clothes of the inhabitants. The women camp followers swooped in behind the troops, "a swarm of beings (not better than harpies). . . . who followed . . . in the character of officers' and soldiers' wives. . . . They were generally mounted on the best horses and side saddles, dressed in the finest and best clothes that could be taken from the inhabitants." The command finally arrived at Wilmington on April 7.[7]

Cornwallis now revealed the strategy that had been maturing in his mind for some time. Clinton had already become disillusioned with Cornwallis. Realizing this the earl had been corresponding directly with Lord Germain in London. The American Secretary had become increasingly preoccupied with the Chesapeake, and it was in compliance with dispatches from London—and much against his better judgment—that Clinton had been feeding forces into the bay area. First, there had been Arnold's raid in December and then the dispatch of additional regiments under General Phillips. The force on the Chesapeake now numbered almost 5,500 men.[8]

The answer to Cornwallis' dilemma was obvious. He had long been obsessed with the "domino strategy." As early as January he had been convinced that the invasion of North Carolina would bring about a collapse of resistance in South Carolina. It followed that an invasion of Virginia would strike at the source of Greene's supplies and reinforcements and that the safety of the Carolinas—the primary concern of Clinton's instructions—would be assured. Cornwallis' own force would be swelled by the troops already in Virginia, and he would then be able to sweep all before him. If this strategy made Clinton unhappy, it would surely find approval in the eyes of Lord Germain. The southern campaign would be brought to a successful conclusion, and, not incidentally, the Earl of Cornwallis would be the hero of the hour.

But Cornwallis' vision went beyond the invasion of Virginia. In a dispatch to General Phillips, he proposed a drastic change in the whole focus of British strategy: "If we mean an offensive war in America we must abandon New York and bring our whole force into Virginia, we must then have a stake to fight for, and a successful battle may give us America . . . let us quit the Carolinas (which cannot be held defensively while Virginia can so easily be armed against us). . . . " His decision made, Cornwallis dared not wait for approval from Clinton in New York. On April 25 he left Wilmington, moving north toward Virginia. But as he did so he figuratively looked back over his shoulder, and what he saw might well have made him hesitate had he not been so obdurately committed to his new strategy.[9]

Greene followed Cornwallis only as far as Ramsey's Mill on the Deep River, but he sent Harry Lee and General John Lillington's North Carolina militia to trail the British "at such a distance as you may think necessary to mask our real design." Greene now made his momentous decision. It would be some time before Cornwallis could again take the field (Greene was not yet aware of the decision to move into Virginia). He therefore determined to return to South Carolina. Although the British still had some 8,000 men in the state, they were scattered in detachments from Augusta on the Savannah River to Georgetown. By moving rapidly on these outposts, Greene hoped to defeat them in detail. If Lord Rawdon, now commanding in Cornwallis' absence, gathered in his detachments to oppose Greene's army, Ninety Six, Augusta, Camden, and the rest of the posts would be stripped of their defenses and exposed to Marion, Pickens, and Sumter.[10]

An integral part of Greene's plan for reconquest was his partisan commanders. When Pickens requested that he be allowed to return to South Carolina before Guilford Court House, Greene had ordered him to place himself under Sumter's command. He hoped not only to use these forces to suppress the Tories but also to raise enough militia so that, when the time came that he must test his strength against Rawdon, he could add these forces to his command and thereby gain a decisive numerical superiority.[11]

By the end of March, Pickens was back in South Carolina, where he hoped to join the Georgian Elijah Clarke and conduct operations between Ninety Six and Augusta. When Pickens caught up with Clarke, the Indian fighter was fresh from a victory over the Tories. Clarke had overtaken a party of the enemy commanded by the Tory raider Major James Dunlap at Beattie's Mill on the Little River. With 180 mounted men at his back, the Georgian had charged the enemy, driven off the dragoons, and surrounded the infantry, killing thirty-four.

Dunlap was among those captured. Almost as notorious as "Bloody Bill"

Cuningham and Thomas Browne, Dunlap had burned Pickens' home in 1780, thereby goading Pickens into renouncing his parole. The two commanders decided to send the prisoners to Gilbert Town, where they would be held until they could be sent on to Virginia. Somewhere on the way Dunlap was murdered. "A set of men chiefly unknown except one Cobb, an over Mountain Man forced the Guard and shot him," reported Pickens to Greene. Pickens also reported the episode to Colonel Cruger, the Loyalist commander at Ninety Six, remarking that Americans regarded the murder with "horror and detestation" but noting that it might have been the result of "the many barbarous massacres committed by those calling themselves [Tory] officers on our people after their capture."

If anything the partisan war was becoming even more desperate. When Patriots and Loyalists clashed, "quarter was seldom given." In the affair at Beattie's Mill in which thirty-four Tories were killed, the Americans suffered no casualties at all. "The country here is in great distress," observed Pickens, "chiefly broken up for want of assistance by the Enemy's marauding parties, and unless something can shortly be done for them I am afraid they will in great measure altogether quit these parts. . . ." On March 31 Cruger sortied from Ninety Six with 500 regulars and Tories in an attempt to establish a strong point on Fair Forest River, but the threat from Pickens and Clarke turned him back. The Patriots now had loose control over the area between Ninety Six and Augusta, but small Tory raiding parties continued to terrorize the countryside.[12]

When Cornwallis heard of Greene's move, he was not only surprised but seemingly offended by his opponent's unorthodox strategy: "Greene took advantage of my being obliged to come to this place [Wilmington], and has marched into South Carolina."[13]

A few days later, Colonel Lee was ordered to break off his pursuit of Cornwallis and find the Swamp Fox, Francis Marion. The combined force moved against Fort Watson, located on the Santee just below its junction with the Congaree. Fort Watson was a small stockade located on a slight elevation surrounded by a formidable abatis. It was defended by a combined force of about 130 Tories and regulars. The commander of the fort, Colonel John Watson, had taken most of his force on a raid. He clashed with Marion some weeks earlier and had retreated to Georgetown. He had, however, been reinforced and was on his way to join Rawdon. The situation of the Americans was awkward. Lee and Marion vastly outnumbered the slender garrison of the fort but had no artillery to breach the abatis and stockade. The first move was to cut off the fort's water supply, which came from a nearby lake, and this was easily done. But the garrison commander countered by sinking a well.

The only means of reducing the fort without heavy losses seemed to be to starve out the defenders. A siege, however, would be too protracted for it would allow Watson and his superior force to come to the fort's relief. The answer to this dilemma was supplied by a South Carolina militia colonel named Hezekiah Maham. Maham proposed to construct and raise a tower from which riflemen could fire into the interior of the fort. It took five days to cut and fit the logs. On the night of April 22 they were carried into position, and the prefabricated structure was raised. At the top of the tower a platform with a log parapet had been built, and from this protected position riflemen poured a deadly fire into the fort as two assault parties attacked the walls. The rifle fire prevented the defenders from manning the walls, and the garrison quickly surrendered. The Americans lost two killed and six wounded. The fall of Fort Watson punched the first hole in Rawdon's line of communication with Charleston.[14]

In the meantime, Greene had been on the march toward Camden, still hoping to surprise the British. Cornwallis in Wilmington had attempted to alert his subordinate, but "my expresses to Lord Rawdon . . . warning him of the possibility of such a movement have all failed. . . ."[15] Greene's men were reasonably well fed thanks to the indefatigable Carrington, who prepared provisions in advance of the march. For the first time in weeks, the army had rum, a gill a day for the men and a quart for the officers. The men had time to wash their clothes and clean their arms but even so the march was swift. The little army traveled 130 miles in thirteen days, including a three-day delay at the crossing of the Pee Dee.

Despite this rapid movement, it was impossible for the American force to go unnoticed, and some time before Greene's arrival on April 19, Rawdon was informed of his approach.[16]

✴ Hobkirk's Hill ✴

Francis Lord Rawdon was a scion of the Irish nobility. At the outbreak of the war he was only twenty-one years old. His family had secured him a commission in the army when he was sixteen, but he had interrupted his military duties to study at Eton and Oxford. He came to America in 1774 with the 5th Regiment and distinguished himself at the battle of Bunker Hill. He continued to perform brilliantly as a combat officer and by 1778 had risen to the rank of lieutenant colonel and became adjutant general of the army when Clinton assumed command. It was perhaps inevitable that Rawdon, a man of forthright honesty and integrity, failed to get along with the commander in chief and found administrative duty "most irksome to me."

Clinton had noticed that many of the Americans who were willing to enlist in the British forces were recent immigrants from Europe, especially from Ireland. To induce more of such people to enlist, Clinton appealed to "the national attachment of the Irish by inviting them into a regiment whose officers should all be from that country, and placing at its head a nobleman of popular character and ability." Lord Rawdon was selected to raise the Volunteers of Ireland, and it soon became one of the outstanding provincial corps. Rawdon proved himself to be one of the ablest of Cornwallis' subordinates, and despite his youth he had obviously earned his commander's confidence.

Rawdon was tall, dark, and vigorous, reputed to be the ugliest officer in the British army. But he is said to have possessed a genial manner and the ability to command the loyalty and trust of his men. With Cornwallis' departure for Virginia, Rawdon assumed command of the British forces in the Carolinas.[17]

Greene moved into a position north of Camden on April 19—six years to the day after the battles of Lexington and Concord. He had under his command two regiments of Continentals from Virginia and two from Maryland, a total of about 1,200 men. In addition, there were 250 North Carolina militia, William Washington's cavalry of fewer than 100 men, Kirkwood's light infantry, and 40 artillerymen. The total American force was just over 1,500 men.

Greene located his camp on Hobkirk's Hill, a sandy ridge about a mile and a half north of Camden. The ridge ran east and west, its eastern end dropping off into a swamp bordering Pine Tree Creek. The western end was heavily forested with second growth timber and underbrush. The road from Camden to the Waxhaw settlements ran north from the town and rose to the center of Hobkirk's Hill. Along it on each side was an open area although the plain was covered with thickets. Only near the town was there a real clearing with a cluster of cabins known as Logtown. The logical approach to the town (or from the town to Greene's position) was along the Waxhaws road and the cleared ground to the east of the road. Since it was difficult to see the approaches from the summit, Greene ordered his men to make their camp with the regiments arranged in the order of his planned defensive line. He also sent out heavy patrols to the west to insure against surprise from that quarter. Thus if the enemy moved swiftly to make a surprise attack it would have to be along the road and his men had only to take up their arms and fall into ranks to form a battle line.[18]

Both commanders were expecting reinforcements. Colonel Watson and 500 men had been detached from Rawdon's command to hunt down Marion and his men. Greene expected that the Swamp Fox, reinforced by Lee's Legion, would be able to deal with Watson at least to the extent of delaying his junction with Rawdon. He was not disappointed for Marion and Lee forced Watson to detour to the crossings of the upper Santee. Greene was also expecting the South Carolina partisans of Thomas Sumter. But "Sumter refuses to obey my orders, and carries off with him all the active force of this unhappy State on rambling, predatory excursions, unconnected with the operations of the army."[19]

Greene therefore did not have a large enough force to bottle up Rawdon

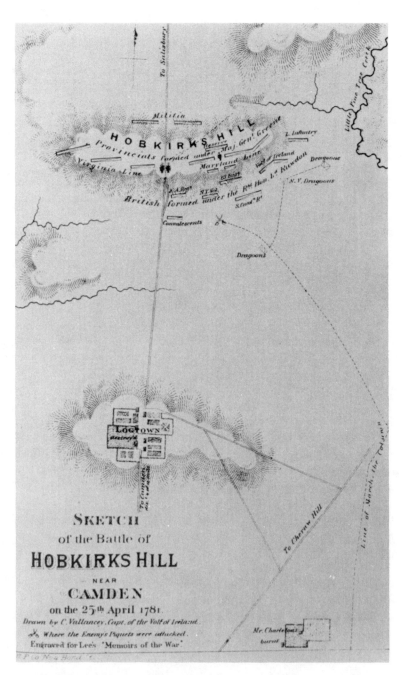

SKETCH
of the Battle of
HOBKIRKS HILL

NEAR

CAMDEN
on the 25ᵗʰ April 1781.
Drawn by C. Vallancey, Capt. of the Volᵗ of Ireland.
Where the Enemys Piquets were attacked.
Engraved for Lee's "Memoirs of the War".

(*From Henry Lee,* Memoirs of the War in the Southern Department
of the United States, *New York: University Publishing Company, 1869;
reprint edition,* The American Revolution in the South,
New York: Arno Press, 1969)

in Camden and starve him into submission. His only hope was that Rawdon would move to the attack and give Greene an opportunity to defeat him in open battle. Perhaps hoping to provoke the Irishman into action, Greene extended his picket line some distance toward Camden and ordered out Robert Kirkwood and his little band of Delaware Continentals to probe Logtown.

On the day after the army encamped, Kirkwood advanced toward Camden under cover of darkness. By midnight he had gotten "full possession of the place [Logtown], a scattering firing was kept all night, and at sunrise next morning had a smart schirmaze, Beat in the Enemy, about two hours afterwards had a Very agreeable Sight of the Advance [works] of the Army." (Since leaving Guilford Court House thirty-three days before, Kirkwood and his light troops had marched 311 miles.) The next day Kirkwood and William Washington conducted a raid west of Camden, "Burnt a House in one of the Enemy's Redoubts . . . took 40 hourses & 50 Head of cattle & returned to Camp."[20]

It is doubtful if these annoyances had much effect on Rawdon's plans. The British commander might be young in years, but he was every bit as battle-tested as his opponent. But Rawdon had several worries. He was concerned that Watson's force had not come to his support. Moreover, the fall of Fort Watson and the presence of Marion and Lee along his line of communication to Charleston threatened his source of supplies, and the force at Camden was none too well provisioned. Rawdon concluded that he must either inflict a crushing defeat on Greene or abandon his post and fall back toward the coast. Camden was the linchpin in the line of British garrisons. To leave it in the hands of the Americans was to threaten Augusta and Ninety Six as well as the minor posts that gave the British a grip on the Carolina backcountry.

On the night of April 25 Rawdon received some welcome intelligence. An American deserter came into the lines and informed the British commander that Greene had sent his guns to the rear and was short of supplies. Both of these bits of information were incorrect, for Carrington was bringing up supplies, and, although Greene had sent a good deal of his baggage back to Lynch's Creek, he still had artillery. The deserter did, however, give a correct account of Greene's numbers and troop dispositions. Rawdon decided to attack.[21]

The British advance took an odd form, dictated by Rawdon's hope for surprise. To achieve it he had to move swiftly over ground where underbrush and thickets concealed his approach. But the concealment also prevented him from deploying his men in line of battle so that the British approach was along a rather narrow front. Three regiments were at the head of the column, the 63rd Regiment on the right, the New York Volunteers in the center, and the King's American Regiment (Fanning's

Regiment) on the left. The line was supported on the right by the Volunteers of Ireland and on the left by a regiment of "convalescents," presumably walking wounded. The reserve was composed of the South Carolina Provincial Regiment and the New York Dragoons.

The Americans had just received their first full ration of food early on the morning of the 25th. Those who had cooked and eaten their meal were busy washing clothes and cleaning weapons. Greene had just settled down for a cup of tea about ten o'clock when shots sounded from the picket line.

Kirkwood immediately advanced his light infantry to the support of the pickets. The Delaware men with the pickets fought a sharp withdrawing action; "his men behaved with a great deal of bravery. . . ."[22] The delay allowed Greene's men to fall into ranks and form a line of battle. To the east of the Waxhaws road the 1st and 2nd Maryland Continentals, commanded respectively by Colonel John Gunby and Colonel Benjamin Ford, formed the American left wing commanded by Colonel Williams. On the other side of the road General Huger commanded the right wing composed of Richard Campbell's 4th Virginia Continentals and Samuel Hawes' 5th Virginia. The reserve consisted of 250 North Carolina militia and William Washington's cavalry. Colonel Charles Harrison posted his guns in the road, masked from the enemy's view by the front ranks of Hawes' Virginians.

As Rawdon advanced up the slope and came within range, the front rank of the Americans stepped clear and Harrison's guns opened with grape. Noting Rawdon's narrow front, Greene ordered the entire front line to charge with the bayonet, believing that his more extended line would overlap the British and present Ford on the left and Campbell on the right with an opportunity to flank the enemy. William Washington's dragoons were ordered to make a wide circuit and attack the enemy from the rear.

Rawdon quickly adjusted to Greene's maneuver, deploying his front rank to the right and left and bringing his rear regiments up to fill the gap in his center. Nevertheless, the blasts of grape and the determined advance of the Continentals caused the British to "begin to give way on all sides, and their left absolutely to retreat." At this point, the most dependable of Greene's men, the veteran 1st Maryland, fell into confusion. As this part of the American line advanced, there was a slight delay in the execution of the order by the companies on the left so that they lagged behind the rest of the regiment. Gunby made the fatal mistake of ordering the advanced elements to halt until the line was straightened. Then Captain William Beatty, who commanded the advance companies, was shot down, and the men faltered. Gunby ordered the entire regiment to fall back in order to reform. This added to the confusion and the regiment broke and retreated. The confusion spread. Colonel Ford, commanding the 2nd Maryland, was shot down. That regiment hesitated and then began to withdraw. Campbell's

Francis Lord Rawdon (Emmet Collection, Engraving by W. Faden, Prints Division, The New York Public Library, Astor, Lenox and Tilden Foundations)

Virginians on the right also broke. Hawes' men were the only ones who remained steady, and their stout behavior prevented the retreat from becoming a rout. By this time the American formations were in utter disorder and Greene was forced to order a general retirement. Harrison's six-pounders were brought off only after a desperate rear guard action in which, it was said, General Greene himself dismounted and helped the men at the drag ropes. Nearly fifty men were killed at the guns, most of them by Captain John Coffin's New York dragoons, before Washington's men arrived to drive them off.

Perhaps the most signal failure of the battle had been Washington's. His wide circuit had brought him into Logtown, where Rawdon's surgeons and commissary troops were drawn up. Instead of driving on against the rear of Rawdon's regiments, the dragoons paused to gather up 200 prisoners. So encumbered—Washington's command counted only about eighty men—they continued their march and arrived after the crisis of the battle had passed.

Greene retreated in good order, and late in the afternoon he sent Kirkwood and Washington back to Hobkirk's Hill. Only Coffin's dragoons occupied the battlefield, and they were ambushed and driven off. The Americans collected the wounded and stragglers and returned to their camp on the old Camden battleground.

The Americans lost 25 killed, including 7 officers, 108 wounded, and 136 missing. The British losses were 258, of whom 38 were killed. One officer was killed and 13 were wounded.[23]

It was a day that would have vexed the most even-tempered of commanders. Greene was furious at the failure of his elite regiments, the Maryland Continentals, and his anger was focused on Gunby. "The troops were not to blame in the Camden affair; Gunby was the sole cause of the defeat; and I found him much more blameable afterwards, then I represented him in my public letters."[24] Gunby asked for a court-martial, and Greene immediately approved, naming General Huger, Colonel Harrison, and Colonel Washington to the board. The court found that "Colonel Gunby's spirit and activity were unexceptionable. But his order for the regiment to retire, which broke the line, was extremely improper and unmilitary, and in all probability the only cause why we did not obtain a complete victory."[25]

"The only cause?" This verdict by both Greene and the court ignores at least two other factors. The first was Greene's decision to attack Rawdon's advancing line. Having an advantage in numbers of almost three to two and the additional weight of Harrison's artillery, Greene would have been better advised to receive Rawdon's attack, inflict as much damage as possible, and then counterattack. In fact, Greene had never displayed a great deal of tactical brilliance. A master of strategy, he had been consistently outfought on the field of battle. He had avoided serious error and had always been guided by the overriding consideration that he must preserve his slender force from any situation that might destroy it. Hobkirk's Hill was therefore something of an aberration since he had committed himself to the tactical offensive.

Another factor, oddly overlooked by the American commander, was the failure of Washington's dragoons. The Virginian had been forced by the broken ground and other obstacles to make a wide circuit to get in position in the British rear. But once in that position he had several alternatives. One was to fall on Rawdon's lightly guarded baggage and stores and destroy them. The other was to press immediately toward the fighting and fall on the rear of the British line. Granted that his force was small, nonetheless a sharp blow, which Washington was capable of delivering, might well have been decisive. Instead, he had encumbered himself with prisoners, even ordering some of them to be mounted behind his men as they finally rode toward the fighting. Yet Washington's lapse was ignored by Greene, who only remarked on the "extraordinary exertions of the cavalry commanded by Lieutenant Colonel Washington."[26]

There was one other failure that Greene did comment on. This was the failure of reinforcements which he had confidently expected and which would have given him such overwhelming superiority that Rawdon's force would have been destroyed. One source of reinforcements was Sumter, whom Greene had ordered to join him before his move to Camden. But Sumter had other ideas, the principal one being to avoid placing himself directly under Greene's command. Colonel Davie, the tireless commissary officer who conferred daily with the general, described Greene's reaction: "General Greene was deeply disgusted with the conduct of General Sumter, who had repeatedly refused to obey his express and urgent orders to join him before Camden. . . ."[27]

The other source of disappointment was the failure to receive reinforcements promised by the state authorities. "The 2,000 Virginia militia I have been expecting to join us have not come out, nor can I learn when they will. . . . Maryland has neglected us altogether; not a man has joined us from that state since I have been in the department."[28]

Yet despite these disappointments Greene soon recovered his usual optimism. Rumors that Cornwallis was returning to the Carolinas instead of invading Virginia caused some alarm, and Greene made plans for such a contingency, but "I am rather inclined to think," he wrote Sumter on May 6, "that he will leave everything here, and move northward. I am led to entertaining this opinion from its being the original plan, and from the earl's being too proud to relinquish his object."[29]

On May 7 Watson finally eluded Marion and Lee and reached Camden. Hobkirk's Hill had not greatly improved Rawdon's situation. Only a week earlier, Colonel Henry Hampton, at the head of a detachment of Sumter's men, overran the guard at Friday's Ferry on the Santee, killing a dozen of the enemy. With Rawdon's line of communications threatened and his supplies dwindling, Watson's reinforcement barely made up for the British losses of April 25. Desperation forced Rawdon to the offensive, and the moment Watson arrived the Irishman took the field to seek a conclusive engagement with Greene. There followed a series of moves and counter-moves as the British commander tried to maneuver into a favorable position. When Greene finally made a stand, Rawdon "found it everywhere so strong, that I could not hope to force it without suffering such a Loss, as must have crippled my Force for any future Enterprize . . . [and] I could not hope that Victory would give us any Advantage. . . ."

Two days later, he began the evacuation of Camden, burning all the supplies he could not take with him and destroying much of the village. Accompanying the British were "Militia who had been with us in Camden . . . also the well affected Neighbours on our Route, together with the Wives, Children, Negroes and Baggage of almost all of them." Rawdon left behind thirty of his men who were too ill to be moved. At Nelson's Ferry he was met by Colonel Balfour, the British commandant at Charleston. Both officers agreed that "the whole interior Country had revolted" and that the defenses of Charleston (where "the disaffection of the Towns People showed itself in a thousand Instances") had deteriorated to the point that the city could not be defended against a major attack. Rawdon therefore continued his withdrawal to Monck's Corner, a bare thirty miles north of the city. From there he sent dispatches to the garrison at Ninety Six ordering its commander, Colonel John Cruger, to abandon the post and go to the assistance of the British post at Augusta.[30]

✶ The War of Posts ✶

Following Rawdon's withdrawal, the countryside was immediately swarming with partisan forces. Sumter, pursuing his independent course, moved against Fort Granby (present-day Columbia) but found it too strongly defended. He then turned on Orangeburg, fifty miles to the south, and by demonstrating before that post with his men and artillery induced eighty-five Tories and regulars of the garrison to surrender. This was on May 11.[31]

Meanwhile, Marion and Lee had laid siege to Fort Motte, one of the principal depots along the supply route from Camden to Charleston. Located just above the confluence of the Wateree and the Congaree, its principal feature was a large house belonging to a Patriot widow, Mrs. Rebecca Motte. It was defended by 150 infantry and was surrounded by a ditch reinforced by a strong abatis. After two days of digging parallels and saps, the Americans were alarmed by the news that Rawdon was on his way to relieve the garrison. Marion and Lee decided that they must resort to the old Indian stratagem of burning the house by using fire arrows. When they regretfully informed Mrs. Motte of their decision, the widow herself furnished them with bow and arrows. The house was set afire, and the garrison soon showed the white flag.

For once, this dark, ugly war was relieved by a spark of old-fashioned chivalry. The British officers were paroled and invited to dine with their captors. Mrs. Motte presided over a "sumptuous dinner" during which the hostess conducted herself "with ease, vivacity, and good sense; . . . the engaging amiability of her manners, left it doubtful which set of officers constituted these defenders."[32]

A little later General Greene arrived at Fort Motte and for the first time met the Swamp Fox face to face. No doubt he repeated the assurance he had previously conveyed in his dispatches that he was "at a loss which to admire most, your bravery and fortitude, or your address and management."[33]

Greene then dispatched his two lieutenants in opposite directions. Marion was ordered to move against Georgetown on the coast, and Lee was sent up the Congaree to reduce Fort Granby. The commander at Granby, Tory Major Andrew Maxwell, was a notorious plunderer and might be induced to surrender if he was allowed to keep the booty he had collected at the fort. When Lee arrived at Granby on May 15, he called on Maxwell to surrender, and the latter promptly complied, afterward being allowed to march out with a considerable convoy of looted goods and slaves. (There were repercussions from this episode. Sumter claimed that since he had left a detachment at Granby to watch it until his return, Lee was preempting his territory. He was indignant enough to offer Greene his resignation, but his injured feelings were soothed. The militia were also resentful that Maxwell escaped with his loot, especially when Lee's men shortly afterward appeared in new clothes).[34]

Marion had no difficulty with Georgetown. On May 23, the British garrison, convinced that this was not just another demonstration, evacuated the town and retreated to Charleston by sea.

There remained the two British strong points in the upcountry, Ninety Six and Augusta. Colonel John Harris Cruger, commanding at Ninety Six, had not received Rawdon's order to abandon his post and reinforce Augusta. The Augusta garrison had for some time been the target of Whig attacks since it was not only a rallying point for Tories on the upper Savannah but was the depot through which the British shipped trade goods to the Indians. In fact, George Galphin, the deputy superintendent of Indian affairs, had just received a stock of goods and was holding them at a small stockade just downriver from Augusta. Immediately following the fall of Fort Granby, Greene detached Lee to go to the assistance of Whig partisans under Pickens and Elijah Clarke, who were about to launch an attack on Augusta. Greene himself advanced toward Ninety Six.

Lee learned of the supply of trade goods at Fort Galphin and set out on a

* See end for anecdote of alleged rebel barbarity at time of Surrender of Ft. Granby

forced march to seize them before they could be moved to Augusta. Mounting his infantry double behind the dragoons of the Legion, he covered the seventy-five miles from Granby to the Savannah in three days and attacked the fort from two sides. Two companies of the defenders were captured and the stores seized.

Lee then joined Pickens and Clarke before Augusta. The post was actually two forts, Cornwallis located in the middle of the town and Grierson about half a mile away. The British commanders were Colonel Grierson, and the famous Tory raider Thomas Browne, whose Florida Rangers had earlier played havoc along the South Carolina and Georgia borders. Grierson and Browne were two of the most hated and feared of the Tory partisans, known on the western frontier for their vengefulness toward Whigs.

On May 23, Lee attacked Fort Grierson to prevent its defenders from joining Browne at Fort Cornwallis. The stockade fell with the first assault, and the eighty defenders were cut down as they tried to reach their comrades. Thirty of them were killed, and almost all the rest were wounded. One of the prisoners was Grierson. He was confined under guard, primarily to prevent the Whigs from harming him, but, as Pickens informed Greene, "information was brought to me that a man had ridden up to the door . . . where Col. Grierson was confined, and, without dismounting, shot him so that he expired soon after, and instantly rode off: and though he was instantly pursued . . . he effected his escape."[35]

Fort Cornwallis was a harder task. Browne commanded 250 Tory militia and 300 Creek Indians. Pickens and Lee began to dig parallels and saps to advance close enough to attempt to storm the works. The Americans also began the erection of a Maham tower. Browne sent out several sorties to halt the sappers and destroy the tower, but they were repulsed. He also mined a building between the fort and the tower, but the powder charges exploded prematurely.

On May 31 a summons was issued calling on Browne to surrender, but he refused. By this time the tower was completed, and the Americans put riflemen onto the platform and also a six-pounder taken at Fort Grierson. The defenders attempted to destroy the tower with their own artillery, but the riflemen drove off the gunners and the six-pounder soon dismounted Browne's guns. Four days later, as the Americans prepared for a final assault, the Tory defenders capitulated. The British losses are uncertain, but more than 300 were captured.

The Tory commander, Thomas Browne, was taken directly to Lee's headquarters for confinement. "This precaution," said Lee, "suggested by the knowledge of the inveteracy with which the operations in this quarter had been conducted on both sides turned out to be extremely fortunate; as otherwise, in all probability, the laurels acquired by the arms of America would have been stained by the murder of a gallant soldier. . . ."[36] Browne was escorted downriver under a heavy guard of North Carolina militia—to prevent his murder as much as to prevent his escape—where he was paroled to the British in Savannah.[37]

"We fight, get beat, rise and fight again," said Greene after the battle of Hobkirk's Hill.[38] This laconic statement scarcely did justice to the incredible performance of the commander of the Southern Department over the past twelve weeks. Faced by an enemy who could muster nearly 8,000 men, Greene had systematically reduced the British posts, forcing not only the abandonment of the posts themselves but a general withdrawal of the occupation troops. Of the British forts in the interior only Ninety Six still held out. Greene's force of Continentals had never exceeded 1,400 men, but he had had considerable aid from the partisan forces commanded by Marion, Pickens, and Sumter. Additional militia (such as the 250 North Carolinians at Hobkirk's Hill) had from time to time reinforced or cooperated with the main army. Yet all these irregular troops had probably never put more than 2,000 men in the field at any one time.

The success had been won partly because of a weakness inherent in the situation of any army of occupation. Although able to get some food and forage from the countryside in the immediate vicinity of their posts, the British were essentially dependent on their supply line to Charleston. This line was vulnerable not only to the attacks of partisans such as Marion but to roaming bands of outlaws and freebooters who pillaged Whigs and Tories alike. As in New York and New Jersey, the British never solved the problem of controlling the interior, although Cornwallis' chain of posts in the Carolina backcountry had come closer to success than any other effort. But with Greene's army marching and countermarching and the rising tide of Whig sentiment that marked his reappearance in South Carolina, it became increasingly difficult for Rawdon either to get supplies from the countryside or to keep open his communications with Charleston. Thus although he might "claim the field" after Hobkirk's Hill, ten days later, "I published to the Troops and to the Militia my design of evacuating Camden. . . ."[39]

13. The Reconquest: Ninety Six to Eutaw Springs

The major factor in the American success was the tenacity and skillful strategy of Nathanael Greene. Although he had still won no major victories, he had frustrated both Rawdon's attempts to destroy the American operating force and his efforts to maintain the British strong points. Greene may have been more sardonic than amused when he noted, "There are few generals that has run oftener, or more lustily than I have done. But I have taken care not to run too far, and commonly have run as fast forward as backward, to convince our Enemy that we are like a Crab, that could run either way."[1]

✳ Frustrations ✳

Greene had long since learned that a commander may be beset not only by the enemy but by complexities and obstacles created by friends. In Virginia Governor Thomas Jefferson and the state council continued to harass him with indignant and carping protests over the seizure of horses. The wearing campaign had taken its toll on both men and animals, and William Washington had sent men to Virginia to impress horses under the authority of General Greene, who had secured permission from Governor Jefferson.

Greene had been careful to specify in his orders to Washington that brood mares and stallions standing at stud were to be exempted, but the hue and cry from the landed gentry of Southside and Tidewater Virginia was too much for the legislature. In a series of resolutions that august body decreed that only horses valued at less than £50 were "proper for dragoons" and that horses seized in violation of this restriction be valued at £5,000 as compensation to the owners. These resolutions and the governor's protest drew from Greene a reply that barely concealed his disgust and irritation. Although some officers had undoubtedly abused their authority, these constituted a small minority. "I observe," Greene continued, "the price fixed for the purchase of horses is very low . . . it would not purchase by voluntary sale a horse that I would trust a dragoon upon."[2] When Jefferson replied by suggesting that Greene send a "remonstrance" to the assembly, he gave full vent to his feelings: "Already we experience in many instances the ill consequences of neglecting the Army when surrounded with difficulties and threatened with ruin. Great expence of blood and treasure have attended this policy. . . . If Horses are dearer to the Inhabitants than the lives of Subjects, or the liberties of the People, there will be no doubt of the Assembly persevering in their late resolution. . . ."[3] This impasse does not seem to have prevented Washington and Lee from keeping their men supplied with good horses. It may have given Greene some wry satisfaction to hear from Joseph Reed a few weeks later that the fine horses denied the southern army were being ridden by Tarleton's dragoons on their plundering raids across the Old Dominion.[4]

It was horses also that almost cost Greene the services of Francis Marion. The urgent need for mounts led Greene to remonstrate sharply with the Swamp Fox: "I am told the militia claim all they take from the Tories; and many of the best horses are collected from the inhabitants on this principle. I cannot think this practice warranted either in justice or in policy. If the object of the people is plunder altogether government can receive but little benefit from them."

The long campaign was stretching frayed nerves taut. Marion's temper flared at the implied rebuke. "The few horses which has been taken from Tories has been kept for the service and never for private property; but if you think it best for the service to dismount the militia now with me, I will direct Colonel Lee and Captain Congers to do so, but am certain we shall never get their service in the future." Then came a shocking addendum: "This would not give me any uneasiness, as I have . . . determined to relinquish my command in the militia. . . . I shall take the opportunity in waiting on you, when I hope to get permission to go to Philadelphia."

Marion could not mean it! Greene remonstrated. "I . . . cannot think you seriously mean to solicit leave to go to Philadelphia. . . . Your State is invaded; your all is at stake; what has been done will signify nothing unless we persevere to the end." Marion was adamant: "I am very serious in my intention of relinquishing my militia command . . . because I found little is to be done with such men as I have, who leave me very often at the point of executing a plan. . . . If I cannot act in the militia, I cannot see any service I can be to remain in the State. . . ." To reassure Greene that his fit of pique had subsided and that he bore his commander no ill feeling, he added, "I send by Major Hyrne a horse for yourself. . . . as far as it is in my power to procure more I will send them."

But Marion ultimately decided to stay. As Greene prepared to attack Ninety Six, he ordered Marion to watch Rawdon and delay him if he attempted to march upcountry. The Swamp Fox dutifully mustered his partisans and moved beyond Orangeburg toward Monck's Corner.[5]

Thomas Sumter was another matter entirely. Marion and Pickens were strong-willed and, at times, stubborn, but both recognized the necessity for a single overall command and both appreciated the necessity for coordinating their movements with those of Greene. Sumter regarded himself not only as an independent commander but as a law unto himself. He was commander of the South Carolina militia, and in the absence of any government authority (the legislature was nonexistent and Governor Rutledge was frequently absent from Greene's headquarters) there was little to curb the Gamecock's willfulness. Although Greene had urged him to bring in his militia before the battle of Hobkirk's Hill, Sumter had remained aloof on the upper Broad River. "General Sumter has got but a few men," Greene wrote to Lee; "he has taken the field, and is pushing after little parties of Tories toward Ninety Six. Major Hyrne is gone to him, if possible to get him to join us; but this I know he will avoid, if he can with decency."[6]

Sumter had also been disgruntled by Lee's actions at Fort Granby. Not only had Light Horse Harry allowed the Tories to retain their plunder but Sumter, who had twice attacked Granby unsuccessfully, regarded the post as his special preserve. "I hope it may not be disagreeable to recall Lieutenant Colonel Lee, as his services cannot be wanted in that place, . . ." he wrote to Greene upon learning that Lee was investing Granby. "I think it for the good of the public to do it [capture the fort] without regulars."

When Lee was not recalled, Sumter responded with a threat to resign: "My indispositon and want of capacity to be of service to this country induces me . . . to beg leave to resign my command, . . ." he wrote to Greene in mid-May, enclosing his commission. Greene was undoubtedly irritated by this troublesome man, but he could not afford to alienate anyone as popular as the Gamecock. ". . . I cannot think of accepting it, and beg you to continue in your command," he replied.[7]

Sumter was mollified, or perhaps he was bluffing and knew that Greene would not call his hand. Far more serious was Sumter's establishment of a new body of state troops. He was disgusted with the militia, whose terms rarely exceeded sixty days and who frequently went home before their enlistments expired. He therefore decided to raise a force of dragoons by offering bounties in the form of slaves seized from Tories. Each man would receive an able-bodied slave for a ten-month enlistment. In addition, the soldier would receive a uniform, a horse, and equipment and would share in two-thirds of all plunder taken from the enemy.

Thus was created "Sumter's Law," decreed solely on his authority as senior militia officer. Marion, ordered by Sumter to raise two regiments of dragoons, refused and questioned Sumter's dictatorial authority. Greene, perhaps realizing that this was a state matter over which he had no authority, made only token objection, saying, "I am a great enemy of plundering," and suggesting that care should be taken to assure that owners of seized property be compensated. But Sumter's Law probably fortified Greene's private opinion that the militia commander was a "freebooter." When Governor Rutledge returned from Philadelphia later in the summer, he immediately issued an order forbidding plundering. Evidently Sumter's recruiting was not very successful for by August 15 only a few hundred men were under his command.[8]

Although his reputation as a partisan fighter had elevated Sumter to the command of the South Carolina state forces, his performance did not match his fame. In February and early March, while Greene was sparring with Cornwallis in North Carolina, he had attempted a raid down the Santee. He obviously hoped that a combination of his reputation and the promise of plunder would attract a large force of militia to his command. He also hoped to get support from Marion, but the latter was operating under orders from Greene and was perhaps not inclined to support a campaign that was ill-conceived and hastily planned. Sumter failed to attract the numbers he had counted on but persisted in his offensive. He attacked in turn Fort Granby, Belleville, and Fort Watson and in each case was repulsed and forced to retire. The campaign ended in a disastrous skirmish at Lynche's River on March 6, when South Carolina Loyalists under the command of Major Thomas Fraser killed or wounded fifty of Sumter's force. The Gamecock retired all the way to the Waxhaws. He had lost a quarter of his command, and the rest of his men were so disgruntled that he sent them home.[9]

His behavior during Greene's campaign against Rawdon's posts during the spring and early summer had led to disputes not only with Greene but with Marion and Lee.

Was the heroic Gamecock a boaster and braggart whose reputation was based on myth? Obviously not, for Sumter's fame as an Indian fighter and partisan leader was well earned. Carolina backcountry folk reserved their admiration for men of proven ability. A tentative conclusion is that the Sumter of the Cherokee wars, Hanging Rock, and Rocky Mount was a changed man after the bloody battle at Blackstocks. A musket ball had torn into his shoulder and back, and it was almost three months before he was able to take the field. He was still complaining that his wounds had not properly healed in the early summer of 1781. Did this experience sap some of the bold courage of the Gamecock? Did he not press his attack with the same hard courage he had once displayed? Probably Thomas Sumter himself could not have answered such questions, but the terrible wound and its painful aftermath may have affected his fighting spirit in ways of which he himself was not aware.[10]

The war was grinding on everyone. Nathanael Greene had been campaigning for six years. Since joining Morgan at Beattie's Ford in January, he had been marching and fighting for four continuous months. They had

Thomas Sumter (Independence National Historical Park Collection)

been months that had strained muscle and nerve to the point of exhaustion. The monumental calm of the Rhode Islander was now broken by flashes of irritation, not only at Sumter but at Marion and Lee. Even Governor Jefferson was not spared, although Greene was quick to soothe and placate those whom he offended. And there were outbursts that came in the privacy of his tent.

"General Greene was deeply disgusted with the conduct of General Sumter," reported Colonel Davie; ". . . to this strange and unmilitary conduct of Sumter, he justly attributed his incapacity to effect the complete investment of Camden; . . . and considering him as a mere Pandour or freebooter, whose sole objective was plunder . . . he would certainly have arrested him but from considerations arising from the state of the country at the time."[11]

Irritation was occasionally mixed with deep pessimism. Not once had Greene had the satisfaction of driving the enemy from the battlefield. The recent successes had been the work of others—Lee, Marion, and Pickens. He was wise enough to see that there was little chance that the British could recoup their losses in the interior, but a report that Rawdon was receiving reinforcements from England brought on a mood of discouragement. "We will dispute every inch of ground that we can, but Rawdon will push me back into the mountains. Lord Cornwallis will establish a chain of posts along the James River, and the southern States thus cut off will die like the tail of a snake."[12]

But these were passing moods. Only one British stronghold remained. If it could be reduced, the last enemy foothold in the backcountry would be gone.

✳ Ninety Six ✳

For a hundred years the Carolinians had alternately traded and fought with the Indians to the west, principally with the Cherokees. The great trading path to the Cherokee towns followed the Santee and the Saluda to Ninety Six, so named because it was ninety-six miles farther to the important Indian town of Keowee. Ninety Six was garrisoned entirely by Loyalists, but most of them were provincial troops of a quality that matched the regulars. The force consisted of 150 men of the 2nd Battalion of De-Lancey's New York Volunteers, 200 New Jersey Volunteers, and 200 South Carolina Loyalist militia.[13]

The commander of the fort was Colonel John Harris Cruger. He came from a prominent family of New York merchants and politicians (a brother, Nicholas Cruger, who managed the firm's branch in St. Croix, sponsored the education of young Alexander Hamilton at King's College). Cruger had been in the South since 1779. He had commanded a regiment of

De Lancey's New York Volunteers at the seige of Savannah and had been at Ninety Six since the summer of 1780.

His effective command of the post had been vastly encouraging to the Loyalists. It was said that they outnumbered the Whigs by five to one and the Patriot partisans had never been very successful in the district. He was a stern disciplinarian and detested the Whigs, but he had refused to engage in the vengeful barbarities that were associated with Thomas Browne and Bloody Bill Cuningham.[14]

Since its days as an Indian trading post, the village had been surrounded by a palisade. Under Cruger's direction it had become a formidable stockade surrounded by a deep ditch, which in turn was protected by an abatis. About eighty yards to the east of the village the stockade was connected to a redoubt called the Star. From its angles crossfires could be directed down two sides of the fort to prevent an enemy lodgment under the walls. To the west and outside the stockade was a smaller outwork that served a similar purpose and also afforded access to the fort's water supply, a rivulet fed by a nearby spring. Covered ways and traverses provided communication from one part of the works to another, and a considerable number of slaves were at hand to provide a labor battalion. Cruger also had three three-pounder guns.

While Pickens and Lee were still engaged in their attack on Augusta, Greene brought his army to Ninety Six. His force consisted of 850 Maryland and Delaware Continentals and perhaps 200 militia. Although this was twice the number of the defenders it was not enough to storm so formidable a defensive work as Cruger had prepared. Greene therefore decided to lay siege to the fort, a kind of operation with which Greene and his men had little experience. This was evident at the beginning of the attack. On May 22 sappers began work on an entrenchment only seventy yards from the Star. By midday Cruger had mounted one of his guns on the wall of the redoubt. It opened fire on the unwary Americans, and under its cover a party of New York Volunteers led by Lieutenant John Roney fell upon the working party and wiped it out. Negroes accompanied the attackers to fill in the trench and carry the tools back to the fort. Cruger was demonstrating a basic lesson in siege warfare: to be successful, the besieged must not remain passive but must seize every opportunity for counterattack.

Greene now began his entrenchment at a more respectable distance. Ten days were consumed in digging regular approaches, and almost every night Cruger sent out small parties to attack the Americans. Not until June 3 did the parallels reach the point where the first trench had been attempted. The Americans then pushed a sap to within thirty yards of the wall of the Star Redoubt. At that point they raised a forty-foot Maham tower, which enabled riflemen to fire over the parapet and silence Cruger's guns. Cruger countered by piling sandbags on top of the wall with loopholes to allow

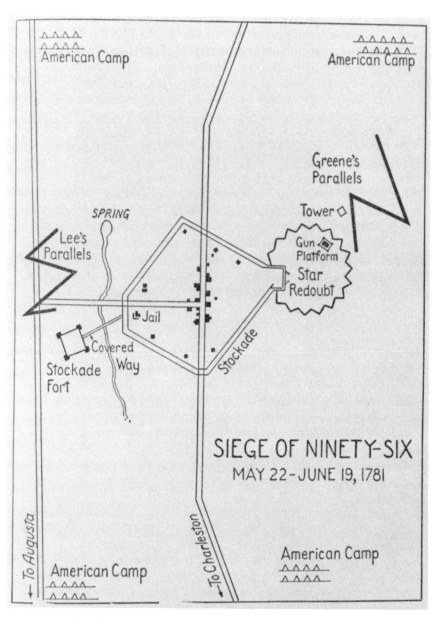

American Camp

American Camp

Greene's Parallels

Tower ◇

SPRING

Gun Platform

Lee's Parallels

Star Redoubt

Jail

Covered Way

Stockade Fort

Stockade

SIEGE OF NINETY-SIX
MAY 22–JUNE 19, 1781

To Augusta

To Charleston

American Camp

American Camp

*(Reprinted with permission of Macmillan Publishing Company
from* The War of the Revolution, *Volume 2, by Christopher Ward.
Copyright 1952 by Macmillan Publishing Company, copyright renewed 1980)*

See Rivington's Royal Gazette 20/4/82
for a Br. eyewitness account.

marksmen to fire at the attackers on the tower. He also tried to set it on fire with red-hot shot from his guns, but without proper furnaces he could not get the cannon balls sufficiently heated. The Americans now adopted the tactics used against Fort Motte. A shower of flaming arrows descended on the roofs of the fort's buildings. Cruger's work parties immediately tore off the roofs of all the buildings.

Inside the fort the garrison and the Tory refugees were suffering from the intense summer heat. Trenches had to be dug to protect the refugees from the rifle fire on the Maham tower. But the resistance continued. Unable to use his guns in the daytime, Cruger moved them into position under cover of darkness and bombarded the tower and the trenches.

On June 8 Harry Lee and Pickens arrived fresh from their success at Augusta. Hoping to discourage the defenders, Lee had the prisoners taken at Augusta paraded in sight of the garrison of the fort. Unfortunately, it seemed to have the opposite effect, rousing the Tories to angry shouts of defiance. (Lee in his *Memoirs* contended that this insulting gesture was the result of a mistake on the part of the officer escorting the prisoners, who had unwittingly taken the road that passed in sight of the fort.)

Greene now did what he undoubtedly should have done at the beginning of the siege: he set about seizing the small redoubt on the west side of the fort guarding the water supply. The intense June heat would surely have brought the garrison to terms if access to water had been interrupted in the beginning of the attack. Lee and the Legion were given this task and immediately began to dig approaches to the stockade defending the spring. The defenders countered with nightly sallies, and bloody little fights erupted in the summer darkness. Although he did not gain control of the stockade, Lee and his men made access to the spring so dangerous that the Loyalists were forced to get their water at night, using the Negroes as carriers under the cloak of darkness. The garrison's water supply was drastically reduced. The defenders now suffered from thirst as well as the summer heat.

On June 11 Greene received ominous news from Sumter. A British fleet had arrived at Charleston with reinforcements for Rawdon. The British commander took only four days to organize a force of 2,000 men and set out to relieve Ninety Six. Rawdon had been on the road four days by the time Sumter's warning was received. Greene immediately sent word to Sumter and Marion to gather as many militia as possible. The partisans were to get on Rawdon's front and do everything possible to delay his march. The American commander probably had doubts about Sumter's willingness to cooperate, but surely Marion could be counted on to hold Sumter to his duty. Incredibly, Sumter and Marion failed. Sumter was convinced that Rawdon would retake the British post at Fort Granby on his way to Ninety Six. He therefore waited for Rawdon's appearance on the Congaree. Whether he overruled Marion or whether the latter agreed to

Sumter's assumption, Rawdon marched by way of Orangeburg. By the time news of his change of direction reached the partisans, it was too late for them to overtake him.

Greene was now faced with some unpleasant choices. Rawdon's approach left him no time to continue a protracted siege. He made an effort to set fire to the stockade, but the incendiaries were discovered and destroyed by a sallying party from the fort. Another attack force of the defenders discovered and thwarted the effort to dig a mine under the Star Redoubt. Greene therefore must either attempt to take Ninety Six by storm or turn and attack Rawdon. The fact that the latter's force consisted almost entirely of regulars and was considerably larger than the American force dictated an attempt on the fort.

On June 12 a courier made his way into Ninety Six bringing the news that the relief column was on the way. The courier approached in a leisurely fashion, chattering with the American soldiers and giving every appearance of a curious countryman. As he neared the front lines, he suddenly spurred his horse into a run and despite a hail of bullets escaped into the fort.

Greene now determined to assault the fort on both sides. On the east side Colonel Richard Campbell was to lead Virginia and Maryland Continentals against the Star Redoubt. A storming party was formed consisting of two groups. The first was to cut a gap through the abatis and fill the ditch with fascines. The second group was to storm the walls with poles to which were attached iron hooks. They were to pull the sandbags from the parapet, thus exposing the defenders to fire from the Maham tower. Under its cover a storming party would climb over the stockade. On the west Lee's Legion and Kirkwood's Delaware troops were to overrun the stockade guarding the water supply and force their way into the town. Cruger would thus be forced to meet two assaults from different directions.

The attack began on the morning of June 18. A forlorn hope led by Captain Michael Rudolph crossed the abatis and ditch and successfully stormed the outwork. Rudolph was followed by Lee's Legion, which then paused to wait for the attack from the west. In front of the Star Redoubt Greene's guns opened fire. The storming party ran forward and cut two gaps in the abatis. Hard on their heels came the hook men, who began pulling the sandbags from the top of the stockade. The defenders countered with rifle fire, but as the sandbags toppled down they were driven from the walls by fire from the Maham tower. For the moment it seemed that the attack would succeed.

But the Loyalists had long since demonstrated that they were not passive defenders. Captain Thomas French of the New York Volunteers led a party of thirty men out of a sally port on one flank of the attack party. Captain Peter Campbell struck at the other flank. For several minutes there was a fierce and bloody struggle mostly with bayonets and clubbed muskets. The two American commanders of the attacking party, Samuel Duval and Thomas Seldon, went down, and the survivors finally fell back to their trenches. General Greene called off the attack.[15]

The Patriots had lost a total of 127 killed and wounded, with 20 missing. The Loyalists' loss was 85 killed and wounded. Rawdon's relief column was now less than thirty miles away. Greene had no choice but to retreat. According to Lee, "gloom and silence pervaded the American camp; every one mortified. Three days more and Ninety-six must have fallen; but this short space was unattainable. . . . Greene alone preserved his equanimity; and highly pleased by the unshaken courage displayed in the assault, announced his grateful sense of the conduct of the troops. . . ."[16]

He laid his failure at Ninety Six to two factors. The first was the failure of his partisan leaders. "It was my wish to have fought Lord Rawdon before he got to Ninety Six," he wrote Marion, "and could I have collected your force and that of General Sumter and Pickens, I could have done it, and am persuaded we should have defeated him. . . . I am surprised the people should be so averse to joining in some general plan of operations." The second factor he laid to his nemesis, Governor Jefferson. This time it involved men, not horses. Two thousand Virginia militia had been raised specifically to reinforce Greene's army. But the threat of the British invasion of Virginia had led Jefferson to countermand their marching orders. Greene was furious: "Nothing could have been more unfortunate than the tardiness of the militia in taking the field and finally in being countermanded. Nor can I conceive the propriety of the governor of any State giving an order that affects the general interest, after the troops are applied and granted for a plan of operations fixed upon, the success of which depends on all parts being directed to the same point."[17]

He was determined somehow to force the British out of Ninety Six, but for the moment this was impossible. In the face of Rawdon's strong force of regulars, he decided to retreat and avoid an engagement. Rawdon was equally determined to seize the opportunity to bring Greene to battle.

As Greene moved northeastward toward Charlotte, the British commander detached enough troops to insure the safety of the Ninety Six garrison and then set out in pursuit. By the time Greene reached the Enoree, Rawdon's van had caught up with the American rear guard, which consisted of Lee's Legion and Kirkwood's sixty light infantrymen. But the British soldiers were done. Since their departure from Charleston seventeen days earlier, the redcoats had been on forced marches, first to reach Ninety Six and then in pursuit of Greene. Clad in their heavy woolen uniforms, unused to the hundred-degree heat and the enervating humidity of the Carolina country, they simply had reached the limit of their endurance. More than fifty of them had died of heat exhaustion. They were short on food and, according to one report, had even run out of salt. Rawdon returned to Ninety Six and ordered its evacuation. Cruger and the garrison troops, reinforced by 500 regulars, were ordered to escort Loyalist evacuees to Charleston. Rawdon hoped to get enough reinforcements to take the offensive against Greene.[18]

When Greene learned of the evacuation of Ninety Six, he immediately turned back to the southeast. Lee had reported the division of the enemy forces, and Greene hoped to find an opening by which he could defeat them in detail. He directed Lee and Kirkwood to try to gain Rawdon's front and requested Marion and Sumter to unite their forces on the lower Congaree. Lee and Kirkwood did get in front of Rawdon, but Marion and Sumter again failed to move with the necessary dispatch. Rawdon was joined by Lieutenant Colonel Alexander Stewart, commanding the 3rd Regiment, the famous Buffs, and halted at Orangeburg, taking a defensive position in several buildings in the small village. Greene arrived before Orangeburg with Washington's dragoons and Lee's Legion. He had also called in Marion and Sumter. For once the Gamecock responded, and Greene now had, with the exception of Pickens, all his elements gathered in one striking force. But a careful reconnoitering of Rawdon's position and the approach of Cruger's force from Ninety Six convinced the American commander that an attack would risk too much.[19]

Greene's command as well as the British were nearly marched out. The Legion and Kirkwood's men were staggering with fatigue. The Delaware troops had marched 323 miles in the twenty-three days since the siege of Ninety Six. And as always the troops were short of rations. ". . . Never did we suffer so severely as during the few days' halt here [Orangeburg]. Rice furnished our substitute for bread, which, although tolerably relished by those familiarized with it . . . was very disagreeable to the Marylanders and Virginians, who had grown up in the use of corn or wheat bread; . . . the few meagre cattle brought to camp as beef would not afford more than two ounces per man. Frogs abounded . . . and on them chiefly did the light troops subsist. . . . Even alligator was used by a few; and very probably, had the army been much longer detained upon that ground, might have rivalled the frog in the estimation of our epicures."[20]

Greene decided to break off the campaign. He led the tired, hungry men to his favorite bivouac in the High Hills of the Santee. This twenty-mile line of sand and clay hills rose some two hundred feet above the north bank of the Santee. The area abounded in grain and was free of the malarial swamps of the lowcountry. Perhaps the air was no cooler, but it seemed to be, and there was almost always a breeze stirring.

For two more weeks the Legion and the partisans harassed the British at Monck's Corner and Dorchester, occupying Nelson's Ferry and Friday's Ferry on the Santee. The British withdrew their forces to the vicinity of Charleston. The Carolinas and Georgia had been cleared of the British except for Charleston, Wilmington, and Savannah.[21]

In late August, Lieutenant Colonel Francis Lord Rawdon sailed for

England. Fifteen months of hard campaigning had broken his health, and he was relieved of his command and furloughed home. He was twenty-seven years old.

✳ "The Fire Ran from Flank to Flank" ✳

As Greene prepared to retire to the High Hills of the Santee, Sumter expressed a wish to continue a harassing campaign against the enemy. Greene assented and assigned Marion and Lee's Legion to his command. Sumter moved toward Monck's Corner. The first objective was a British force at Biggin Church northeast of Monck's Corner. Colonel John Coates, leading the 19th Regiment to Rawdon's support, had a clash with Colonel Peter Horry of Marion's command. Mistaking Horry's dragoons for the van of Greene's army, Coates began retiring toward Charleston. Lee's Legion and Wade Hampton's South Carolina dragoons pursued Coates, who finally decided to make a stand at Quimby, a plantation near the upper Cooper River. Coates stationed his men in the house and its outbuildings, mounting a howitzer in the center of his line. Marion and Lee soon came up but decided the position was too strong to attack without artillery. When Sumter arrived with the main body of infantry, he immediately ordered an attack. Lee and Marion urged him to wait until a six-pounder that had not yet arrived could be brought into action. Sumter persisted in his determination to attack.

The troops were formed into a concave line and ordered forward, but the advance was brought to a standstill by the concentrated fire of muskets and artillery. Sumter ordered Colonel Thomas Taylor to seize a fence in front of the main building. Taylor succeeded but only after heavy losses. Marion came to his support, but both commands were driven off by a bayonet charge from the defenders. In the repulse the Americans lost thirty killed and thirty wounded, most of them Taylor's and Marion's men. Taylor swore he would never fight under Sumter's command again. There is no record of Marion's reaction, but he soon separated his command from Sumter.

Feeling his wounds and too ill to ride, Sumter petulantly ordered his troops to disband until October. Greene was furious. To Colonel John Henderson, who had been ordered to Sumter's command, he exploded, "If he [Sumter] supposes himself at liberty to employ these troops, independently of the Continental army, it is time he should be convinced to the contrary."[22]

By August 22 Greene believed his army was strong enough to take the field. He now had 1,250 Continentals, 300 dragoons under Washington and Lee, 150 South Carolina state troops (ten-month men) about equally divided between infantry and cavalry, 300 partisans under Pickens, and

250 under Marion. In addition, 150 North Carolinians had joined his command. His total force amounted to 2,400 men of whom about three-fourths were either Continentals or seasoned veterans. It was the most formidable body of troops that Greene had had under his command since Guilford Court House.

The British were now commanded by Colonel Stewart. His operating force consisted of 300 light infantry and grenadiers commanded by Major John Marjoribanks, the 3rd, 63rd, and 64th regiments, Cruger's New York and New Jersey Volunteers, and a cavalry force commanded by Major John Coffin. His total rank and file was about 2,000 men. Stewart also had five guns ranging from small swivels to two six-pounders.[23]

The British were also on the move. They had come out from Charleston and marched northwest to the forks of the Santee. Here the two forces were less than twenty miles apart but separated by the swollen waters of the river. Greene had to march all the way to Camden to find a crossing. By the first week in September he had descended the right bank of the Congaree and was approaching Stewart, who was encamped near Eutaw Springs. By this stage of the war an interesting phenomenon was becoming evident. In Greene's army many of the Continentals were deserters from the British army, and among Cruger's Tories a large proportion were deserters from the American army. Greene noted, "At the close of the war, we fought the enemy with British soldiers, and they fought us with those of America." This may also account for the stubbornness of the fighting on both sides. Deserters, if they were recaptured by either army, were summarily hanged; neither Greene nor his British counterpart was inclined to show leniency in such cases.[24]

The Eutaw Springs are actually the appearances above the surface of an underground river. Stewart was camped near a large two-story brick mansion that had several outbuildings and a palisaded garden near the bank of Eutaw Creek. Stewart had trouble locating Greene's force because partisans "rendered it impossible [to scout], by waylaying the bye-paths and passes through the different swamps." Chronically short of food, Stewart sent out an unarmed party to dig for sweet potatoes on the morning of September 8. Whether it was these men or deserters from the North Carolina troops that first reported Greene's presence, Stewart sent Coffin and his cavalry to reconnoiter. Greene's van was led by Colonel John Henderson and consisted of South Carolina troops and Lee's Legion. Coffin struck this body and charged it. His rashness was costly, for Henderson emptied forty saddles before the British fell back.[25]

Whether Stewart was totally surprised or not he had time to establish a defensive line by the time Greene came up to his camp. On his left flank the British commander posted Coffin's command of cavalry. The left wing consisted of the 64th, the 63rd, and Cruger's Loyalists. On the right was

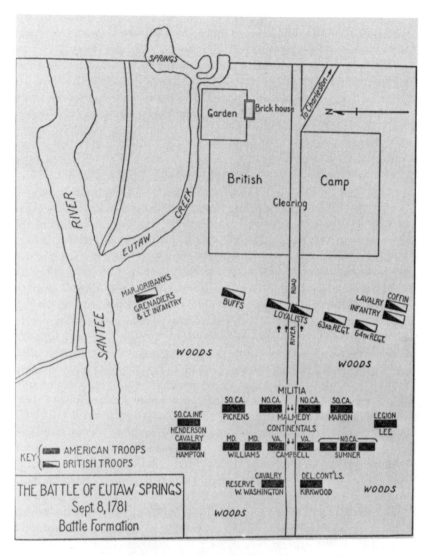

(Reprinted with permission of Macmillan Publishing Company
from The War of the Revolution, Volume 2,
by Christopher Ward. Copyright 1952 by Macmillan Publishing Company,
copyright renewed 1980)

the 3rd Regiment, and on the right flank hidden in a blackjack thicket and formed at an obtuse angle to Greene's approach was Marjoribanks' command of light infantry and grenadiers.

Greene made his advance in two divisions. In the front line were the South Carolina militia under Henderson and Pickens on the left. In the center were North Carolina troops under a French officer, the Marquis de Malmady. On the right was Marion with his South Carolina partisans. Lee's Legion was on the right flank, and the South Carolina dragoons under Wade Hampton covered the left. The second line contained the Continentals of Maryland, Virginia, and North Carolina commanded by Williams, Richard Campbell, and the North Carolina veteran, General Jethro Sumner. William Washington and Kirkwood formed the reserve. The American force advanced through open woods toward the British, driving in the advance guard. About nine o'clock the Americans had advanced their front line and engaged the enemy's main body. If Greene expected the militia of the front line to give a few volleys and fall back, he was pleasantly surprised. "The militia advancing with alacrity, the battle became warm. . . . The fire ran from flank to flank; our line still advancing, and the enemy adhering to his position. . . ." After some minutes of stubborn fighting, Malmady's North Carolina men fell back. Greene immediately restored his line by bringing up Sumner's North Carolina Continentals. On the left Henderson's men faltered when their commander was shot down, but Colonel Hampton took over command and steadied the line.[26]

The British now vigorously attacked Sumner, and the North Carolinians gave way. As the British pressed forward they found themselves facing Williams and his Maryland Continentals and Campbell's Virginians. The Americans rammed home a bayonet charge, and Captain Rudolph commanding the Legion infantry delivered a destructive fire into the left flank of the redcoats. The British charge was abruptly halted. The line fell back, "thrown into irretrievable disorder. But their centre and right still remained; greatly outnumbering the assailing party and awaiting the impending charge. . . . If the two lines on this occasion did not actually come to the mutual thrusting of the bayonet, it must be acknowledged that no troops ever came nearer. . . . so near that their bayonets clashed and the officers sprang at each other with their swords. . . ." Stewart's line gave way along its entire front except for Marjoribanks on the extreme right.[27]

Stewart now pulled some of his men back to the protection of the brick house and its outbuildings. In the race for control of these vital points, the British barely won, barring the doors in the faces of their comrades. The rest of the British line collapsed.

But the redoubtable Marjoribanks could not be pried out of his position in the blackjack thicket on the right. Washington's cavalry charged it but could not penetrate. The big cavalryman then attempted to drive between the British right and Eutaw Creek. In doing so, he wheeled his dragoons across the enemy front. A blast of fire from the grenadiers and light infantry cut the dragoons to shreds. Washington himself was wounded and captured. There was savage fighting as Hampton brought up his South Carolina dragoons in support. He tried to collect what was left of Washington's command while Kirkwood's men pushed forward with the bayonet to prevent a redcoat counterattack. All was confusion, "horses plunging as they died, or coursing the field without their riders. . . . the road strewn with the bodies of men and fragments of dismounted artillery."[28]

In the center the British line was completely broken and in mad retreat. The British began destroying their stores, and fugitives crowded the road to Charleston.

Then the advancing Continentals in the center struck a snag as effective as Marjoribanks or the fortified buildings. The line of the enemy retreat led directly through the British camp, which was filled with equipment, food, and drink. The hungry, thirsty troops could not be denied. Discipline collapsed. "When their officers had proceeded beyond their encampment, they found themselves nearly abandoned. . . ." The looters scarcely noticed the deadly fire from the plantation house that swept the encampment. The Americans "fastened upon the liquors and refreshments . . . and became completely unmanageable."[29] Coffin now led a charge on the disorderly mob, and only an alert counterattack by Hampton's dragoons prevented a rout. Marjoribanks sallied from the blackjack thicket, seized most of the American guns, and brought them under the covering fire of the house.

The fighting had now been going on for almost three hours. The heat was intense, and the soldiers were almost mad with thirst. Stewart managed to restore part of his line as Greene ordered a retreat. The British did not pursue, remaining in the cover of the house and the palisaded garden.

It was the bloodiest battle of the southern campaign. Greene put his losses at 139 killed, 375 wounded, and 8 missing, almost one-quarter of the force he had on the field. Henderson and Pickens were wounded, and Richard Campbell was killed. Stewart's losses were catastrophic. Of 1,800 men he committed to action, 85 were killed, 351 were wounded, and 430 were missing, most of the latter prisoners of the Americans. He had lost 42 percent of his force. Among the casualties was gallant John Marjoribanks, mortally wounded in the last moments of the battle.[30]

The battle of Eutaw Springs was the last major engagement in the campaign for the Carolinas. Although the British claimed the field, Greene noted that "we collected all our wounded except those too far forward under the fire of the house. . . . I left upon the field of battle a strong picket." The Americans also held 400 prisoners. But the decisive fact was that on the night of September 9 Stewart abandoned his position and moved toward Monck's Corner. With Marion and Lee hanging on his rear, he paused there briefly and then continued on to Charleston.[31]

Greene once more took his little army to the High Hills of the Santee. The interior of the Carolinas was now cleared of the enemy. From Virginia to Florida only Wilmington, Charleston, and Savannah remained in possession of the British. But the war was not over.

Eutaw Springs the bloodiest
battle of the S. Campaign.
Americans suffered 24% casualties
British suffered 42% casualties

14. "If Ponies Rode Men"

As the British occupying forces withdrew from the backcountry Nathanael Greene began to think of shifting his field of operations northward and once more engaging his old enemy, Cornwallis. "The benefit resulting from our operations will, in great measure, depend on the proper management of our affairs in Virginia," he had written early in May 1781. "If the principal officer in the enemy's interest is there who should be opposed to him? Which will be more honorable, to be active there, or laying, as it were, idle here? . . . More advantage will result from [my] going than staying; for [I] can serve . . . more effectually yonder than here."

He was not without pride. He sensed that the situation that was developing in Virginia might produce dramatic results, and he believed himself able to "oppose the enemy more effectually there than those that will command if he don't go."[1] But he did not go. Perhaps he recognized that only a strong hand could keep the Carolina campaign from unravelling, perhaps because there was no one among his brilliant but willful subordinates to whom he could entrust the command. Joseph Reed may have been right when he observed that if Greene "cannot preserve the Country, it cannot be preserved."[2]

✳ Yorktown ✳

Virginia had scarcely felt the full force of the war. But as the spring of 1781 turned to summer, it attracted the attention of both the British and the Americans. Virginia was the largest of the states and along with Massachusetts had been the center of the revolutionary movement. Unlike those in Massachusetts, Virginia Whigs had little difficulty in overturning royal authority because most of its colonial leaders were in the forefront of the revolutionary movement. It could almost be said that the government of the colony overthrew itself. The British had therefore never found much Loyalist support in the Old Dominion. Three considerations had led

Clinton to send expeditions to the Chesapeake. The first was that the anchorage at Hampton Roads offered a superb naval base from which elements of the British fleet could operate. Second, Virginia was an important source of men and supplies, especially for the southern army. Although Sir Henry never subscribed to Cornwallis' theory that the fall of Virginia would mean the automatic collapse of the Carolinas, he did recognize the importance of interdicting the logistical support of Greene's army. The third factor was Lord George Germain's insistence that the Chesapeake was an important strategic area.

The familiar story of Cornwallis' road to Yorktown is quickly told. When the earl reached Petersburg on May 20 he found himself in command of a combined force of just over 7,000 men. George Washington's reaction to the invasion of his native state was to detach the Marquis de Lafayette with 1,200 Continentals to the support of the tiny force under Steuben. When the Frenchman arrived in Virginia at the beginning of May, he was reinforced by 2,000 Virginia militia of dubious quality. Lafayette was under no illusions about his situation, especially after Cornwallis arrived with his army from the Carolinas. "Were I to decline fighting, the country would think itself given up. I am therefore determined to skirmish, but not to engage too far. . . ." He added ruefully, "I am not strong enough even to get beaten."[3]

Cornwallis moved north to force Lafayette out of Richmond. The latter retreated before the British advance not only to avoid an engagement but to link up with an additional reinforcement consisting of "Mad Anthony" Wayne's Pennsylvania Continentals. The withdrawal took Lafayette all the way to the Rapidan. Cornwallis did not press the pursuit but instead sent his two mounted corps on raids to the west.

Colonel John Simcoe and his Queen's Rangers caught up with Steuben, who was attempting to escort stores and supplies out of reach of the enemy. Simcoe forced the doughty Prussian to abandon the supplies although Steuben and his men escaped. Tarleton conducted a sweep to the westward that had as its principal objective Governor Thomas Jefferson and the Virginia legislature, who had sought refuge in Charlottesville. Warned of the British approach, the legislature crossed the Blue Ridge to the safety of Staunton. Jefferson's term as governor was at an end, so he retreated to his estate at Poplar Forest in Bedford County.[4]

After this whirlwind of meaningless action Cornwallis withdrew to Richmond and thence down the Peninsula (the neck of land between the James and York rivers). Lafayette followed. Cornwallis then decided to cross the James at Greenspring and occupy Portsmouth so he could embark 2,000 men that Clinton had ordered back to New York. Lafayette thought he saw an opportunity to strike the enemy while it was divided by the river crossing. Cornwallis set a trap, luring the Frenchman into thinking that most of his army had made the crossing and that only a rear guard was on the north bank. On July 4 Lafayette sent Wayne's Pennsylvanians in to attack although the marquis did not commit his entire army. As Wayne advanced, he was suddenly confronted by the entire British force. Immediately aware of his peril, the fiery general launched an attack with the bayonet. This surprise move threw the redcoats into momentary confusion, and Wayne was able to extricate his command. It was a nice maneuver, but at least one of the rankers failed to appreciate it. "Mad A——y, by G——d, I never knew such a piece of work heard of—about eight hundred troops opposed to five or six thousand. . . ." Cornwallis failed to pursue but continued to Portsmouth, where he received dispatches from Clinton telling him that the 2,000 men were not needed after all.[5]

Cornwallis was directed to take a suitable position that would provide security for a naval anchorage. Since Portsmouth was virtually indefensible, the earl, after consulting his engineers and naval officers, decided to occupy and fortify Yorktown and Gloucester. On August 1 his army arrived at Yorktown and began construction of defensive works.[6]

It may be wondered what strategic purpose lay behind this marching and countermarching. The answer is that no strategy had been determined. Military doctrine in the late eighteenth century had not yet accepted the formal principle of a chain of command running from Lord George Germain to Sir Henry Clinton to the Earl of Cornwallis. Even if such a theoretical principle had existed, it would probably not have prevented the strategic miasma that hung over British operations in America. Germain was fighting for his political life, all too aware of the inadequacies of his commander in chief, lacking the will to dismiss him, yet lending a sympathetic ear to Sir Henry's subordinate. Clinton remained irresolute and querulous, equally unwilling to impose his will on his subordinate. And Cornwallis had not only submitted a strategic plan of his own directly to Germain but heeded the orders of his superior in New York only when it suited him.

When Cornwallis first arrived at Petersburg in May, he found a dispatch from Clinton (directed to Phillips, who had died a few days before) outlining a new plan of campaign. Clinton wanted to repeat north of the Delaware "the same experiment (which has hitherto unfortunately not succeeded to the southward); . . .the inhabitants of Pennsylvania on both sides of the Susquehannah, York, Lancaster, Chester, and the Peninsula between Chesapeake and Delaware [bays] are represented to me to be friendly. There, or thereabouts, I think this experiment should now be tried. . . ."[7]

Cornwallis' reaction to Clinton's proposal was as flat a veto as a subordinate could deliver to a superior. The plan bore "too strong a resemblance to those emissaries from North Carolina to give me much confidence. . . . By the vigorous exertions of the present Governors of America, large Bodies of men are soon collected, and I have too often observed, that when the Storm appears, our friends disappear." He then reverted to his favorite theme: "I shall take the liberty of repeating, that if an offensive War is intended, Virginia appears to me, to be the only Province, in which it can be carried on, and in which there is a Stake. . . ."[8]

In mid-July, Clinton received Germain's dispatch of May 2 urging "the Prosectuion of the War . . . from South to North. . . ." Its Delphic overtones must have infuriated Clinton as much as Cornwallis' obstinacy. Germain's insistence on a campaign based in Virginia seemed to support Cornwallis. But in the next breath he seemed to agree with Clinton's Pennsylvania plan (which had not yet reached Whitehall). Germain wrote that "as it may be hazardous to the health of the Troops to carry on offensive operations to the South of the Delaware in the Summer Months . . . His Majesty leaves you at full Liberty to employ the Troops in any offensive Undertaking to the North of the Delaware. . . ."[9]

Germain's strictures, however, were so out of date as to be irrelevant. On June 2 (by which time Clinton had proposed and Cornwallis had disposed of the Pennsylvania plan) he was writing to Cornwallis that it was "a MATTER OF ASTONISHMENT to all Europe" that he had defeated Greene at Guilford Court House. Cornwallis had not hinted at, nor had Germain grasped, either the hollow nature of the victory or the fact that the Carolinas were as yet unconquered.

Thus the sum of British strategy at the beginning of August 1781 was that Clinton was sulking in New York writing long-winded dispatches of self-justification to Cornwallis and Germain while the British forces in Virginia, more than 7,000 strong, dug in at Yorktown to protect an anchorage in which there were no ships.[10]

Ever since the entry of the Bourbon allies into the war, the enemy had posed serious threats to British naval supremacy. It was unthinkable that Britain should lose control of the seas, or so the conceit and arrogance in England permitted its leaders to believe. Both Clinton and Cornwallis appreciated the importance of sea power and specifically the danger to which Cornwallis was exposed if the allies gained the upper hand in the North Atlantic. The position on the Chesapeake, observed the earl, "is ever liable to become a prey to a foreign Enemy, with a temporary superiority at Sea." French mistakes and good luck had so far prevented calamity. In 1781 British luck ran out and the French made no mistakes.[11]

The threat came in the form of a French reinforcement under Admiral the Comte de Grasse. Unlike his predecessor, the French commander was belligerent and aggressive. His departure for America, however, caused little concern in England. Germain informed Clinton in July that Admiral Sir George Rodney, commanding British forces in the West Indies, would be given precise instructions "to proceed directly to North America whenever Mr. De Grasse quits the Leeward Islands." Moreover, a successor had finally been appointed to replace Arbuthnot. Admiral Robert Digby would sail shortly with three ships of the line to augment British forces in the western Atlantic.[12]

De Grasse arrived in the West Indies and took command of a force of twenty-eight line-of-battle ships. There were eight more French capital ships at Newport under Admiral the Comte de Barras, presumably bottled up by the New York squadron commanded by Admiral Sir Thomas Graves. Soon after his arrival in the Caribbean, de Grasse received dispatches from Rochambeau and Washington urging him to cooperate in an attack on the Chesapeake. De Grasse showed himself to be not only aggressive but generous. He agreed to the plan and also promised to commit his entire command and to furnish 3,000 troops. He would, he said, remain in the North Atlantic until the middle of October.

Ten of the French capital ships had been ordered home for overhaul, but de Grasse ignored the orders. The West Indian merchant ships were due to be convoyed back to France. De Grasse ordered them to the shelter of Santo Domingo, where they remained for the rest of the year. All twenty-eight of the admiral's capital ships stood northward for the Chesapeake.[13]

The British now committed a series of blunders. The French departure was not noted for some time because de Grasse took his force through the Old Bahama Channel to conceal his movement. When Rodney found his adversary had given him the slip, he refused to believe that the Frenchman would not leave some of his force on station in the West Indies. Rodney therefore detached only fourteen ships of the line under Admiral Samuel Hood to follow de Grasse. In fact, because of de Grasse's indirect route Hood reached the Chesapeake ahead of him. Finding the bay empty, he continued on to New York—and missed Barras and his eight ships of the line, which had eluded Graves and were on their way to join de Grasse.

Contrary to British blundering, allied operations proceeded with clockwork precision. Washington and Rochambeau received word of de Grasse's cooperation on August 14. In a week the Americans were on the road with their French allies, a combined force of just over 8,000 men. Barras was bringing provisions and siege artillery from Newport. De Grasse's transports were to meet the army at the head of the Chesapeake on September 1.[14]

The army's passage through New Jersey was designed to convince Clinton that the allies were maneuvering to attack New York; Washington even ordered the laying out of an encampment opposite Staten Island. Whether the deception was exceptionally clever or whether Clinton believed what he wanted to believe is difficult to say. Spies deluged his headquarters with reports that the allied army was abandoning New York, but on September 1 Clinton wrote to Cornwallis that "unless Mr. Washington should send a considerable part of his army to the southward, I shall not judge it necessary to detach [reinforcements] thither." On September 2 the American and French troops were parading through Philadelphia.

True to his word, de Grasse arrived off the Chesapeake Capes on August 26. He sent transports up the bay to fetch Washington's army, and on September 2 he began putting ashore his own troops on the south side of the Peninsula. By September 18 the transports had reached the Head of the Elk and had embarked the allied army.[15]

September 1 is the first critical date in the chain of circumstances that led to the British disaster at Yorktown. On that date Cornwallis must have known that his position was becoming dangerous. The previous day, "A Lieutenant of the Charon who . . . went to Old Point Comfort, reports that there are between 30 and 40 [French] sail within the Capes, mostly ships of War & some of them very large." Although Cornwallis knew that Admiral Graves was on his way from New York to the Chesapeake he did not know that Hood had arrived with the West Indian reinforcement. Did he expect that Graves, with no more than ten ships of the line, could disperse the formidable enemy force of "between thirty and forty sail"? The earl did not know that Washington and Rochambeau were on their way south, but he had reports that boats from the French fleet were on their way up the James carrying regiments from de Grasse's transports. Surely under such circumstances he must rely on his own resources for he could not expect prompt assistance from Clinton. Simple prudence dictated that he put himself in a position to extricate himself from possible entrapment. The Yorktown position, originally established to protect the naval anchorage, now ceased to have any value. yet the man who had harried the Carolinas and pursued Nathanael Greene so relentlessly did nothing. General Claude Saint Simon landed his 3,000 men and marched them to join Lafayette without the slightest interference from the British. So Cornwallis stayed where he was. He was later to claim that Clinton's orders bound him to holding the Yorktown position. This from a general who for the past year had obeyed his superior only when it suited him.[16]

Graves was indeed on his way from New York. Counting Hood's addition, his force numbered nineteen ships of the line. On September 5 the British fleet arrived off the Chesapeake Capes. Although Barras had not yet arrived from Newport, de Grasse's battle line consisted of twenty-eight capital ships. Leaving four of these to guard his transports, the French commander sortied. The two fleets fought a confused engagement in which de Grasse nonetheless never lost sight of his strategic objective, which was to deny the British access to the Chesapeake. During the fighting and maneuvering, Barras finally arrived from the north and entered the bay, bringing the French force to a strength of thirty-six ships of the line. By September 14 Graves recognized that his situation was hopeless and set sail for New York. Cornwallis was now trapped in the cul-de-sac of the Yorktown peninsula.[17]

Or was he? September 14 is the second crucial date in the fate of Cornwallis' army. By then he knew that an overwhelming allied army was descending on him from the north, an army that, combined with Lafayette's, would outnumber him by better than two to one. But that force was still on the upper reaches of the Chesapeake and would not arrive for another twelve days.[18] His army still equaled the combined force of Lafayette and Saint Simon, and his troops were of better quality. Cornwallis had not hesitated to attack Gates at Camden or Greene at Guilford Court House when the odds against him were three to two and two to one respectively.

The Englishman seems finally to have been aroused from his torpor by Tarleton. The Legion commander had reconnoitered all the way into Williamsburg and found Lafayette's position exposed and his sentries and outposts carelessly manned. He pressed Cornwallis to strike at the enemy, and at his urging an attack was planned. On that day, however, a dispatch arrived from New York. Clinton informed Cornwallis that help was on the way, "with all the force that can be spared from hence, which is about 4,000 men." The dispatch was dated September 6. Clinton did not then know of Graves' repulse off the Chesapeake Capes, nor did he know the full strength of de Grasse's fleet. Of all the commanders involved, only Cornwallis knew all the facts: de Grasse had thirty-six sail of the line (Graves thought that Barras had joined de Grasse before the Battle of the Capes and that the French total was twenty-eight); Graves had been defeated and even if reinforced would have little chance of breaking through the overwhelming French force; the 4,000 men promised, even if they could be landed, would still leave Cornwallis outnumbered three to two. Clinton's promise was an empty one. Tarleton stated the obvious: "There existed no substantial reason to believe that the British Commander in Chief would be able . . . to give serious assistance to the King's troops in Virginia." But Cornwallis called off the attack on Lafayette. The dispatches, he said, left him no choice but to hold his post. Such rigid adherence to orders was not only uncharacteristic but flew in the face of the traditional discretion allowed a commander on the spot.[19]

From first to last Cornwallis' behavior since coming to Virginia seems incomprehensible. Why had he not run Lafayette to earth in July? If Lafayette was elusive there had certainly been an opportunity at Greenspring to punish him severely. After de Grasse's arrival, as the trap began to close, why did he not break out of the encirclement or at least abandon the static position at Yorktown the occupation of which now had no useful purpose? Did he share the arrogant and blind assumption of British naval invincibility even in the face of the brutal fact of de Grasse's fleet? Cornwallis surely knew too much of the fumbling hesitancy of the naval command and of his own superior Clinton to place much reliance on the promise of prompt relief. If he did not, he was soon to be treated to a demonstration.

One explanation, put forward with caution, may account for Cornwallis' malaise. The force that he took command of when he arrived in Virginia was more than twice as large as any *operational* force that he had ever commanded in the absence of a superior officer. There have been numerous instances in military history in which extremely capable officers in smaller commands have been incapable of handling larger ones. Brilliant regimental colonels sometimes floundered hopelessly when promoted to the direction of a brigade or corps. So Cornwallis, never commanding more than 3,000 men in the field, now found himself at the head of a force of more than 8,000 (he reported 8,885 men at the beginning of the siege). Such numbers may have been beyond his capacity to maneuver and control.[20]

Another possible explanation is that Cornwallis was physically exhausted. It will be recalled that he had been so ill in October 1780 that he could not even attend to his correspondence. Since December he had been continuously on the march—seven months of the hardest kind of campaigning. It is possible that the iron will that had driven him so relentlessly in the past was finally faltering under the stress of physical debility.

On September 28 Washington and Rochambeau brought their troops to the Peninsula and invested Yorktown. The total allied force now numbered over 16,000 men. On October 6 the allies began to dig parallels and approaches to advance their artillery into position to bombard the British defensive works.

In New York Clinton continued to fumble. On September 24 he wrote to Cornwallis that "it is determined that above five thousand men rank and file shall be embarked . . . and the joint exertions of the navy and the army made in a few days to relieve you. . . ." On September 25 "the necessary repairs of the fleet will detain us here to the 5th day of next month; and your Lordship must be sensible to the unforeseen accidents that may lengthen it out a day or two longer." On September 30, "assurances [have been] given me this day by Admiral Graves, that we may pass the bar by the 12th of October, if the winds permit. . . ."

On October 9 the allies opened a devastating bombardment on the British position. It is ironic that this final and climactic battle of the War of American Independence should be the one which, of all the battles of this long war, most strictly conformed to eighteenth-century military orthodoxy. The great military engineer Vauban would have been highly gratified at the leisurely and orderly advance of the parallels, the precise location of the guns, and the massive bombardment that inexorably destroyed Cornwallis' defensive works.

On October 18 Clinton wrote from Sandy Hook, "The fleet is assembled, the troops embarked on board, and the whole will go to sea, if the wind continues fair, tomorrow morning."[21]

Two days later Lord Cornwallis reported to his commander in chief, "I have the mortification to inform your Excellency that I have been forced to give up the posts at York and Gloucester, and to surrender the troops under my command. . . ."[22] Tradition has it that as the British marched out of their shattered defenses to the surrender ground the musicians played "The World Turned Upside Down":

> If ponies rode men, and if grass
> >   ate cows,
> And cats should be chased in holes
> >   by the mouse . . .
> Summer were spring, and the
> >   other way 'round,
> Then all the world would be
> >   upside down.[23]

✳ London ✳

The American victory at Yorktown came as the bitter climax of a second British plan to conquer her rebellious colonies. Unlike the defeat of Burgoyne at Saratoga in 1777, Yorktown was the final disaster of a campaign that had been marked by the steady deterioration of England's fortunes. Yet the American victory in the South attained real significance only if it destroyed English will to resist. And that will was a collective one that consisted of Parliament, the ministry, and the King.

As the summer of 1781 drew to its close, the news from America was increasingly gloomy for anyone who did not wear the rose-tinted glasses of Lord George Germain. It was obvious that despite the reportedly decisive victory of Cornwallis at Guilford Court House, two salient and indisputable facts had emerged. The news of the marching and countermarching by Greene and Cornwallis made it clear that the American army was still in the field, giving the lie to Germain's assertion that "no resistance on their part . . . can materially obstruct the progress of the King's arms in the speedy suppression of the rebellion."

Equally important was the fact that in the Carolinas the Loyalists had not rallied to the King's standard. The ministry was careful not to publish Cornwallis' dispatch of April 1781 in which he reported the utter lack of Loyalist support following Guilford Court House, for this would have fatally undermined Germain's principal justification for continuing the war. Yet the Opposition sensed the truth. When Germain told the Commons that "a great proportion of the inhabitants were inclined to compromise with the mother country" and that only lack of arms prevented the Loyalists from resisting, Charles James Fox refused to believe him. Cornwallis, he said, had defeated Greene, but "he had found no one good consequence of his success, not being joined by any body of Americans as he had expected." Fox scored Germain for the continued failure of his policies: "It was undeniable that the project was a vain one, similar to all other enterprises we had formed during the course of the war."[24]

It was evident that the position of Lord North's ministry was far graver than after Saratoga. In the four years since 1777 England had been drawn into an ever-widening conflict. For the first time in a century England faced her enemies alone. The bulk of her army was mired in the morass of the war in America. Her navy was stretched to its limit—perhaps beyond—to fend off the combined Bourbon fleets. And to what purpose was the war to be continued? Germain had acknowledged that the rebellion could not be suppressed without a rising of the Loyalists and reiterated that England could not abandon her friends in America. But the argument was wearing thin.

By midsummer of 1781, then, the ministry's position was becoming more and more difficult to defend. But although the Opposition pressed its attack with increasing boldness, the North government stood firm. It might yield points in debate, even stand silent in the face of denunciation, but it still mustered the necessary votes to beat back its enemies on the three principal issues of financial reform, reform of Parliament, and the continuation of the war.[25]

To understand why this was so it is necessary to understand the nature of parliamentary representation and the variety of sources from which the ministry drew its support. It is also necessary to remember that the party system in England was virtually nonexistent so that the usual pattern of party leadership and discipline did not exist. The formation of the North ministry in 1770 resulted from a coalition of cliques and blocs that had been fashioned by the King after a decade of political chaos during which half a dozen ministries had come and gone.

Something over 200 seats in Parliament were controlled by the great landowners and heads of families, who by the sheer weight of money and place were able to retain their seats or dictate who should occupy them. The great magnates often controlled several seats (although usually not more than three or four). These might be pledged to the government in return for royal favors, or because of straightforward loyalty to the crown, or for a financial consideration. The latter votes were purchased at election time out of a special fund maintained by the King and dispensed by Lord North or his aides. There were also those who controlled "rotten boroughs," where only two or three people were qualified to vote, but such boroughs were not so numerous as their notoriety in history suggests.

There were also the close boroughs whose control was just as complete though more complex. There were close boroughs in which the government's direct interest represented by a dockyard or ordnance depot gave it control. There were twenty-four such seats, and they were assigned from North's office. About one-third of these were occupied by government administrators such as Charles Jenkinson, Secretary at War, and John Robinson, who was North's principal aide in the treasury.[26]

Other close boroughs were controlled by great magnates who owned the residences whose occupants were qualified to vote. Sir James Lowther, a member of the Opposition, bought all such homes in Haslemere and sent workers from his colliery to occupy them at election time. They dutifully voted for Lowther's candidate and then returned to the mines.

It was possible for a candidate to stand for election from more than one constituency. This was done primarily to insure the retention of one's seat in Parliament, but if he was fortunate enough to win two or three elections the member might dispose of the extra seats to his associates or sell them, either to the government or to another member who wished to increase his influence. These seats were avidly sought by the government for their control enabled North to retain in Parliament a supporter who had failed to be reelected from his own district.[27]

If the modern reader is dismayed by this system of buying and selling representation, it may only be pointed out that it was done more or less openly and that it was done by all parties. North and his political adviser, John Robinson, disbursed about £100,000 from the King's election fund in 1780 in about forty campaigns, an average of a little more than £2,000 per candidate. Candidates themselves often spent as much as £15,000, and in one election in Cambridge it was estimated that three candidates spent £50,000.

For all the dirty smell of money, there existed a remarkable degree of principle. Men who bore the names of Suffolk and Salisbury and Gower had not forgotten entirely the patriotism and idealism of their English heritage. Owing one's seat in Parliament to a patron or minister did not bind the member to blind obedience. The policy or actions of the ministry might become so offensive that a member would be driven into the Opposition regardless of his obligation.[28]

Finally, there were the independents. Sometimes called the "country gentlemen," they were never exclusively from the country nor were they of a particular social class. James Martin of Tewkesbury was head of one of the great banking houses of England, and four independents sat for the city of London. These independents sought no patronage or financial gain and studiously avoided any commitment to the ministry or to any of the various political factions. They were guided only by the local interests of their constituents and by their own judgment. Although accused of provincialism, they claimed that theirs was the only truly imperial view. They were regarded with considerable deference because, although there was a strong strain of conservatism in their makeup, their ability was acknowledged on all sides, and they represented an uncommitted group from which both the government and the Opposition hoped to gain support.

Although some came from close boroughs or rotten boroughs, most represented popular constituencies with sizable electorates. They were careful to protect the local interests of their supporters, but such interests were seldom related to the great questions of the American war, executive influence, or parliamentary reform. Among them, something like a popular will or national interest found expression. Because they held more than 200 seats, no ministry could stay in power without considerable support from the country gentlemen; and the Opposition could never unseat the North ministry without their support. Independent they might be, but they considered themselves patriots and therefore loyal to the King, whom they would not lightly abandon.[29]

Several factors were at work to raise serious doubts among the country gentlemen when Parliament convened for a brief pre-Christmas session following the news of Yorktown. What if the policy put forward by the King was obviously detrimental to the nation? As had happened frequently in England's long history, the prestige of the crown was being severely tested when the royal will was set against the well-being of the empire. There was also the concomitant question of budget reform. The most important source of government revenue was the land tax, which bore most heavily on large propertyholders. To continue the war, additional funds must be raised. Lord North, aware of the explosive potential inherent in a request for increased taxes, had warned his colleagues ten months earlier that the war could not be financed for more than a year.[30]

In the December session North himself moved to the position that if the war was to be ended, America must be abandoned. Little was accomplished before the holiday adjournment, but it was obvious that the great issue was the Opposition's insistence that the ruinous war must be concluded. The King and his principal supporter, Germain, contended that "we can never continue to exist as a great or powerful nation after we have lost or renounced the sovereignty of America"; not only would the geographic entity be lost but the American trade and American bases from which to defend the West Indies, Canada, and the Maritime Provinces. In the last resort Britain should at least retain what it already held, New York, Charleston, and Savannah. Germain declared that the ministry was unanimous against abandoning America, but the cabinet had already determined to send only recruit replacements to Clinton. Sandwich, the head of the Admiralty, shared with Germain the blame for Yorktown, and these two became the principal targets of the Opposition attack. Lord North, as though seeking to get out of the line of fire, left the Treasury bench during the debate and took a seat behind it.[31]

To complicate matters, Clinton had finally asked to be recalled. His obvious successor would be Sir Guy Carleton, the governor-general of Canada, but he was an inveterate enemy of Germain, who refused to continue in office if Carleton were given the American command. The King had no objection to replacing Germain so long as his successor was committed to opposing American independence. It would be well nigh impossible to find such a man. North put the matter succinctly: "You see there is no great objection to changing men, but a very great one to changing measures. . . ." Yet only by changing measures could the ministry maintain itself against the growing forces of the Opposition.

In the interim following Parliament's adjournment for Christmas, Germain sought a decision from the King, declaring that he would leave office rather than abandon America. He received no assurances from George III, who, in effect, passed the buck to North. North told Germain flatly that it was impossible to continue the war and that American independence was a foregone conclusion. When a few days later Germain reminded North that his position must be confirmed if he was to write instructions for the coming campaign, North was evasive, saying that no successor had been found. But Germain considered his authority at an end, and on February 9 he finally left office.[32]

The Opposition had apparently spent the holiday consolidating its position. Although it was obvious that neither the public nor the ministry supported the continuance of the war, the obstinacy of the King blocked every effort to act. When Parliament reassembled in January 1782, it was clear that the country gentlemen had deserted both the ministry and the King. The Commons voted to abandon the coercion of America by a majority of nineteen. The King found himself faced by the leaders of the Opposition, Fox, Lord Rockingham, and Shelburne, all of whom refused to accept a coalition ministry under North. Rockingham, spokesman for the dissidents, announced that they would accept nothing less than a clean sweep of men and measures. The decisive point was reached when Thomas Grovesnor informed North that the country gentlemen could no longer support the King. On March 20 a vote on the removal of the ministry was scheduled. North determined to avoid disgrace, and having finally obtained the King's permission, he resigned.[33]

The new ministry headed by the Marquis of Rockingham took office at the end of March 1782. Fox became foreign secretary and Shelburne Secretary of State, heading a new department charged with Irish, domestic, and colonial affairs. It was he who was to supervise the ending of the war, including peace negotiations and the evacuation of the British army in America. The new ministry was determined to institute great changes in men and measures but did not possess the knowledge or skill to effect policy. As a minor example, Admiral Rodney returned from the West Indies after having won the most decisive naval victory of the war, defeating a French fleet under de Grasse at the battle of the Saintes. Unaware of this the new leaders had purged the navy and replaced Rodney with Admiral Hugh Pigot. An embarrassing scene ensued when the greatest naval hero of the war came home to find that he had been stripped of his command. The ministry lamely conferred a peerage on Rodney, and Parliament voted him a pension of £2,000.[34]

Shelburne opened negotiations with the American diplomats in Paris, and preliminary articles of peace between England and America were signed on November 21, 1782. The story of the conclusion of the treaty has been told elsewhere, but it was some time before the British occupation ended. The ineptness of the new ministry (complicated by the death of Rockingham in July 1782) was seen in the fact that no provision was made for assembling the shipping necessary to evacuate the British army, its vast stores and artillery, and Loyalists who wished to leave America. In fact, even after it was decided that the army was to be withdrawn, the implacable bureaucracy shipped fifteen months' stores and provisions *to* America; nor were captains given orders to make their ships available for the evacuation. It was estimated that 85,000 tons of shipping would be necessary to evacuate New York alone, three times the amount that was available. Thus it was not until November 23, 1783, a full year after the signing of the articles of peace, that the great port which had been headquarters for the British army for seven years saw the enemy fleet weigh anchor and put to sea.[35]

✳ Charleston ✳

After the battle of Eutaw Springs, Greene hoped to take advantage of the enemy's weakened condition and resume the offensive. But the battle, coming at the climax of several weeks of marching and maneuvering, had reduced the Americans to an impotence that matched that of their opponents. Even the seemingly indestructible corps of Kirkwood and Washington were exhausted. Greene therefore pulled his army back to the High Hills of the Santee. There the slow process of recovery began, but the commanding general was still beset with chronic problems of sickness, discipline, and the steady erosion of manpower. The tireless Kirkwood had finally succumbed to malaria. The hospital contained 350 wounded Americans and 250 redcoats whom Stewart had left behind on the battlefield. Greene had fewer than 1,000 men fit for duty at the end of October when he reported to Washington, "We can attempt nothing further except in a partisan way. . . . I look forward with pain to December when the whole Virginia [Continental] line will leave us."

It is an article of military faith that nothing—not even casualties on the battlefield—so erodes troop morale as bad food and no pay. In both these respects the tolerance of Greene's army had been stretched almost to its limit. "An army which has received no pay for more than two years," said Greene, ". . . subsisted without spirits, and often short in the usual allowances of meat and bread, will mutiny. . . ." Mutiny was in the air, and the seriousness of the threat was underscored by the fact that the discontent centered among the veterans of the Maryland Continentals. They submitted petitions to Greene pointing out that of the seven Maryland regiments that had begun the campaign there were now only 200 survivors. They were unpaid, hungry, and nearly naked. Their discontent spread to other regiments and came to a boil when a South Carolina soldier, emboldened by an excess of drink, appeared on parade urging the men to defy their officers. He was immediately seized, court-martialed, and shot in the presence of the entire army. This had a salutary effect, and the threat was averted.[36]

Greene was also aware of the spread of anarchy in the countryside that was intensified by the withdrawal of the British from the interior of the Carolinas. In September a Tory raiding party led by Hector McNeil struck suddenly at Hillsborough, capturing North Carolina Governor Thomas Burke. The Whigs quickly retaliated, dispersing the Tories and killing McNeil, but Burke remained a prisoner of the British. Rumors reached headquarters that the Whigs were carrying out savage reprisals against the Loyalists that were sanctioned by North Carolina leaders. Greene was quick to issue stern orders to Jethro Sumner and Griffin Rutherford. Persecution of the Tories would stiffen their resistance, he said, and would brand Americans with the same evil reputation that had discredited the British: "You cannot treat the inhabitants with too much delicacy, nor should the least encouragement be given to the soldiers, either to invade the property of the people, or offer them any personal insults— This conduct it is which had made the British so very odious."[37]

In the last week of October the news of Cornwallis' surrender reached army headquarters. There was, of course, a wild celebration. Even Thomas Sumter, who had only a short while before protested his inability to take the field, came galloping into camp to join the revelry. But Greene was as usual not carried away by this sensational turn of events. Cornwallis' army was, after all, only a fraction of the British forces remaining in America. Wilmington, Charleston, and Savannah were still held by the British. Greene's immediate reaction was to urge Washington to send reinforcements that would enable him to complete the reconquest of the South. Already 700 men from Maryland who had been on their way to Greene were diverted to Yorktown by order of the commander in chief, drawing from Light Horse Harry Lee the sardonic observation that there was "a perfect monopoly . . . of men and supplies, to fight a small, deranged army." Greene even entertained a hope that de Grasse's naval force would blockade Charleston and thereby repeat the strategy that had destroyed Cornwallis. But de Grasse had already overstayed his leave and felt obliged to return and guard the West Indies. The best that Washington would promise was the 700 troops from Maryland and the Pennsylvania Line of Mad Anthony Wayne. It would be two months before these troops could join the southern command.[38]

By the middle of November, Greene felt strong enough to resume the offensive. He intended to keep pressure on the enemy and confine his operations as much as possible. The immediate objective was the British outpost at Dorchester, about thirty miles from Charleston. The village was held by 850 enemy troops commanded by Major John Doyle. Greene hoped to surprise them and cut them off, and he himself accompanied a reconnaissance force of 400 cavalry and infantry led by Lee and Washington. As the force approached Dorchester and began to skirmish, Greene was recognized and Doyle assumed that he was confronted by the main American army. He hastily destroyed his stores, sank his guns in the Ashley River, and retreated to the vicinity of Charleston. There was wild alarm in the city, and the British prepared for an assault by the Americans which, of course, never came.

A similar panic overtook the British commander at Wilmington. Hearing of the approach of Wayne's Pennsylvanians, who were finally en route to the Southern Department, he ordered the port evacuated. By the first of the year only Charleston and Savannah were controlled by the British. General Leslie, who had taken command at Charleston early in November, was thoroughly frightened by Greene's aggressive strategy and bent every effort to strengthen the defense of the city. The Americans pushed down the Ashley to Round O, where the army now lay across the land communication with Savannah. Marion patrolled the Cooper River with his headquarters at Monck's Corner.[39]

The first week in January marked the departure of the officers of the Delaware line. Among them was Robert Kirkwood, who had led his men through six continuous years of fighting. Almost ten years later he volunteered to serve under General Arthur St. Clair in his campaign against the Indian tribes of the Old Northwest. On November 4, 1791, he was killed in action on the Miami River. It was his thirty-third battle. The two Delaware companies were added to William Washington's dragoons to form another legion.

Lee and Marion now pushed their patrols down the Cooper as Greene continued to apply pressure on Charleston from the west. The troops enjoyed the relative luxury of plentiful food, although they complained that rice was no substitute for flour. Clothing was still in short supply. Greene reported that 600 of his men had only breech clouts "and never came out of their tents; and the rest are as ragged as wolves."

Greene had hoped that the American victory at Yorktown would induce Washington to release sizable reinforcements to the Southern Department. Information was received that the British planned to reinforce Leslie and resume a southern offensive. Greene begged Washington and Rochambeau to send more regiments, but both refused, the former citing the need to keep Virginia secure. The commander in chief seemed at times as myopic as Clinton in his failure to see beyond his own command.[40]

The rumors of Leslie's reinforcement proved false, but Greene confessed that he had been "confoundedly scared," and he laid before Governor Rutledge a proposal to raise 2,000 Negro troops. He was supported in his request by Colonel John Laurens, son of Henry Laurens, a South Carolina merchant and planter who had been president of the Continental Congress. In 1779 Congress had authorized the enlistment of 3,000 black troops in the South offering to pay slave owners $1,000 for each recruit (it was assumed that the black soldiers would be freed after their service). Greene's proposal, however, was refused by the recently assembled legislature, drawing from General Washington the observation that the spirit of freedom that had existed at the start of the war "has long since subsided and every selfish feeling has taken its place."[41]

Political as well as military considerations lay behind the steady pressure that Greene was exerting on the enemy. He was as anxious as Governor Rutledge to reestablish civil government, not only because of the generally salutary effect that it would have for the Whig cause but because he was increasingly confronted with problems that he felt were outside the province of military authority. General elections were held, and on January 18, 1782, the South Carolina General Assembly convened at Jacksonboro. The town was a scant thirty miles from Charleston. By establishing the seat of government on the enemy's doorstep, Greene was demonstrating that British power in South Carolina was at an end. Among the members of the assembly were Marion, Pickens, and Sumter.[42]

Greene had assigned the task of clearing the enemy from Georgia to Wayne and his Pennsylvanians. Wayne was charged with confining the British to Savannah and suppressing a British-inspired Indian uprising. Between January and July he conducted a vigorous campaign that culminated in a battle with the Creeks on June 24 in which the principal chief, Emistasigo, was killed. A month later Savannah was evacuated.[43]

As the war wound down, Greene's problems seemed to increase. The British in Charleston posed no threat except for occasional raids that were primarily foraging expeditions. But there were several thousand Loyalists in hiding who had to be routed out or induced to surrender. Sumter estimated that there were 1,500 in the swamps along the Edisto River alone. Both Greene and Rutledge issued proclamations promising amnesty to those who came in voluntarily and agreed to serve with the army. Many hundreds of these former enemies responded; indeed, for many Loyalists enlistment in the army was their best assurance of protection.[44]

Most of the senior officers were leaving the army. Marion left to serve in the newly elected assembly and this sparked a quarrel between Peter Horry and Captain Hezekiah Maham over rank. Otho Holland Williams and John Eager Howard returned to Maryland. Light Horse Harry Lee retired, and the officers of the Legion were outraged when Greene appointed an "outsider," John Laurens, to the command. They threatened to resign unless one of their own was appointed, but the commanding general accepted their resignations. Greene had no intention of allowing even the officers of the Legion "to cram the thing down my throat. . . ." The officers, surprised and embarrassed, withdrew their resignations. On several occasions General Leslie asked for a truce to allow his men to forage for supplies. Greene refused. If Leslie was out of provisions, he could surrender. The American commander was still suspicious of British good faith.[45]

The long summer of 1782 slowly passed. Hot weather brought sickness and death to the American camp; nearly 200 soldiers perished. By fall news came that the preliminary peace with England had been concluded. In August Leslie received orders to evacuate Charleston, but transports did not arrive until October, and Leslie took care first to evacuate those Loyalists who wished to leave South Carolina. Not until December 13 were the British ready to complete their evacuation of the city.

Greene had finally agreed to a truce but insisted that American troops enter the city literally on the heels of the British withdrawal. As Leslie's rear guard marched toward the docks, they were followed at a 200-yard interval by Wayne's corps of light infantry. The city seemed deserted except for the two armies. Later in the day General Greene, escorted by the Legion and accompanied by the new governor, John Mathews, led a column of Continentals in a parade down King Street. Now the townspeople turned out and accompanied the soldiers through the city. Greene established the last headquarters of the Southern Department at the home of John Rutledge.[46]

The long war was over.

Conclusion

Most of the conflicts that constituted what is known as the Second Hundred Years' War could be fairly characterized as limited wars for limited victories. However intricate the military strategy, however dramatic the victories or defeats, the game of war was played to achieve a diplomatic objective. Victory was won when the enemy no longer had the will to resist. In the conflicts of the eighteenth century the decision for peace or war usually resided in the single will of an absolute monarch. A Louis or a Frederick might decide that the price of peace—a bit of territory or an economic concession—was not too high if it brought relief from an expensive and destructive war.

The War of American Independence broke this pattern in that for both participants the will to resist was a collective one. It is conceivable that in America, even if Congress and the army had given up the struggle, some or all of the states might have continued to fight.

The American victory at Yorktown finally broke the collective will of Parliament, the ministry, and the King. But the effect of Yorktown can be understood only if it is placed in the context of the entire southern campaign. While it is true that Washington and his French allies were the architects of the victory on the Chesapeake, Nathanael Greene and his southern army could claim a large share in the victory as surely as if they had been present at the surrender field.

In the parliamentary session in the late summer of 1781 Charles James Fox spoke for the growing numbers of the Opposition when he attacked the ministry for continuing the American war. "Had our army been vanquished [at Guilford Court House] what course would they have taken? Certainly they would have abandoned the field of action, and flown for refuge to the sea-side; now these are precisely the measures we were obliged to adopt after Guilford, the victorious army leaving the field, abandoning the future object of its expedition, and returning to the fleet." Sir Thomas Clarges, a member of the independents on whom the government relied heavily, announced his defection from the ministerial ranks. He was joined by two of Lord North's hitherto most firm supporters, Richard Rigby and George Onslow.[1]

When Parliament convened for the brief pre-Christmas session, it was known not only that Cornwallis' army was lost but that the British hold on the South had been reduced to Wilmington, Charleston, and Savannah. Lord Rockingham, the most powerful leader in the Opposition, noted: "The most calamitous events were perhaps upon the eve of happening [so] that even a victory at sea, the being able to extricate Lord Cornwallis' army (which would almost be miraculous) would probably only *postpone* our final extirpation from the continent of America." Yorktown was the denouement of a drama that began in the Carolina backcountry in the fall of 1780.[2]

This war also broke the pattern of the eighteenth century in that there were no strategic towns or fortresses the occupation of which would provide the keys to victory. Ticonderoga, considered even by Washington as the Gibraltar of North America, fell to the British with no dire consequences. When the capital of the new nation was threatened, Congress simply packed its bags, and the British found, as Benjamin Franklin put it, that "Philadelphia has taken Sir William Howe." The occupation of New York, Charleston, and Savannah gave the British strategic naval bases from which to operate, but the British fleet could not prevent supplies and troops from landing at Boston or Newport or the Chesapeake. Thus the European strategic doctrine of a war of posts did not apply. From a military point of view, the redcoats had not only to win battles but to follow up by occupying territory.

Could England have won the war for America? There is, of course, no way of knowing whether the British could have eventually overcome the inherent difficulties of geography and distance, of communications, and of operating in the interior of a hostile countryside.

An important factor in England's failure was its flawed leaders. This war did not produce a Marlborough or a Wellington, but wars have been won with mediocre generals. The fatal characteristics of English leadership from 1776 to 1781 were a paralysis of will and lack of energy. Clinton owed his appointment to the fact that he was virtually the only candidate available, and it was clear from the outset that Germain did not have great confidence in his American commander's abilities. Yet Germain seems to have been unable either to give him a theater commander's freedom of action or to dismiss him after Cornwallis became available (the reader is reminded that in 1758 Pitt replaced two American commanders in nine months).

For his part Clinton displayed the same paralysis of will. He could not bring himself either to hold Cornwallis on a tight rein or to give him the discretion—and the responsibility—of an independent commander in the South. The final absurdity was that although Cornwallis went to Virginia without Clinton's approval, he justified the disaster at Yorktown on the ground that Clinton forbade him to leave his post.

In the war at sea there was similar indecision. After the entrance of Spain and France, England never had naval superiority. Yet English leaders seemed incapable of acknowledging the navy's limitations even in the face of evidence to the contrary. The loss of Grenada and St. Vincent in the West Indies and Minorca in the Mediterranean as well as near-disasters that were averted only by good luck or French incompetence failed to penetrate the myth of the "mistress of the seas." Reality dictated that only bold and decisive leadership could fully utilize the limited resources of the navy. It seems incredible that the ministers' choice for the direction of American operations was Admiral Arbuthnot, a man disqualified by age, lack of experience, and temperament. It may be argued that more capable leaders such as Hood and Rodney were needed elsewhere, but the fact remains that the war was lost in the waters of North America and that Rodney's defeat of de Grasse in 1782 did not materially affect the outcome. Even when the ministry decided that Arbuthnot should be replaced, it would not name a successor and it was nine months before the old admiral left New York. And again there was a final absurdity. As the Yorktown campaign reached its climax, three admirals converged on New York: Graves, who was commanding pending the arrival of Arbuthnot's replacement, had no experience in fleet command; Hood, the ablest, was also the most junior in rank; Digby, Arbuthnot's successor, was so recently arrived that he professed not to understand the circumstances and deferred to Graves. So it was Graves who commanded in the final crisis.

In the southern campaign, at least it could be said that the British command did not lack boldness and energy. Cornwallis' flaw was that he too often made assumptions about what the enemy would do instead of calculating what he could do. In the aftermath of the battle of the Cowpens the earl assumed that Morgan would retreat westward to the mountains and so allowed Greene to reunite his command. Cornwallis then assumed that Greene would not be able to cross at the fords on the lower Dan and thereby missed the opportunity of bringing him to battle before he could receive reinforcements. Finally, in the stubborn pursuit of his "domino" strategy, the Englishman went to Virginia with only the most cursory warning to Rawdon of the danger to the South Carolina garrisons. The larger disaster at Yorktown overshadowed the casual indifference with which Cornwallis abandoned his subordinate, a dereliction far more reprehensible than Howe's failure to support Burgoyne in 1777.

In planning the southern campaign Germain recognized that a principal means of victory might be found in the utilization of American Loyalists. The most obvious use would be to supply some of the military manpower that Britain needed to bring about a counterrevolution. Paradoxically,

Germain and his generals overestimated the numbers and strength of the Loyalists and failed to make use of the support that was available.

English arrogance and contempt for Americans in general fostered the belief that Loyalists would not make good soldiers. Despite the demonstrated ability of such units as Tarleton's Legion, Simcoe's Queen's Rangers, Rawdon's Volunteers of Ireland, and Cruger's New York Volunteers, the British refused to incorporate Loyalist regiments into the regular army or to give something like equal status to American officers. Even regular officers such as Rawdon and Ferguson had to accept temporary "provincial" rank because they did not command regular regiments. Lesser discriminations (such as the refusal to grant half-pay pensions) and failure to adequately supply and equip Loyalist regiments discouraged many who would have been eager to fight for their country.

Even more disastrous was the failure of the army to support Loyalists who organized counterrevolutionary efforts of their own. From Moore's Creek Bridge in 1776 to the slaughter of Pyle's regiment in 1781 Loyalists learned the bitter lesson. Assurances of support by the redcoats, even if they materialized, were always temporary. The regulars eventually moved on, leaving the King's friends to the mercy of their Whig neighbors. Small wonder that Tarleton, commenting on visitors to the British camp in 1781, observed, "The generality of these visitants seemed desirous of peace, but averse to every exertion that might procure it; . . . the dread of violence and persecution prevented their taking a decided part in a cause that yet appeared dangerous."[3]

After the fall of Charleston the British for the first time attempted an occupation policy. They established the chain of posts in the interior, and Clinton ordered the organization of a peacekeeping force under Major Patrick Ferguson. But the pacification program broke down in the face of partisan resistance mounted by Sumter, Marion, and other Whig leaders. To this was added the inveterate plundering of the redcoats and the vengeful spirit of the Tories, who were more interested in settling old scores than in keeping the peace.

There was also the failure of the American Secretary to implement the political strategy to which he had paid lip service before Parliament. Despite the urgings of Arbuthnot and Simpson, Germain rejected the notion of establishing civil government. There were a number of prominent leaders, such men as the elder Pinckney, Lowndes, and Daniel Huger, whose experience and prestige would have given a reconstituted government respect and authority. Yet no attempt was made to revive "the British Constitution and the free operation of the laws."

Whether or not the Carolinas teemed with Loyalists, as Germain supposed, is beside the point. The fact was that the loyalty of most Carolinians to either side did not run deep. In the aftermath of the fall of Charleston it was evident that those who did not support the crown were not irrevocably committed to resistance, as the initial submission of Pickens, Williamson, and others demonstrated. It seems clear that if the occupation of the interior posts had been accompanied by the establishment of civil government, including a system of courts, and if the Loyalist militia had pursued an evenhanded policy in executing Clinton's instructions "for the maintainance of peace and good order," then there might well have been a return to the King's peace.

Nathanael Greene never lost sight of the fact that he was fighting a political war. Soon after he assumed command he wrote, "There is no mortal more fond of enterprise [partisan warfare] than myself; but this is not the basis on which the fate of this country depends. It is not a war of posts, but a contest for States dependent on public opinion."[4]

Theodore White, in his *In Search of History* and writing in the context of the Chinese Revolution, observed, ". . . People accept government only if government accepts its first duty—which is to protect them. This is an iron rule running from the bombed-out streets of Chunking to the feudal communities of the Middle Ages to the dark streets of New York and Rome where the helpless are so often the prey."[5] Let it be added that the iron rule runs also to the Carolina backcountry. In the struggle for dominance against the backdrop of revolution, war becomes politics in that victory will be determined by the side that convinces the people that it can protect lives and property. Generals who ignore the iron rule are foredoomed to failure. The British high command dimly perceived this but failed to recognize its supreme importance. And Germain intrusted the war to his generals without giving them any instruction as to how to deal with the war's political problems. The British may have had the best army, but they could never convince the people that the redcoats could be the guarantors of "life, liberty, and the pursuit of happiness."

✳ ✳ ✳ Notes ✳ ✳ ✳

ABBREVIATIONS

AR   Sir Henry Clinton, *The American Rebellion: . . . Narrative of His Campaigns, 1775–1782, with an Appendix of Original Documents,* ed. William B. Willcox, New Haven, Conn., 1954

BHP   Sir Guy Carleton Papers, more familiarly known as the British Headquarters Papers, Colonial Williamsburg

CL   The William L. Clements Library, Ann Arbor, Michigan

GHQ   *Georgia Historical Quarterly*

HMC   Historical Manuscripts Commission

JSH   *Journal of Southern History*

LC   Library of Congress

NCSR   *North Carolina State Records*

NYHS   New York Historical Society

PMHB   *Pennsylvania Magazine of History and Biography*

SCHGM   *South Carolina Historical and Genealogical Magazine*

SCLC   South Carolina Loyalists Claims. Volumes 52–57 are in the British Public Records Office; Volume 25 is in the Ontario Archives

WMQ   *William and Mary Quarterly*

CHAPTER I

1. Piers Mackesy, *The War for America, 1775–1783* (Cambridge, Mass., 1965), chap. 8, esp. pp. 165–70; see also Geoffrey Marcus, *A History of the British Navy: The Formative Years* (London, 1961).

2. Edward J. Lowell, *The Hessians and Other German Auxiliaries of Great Britain in the Revolutionary War* (1884; new ed., Williamstown, Mass., 1970), pp. 17–20.

3. R. Arthur Bowler, *Logistics and the Failure of the British Army in America* (Princeton, 1975), p. 9.

4. Mackesy, *War for America,* chap. 10; Sir Henry Clinton, *The American Rebellion: Sir Henry Clinton's Narrative of His Campaigns, 1775–1782, with an Appendix*

of Original Documents, ed. William B. Willcox (New Haven, 1954), pp. 99–101 (hereafter cited as *AR*.)

5. Mackesy, *War for America*, pp. 216–19; *AR*, pp. 102–06.

6. Mackesy, *War for America*, pp. 221–22, 237–45; *AR*, pp. 105–07.

7. Mackesy, *War for America*, pp. 249–51, 257–60.

8. Germain to Clinton, Mar. 8, 1778, British Headquarters Papers, Colonial Williamsburg (hereafter cited as BHP); Memorandum, Dec. 5, 1778, Germain Papers, Supplemental Dispatches, Clements Library, Ann Arbor, Mich. (hereafter cited as CL).

9. Germain to Clinton, Jan. 23, 1779, *AR*, pp. 398–99. Clinton noted that of his 22,000 men only 18,900 were present and fit for duty.

Germain's letters in the Clinton Papers, CL, contained passages that are underlined, in all probability by Clinton. I have taken the liberty of omitting the italics in order that the reader might not confuse Clinton's emphases with Germain's.

10. Clinton to Germain, May 22, 1779, *AR*, pp. 407–08; ibid., p. 127. Although the *Narrative* was written some years after the events described, it reflects Clinton's state of mind at the time of the events, as evidenced by his letters of May 14 and 22 (ibid., pp. 405–08). Clinton's account is valuable not only because his record of events (with a very few highly significant exceptions) is accurate but also because the feelings and opinions expressed are those that he had at the time of the events. Obviously, Clinton had his voluminous notes and correspondence at hand as he wrote so that his recollections of both events and sentiments could be verified.

11. For a more elaborate analysis of Clinton see William Willcox, *Portrait of a General: Sir Henry Clinton in the War of Independence, 1775–1782* (New York, 1964), chap. 12, and William Willcox and Frederick Wyatt, "Sir Henry Clinton: A Psychological Exploration in History," *WMQ*, 3d ser., 16 (1959): pp. 3–26.

12. Clinton to Germain, May 14, 1779, *AR*, p. 405; ibid., pp. 120–22.

13. George Washington, *The Writings of George Washington, from the Original Manuscript Sources, 1775–1799*, ed. John C. Fitzpatrick, 39 vols. (Washington, 1931–44), 15: p. 292; Christopher Ward, *The War of the Revolution*, ed. John R. Alden, 2 vols. (New York, 1952), 2: p. 867; *AR*, pp. 123–24.

14. *AR*, p. 124.

15. Ward, *Revolution*, 2: p. 619; Tryon to Clinton, July 20, 1779, *AR*, p. 414; Benjamin F. Stevens, ed., *Facsimiles of Manuscripts in European Archives Relating to America*, 26 vols. (London, 1889–98), 10: no. 1006; Willcox, *Clinton*, pp. 277–78.

16. Ward, *Revolution*, 2: chaps. 49 and 50; *New York Journal*, Aug. 2, 1779, quoted in Frank Moore, ed., *Diary of the American Revolution* (New York, 1860), p. 193.

17. *AR*, pp. 137, 140–41.

18. For the Rhode Island episode see Willcox, *Clinton*, pp. 290–92, and the correspondence between Clinton and Arbuthnot, Oct. 6–29, in *AR*, pp. 424–32.

19. *AR*, p. 147.

CHAPTER 2

1. *AR*, p. 140.

2. For the background of the Revolution in North Carolina, see Robert DeMond,

Loyalists in North Carolina during the Revolution (Chapel Hill, 1964), esp. chap. 3; Hugh F. Rankin, *The North Carolina Continentals* (Chapel Hill, 1971), chap. 1; Robert M. Calhoon, *Loyalists in Revolutionary America* (New York, 1973), pp. 441–42.

3. For the background of the Regulator movement, see James K. Huhta and Thomas J. Farnham, eds., *The Regulators in North Carolina, A Documentary History* (Raleigh, 1971); Marvin L. Michael Kay and Lorin Lee Cary, "Class, Mobility, and Conflict in North Carolina on the Eve of the Revolution," in Jeffrey J. Crow and Larry E. Tise, eds., *The Southern Experience in the American Revolution* (Chapel Hill, 1978), pp. 109–51. Charles G. Sellers, "Private Profits and Colonial Policy: Speculations of Henry McCullock," *WMQ*, 3d ser., 8 (1951): pp. 535–51; Earl of Dartmouth to William Howe, *Parliamentary Register, or History of the Proceedings and Debates in the House of Commons*, John Almon and John Debrett, eds., 17 vols. (London, 1802), 10: pp. 262–64.

4. Rankin, *North Carolina Continentals*, chap. 2; James Moore to the North Carolina Council, Mar. 2, 1776, quoted in Henry Steele Commager and Richard Morris, eds., *The Spirit of 'Seventy-Six: The Story of the American Revolution as Told by Participants* (New York, 1975), p. 115.

5. Peter Force, ed., *American Archives, Fourth Series, Containing a Documentary History of the English Colonies . . . to the Declaration of the Independence of the United States*, 6 vols. (Washington, 1837–46), 5: p. 1342; *AR*, pp. 24–38, 371–79 (quotations on pp. 27, 28, 29).

6. Force, ed., *American Archives*, 4th ser., 4: p. 297: William Moultrie, *Memoirs of the American Revolution . . . Related to the States of North and South Carolina, and Georgia*, 2 vols. (New York, 1802), 1: pp. 174–81. Clinton learned that the crossing to Sullivan's Island could not be made and offered to occupy Haddrell's Point. Parker refused to support the move on the ground that the water was too shallow to allow for the approach of his ships. The fort on Sullivan's Island was later named Fort Moultrie.

7. Willcox, *Clinton*, pp. 83–84, 87–92. The quotations are on pp. 83–84.

8. Burgoyne to Germain, Aug. 20, 1777, John Burgoyne, *A State of the Expedition from Canada as Laid before the House of Commons . . .* (London, 1780), pp. xxv–xxvi; Howe to Germain, Dec. 20, 1776, Historical Manuscripts Commission, *Report of the Manuscripts of Mrs. Stopford-Sackville of Drayton House, Northhamptonshire*, 2 vols. (London, 1910), 2: pp. 52–53; Howe to Germain, Jan. 20, 1777, *Parliamentary Register*, 10: pp. 377–78; Paul H. Smith, *Loyalists and Redcoats* (Chapel Hill, 1964), pp. 29–30. Wright is quoted in ibid., p. 89.

9. Worthington C. Ford, "Parliament and the Howes," *Proceedings of the Massachusetts Historical Society*, 44 (1910–11): p. 142; but see Smith, *Loyalists and Redcoats*, p. 120; *Parliamentary Register*, 13: pp. 22, 31. Loyalist support referred to here would consist not only of reinforcements to the army but of militia to provide a sort of police force to insure continued British control after the army was withdrawn. Having observed the effectiveness of the Whig militia in suppressing Loyalism, the British were beginning to see the necessity for a similar "infrastructure."

10. Sir John Fortescue, ed., *The Correspondence of King George the Third*, 6 vols. (London, 1927–28), 4: no. 2630; *Parliamentary Register*, 13: p. 322; Smith, *Loyalists and Redcoats*, pp. 95–99.

11. Simpson to Germain, Aug. 28, 1779, Alan S. Brown, "James Simpson's Reports on the Carolina Loyalists," *JSH*, 21 (1955): pp. 316–17.

12. Kenneth Coleman, *The American Revolution in Georgia* (Athens, 1958), chaps. 5 and 6, esp. pp. 96–98, 103–08; Gaillard Hunt, ed., *Journals of the Continental Congress*, 34 vols. (Washington, 1921–36), 5: pp. 521–22, 607, 761–63; 12: pp. 937–39; Alexander A. Lawrence, "General Lachlan McIntosh and His Suspension from Continental Command . . ." *GHQ*, 38 (1954): pp. 107–18; Lee to Col. John Armstrong, Aug. 27, 1776, "Lee Papers," *New York Historical Society Collections*, 2 vols. (1872), 1: p. 246.

13. *AR*, pp. 116–17; Coleman, *Georgia*, pp. 116–27.

14. Campbell to Clinton, Mar. 4, 1779, BHP; Otis Ashmore and Charles Olmstead, "The Battles of Kettle Creek and Brier Creek," *GHQ*, 10 (1926): pp. 85–125.

15. Smith, *Loyalists and Redcoats*, pp. 104–05; Prevost to Clinton, May 21, 1779, BHP; Moultrie, *Memoirs*, 1: pp. 423–36. Richard Barry, *Mr. Rutledge of South Carolina* (New York, 1942), pp. 257–62, says that Rutledge was stalling to give Lincoln time to return from Augusta. If so, he did not tell his commanding general, Moultrie.

16. Alexander A. Lawrence, *Storm over Savannah* (Athens, 1951) is the definitive story of the siege of Savannah.

17. Germain to Clinton, June 25, 1779, BHP; Clinton to Germain, Aug. 20, 1779, ibid.

CHAPTER 3

1. Walter Lowrie and Matthew St. Clair, eds., *The American State Papers, Military Affairs*, 7 vols. (Washington, 1832–61), 1: pp. 14–19. But see Charles Lesser, ed., *The Sinews of Independence: Monthly Strength Reports of the Continental Army* (Chicago, 1976), esp. pp. xxxiii–xxxv; John Hastings Gwathmey, ed., *Historical Register of Virginians in the Revolution, Soldiers, Sailors, Marines* (Richmond, 1938), p. 602.

2. Lesser, ed., *Sinews of Independence*, p. 85.

3. Edmund E. Curtis, *The Organization of the British Army in the American Revolution* (New Haven, 1926), pp. 1–2.

4. Ibid., pp. 57–62; quotations on pp. 60, 63.

5. Mackesy, *War for America*, pp. 61–62; Louise Hall Tharp, *The Baroness and the General* (Boston, 1961), p. 13. In a typical agreement concluded between the ministry and the Duke of Brunswick in January 1776, England agreed to pay £7 4s. 7½d. per man plus an annual subsidy of £11,500 and a payment of £46,000 when the troops completed their service. The duke was also compensated for men who were killed and wounded. The 5,700 troops hired under this agreement cost the English treasury about £750,000. Of a total of more than 29,000 German troops sent to America, only 60 percent returned. Seventy-five hundred died in America and about 5,000 deserted (Lowell, *Hessians*, pp. 30, 16–18, 20, 39–40, 138, 300).

For most of the southern campaign Cornwallis had 100 jägers and Regiment Bose, about 350 rank and file (Bernard Uhlendorf, ed., *The Siege of Charleston with an Account of the Province of South Carolina . . .* [Ann Arbor, 1938], p. 13; Benjamin

Franklin Stevens, *The Campaigns in Virginia 1781: An Exact Reprint of Six rare pamphlets on the Clinton-Cornwallis Controversy with very Numerous Important unpublished manuscript notes by Sir Henry Clinton K.B. . . . ,* 2 vols. [London, 1888], 1: p. 376).

6. Stevens, ed., *Clinton-Cornwallis Controversy,* 1: p. 376; Rawdon to the Earl of Huntingdon, Jan. 13, 1776, HMC, *Report on the Manuscripts of the late Reginald Rawdon Hastings,* 4 vols. (London, 1931–47), 3: p. 167.

7. Much of what is said about the regimental organization of the British army was also true of the American Continental Line. Washington and other officers with military experience had served with the British army, and most of them admired the redcoats. At least one Loyalist suggested that American officers could be completely suborned if they were offered commissions in the British regular establishment (unknown to Col. Edmonton, Oct. 18, 1780, Germain Papers, CL). In formation and tactics, the American commander in chief and his generals may have been political revolutionaries but in military matters they were orthodox European.

"Battalion" and "regiment" are, as nearly as I can tell, used interchangeably although "battalion" was used on occasion to designate subdivisions of oversize regiments (such as the 71st and the Guards regiments in Cornwallis' command in 1781). See Curits, *British Army,* pp. 3–6; Stevens, *Clinton-Cornwallis Controversy,* 1: p. 376.

8. Greene to Sumter, Dec. 15, 1780, quoted in Theodore Thayer, *Nathanael Greene: Strategist of the Revolution* (New York, 1960), p. 297; Stevens, *Clinton-Cornwallis Controversy,* 1: p. 376; Curtis, *British Army,* pp. 5–6.

9. Harold L. Peterson, *The Book of the Continental Soldier: Being a Compleat Account of the Uniforms, Weapons, and Equipment with which He Lived and Fought* (Harrisburg, 1968), pp. 24, 26–29, 61–62, 64–69; Curtis, *British Army,* pp. 16–20.

10. Tests conducted by the navy in World War II demonstrated that gun crews that were 100 percent efficient in training lost 35 percent of their efficiency in their first performance in combat.

11. Harold L. Peterson, *Round Shot and Rammers* (Harrisburg, 1969), pp. 33–48; Captain Georg Pausch, *Journal of Captain Pausch,* ed. William L. Stone (Albany, 1886), p. 126.

12. Curtis, *British Army,* p. 6; Henry Lee, *Memoirs of the War in the Southern Department of the United States,* ed. R. E. Lee (New York, 1869), p. 212. This edition hereinafter cited as Lee, *Memoirs.*

13. Curtis, *British Army,* pp. 54–57, 59, 60.

14. Ibid., pp. 77–80.

15. Ibid., pp. 22–24. The quotation is on p. 24.

16. Ibid., pp. 28–30; Franklin and Mary Wickwire, *Cornwallis: The American Adventure* (Boston, 1970), p. 70; cf. H. C. B. Rogers, *The British Army in the Eighteenth Century* (New York, 1977), pp. 63–65.

17. Curtis, *British Army,* pp. 28–32; Stephen Kemble, *Papers,* 2 vols., *Collections of the New York Historical Society,* 16 and 17 (1883–84), 1: pp. 269–70.

18. Curtis, *British Army,* p. 11; R. Lamb, *An Original and Authentic Journal of Occurrences in the Late American War from its Commencement to the Year 1783* (Dublin, 1809), pp. 184–88; Kemble, *Papers,* 1: p. 386.

19. Curtis, *British Army,* p. 160. Burgoyne wrote a treatise on the duties of officers

in which he recommended that enlisted men be treated as patriotic, intelligent human beings. He practiced what he preached, and it was the rankers who dubbed him "Gentleman Johnny." Howe had produced a study on light infantry tactics thought to be ideal in training troops for the war in America. Clinton's *American Rebellion*, although written as a defense of his conduct as commander in chief, is still one of the most important primary sources for the war.

20. Charles M. Clode, *Military Forces of the Crown and Their Administration and Government*, 2 vols. (London, 1869), 1: p. 70; 2: p. 62; Wickwire, *Cornwallis*, p. 52.

21. Force, *American Archives*, 4th ser., 2: p. 62; Edmund C. Burnett, ed., *Letters of Members of the Continental Congress* (Washington, 1921– 36), 1: p. 29.

22. Elbridge Gerry to John Adams, Dec. 15, 1775, Force, *American Archives*, 4th ser., 4: pp. 255– 56; Hunt, ed., *Journals of the Continental Congress*, 5: p. 762.

23. Jared Sparks, ed., *Correspondence of the Revolution; Being Letters of Eminent Men to George Washington*, 4 vols. (Boston, 1853), 1: pp. 348– 49; Burnett, ed., *Letters of Members of Congress*, 1: p. 360; Don Higginbotham, *The War of American Independence: Military Attitudes, Policies, and Practices, 1763–1789* (New York, 1971), pp. 390– 91.

24. Joseph Plumb Martin, *Private Yankee Doodle: Being a Narrative of Some of the Adventures, Dangers, and Sufferings of a Revolutionary Soldier*, ed. George F. Scheer (Boston, 1962), pp. 14, 56– 60.

25. Hunt, ed., *Journals of Congress*, 5: 762– 63, 788.

26. Washington, *Writings*, ed. Fitzpatrick, 10: p. 366; William Davie to Greene, Apr. 16, 1781, quoted in William Johnson, *Sketches of the Life and Correspondence of Nathanael Greene . . .* , 2 vols. (Charleston, 1822), 2: p. 40.

27. Washington, *Writings*, ed. Fitzpatrick, 4: p. 194; Benjamin Quarles, *The Negro in the American Revolution* (Chapel Hill, 1961), pp. 55– 57.

28. Quarles, *Negro in the Revolution*, pp. 53, ix, 72, 70; Benjamin Harrison to Thomas Dabney, Oct. 7, 1783, Thomas Jefferson, *The Papers of Thomas Jefferson*, ed. Julian P. Boyd (Princeton, 1950–), 6: pp. 430– 31; William A. Hening, ed., *Statutes at Large, Being a Collection of All the Laws of Virginia* (Richmond, 1809– 23), 11: pp. 308– 09.

29. "Some Extracts from the Papers of General Persifor Frazier," *PMHB*, 31 (1907): p. 134; Washington, *Writings*, ed. Fitzpatrick, 6: p. 83; 3: p. 309, 382.

30. Washington, *Writings*, ed. Fitzpatrick, 7: p. 264; 8: p. 452; George W. Greene, *Life of Nathanael Greene, General in the Army of the American Revolution*, 3 vols. (New York, 1867– 71), 3: pp. 54, 267.

31. Greene to Davie, Apr. 10, 1781, Greene, *Greene*, 3: p. 408; Washington, *Writings*, ed. Fitzpatrick, 6: p. 13; Thayer, *Greene*, p. 63.

32. Washington, *Writings*, ed. Fitzpatrick, 6: pp. 107– 10; Thayer, *Greene*, pp. 44– 45; 50.

33. Greene, *Greene*, 3: pp. 68– 70; Johnson, *Greene*, 2: pp. 2– 3; Ward, *Revolution*, 2: pp. 749, 784.

34. Robert Kirkwood, *Journal and Orderly Book*, Papers of the Historical Society of Delaware, no. 16 (Wilmington, 1910); Ward, *Revolution*, 2: p. 735; Caleb P. Bennett, "Narrative of . . . the Delaware Regiment," *PMHB*, 9 (1885): pp. 451– 62.

35. Banastre Tarleton, *A History of the Campaigns of 1780 and 1781 in the Southern Provinces of North America* (London, 1787), pp. 8, 27; Lee, *Memoirs*, pp. 212, 353; Ward, *Revolution*, 2: p. 253.

36. Greene, *Greene*, 3: p. 55.

37. John Adams, "Autobiography," in Charles Francis Adams, ed., *Works of John Adams . . .*, 10 vols. (Boston, 1850–56), 3: p. 48.

38. John Shy, "A New Look at Colonial Militia," *WMQ*, 3d ser., 20 (1963): pp. 175–85.

39. Peterson, *Continental Soldier*, pp. 41–43.

40. Shy, *WMQ*, 3d., 20: p. 179; Walter Millis, *Arms and Men* (New York, 1956), pp. 34–35.

41. John S. Pancake, *1777: The Year of the Hangman* (University, Ala., 1977), p. 81.

42. Arthur J. Alexander, "Pennsylvania Revolutionary Militia," *PMHB*, 49 (1945): pp. 15–25, 53.

43. Washington, *Writings*, ed. Fitzpatrick, 6: pp. 110–11.

44. Johnson, *Greene*, 1: p. 344.

45. Clyde R. Ferguson, "Functions of the Partisan Militia in the South during the American Revolution," in *The Revolutionary War in the South: Power, Conflict and Leadership*, ed. W. Robert Higgins (Durham, N.C., 1979), pp. 239–58.

46. Robert Bass, *Gamecock: The Life and Campaigns of General Thomas Sumter* (New York, 1961), p. 88; Clyde R. Ferguson, "General Andrew Pickens" (dissertation, Duke University, 1960), pp. 151, 156.

47. Ferguson, "Partisan Militia," *Revolution*, ed. Higgins, pp. 245, 257–58.

48. Smith, *Loyalists and Redcoats*, pp. 33–36, 48–50, and see esp. chap. 6.

49. Lowell, *Hessians*, p. 40. Sylvia R. Frey, in *The British Soldier in America: A Social History of Military Life in the Revolutionary Period* (Austin, Texas, 1981), has found that the traditional notion that redcoats came from the dregs of English society has to be altered because a considerable percentage of wartime recruits (who enlisted for the duration of the war rather than for life) were unemployed artisans who were victims of economic hard times. The basic fact remains that the redcoats were mostly "losers," who could not obtain the necessities of life anywhere else. One suspects also that the contempt in which the soldier was held was the result of the general condemnation of a society that looked upon the unemployed as possessing basic deficiencies of character that accounted for their failure.

50. Alexander Graydon, *Memoirs of His Own Time*, John Littell, ed. (Philadelphia, 1846), p. 135.

CHAPTER 4

1. *AR*, pp. 155, 158.

2. Brown, *JSH*, 21: p. 317; Clinton to William Eden, Dec. 11, 1779, Stevens, ed., *Facsimiles*, 10, no. 1034; *AR*, p. 142n.

3. Troop returns are in Uhlendorf, ed., *Siege of Charleston*, p. 108; G. Damer to Germain, Sept. 7, 1781, *Report of the Manuscripts of Mrs. Stopford-Sackville*, 2: p. 213. For fuller accounts of Cornwallis see Hugh F. Rankin, "Charles Lord Cornwallis: A Study in Frustration," in George Athan Billias, ed., *George Washington's Opponents: British Generals and Admirals in the American Revolution* (New York, 1969), pp. 193–232; Wickwire, *Cornwallis*.

4. Quoted in Rankin, *George Washington's Opponents*, ed. Billias, p. 201; Willcox, *Clinton*, pp. 281–83; Clinton to Germain, Aug. 20, 1779, BHP.

5. The only biography of Tarleton is Robert Bass, *The Green Dragoon: The Lives of Banastre Tarleton and Mary Robinson* (New York, 1957). See also Tarleton, *Campaigns*. Tarleton held the provincial rank of colonel.

6. Henry Manners Chichester, "Patrick Ferguson," *Dictionary of National Biography*, eds. Sir Leslie Stephens and Sir Sidney Lee, 63 vols. (London, 1895–1901), 6: pp. 1212–14; see also Mark M. Boatner III, *Encyclopedia of the American Revolution* (New York, 1966), pp. 364–65.

7. Uhlendorf, ed., *Siege of Charleston*, pp. 125, 129.

8. *AR*, pp. 159–61.

9. Prevost to Clinton, Mar. 30, 1780, BHP; Wright to Clinton, Apr. 6, 1780, ibid.; Prevost to Clinton, Apr. 12, 1780, ibid.; Howard Peckham, ed., *The Toll of Independence: Engagements & Casualties of the American Revolution* (Chicago, 1974), pp. 68–69.

10. *AR*, pp. 161–63.

11. Tarleton, *Campaigns*, pp. 5–6, 9–10; Uhlendorf, ed., *Siege of Charleston*, pp. 223–31. When undertaking a "regular approach" (as opposed to an immediate assault) on enemy defenses, the attacking force dug a trench or parallel across the front of the enemy's works. A sap was then dug diagonally toward the enemy line and then a second parallel was extended. The repeated extension of saps and parallels resulted in a zigzag line of trenches which concealed the attacker's troops and workmen until his guns were close enough to the defensive works to bring them under fire at effective range.

12. Charles Pinckney to his mother, Mar. 28, 1779, R. W. Gibbes, ed., *A Documentary History of the American Revolution . . . Chiefly in South Carolina*, 3 vols. (New York, 1857), 2: p. 112; Charles Pinckney, Jr., should not be confused with his older cousin, Charles Cotesworth Pinckney, or his father, Charles Pinckney, Sr.

13. Moultrie, *Memoirs*, 2: p. 114. It is difficult to be certain about the militia. Moultrie says that at the surrender when it was discovered that the British intended to parole the militia and threatened "having the grenadiers turned in among them" if they did not surrender their arms, "the aged, the timid, the disaffected, and the infirm, who had never appeared in the whole siege [turned out] . . . three times the number of men we had on duty." Ibid., 2: p. 209. Washington, *Writings*, ed. Fitzpatrick, 8: p. 299; *AR*, pp. 163–67 (quotation, p. 164).

14. Tarleton, *Campaigns*, pp. 8, 15–17.

15. Moultrie, *Memoirs*, 2: p. 70; A carcass was a mortar shell filled with a highly combustible charge designed to set fire to buildings or wooden fortifications.

16. Yates Snowden, *History of South Carolina*, 2 vols. (Chicago, 1920), 1: p. 378; Moultrie, *Memoirs*, 2: pp. 68–70; Uhlendorf, ed., *Siege of Charleston*, pp. 70–71, 259–65.

17. Willcox, *Clinton*, p. 306; Moultrie, *Memoirs*, 2: pp. 96–97. The correspondence between Clinton and Lincoln and the surrender terms (including Lincoln's proposals and Clinton's modifications) are conveniently reproduced in ibid., 2: pp. 87–105.

18. British casualties are in Tarleton, *Campaigns*, pp. 45–46, Americans in Peckham, ed., *Toll of Independence*, p. 70. The magazine explosion is in Moultrie, *Memoirs*, 2: p. 109, and Uhlendorf, ed., *Siege of Charleston*, pp. 89, 297–99. Captain Ewald says that more than 200 people were killed (p. 89). Captain Johann

Hinrichs says that "the best and most skillful artificers and gunners . . . were carried off in a most inglorious manner" (p. 299). Moultrie, *Memoirs*, 2: pp. 100, 102.

19. See note 17 *supra*.

20. Germain to Clinton, July 5, 1780, BHP; Mackesy, *War for America*, pp. 359–63.

21. Tarleton, *Campaigns*, pp. 70–72. Clinton to Eden, May 30, 1780, quoted in Willcox, *Clinton*, p. 313; *AR*, p. 182. The Carlisle Commission had proposed the repeal of the Tea Act and the Coercive Acts, the suspension of all acts of Parliament passed after 1763, and a pledge that Parliament would not tax the colonies for revenue. See Weldon S. Brown, *Empire or Independence: A Study in the Failure of Reconciliation* (Baton Rouge, 1964), chaps. 9 and 10.

22. George S. McCowan, Jr., *The British Occupation of Charleston, 1780–82* (Columbia, S.C., 1972), pp. 13–19; Simpson to Clinton, July 16, 1780, BHP; Germain to Cornwallis, Nov. 9, 1780, ibid.; Germain to Clinton, Jan. 23, 1779, *AR*, pp. 397–400.

23. Tarleton, *Campaigns*, pp. 69–70; Clinton to Ferguson, May 22, 1780, BHP.

24. Tarleton, *Campaigns*, pp. 26, 86–87; David D. Wallace, *History of South Carolina*, 3 vols. (New York, 1934), 2: pp. 204–07; *AR*, p. 176.

25. Willcox, *Clinton*, pp. 114, 314–21; *AR*, pp. 183–87; Clinton to Cornwallis, June 1, 1780, BHP.

26. *AR*, p. 181; Tarleton, *Campaigns*, pp. 73–76, conveniently reproduces the text of the proclamation.

27. Tarleton, *Campaigns*, pp. 29–32; Robert Brownsfield to William D. James, June 7, 1782, William D. James, *A Sketch of the Life of Brig. Gen. Francis Marion and a History of His Brigade* (Charleston, 1821), appendix, pp. 1–5. Many of the so-called rules of war were not understood by most Americans. When an enemy offered quarter it was understood that this was done to avoid casualties on both sides. When quarter was refused (especially if a town or fort were besieged) it was understood that the defender was at the mercy of the attacker and must suffer the consequences of his refusal, however severe. It also seems probable that some of Buford's men continued to fire after others had raised the white flag.

28. These engagements are detailed in chapter 6.

29. Clinton to Germain, June 4, 1780, BHP; Tarleton, *Campaigns*, p. 80; Germain to Clinton, July 4, 1780, BHP.

CHAPTER 5

1. Greene to the President of Congress, Dec. 28, 1780, letterbook, Greene Papers, LC.

2. Edward McCrady, *The History of South Carolina in the Revolution, 1775–1780* (New York, 1902), pp. 2–6. This is the first of two volumes, the second covering the period from December 1780 to 1783. For convenience these will be cited respectively as volumes 1 and 2. William Dabney and Marion Dargen, *William Henry Drayton and the American Revolution* (Albuquerque, 1962), p. 77. The Association agreement appears in "Miscellaneous Papers of the General Committee, Secret Committee and Provincial Congress, 1775," *SCHGM*, 7 (1907): pp. 141–42.

3. McCrady, *South Carolina in the Revolution*, 1: pp. 5–7.

4. Ibid., pp. 10–16, 100–10; Jerome J. Nadelhaft, *The Disorders of War: The Revolution in South Carolina* (Orono, Me., 1981), pp. 21–33.

5. McCrady, *South Carolina in the Revolution*, 1: pp. 33–34; Dabney and Dargen, *Drayton*, pp. 91–92.

6. Dabney and Dargen, *Drayton*, pp. 93–103; McCrady, *South Carolina in the Revolution*, 1: pp. 41–42, 47–51; "Papers of the First Council of Safety," *SCHGM*, 2 (1901): pp. 104, 262, 267.

7. McCrady, *South Carolina in the Revolution*, 1: pp. 86–92, 94–99.

8. Ibid., pp. 186–99.

9. Ibid., pp. 168–77.

10. Ibid., pp. 179–81.

11. Ibid., pp. 236–39.

12. Ibid., pp. 266–74; Robert W. Barnwell, Jr., "Loyalism in South Carolina" (dissertation, Duke University, 1941), chap. 5, esp. pp. 171–75. Lest the reader get the impression that all Carolinians were wavering and indecisive, it must be noted that many hundreds on both sides were unswerving in their loyalty regardless of which side was in the ascendancy. From random samples taken from Alexander S. Salley, *Stub Entries to Indents in Payment of Claims against South Carolina . . .* (Columbia, S.C., 1915–18), Books O–Q and R–T, of 450 militiamen, 92 or more than 20 percent, served more than 250 days. Thomas Franklin served 558 days; John Garrarde, 706 days; Thomas Dunlap, Thomas Dunlap, Jr., and George Dunlap served continuously from 1779 to 1782.

13. Transcripts of Loyalist claims from the British Public Record Office, New York Public Library, vol. 55, pp. 91–93. There is also a collection of Loyalist claims in the Ontario Department of Archives and History, Toronto. South Carolina Loyalists' claims are in vols. 52–57 of the PRO collection and in vol. 25 of the Ontario Archives collections. The latter are available on microfilm in the South Carolina Department of Archives and History, Columbia (hereafter cited as SCLC). Barnwell. "Loyalism in South Carolina," provides an invaluable guide to these collections. SCLC, 56: p. 576; John Smythe's petition to the Senate of South Carolina, 1783, South Carolina Historical Commission MSS, Department of Archives and History; SCLC, 53: p. 491; ibid., pp. 133–34; ibid., 25: pp. 184–85; ibid., pp. 707–08.

14. Barnwell, "Loyalism in South Carolina," pp. 246–47; McCrady, *South Carolina in the Revolution*, 1: p. 536.

15. Charles Pinckney, Sr. to Lt. Col. Nisbet Balfour, PRO, C.O. 5/178 (microfilm), p. 177; Middleton to Balfour, ibid., pp. 185–86; Lowndes to Balfour, ibid., pp. 183–84; Horry to Balfour, ibid., pp. 175–76.

16. McCrady, *South Carolina in the Revolution*, 1: pp. 540–41; Richard B. Morris, *The Peacemakers: The Great Powers and American Independence* (New York, 1965), pp. 171, 178–79.

17. J. B. O. Landrum, *Colonial and Revolutionary History of Upper South Carolina* (Spartanburg, S.C., 1897), p. 104; Anne K. Gregorie, *Thomas Sumter* (Columbia, S.C., 1931), p. 76. Whatever Sumter might have done his mind was made up for him when raiders burned his house and turned out his family.

18. Balfour to Cornwallis, June 24, 1780, Cornwallis Papers, LC (microfilm); McCrady, *South Carolina in the Revolution*, 1: pp. 529–32.

19. Brown, *JSH*, 21: pp. 318–19.

20. Clinton to Cornwallis, May 29, 1780, Cornwallis Papers; Balfour to Cornwallis, June 24, 1780, ibid.

21. Balfour to Cornwallis, June 12, 1780, Cornwallis Papers; Robert Gray, "Robert Gray's Observations on the War in Carolina," *SCHGM*, 11 (1910): p. 171.

22. Col. George Turnbull to Cornwallis, June 16, 1780, Cornwallis Papers; Ferguson to Cornwallis, July 20, 1780, ibid.; Lyman C. Draper, *King's Mountain and Its Heroes: A History of the Battle of King's Mountain, October 7, 1780* (Cincinnati, 1871), pp. 353–54.

23. Zachariah Gibbes to Cornwallis, June 16, 1780, Cornwallis Papers; Moses Kirkland to Cornwallis, Oct. 12, 1780, ibid.; Cornwallis to Clinton, Aug. 6, 1780, BHP.

24. Zachariah Gibbes to Cornwallis, Oct. 12, 1780, Cornwallis Papers; Thomas Phepo to Loyalist Commission, SCLC, 57: p. 238; Phepo to the General Assembly of South Carolina, Jan. 28, 1787 (petition no. 28), South Carolina Archives.

25. After the conquest of Georgia by the British in 1778 the South Carolina government began to take more severe measures to suppress the Loyalists. A number were tried and executed, but an even larger number were either acquitted or pardoned after conviction. Most of those executed were convicted of crimes beyond mere disloyalty, i.e., arson, murder, or plotting an Indian uprising. See Barnwell, "Loyalism in South Carolina," chap. 5. Simpson to Clinton, May 15, 1780, BHP.

26. Most of these engagements are detailed elsewhere in this work. For Musgrove's Mill see Louise Frederick Hays, *Hero of Hornet's Nest: A Biography of Elijah Clark* (New York, 1946), pp. 93–94; Peckham, ed., *Toll of Independence*, p. 74. The quotation is from the Davie-Weems Collection, University of North Carolina, no. 2540.

Thomas Browne's notorious career was first depicted by David Ramsay in his *History of the Revolution in South Carolina* (Trenton, 1785). The book brought a rejoinder from Colonel Browne in which he defended his conduct. See Gary D. Olson, "Dr. David Ramsay and Lt. Colonel Thomas Brown: Patriot Historian and Loyalist Critic," *SCHM*, 77 (1976): pp. 257–67. Browne's name is spelled both with and without the "e." The colonel himself signed his name both ways.

27. Joseph Graham, "Battle of King's Mountain," in Draper, *King's Mountain*, p. 550; Campbell's general orders, Oct. 11, 15, 1780, ibid., pp. 553–54; Ensign Robert Campbell's account, ibid., pp. 539–40; Lt. Anthony Allaire, "Diary of Anthony Allaire," ibid., pp. 510–11. Allaire was a Loyalist who was captured.

28. Landrum, *Revolutionary South Carolina*, pp. 114, 120, 126, 176; Draper, *King's Mountain*, pp. 156–64. See also chapter 12 below.

29. Draper, *King's Mountain*, pp. 134–39.

30. Hugh F. Rankin, *Francis Marion: The Swamp Fox* (New York, 1973), pp. 88–89; Alexander Gregg, *History of the Old Cheraws* (New York, 1867), p. 354.

31. Hays, *Clark*, pp. 82–85. It is difficult here, as in many cases, to separate fact from fiction. There is, however, an interesting footnote to the Nancy Hart legend. In 1912 workmen laying the track for the Elberton and Eastern Railway through the site of the Hart cabin uncovered a grave containing six corpses.

32. Samuel Curwen, *Journals and Letters of Samuel Curwen during the American*

Revolution, ed. George A. Ward (New York, 1845), pp. 638– 48; Landrum, *Revolutionary South Carolina*, pp. 350– 59. McCrady, among others, spells all the Cuninghams with one "n."

33. E. W. Caruther, *Interesting Revolutionary Incidents . . . Chiefly in the Old North State* (Philadelphia, 1856), pp. 253– 54, 262.

34. John C. Dann, ed., *The Revolution Remembered: Eyewitness Accounts of the War of Independence* (Chicago, 1980), p. 189.

The British execution of Colonel Isaac Hayne in August 1781 became a cause célèbre in the history of British "atrocities." Hayne had been captured at Charleston and had taken the oath of allegiance in order to be with his family who were ill with smallpox (his wife and children subsequently died of the disease). After the battle of Ninety Six and the British retreat to the low-country Hayne considered himself released from his oath and took the field with Greene's army. He was captured by the British, and a court of inquiry ordered his execution. His position as a member of the South Carolina aristocracy brought outraged protest from prominent Charlestonians, but Balfour and Rawdon refused to reprieve him. His execution brought threats of reprisals from Greene (which were never carried out), and questions were asked on the floor of Parliament. A judicious evaluation of the episode is in Boatner, *Encyclopedia of the Revolution*, pp. 495– 97. Lee, *Memoirs*, pp. 449– 62, 613– 20, contains a detailed account and reproduces pertinent documents. See also Gibbes, *Documentary History*, 3: pp. 108– 16, 133– 34.

35. Gray, *SCHGM*, 11: p. 171.

36. Balfour to Cornwallis, June 7, 1780, Cornwallis Papers.

37. Cornwallis to General James Pattison, June 10, 1780, Charles Ross, ed., *Correspondence of Charles, First Marquis Cornwallis*, 2 vols. (London, 1859), 1: p. 46.

38. Rawdon to Cornwallis, July 7, 1780, Cornwallis Papers.

39. Germain to Clinton, Sept. 27, 1779, BHP.

CHAPTER 6

1. Cornwallis to Clinton, June 30, 1780, BHP; Balfour to Cornwallis, July 12, 1780, Cornwallis Papers; Tarleton, *Campaigns*, p. 87. John Harris Cruger, also a colonel in the New York Volunteers, replaced Balfour at Ninety Six in late July. Of the officers who served in these commands, only Balfour, Ferguson, and Rawdon were officers in the British regular army, and Rawdon had accepted a colonelcy in the Provincial Corps because he was refused promotion in the regular establishment. The New York Volunteer Regiments were raised by a wealthy New York Loyalist, Oliver DeLancey, Sr. One of these regiments remained in New York; the other two were commanded by Cruger and Turnbull.

2. Balfour to Cornwallis "Friday" [June 2?], 1780, Cornwallis Papers. I have taken the liberty of editing out some of Colonel Balfour's copious commas.

3. Turnbull to Cornwallis, June 16, 19, 1780, Cornwallis Papers.

4. Greene is quoted in Higginbotham, *War of Independence*, p. 385; Washington, *Writings*, ed. Fitzpatrick, 7: p. 33.

5. In the "patriotic gore" that characterizes most of the recollections and memoirs, as well as most of the nineteenth-century histories of the War of Indepen-

dence, it is difficult to detect Patriots as villainous as Bloody Bill and Plundering Sam, but almost certainly they existed. See especially Draper, *King's Mountain*, a valuable source but one that must be used with great caution.

6. Orangeburg association articles reproduced in Barnwell, "Loyalism in South Carolina," p. 203.

7. Balfour to Cornwallis, June [2?], 1780, Cornwallis Papers.

8. Balfour to Cornwallis, dated "Tuesday," probably May 30 or June 6, 1780, ibid.; Balfour to Cornwallis, June 24, 1780, ibid.; Rawdon to Cornwallis, June 25, 1780, ibid.

9. Balfour to Cornwallis, June 7, 1780, ibid.

10. Cornwallis' proclamation, July 18, 1780, in Tarleton, *Campaigns*, pp. 121–22; Cornwallis to Clinton, June 30, 1780, BHP.

11. Balfour to Cornwallis, July 4, June 27, 1780, Cornwallis Papers.

12. Balfour to Cornwallis, June [2?], 1780, ibid.; Kemble, *Papers*, 1: pp. 269–70.

13. Cornwallis to Clinton, June 30, 1780, BHP.

14. Ibid.; DeMond, *Loyalists in North Carolina*, pp. 126–27.

15. Cornwallis to Clinton, June 30, 1780, BHP.

16. Gregorie, *Sumter*, pp. 83–85; General Joseph Graham, "Narrative of the Revolutionary War," in W. H. Hoyt, ed., 2 vols., *The Papers of Archibald D. Murphey* (Raleigh, N.C., 1914), 2: pp. 230, 242, 245; Huck's name is also spelled Hook, Houck, and Houyck.

17. Draper, *King's Mountain*, pp. 73–83; Wallace, *South Carolina*, 2: pp. 211–12.

18. Gregorie, *Sumter*, pp. 87–90; William Hill, *Memoirs of the Revolution*, ed. A. S. Salley (Columbia, S.C., 1921), pp. 11–12; William R. Davie, "Recollections," in the Davie-Weems Collection, no. 2540; Wallace, *South Carolina*, 2: p. 212; Draper, *King's Mountain*, pp. 87–88.

19. Gregorie, *Sumter*, pp. 91–96; Tarleton, *Campaigns*, pp. 94–96; Allaire, "Diary," in Draper, *King's Mountain*, p. 510; Sumter to Charles Pinckney, Aug. 10, 1780, *North Carolina State Records*, ed. Walter Clark (Winston-Salem, 1895–1905), 14: pp. 540–43 (hereafter cited as *NCSR*).

20. Cornwallis to Clinton, July 14, 1780, BHP.

21. Ibid.

22. The estimated population of the backcountry in 1770 was thirty-five thousand of a total population of 50,000. Richard M. Brown, *The South Carolina Regulators* (Cambridge, Mass., 1963), p. 182; Bureau of the Census and the Social Science Research Council, *Statistical History of the United States* (Stamford, Conn., 1965), p. 756. The census of 1790 shows the backcountry white population to be four times that of the lowcountry. Cornwallis to Clinton, Aug. 6, 1780, BHP.

23. Cornwallis to Clinton, Aug. 6, 1780, BHP.

24. For de Kalb see Frank Monaghan, "Johann Kalb," *Dictionary of American Biography*, ed. Allen Johnson and Dumas Malone (New York, 1943–53), 10: pp. 253–54. For Kirkwood, see his *Journal and Orderly Book*; and Ward, *Revolution*, 2: p. 735.

25. For the Camden campaign the best primary sources are Otho Holland Williams (colonel of the 6th Maryland and Gates' adjutant), "Narrative," in Johnson, *Greene*, 1: Appendix B (hereafter cited as Williams in *Greene*); Tarleton, *Campaigns*, pp. 104–10; Cornwallis to Germain, Aug. 21, 1780, BHP; Gates to the President of Congress, Aug. 28, 1780, Papers of the Continental Congress, Na-

tional Archives. Secondary accounts are Paul David Nelson, *General Horatio Gates: A Biography* (Baton Rouge, 1966), pp. 221– 35; Wickwire, *Cornwallis*, chap. 7. Subsequent notes will not repeat the works cited above except to identify quotations.

26. Nelson, *Gates*, pp. 215– 20. Nelson is kinder to Gates than I am, but his treatment is eminently fair.

27. Gates to Caswell, July 29, 30, Aug. 3, 5, 1780, John S. Stevens, "The Southern Campaign of 1780, Letters of Major General Gates," *Magazine of American History*, 5 (1880– 81): pp. 292– 98; Sumter to de Kalb, July 17, 1780, *NCSR*, 14: pp. 505– 07. A copy of this letter went to Gates.

28. Williams in *Greene*, 1: pp. 486– 87.

29. Gates' circular letter, "July & Aug., 1780," Stevens, *MAH*, 5: p. 293.

30. Gates' orders of July 28 and Aug. 2, 1780, ibid., pp. 312– 13; Williams in *Greene*, 1: pp. 486– 87.

31. Williams in *Greene*, 1: p. 488.

32. Ibid., pp. 492– 93.

33. Gates' order of July 30, 1780, Stevens, *MAH*, 5: p. 312; Gates to John Adams, July 23, 1776, Bernard Knollenberg, ed., "Correspondence of John Adams and Horatio Gates," *Proceedings of the Massachusetts Historical Society*, 67 (1941– 44): pp. 140– 41.

34. Cornwallis to Germain, Aug. 21, 1780, BHP; troop return of Aug. 15, 1780, Tarleton, *Campaigns*, p. 136.

35. Williams in *Greene*, 1: p. 494.

36. Ibid., p. 495. One is inclined to trust a man who acknowledges his own mistakes (rare among officers of either army). Williams clearly admits his error: "The right wing [British] was soon discovered *in line* of battle. . . ." Italics are Williams'.

37. Ibid., p. 496. Williams says he saw Dixon's men fire "two or three rounds of cartridges. . . ."

38. Ibid., p. 497.

39. Gates to Congress, Aug. 10, 1780, Stevens, *MAH*, 5: pp. 303– 04; Gregorie, *Sumter*, pp. 100– 02; Tarleton, *Campaigns*, pp. 113– 15; Peckham, ed., *Toll of Independence*, p. 74.

CHAPTER 7

1. Cornwallis to Clinton, Aug. 23, 1780, BHP.

2. For early references to the Chesapeake objective see Germain to Clinton, Jan. 23, 1779, *AR*, pp. 398– 99; Mathews expedition, ibid., pp. 123– 24, 406– 07; Germain to Clinton, Sept. 27, 1779, ibid., p. 423; Clinton's instructions to Cornwallis, June 13, 1780, BHP.

3. Cornwallis to Clinton, Aug. 31, 1780, BHP.

4. Clinton's view here was consistent with the original strategy behind the southern campaign of piecemeal reduction of separate colonies. Mackesy, *War for America*, p. 252; *Stopford-Sackville Mss.*, 2: p. 98.

5. Clinton to Germain, Aug. 30, 1780, *AR*, p. 455; to Leslie, Oct. 12, 1780, ibid., p. 467.

6. Cornwallis to Clinton, Aug. 23, 6, 1780, BHP.

7. Rankin, *Marion*, pp. 65– 66; Cornwallis to Clinton, Aug. 29, 1780, BHP.

8. Rankin, *Marion*, esp. pp. 22–27, 56–60, 298–99.

9. Cornwallis to Clinton, Aug. 29, 1780, BHP.

10. Hays, *Clark*, p. 105. Hays has discussed in detail her reasons for spelling "Clark" without the "e." A number of names are spelled in various ways (Sumter, for example, signed at least one of his letters "Sumpter"). The overwhelming majority of contemporary sources, however, spell the Georgian's name "Clarke."

11. Ibid., pp. 90–94; Peckham, ed., *Toll of Independence*, p. 74; Draper, *King's Mountain*, pp. 99–101 (Wofford's Iron Works), 103–11 (Musgrove's Mill).

12. Hays, *Clark*, pp. 95–102; Tarleton, *Campaigns*, pp. 161–64; Coleman, *Revolution in Georgia*, p. 34; Samuel C. Williams, "Colonel Elijah Clarke in the Tennessee Country," *GHQ*, 25: pp. 151–58.

13. Cornwallis to Germain, Aug. 20, 1780; to Clinton, Aug. 29, 1780, BHP.

14. Rush to John Adams, Oct. 23, 1780, Benjamin Rush, *Letters*, . . . ed., Lyman H. Butterfield (Princeton, 1951), I: p. 255; Williams in *Greene*, I: pp. 504–06; Nelson, *Gates*, pp. 241–42. That this ability to come back after defeat was not uncommon, see Pancake, *1777: Year of the Hangman*, p. 174.

15. Don Higginbotham, *Daniel Morgan: Revolutionary Rifleman* (Chapel Hill, 1961), pp. 103–05, 108–11; James Grant Wilson and John Fiske, eds., *Appleton's Cyclopaedia of American Biography* (New York, 1889), 6: p. 384; Ward, *Revolution*, 2: pp. 734–35; Christopher Ward, *The Delaware Continentals, 1776–1783* (Wilmington, Del., 1941), pp. 355–57. The 1st and 3rd Maryland were divided between the new 1st and 2nd regiments (as they were subsequently called); the 5th and 7th Maryland went to the 1st and the 4th and 6th to the 2nd.

16. Gates to Jefferson, Sept. 20, 1780, Gates Papers, NYHS; Nelson, *Gates*, pp. 245–46; Chalmers G. Davidson, *Piedmont Partisan: The Life and Times of Brigadier General William Lee Davidson* (Davidson, N.C., 1951), pp. 66–75.

17. Cornwallis to Clinton, Aug. 29, Sept. 22, 1780; Rawdon to Leslie, Oct. 24, 1780, BHP.

18. Davie, "Recollections," Davie-Weems Collection, no. 2540; Tarleton, *Campaigns*, pp. 159–60.

19. Draper, *King's Mountain*, pp. 200–04; Allaire, "Diary," ibid., pp. 508–09; ibid, p. 169; Isaac Shelby, "Narrative, . . ." *NCSR*, 15: pp. 105–06.

20. Draper, *King's Mountain*, pp. 170–77; Allaire, "Diary," ibid., pp. 509–11; Ferguson to Cornwallis, n.d., 1780, Tarleton, *Campaigns*, p. 193, and Draper, *King's Mountain*, pp. 207–08. Tarleton says, "published by the Americans," indicating that Ferguson's dispatch was intercepted.

21. There is a wealth of material on King's Mountain, the best of which is still Draper, *King's Mountain*, but caution is necessary. Draper has reprinted several firsthand accounts in his appendix. The election of Campbell and the decision to make the forced march are in ibid., pp. 187–88, 216, 227; see also "Official Report" by Shelby, Cleveland, and Campbell in ibid., p. 522.

22. [James P. Collins], *Autobiography of a Revolutionary Soldier* (Clinton, La., 1859), p. 52; Draper, *King's Mountain*, pp. 210–11.

23. [Isaac Shelby], *Battle of King's Mountain* (n.p., 1823), p. 6.

24. Ward, *Revolution*, 2: p. 745; Peckham, ed., *Toll of Independence*, p. 76; Collins, *Autobiography*, p. 53.

25. Davidson to Sumner, Oct. 10, 1780, quoted in Draper, *King's Mountain*, p. 520; Rawdon to Clinton, Oct. 24, 1780, BHP; Collins, *Autobiography*, p. 53.

26. Rawdon to Clinton, Oct. 29, 1780, BHP.

CHAPTER 8

1. Rawdon (for Cornwallis, who was ill) to Leslie, Oct. 24, 1780, BHP; Rankin, *Marion*, p. 89.

2. Rankin, *Marion*, pp. 88–89.

3. Ibid., pp. 103–07.

4. Ibid., pp. 105–06; Ross, ed., *Cornwallis Correspondence*, 1: pp. 67–68; Cornwallis to Tarleton, Nov. 5, 1781, [misdated], Tarleton, *Campaigns*, p. 198.

5. Rankin, *Marion*, pp. 11–14; Tarleton, *Campaigns*, pp. 171–72. At the end of the chase Tarleton is said to have exclaimed, ". . . As for this damned fox, the Devil himself could not catch him." Hence, the sobriquet, "Swamp Fox" (Rankin, *Marion*, p. 113).

6. Cornwallis to Clinton, Dec. 3, 1780, BHP; Rankin, *Marion*, pp. 130–34; Greene to Marion, Dec. 4, 1780, Greene, *Greene*, 3: pp. 80–81.

7. Cornwallis to Clinton, Dec. 3, 1780, BHP; Gregorie, *Sumter*, pp. 110, 114–17.

8. Cornwallis to Tarleton, Nov. 10, 11, 1780, Tarleton, *Campaigns*, pp. 201–02; Gregorie, *Sumter*, pp. 121–24; Samuel Hammond, "The Battle of Blackstocks, November 20th, 1780," in Joseph Johnson, *Traditions and Reminiscences Chiefly of the Revolution in the South* (Charleston, 1851), pp. 522–26. The American casualties seem incredibly light for such a sharp engagement. American reports may have been exaggerated, but Sumter's position was strong, and most of his men were armed with rifles, effective at more than twice the range of the British muskets (Peckham, ed., *Toll of Independence*, p. 77).

9. Gregorie, *Sumter*, pp. 126–27; Greene to Morgan, Dec. 16, 1780, Greene Papers, CL; see also note 25, below.

10. Washington to Greene, Oct. 14, 1780, Washington, *Writings*, ed. Fitzpatrick, 20: pp. 181–82; Greene to Washington, Oct. 16, 1780, Greene Papers, LC.

11. For Greene's career before his assumption of the command of the Southern Department, see Thayer, *Greene*.

12. Ibid., pp. 283–90; Greene to Jefferson, Nov. 20, 1780, Jefferson, *Papers*, ed. Boyd, 4: p. 132.

13. Greene to General Edward Stevens, Dec. 1, 1780, Greene Papers, LC.

14. Washington to Greene, Oct. 22, 1780, Washington, *Writings*, ed. Fitzpatrick, 20: p. 238; Greene, *Greene*, 3: pp. 71, 74; Greene to General Henry Harrington, Dec. 4, 1780, Greene Papers, LC; Greene to Colonel Long, Dec. 6, 1780, ibid.

15. Greene to Harrington, Dec. 4, 1780, Greene Papers, CL.

16. Polk to Greene, Dec. 10, 1780, ibid.; Greene to Davie, Dec. 16, 1780, Greene, *Greene*, 3: pp. 75–76.

17. Greene to Marion, Dec. 4, 1780, Greene Papers, LC.

18. Greene to Lafayette, Dec. 29, 1780, Greene, *Greene*, 3: p. 70; Greene to Alexander Hamilton, Jan. 10, 1781, Alexander Hamilton, *Papers*, ed. Harold C. Syrett and Jacob Cooke, 26 vols. (New York, 1961–79), 2: p. 532.

19. William Gordon, *The History of the Rise, Progress, and Establishment of the United States . . .* , 4 vols. (London, 1788), 4: p. 28.

20. Greene to Washington, Dec. 28, 1780, Sparks, ed., *Correspondence*, 3: p. 190; Greene to Morgan, Dec. 29, 1780, Greene Papers, CL.

21. Cornwallis to Clinton, Dec. 3, 1780, BHP; Greene to Washington, Dec. 28, 1780, Sparks, ed., *Correspondence of the Revolution*, 3: p. 190; Ferguson, "Pickens," pp. 123–24, 127.

22. Greene to Washington, Dec. 28, 1780, Greene, *Greene*, 3: pp. 131–32.

23. Tarleton, *Campaigns*, p. 210; Rankin, *Marion*, pp. 151–55, 157.

24. James Graham, *Life of Daniel Morgan with Portions of His Correspondence* (New York, 1856), pp. 268–69; Thayer, *Greene*, p. 299.

25. Higginbotham, *Morgan*, pp. 126–28; Greene to Sumter, Jan. 18, 1781, McCrady, *South Carolina in the Revolution*, 2: pp. 67–68; Gregorie, *Sumter*, p. 130.

26. Cornwallis to Clinton, Jan 18, 1781, BHP; Cornwallis' brief dispatches to Tarleton are in Tarleton, *Campaigns*, pp. 244–48.

27. Cornwallis to Tarleton, Jan 11 and 14, 1781, Tarleton, *Campaigns*, pp. 248–49; Higginbotham, *Morgan*, pp. 129–30.

28. Tarleton, *Campaigns*, pp. 212–13; Higginbotham, *Morgan*, pp. 130–31.

30. The best accounts of the battle of the Cowpens are in Higginbotham, *Morgan*, chap. 9; Ward, *Revolution*, 2: chap. 69; George F. Scheer and Hugh F. Rankin, *Rebels and Redcoats*, (New York, 1957), chap. 35. Eyewitnesses' accounts are in Tarleton, *Campaigns*, pp. 215–23; John Eager Howard in Henry Lee, *The Campaign of 1781 in the Carolinas* (Philadelphia, 1824), pp. 97–98 (hereafter cited as Lee, *Campaign*); Morgan to Greene, Jan. 19, 1781, Graham, *Morgan*, pp. 467–70; Thomas Young, "Memoir of Thomas Young," *Orion*, 3 (October 1843): pp. 86–101; William Seymour, "A Journal of a Southern Expedition," *PMHB*, 7 (1883): pp. 294–95; [Collins], *Autobiography*, pp. 264–65. The quotations are from Young, Tarleton, Seymour, Collins, Howard, and Young respectively. Seymour was sergeant-major of Washington's dragoons; Collins was the North Carolina lad whom the reader has already met at King's Mountain. Samuel Hammond has a detailed account of Morgan's meeting with his officers in "The Battle of the Cowpens," in Johnson, *Traditions of the Revolution*, pp. 527–28. Young's account relates Morgan's exhortations to his men on the eve of the battle.

31. Higginbotham, *Morgan*, p. 142; Tarleton, *Campaigns*, p. 218; Cornwallis to Clinton, Jan. 18, 1781, BHP, reported 400 killed, wounded, and captured, but to Germain on Mar. 17, 1781, he said, "our losses did not fall short of 600 men" (ibid.); Peckham, ed., *Toll of Independence*, p. 79.

32. Tarleton, *Campaigns*, p. 221; Lee, *Campaign of 1781*, p. 98.

33. *Maryland Gazette* (Annapolis), Aug. 2, 1781.

34. Greene to Jefferson, Nov. 20, 1780, Jefferson, *Papers*, ed., Boyd, 4: pp. 130–31.

CHAPTER 9

1. *AR*, p. 237; Germain to Clinton, Mar. 7, 1781, BHP; Washington to John Laurens, Apr. 9, 1781, Washington, *Writings*, ed. Fitzpatrick, 21: p. 439. This passage is written in code.

2. *AR*, p. 35n; cf. Willcox, *Clinton*, p. 314.

3. The persistence of the Chesapeake theme may be noted in Germain's letters to Clinton, July 4, 1780, *AR*, p. 442; Oct. 4, 1780, Germain Papers, Supplemental Dispatches, CL; to Cornwallis, Nov. 9, 1780, BHP; to Clinton, Jan. 3, 1781, ibid., Germain to Clinton, Jan. 3, 1781, *AR*.

4. Willcox, *Clinton*, pp. 323–24; Mackesy, *War for America*, pp. 346–47.

5. Willcox, *Clinton*, pp. 325–28; *AR*, pp. 198–99.

6. *AR*, pp. 199–201; Arbuthnot to Clinton, July 18, 1780, ibid., p. 444.

7. Ibid., p. 202; Arbuthnot to Clinton, Aug. 3, 1780, ibid., pp. 447–48.

8. Ibid., p. 203n; Willcox, *Clinton*, pp. 331–32.

9. *AR*, pp. 204–05; Clinton to Arbuthnot, Aug. 18, 1780, ibid., p. 451; minute of conversation between Arbuthnot and Generals Mathew and Dalrymple, Aug. 19, 1780, ibid., p. 452.

10. Willcox, *Clinton*, p. 335.

11. Ibid., pp. 338–40; *AR*, pp. 213–14; Clinton to Rodney, Sept. 18, 1780, ibid., p. 457.

12. See, for example, Vergennes' letter to the King, Sept. 27, 1780, which documents his strenuous effort to dissuade Louis XVI from opening peace negotiations. The letter is quoted in Edwin S. Corwin, *French Policy and the American Alliance* (Princeton, 1916), p. 284.

13. Clinton to Leslie, Oct. 12, 1780, *AR*, p. 467; Clinton to Cornwallis, Nov. 6, 1780, BHP; Clinton to Leslie, Nov. 2, 1780, ibid.

14. Cornwallis to Clinton, Sept. 22, 1780, BHP; Clinton to Germain, Oct. 30, 1780, ibid. Clinton may have received a copy of Cornwallis' (i.e., Rawdon's) dispatch to Leslie as early as Nov. 12, but he did not receive the dispatch of Oct. 24 until Dec. 2. See Clinton to Leslie, Nov. 12, and to Cornwallis, Dec. 13, 1780, ibid.

15. Clinton to Leslie, Nov. 2, 1780, ibid.; Rawdon to Leslie, Oct. 31, 1780, ibid.; Leslie to Clinton, Nov. 12, 19, 1780, ibid.; Balfour to Leslie, n.d. [1780], ibid.. Leslie decided to leave on Nov. 7 but the British did not actually get under way until the 18th.

16. Cornwallis to Leslie, Nov. 12, 1780, ibid.; Rawdon to Clinton, Oct. 31, 1780, ibid.; Cornwallis to Clinton, Dec. 3, 1780, ibid. There is a Cape Fear and a Cape Fear River.

17. Germain to Cornwallis, Nov. 9, 1780, ibid.

18. Clinton to [?], Nov. 12, 1780, Clinton Papers, CL, also quoted in Willcox, *Clinton*, p. 350; Germain to Clinton, Jan. 3, 1781, Germain Papers, Supplemental Dispatches, CL.

19. Clinton to Arnold, Dec. 14, 1780, BHP.

20. Arnold to Clinton, Jan. 23, 1781, ibid. Phillips elaborated on the problem to Clinton, Apr. 3, 1781, ibid.

21. Quoted in Willcox, *Clinton*, p. 358.

22. Ibid., p. 357; *AR*, p. 205.

23. Cornwallis to Germain, Aug. 21, 1780, BHP. Clinton believed that he was being undercut by Cornwallis when the latter communicated directly with Germain (Willcox, *Clinton*, pp. 370–71).

24. Germain to Clinton, Oct. 13, 1780, Germain Papers, Supplemental Dispatches, CL; Earl of Sandwich, *Private Papers of John, Earl of Sandwich, First Lord of the Admiralty, 1771–1782*, ed. G. R. Barnes and J. H. Owen, 4 vols. (London, 1932–38), 3: p. 255.

25. Willcox, *Clinton*, p. 360.

26. Mackesy, *War for America*, pp. 325–29.

27. Clinton to Germain, May 22, 1779, *AR*, pp. 407–08.

28. Quoted in Willcox, *Clinton*, p. 367.

29. Cornwallis to Clinton, Jan. 6, 18, 1781, BHP; Cornwallis to Germain, Mar. 17, 1781, ibid.; Arnold to Clinton, Feb. 25, 1781, ibid. In his letter to Clinton of May 2, 1781, Germain acknowledged receipt of Clinton's dispatches from Feb. 28 to Mar. 9. Clinton must have included copies of Cornwallis' January dispatches (see note 31 below) but since Clinton had heard nothing from Cornwallis for three months, Germain's next word from the South was Cornwallis' dispatch of Mar. 17, which the American Secretary did not receive until June 2.

30. Clinton to Phillips, Mar. 10, 1781, BHP.

31. Germain to Clinton, May 2, 1781, Germain Papers, Supplemental Dispatches, CL; italics added.

32. Cornwallis to Clinton, Apr. 10, 1781, BHP. For Germain, Cornwallis was more cautious, saying only that "a serious attempt upon Virginia would be the most solid plan" (Apr. 18, 1781, ibid.). Three months later, on July 14, Germain wrote to Clinton, ". . . They [reinforcements] will enable Lord Cornwallis to form a separate Army for the Delaware Peninsula, while he moved on to the head of the Elk with his own, which would be the most certain means of succeeding throughout, & would Effect the Compleat Execution of your Plan. . . . I cannot resist the strong Impulse to repeat to you my most earnest Wishes, that Nothing may divert you from the steady Pursuit of this Plan until you have accomplished it, and then I shall consider the great Work of recovering America nearly compleated" (Germain Papers, Supplemental Dispatches, CL).

33. Gerald Stourzh, *Benjamin Franklin and American Foreign Policy* (New York, 1958), pp. 158–66, 299.

34. For more detail on the problems discussed here see Higginbotham, *War of American Independence*, chap. 12, and Edmund Cody Burnett, *The Continental Congress* (New York, 1941), chaps. 20, 21, 22, and 24. The quote is from Washington to James Duane, Dec. 26, 1780, Washington, *Writings*, ed. Fitzpatrick, 21: p. 14.

35. Douglas Southall Freeman, *George Washington: A Biography*, 7 vols. (New York, 1948–57), 5: pp. 187–95; Washington to Lafayette, Oct. 30, 1780, Washington, *Writings*, ed. Fitzpatrick, 20: pp. 266–67.

36. Freeman, *Washington*, 5: pp. 196–222; Thomas Flexner, *The Traitor and the Spy* (New York, 1953), p. 371.

37. Carl Van Doren, *Mutiny in January* (New York, 1943); Washington to Greene, Jan. 9–11, 1781, Washington, *Writings*, ed. Fitzpatrick, 21: p. 86; to Wayne, Jan. 3–4, 1781, ibid., p. 56; Sparks, ed., *Correspondence of the Revolution*, 3: p. 193.

38. Washington to Greene, Oct. 22, 1780, Washington, *Writings*, ed. Fitzpatrick, 20: p. 239. Lee did not finally report to Greene until the first of the year. Washington to Jefferson, Dec. 10, 1780, ibid., 20: p. 450; Washington to the President of Congress, Jan. 2, 1781, ibid., 21: p. 51.

39. Washington to Rochambeau, Jan. 29, 1781, ibid., pp. 152–53; Washington to John Laurens, Jan. 31, 1781, ibid., pp. 161–62.

40. Washington to Rochambeau, Feb. 7, 1781, ibid., p. 197; Freeman, *Washington*, 5: pp. 261–64.

41. Greene to Washington, Jan. 13, Feb. 9, 1781, Sparks, ed., *Correspondence of the Revolution*, 3: pp. 207–08, 227.

42. Clinton's note on Cornwallis' letter of Jan. 17, 1781, when he was informed that Cornwallis would pursue Greene into North Carolina, Stevens, ed., *Clinton-Cornwallis Controversy*, 1: p. 321.

CHAPTER 10

1. Graham, *Morgan*, pp. 324–25; Higginbotham, *Morgan*, p. 145.

2. Cornwallis to Germain, Mar. 17, 1781, BHP.

3. Williams to Morgan, Jan. 25, 1781, Graham, *Morgan*, p. 323; Scheer and Rankin, *Rebels and Redcoats*, p. 500.

4. Hunt, ed., *Journals of Congress*, 9: pp. 246–47; General Orders, Feb. 13, 1781, Washington, *Writings*, ed. Fitzpatrick, 21: p. 224; Greene, *Greene*, 3: p. 152.

5. Johnson, *Greene*, 1: p. 394; Greene, *Greene*, 3: p. 152.

6. Scheer and Rankin, *Rebels and Redcoats*, p. 501; Lee, *Memoirs*, pp. 232–33; Higginbotham, *Morgan*, pp. 149–50; Johnson, *Greene*, 1: p. 394.

7. Wickwire, *Cornwallis*, pp. 268–69; Tarleton, *Campaigns*, p. 220; McJunkin Narrative, Draper Mss., 23 VV 193, Wisconsin State Historical Society, Madison.

8. Tarleton, *Campaigns*, p. 222; Wickwire, *Cornwallis*, pp. 268–69; Tarleton, *Campaigns*, p. 252.

9. Cornwallis to Clinton, Jan. 18, 1781, BHP.

10. Ibid.; Wickwire, *Cornwallis*, pp. 276–77; Higginbotham, *Morgan*, pp. 147–50; Graham, *Morgan*, p. 343.

11. Tarleton, *Campaigns*, pp. 252–53; Graham, *Morgan*, pp. 342–43; Johnson, *Greene*, 1: pp. 398, 403; Higginbotham, *Morgan*, p. 150; Thayer, *Greene*, pp. 310–11.

12. Thayer, *Greene*, pp. 311–12; Higginbotham, *Morgan*, p. 150; Johnson, *Greene*, 1: p. 413; Graham, *Morgan*, p. 344.

13. Lee, *Memoirs*, p. 232; Higginbotham, *Morgan*, p. 147; Wickwire, *Cornwallis*, pp. 276–77; Cornwallis to Germain, Mar. 17, 1781, BHP.

14. Cornwallis to Germain, Mar. 17, 1781, BHP; Graham, *Morgan*, p. 345; Ward, *Revolution*, 2: p. 767; Wickwire, *Cornwallis*, pp. 278–79; Higginbotham, *Morgan*, pp. 151, 149; Davidson, *Davidson*, pp. 110–11.

15. Davidson, *Davidson*, pp. 15, 36–37, 46, 57, 59, 61, 64.

16. Higginbotham, *Morgan*, p. 150; Davidson, *Davidson*, pp. 111–12; Johnson, *Greene*, 1: p. 414; Scheer and Rankin, *Rebels and Redcoats*, p. 502; Thayer, *Greene*, p. 312.

17. Cornwallis to Germain, Mar. 17, 1781, BHP.

18. Ward, *Revolution*, 2: pp. 767–68; Graham, *Morgan*, p. 344; Cornwallis to Germain, Mar. 17, 1781, BHP; Greene, *Greene*, 3: p. 156.

19. Ward, *Revolution*, 2: p. 768; Scheer and Rankin, *Rebels and Redcoats*, p. 503; Davidson, *Davidson*, p. 119.

20. Cornwallis to Germain, Mar. 17, 1781, BHP; Thayer, *Greene*, pp. 312–13; Greene, *Greene*, 3: p. 160; Scheer and Rankin, *Rebels and Redcoats*, p. 505; Davidson, *Davidson*, pp. 167–68.

21. Scheer and Rankin, *Rebels and Redcoats*, p. 505; Thayer, *Greene*, p. 313; Higginbotham, *Morgan*, pp. 152–53.

22. Johnson, *Greene*, 1: p. 418; Higginbotham, *Morgan*, pp. 151–52; Wickwire, *Cornwallis*, p. 282; Thayer, *Greene*, p. 314; Johnson, *Greene*, 1: p. 418.

23. Cornwallis to Germain, Mar. 17, 1781, BHP; Davidson, *Davidson*, p. 120; Tarleton, *Campaigns*, p. 227; Wickwire, *Cornwallis*, pp. 282–83; Greene, *Greene*, 3: p. 160.

24. Greene, *Greene*, 3: pp. 160–61; Johnson, *Greene*, 1: p. 419; Thayer, *Greene*, pp. 314–15.

25. Lee, *Memoirs*, p. 236; Johnson, *Greene*, 1: pp. 407, 425.

26. Thayer, *Greene*, p. 315; Tarleton, *Campaigns*, pp. 227–28; Johnson, *Greene*, 1: p. 416; Wickwire, *Cornwallis*, p. 284.

27. Tarleton, *Campaigns*, p. 228; Johnson, *Greene*, 1: p. 421.

28. Johnson, *Greene*, 1: pp. 429, 425–26; Thayer, *Greene*, p. 316.

29. Johnson, *Greene*, 1: pp. 428–31; Thayer, *Greene*, pp. 316–17; Johnson, *Greene*, 1: pp. 412–13; Graham, *Morgan*, pp. 395–96; Higginbotham, *Morgan*, pp. 152–55.

30. Thayer, *Greene*, p. 317; Lee, *Memoirs*, pp. 237–38; Johnson, *Greene*, 1: p. 435; Tarleton, *Campaigns*, pp. 228–29; Cornwallis to Germain, Mar. 17, 1781, BHP.

31. Thayer, *Greene*, pp. 317–18; Lee, *Memoirs*, pp. 238–39.

32. Lee, *Memoirs*, p. 238; Johnson, *Greene*, 1: pp. 238–39.

33. Cornwallis to Germain, Mar. 31, 1781, BHP; Ward, *Revolution*, 2: pp. 775–76; Lee, *Memoirs*, pp. 239–47. The quotation is on p. 244.

34. Greene, *Greene*, 3, pp. 172–73; Johnson, *Greene*, 1: p. 431; Ward, *Revolution*, 2: p. 776.

CHAPTER 11

1. Cornwallis to Germain, Mar. 17, 1781, BHP; Tarleton, *Campaigns*, pp. 230–31.

2. Tarleton, *Campaigns*, p. 232; Ward, *Revolution*, 2: pp. 778–79; Johnson, *Greene*, 1: p. 435.

3. Lee, *Memoirs*, p. 258; Thayer, *Greene*, pp. 322–23.

4. Greene to Pickens, Feb. 26, 1781, Johnson, *Greene*, 1: p. 457.

5. Tarleton, *Campaigns*, pp. 232–33; Seymour, *PMHB*, 7, p. 298.

6. Johnson, *Greene*, 1: pp. 444–45; Thayer, *Greene*, pp. 319–20; Jefferson to Greene, Feb. 19, 1781, Jefferson, *Papers*, ed. Boyd, 4: pp. 654–55; same to same, April 5, 1781, ibid., 5: p. 356; Greene to Jefferson, Apr. 6, 1781; ibid., pp. 360–61; same to same, April 28, 1781, ibid., pp. 567–69.

7. Ward, *Revolution*, 2: p. 780; Johnson, *Greene*, 1: pp. 438, 444; Thayer, *Greene*, 320–21; Ferguson, "Pickens," pp. 190–91.

8. Lee, *Memoirs*, p. 261; Thayer, *Greene*, pp. 321–22; Johnson, *Greene*, 1: pp. 448–49, 451–52.

9. Lee, *Memoirs*, p. 264; Tarleton, *Campaigns*, pp. 234–36.

10. Cornwallis to Germain, Mar. 17, 1781, BHP; Wickwire, *Cornwallis*, p. 446.

11. Tarleton, *Campaigns*, pp. 237–38; Lee, *Memoirs*, p. 267.

12. Thayer, *Greene*, pp. 326–27; Ward, *Revolution*, 2: pp. 784–85; Scheer and Rankin, *Rebels and Redcoats*, p. 512; Greene to Jefferson, Mar. 10, 1781, Jefferson, *Papers*, ed. Boyd, 5: pp. 111–12.

13. Cornwallis to Major Craig, Feb. 21, 1781, Cornwallis Papers; Cornwallis to Rawdon, Apr. 2, 1781, ibid.; Tarleton, *Campaigns*, pp. 270–71; Johnson, *Greene*, 2: p. 4; Lee, *Memoirs*, pp. 274–75; Ward, *Revolution*, 2: pp. 785–86; Johnson, *Greene*, 1: p. 425.

14. Lee, *Memoirs*, p. 275; Ward, *Revolution*, 2: pp. 785–86; Morgan to Greene, Feb. 20, 1781, Graham, *Morgan*, p. 370; Johnson, *Greene*, 2: p. 5; Ward, *Revolution*, 2: p. 784.

15. Johnson, *Greene*, 2: p. 6; Ward, *Revolution*, 2: pp. 784, 789–93.

16. Johnson, *Greene*, 2: p. 8; Ward, *Revolution*, 2: p. 787; Cornwallis to Clinton, Mar. 17, 1781, BHP; Lamb, *Journal*, p. 357.

17. David Schenck, *North Carolina, 1780–1781* (Raleigh, 1889), chap. 7; Lamb, *Journal*, p. 361; Schenck, *North Carolina*, pp. 350, 352.

18. Johnson, *Greene*, 2: pp. 8–9; Lee, *Memoirs*, pp. 277–78; Williams' casualty report, Mar. 17, 1781, quoted in Tarleton, *Campaigns*, p. 319.

19. Lee, *Memoirs*, p. 278; Ward, *Revolution*, 2: p. 788; Johnson, *Greene*, 2: p. 9.

20. Cornwallis to Germain, Mar. 17, 1781, BHP; Ward, *Revolution*, 2: p. 790; Johnson, *Greene*, 2: pp. 9–10; Lee, *Memoirs*, pp. 278–79.

21. Johnson, *Greene*, 2: pp. 9–10; Lee, *Memoirs*, p. 278; Ward, *Revolution*, 2: p. 790.

22. Johnson, *Greene*, 2: p. 11; Tarleton, *Campaigns*, p. 273; Ward, *Revolution*, 2: p. 791.

23. Ward, *Revolution*, 2: p. 791; Tarleton, *Campaigns*, p. 274; Johnson, *Greene*, 2: pp. 11–12; Thayer, *Greene*, p. 329; Tarleton, *Campaigns*, p. 275; Cornwallis to Germain, Mar. 17, 1781, BHP.

The two best witnesses to the battle are Light Horse Harry Lee (*Memoirs*) and Colonel John Eager Howard (quoted in Andrew A. Gunby, *Colonel John Gunby of the Maryland Continental Line* . . . [Cincinnati, 1902]). Lee was not on this part of the field, but he undoubtedly compared notes with other officers after the battle. Lee is often suspect when the Legion is involved, but otherwise he is a reliable witness.

Lee describes the order of battle and places the Maryland regiments on the left (p. 279). But when Webster advanced against the Continentals, he "approached its *right* wing. Here was posted the first regiment of Maryland . . ." (p. 279; italics added). This inconsistency is understandable if the arrangement was as it is in the sketch. He also notes that the counterattack of the 1st Maryland was "supported by Hawes's regiment of Virginia and Kirkwood's company of Delawares . . ." (p. 282). After Webster was driven back and had reformed, he "recrossed the ravine and attacked Hawes's regiment of Virginia supported by Kirkwood's company" (p. 282), indicating that these latter units may not have followed Washington and Howard in the flank attack on the Guards. Colonel Green's Virginia Continentals never got into this part of the action, probably because General Greene was holding them in reserve. Only after the retreat began did Green move to check the British pursuit (p. 282).

Howard says that the fight between Webster and the 1st Maryland was obscured by woods from Stuart and the Guards when they broke the 2nd Maryland. Howard, from higher ground, saw the opportunity and informed Gunby, who promptly attacked. Gunby's horse was shot down and Howard took direction of the regiment. Howard says that Washington's cavalry "first charged and broke the enemy. My men followed, and we passed through the Guards . . ." (Gunby, *Gunby*, pp. 50– 51).

24. Lee, *Memoirs*, p. 281; Tarleton, *Campaigns*, p. 276; Johnson, *Greene*, 2: pp. 16– 17 and note.

25. Thayer, *Greene*, pp. 329– 30; Johnson, *Greene*, 2: p. 15; Cornwallis to Germain, Mar. 17, 1781, BHP.

26. Judge Johnson, who had access to Greene's papers and who talked to many survivors of the war, gives the number of militia missing (*Greene*, 2: p. 18). Lee (*Memoirs*, p. 285) says the militia suffered a total of 17 killed and 60 wounded. Most sources, including Peckham (*Toll of Independence*, p. 82), agree that the loss of the Continentals was 78 killed and 183 wounded. Peckham estimates 1,000 total missing.

27. Ward, *Revolution*, 2: p. 793; Lee, *Memoirs*, p. 285; Tarleton, *Campaigns*, p. 276.

28. Greene, *Greene*, 3: p. 187; Thayer, *Greene*, p. 332; Greene to his wife, Mar. 16, 1781, Johnson, *Greene*, 2: p. 22.

29. Greene to Joseph Reed, Mar. 18, 1781, W. B. Reed, *Life and Correspondence of Joseph Reed*, 2 vols. (Philadelphia, 1847), 2: p. 351.

30. Cornwallis to Germain, Apr. 18, 1781, BHP.

CHAPTER 12

1. Johnson, *Greene*, 1: pp. 406– 07; Greene to Huger, Jan. 30, 1781, Greene Papers, CL.

2. Cornwallis to Germain, Mar. 17, 1781, BHP; Wickwire, *Cornwallis*, p. 309; Cornwallis to Clinton, Apr. 18, 1781, BHP.

3. Cornwallis to Germain, Mar. 17, 1781, BHP; Greene, *Greene*, 3: p. 206.

4. Cornwallis to Germain, Apr. 23, 1781, BHP; Cornwallis to Balfour, Apr. 24, 1781, Cornwallis Papers; Cornwallis to Clinton, Apr. 23, 1781, BHP; Cornwallis to Phillips, Apr. 24, 1781, Cornwallis Papers.

5. Cornwallis to Germain, Mar. 17, 1781, BHP; William Dickson to Robert Dixon, Nov. 30, 1784, James O. Carr, ed., *The Dickson Letters* (Raleigh, N. C., 1901), p. 15.

6. Greene, *Greene*, 3: p. 210.

7. Carr, ed., *Dickson Letters*, p. 15.

8. See Chapter 9, note 3.

9. Cornwallis to Phillips, Apr. 10, 1781, Cornwallis Papers; Greene to Lee, Apr. 4, 1781, Greene, *Greene*, 3: pp. 233– 34.

10. Lee, *Memoirs*, pp. 287– 90; Thayer, *Greene*, pp. 332– 34.

11. Greene to Sumter, Mar. 30, 1781, Draper Coll. 7, VV, p. 230.

12. Ferguson, "Pickens," pp. 195– 98.

13. Cornwallis to Phillips, Apr. 24, 1781, Cornwallis Papers.

14. Lee, *Memoirs*, pp. 330– 31; Marion to Greene, Apr. 23, 1781, Gibbes, ed., *Documentary History*, 3: pp. 57– 58.

15. Cornwallis to Phillips, Apr. 24, 1781, BHP.

16. Greene, *Greene*, 3: pp. 231– 33.

17. W. H. Wilkinson, *Some British Soldiers in America* (London, 1914), pp. 74– 83; *AR*, pp. 110– 11.

18. Greene, *Greene*, 3: pp. 239– 41; Ward, *Revolution*, 2: p. 803.

19. Davie, "Memoirs," quoted in Greene, *Greene*, 3: p. 265.

20. Kirkwood, *Journal and Orderly Book*, p. 16. This was about 90 miles more than the rest of the troops had marched.

21. Lee, *Memoirs*, p. 335.

22. Greene to Congress, Apr. [25?], 1781, Tarleton, *Campaigns*, p. 467.

23. The best primary sources for the battle of Hobkirk's Hill are Greene's report to Congress, ibid.; Lee, *Memoirs*, pp. 337– 40 (although Lee was not present at the battle); "Samuel Mathis to General W. R. Davie, June 16, 1819," in Benson J. Lossing, ed., *American Historical Record* (Philadelphia, 1873), 2: pp. 106– 09; Charles Stedman, *The History of the Origin, Progress and Termination of the American War* (London, 1794), 2: pp. 356– 58. Stedman was not present, but he was a member of Cornwallis' staff during the southern campaign and no doubt had access to Rawdon's dispatches. Secondary sources are Ward, *Revolution*, 2: chap. 75; Greene, *Greene*, 3; pp. 243– 50. The quotation is from Greene's report to Congress, Tarleton, *Campaigns*, p. 467.

24. Greene to Reed, July 6, 1781, Reed, *Reed*, 2: p. 362.

25. Greene, *Greene*, 3: p. 252.

26. Ibid., p. 250.

27. Davie, "Memoir," quoted in ibid., p. 253.

28. Ibid., p. 264.

29. Ibid., p. 273.

30. Peckham, ed., *Toll of Independence*, p. 85; Rawdon to Cornwallis, May 24, 1781, Stevens, ed., *Clinton-Cornwallis Controversy*, 1: pp. 482– 85.

31. Gregorie, *Sumter*, pp. 156– 57.

32. Lee, *Memoirs*, pp. 345– 49, 349n.

33. Gibbes, ed., *Documentary History*, 3: p. 59.

34. Lee, *Memoirs*, pp. 350– 52; Greene, *Greene*, 3: pp. 28– 81; Johnson, *Greene*, 2: pp. 121– 23. In my ed. of Lee pp are 2:81-83

35. Pickens to Greene, June 7, 1781, Gibbes, ed., *Documentary History*, 3: p. 91.

36. Lee, *Memoirs*, p. 370.

37. For the entire campaign around Augusta, May 23 to June 5, Lee, *Memoirs*, pp. 353– 70; Ferguson, "Pickens," pp. 209– 26.

38. Greene, *Greene*, 3: p. 253.

39. Rawdon to Clinton, May 24, 1781, BHP.

CHAPTER 13

1. Greene to Henry Knox, July 18, 1781, Thayer, *Greene*, p. 367.

2. Greene, *Greene*, 3: pp. 283– 89; Greene to Jefferson, Apr. 6, 1781, Jefferson Papers, McGregor Library, University of Virginia.

3. Greene to Jefferson, Apr. 28, 1781, Jefferson Papers, University of Virginia.

4. Thayer, *Greene*, p. 339.

5. Greene, *Greene*, 3: pp. 291– 94; Thayer, *Greene*, p. 355.

6. To Lee, Apr. 23, 1781, Greene, *Greene*, 3: pp. 256–57.

7. Ibid., pp. 295, 297.

8. Gregorie, *Sumter*, pp. 148–50; Sumter to Marion, Mar. 28, 1781, Gibbes, ed., *Documentary History*, 3: pp. 44–45; Richard Hampton to John Hampton, April 2, 1781, ibid., pp. 47–48; Greene, *Greene*, 3: p. 345.

9. Peckham, ed., *Toll of Independence*, p. 81; Gregorie, *Sumter*, pp. 136–43.

10. Attention is drawn to the behavior of General Horatio Gates at Camden. He had been wounded in the Seven Years' War and had never afterward been under fire until Camden. In the Civil War, General Richard Ewell's hesitancy on the first day of Gettysburg was uncharacteristic of this formerly aggressive lieutenant of Stonewall Jackson. Ewell had just returned to duty after having his leg amputated.

11. Greene, *Greene*, 3: p. 257.

12. Ibid., p. 266.

13. Ward, *Revolution*, 2: p. 817.

14. Boatner, *Encyclopedia of the Revolution*, pp. 310–11; Thayer, *Greene*, p. 357.

15. I know of no better account of the siege of Ninety Six than that contained in Kenneth Roberts, *Oliver Wiswell* (New York, 1940), pp. 667–724. The reader must, of course, be wary of the novelist's sympathetic treatment of the defenders. Also I can find no other reference to the tower similar to the Americans' Maham tower that Roberts had the defenders of the fort erect. Other secondary accounts are Ward, *Revolution*, 2: chap. 77; Greene, *Greene*, 3: pp. 301–16. Primary sources are Lee, *Memoirs*, pp. 371–78; Stedman, *American War*, 2: pp. 364–73. For the failure of Marion and Sumter, see Greene to Sumter, June 10, to Congress, June 20, and to Lafayette, June 23, 1781, Greene, *Greene*, 3: p. 311.

16. Ward, *Revolution*, 2: p. 822; Lee, *Memoirs*, p. 378.

17. Greene, *Greene*, 3: pp. 321–22.

18. Thayer, *Greene*, p. 362; Tarleton, *Campaigns*, p. 323; Balfour to Clinton, July 20, 1781, BHP.

19. O. H. Williams to Major Nathaniel Pendleton, July 16, 1781, Gibbes, ed., *Documentary History*, 3: pp. 105–06; Greene to Congress, July 17, 1781, Greene, *Greene*, 3: pp. 331–32.

20. Kirkwood, *Journal and Orderly Book*, pp. 19–20; Lee, *Memoirs*, p. 386.

21. Lee, *Memoirs*, p. 387; Kirkwood, *Journal and Orderly Book*, pp. 20–21.

22. Johnson, *Greene*, 2: pp. 168–77; Gregorie, *Sumter*, pp. 176–79; Lee, *Memoirs*, pp. 387–93; Greene, *Greene*, 3: p. 380.

23. Ward, *Revolution*, 2: pp. 825–26.

24. Ibid., pp. 826–27; Johnson, *Greene*, 2: p. 220.

25. Stewart's report to Cornwallis, Sept. 9, 1781, Gibbes, ed., *Documentary History*, 3: p. 137; Greene's report to Congress, ibid., pp. 141–44; account of Otho Holland Williams "with additions by Cols. W. Hampton, Polk, Howard, and Watt," ibid., pp. 144–58; Lee, *Memoirs*, pp. 466–74.

26. Lee, *Memoirs*, p. 468.

27. O. H. Williams to Major Nathaniel Pendleton, July 16, 1781, Gibbes, ed., *Documentary History*, 3: p. 150.

28. Ibid., p. 152.

29. Ibid., p. 154.

30. Ward, *Revolution*, 2: p. 834; Greene in Gibbes, ed., *Documentary History*, 3: p. 144, which includes only Continentals; Stewart in ibid., p. 139, probably reports

only the casualties of the regulars. He reports 224 missing, but Greene reported taking 400 prisoners (Peckham, ed., *Toll of Independence,* p. 290).

31. Greene, in Gibbes, ed., *Documentary History,* 3: pp. 143–44.

CHAPTER 14

1. Greene, *Greene,* 3: p. 275.

2. Thayer, *Greene,* p. 253.

3. Ward, *Revolution,* 2: p. 872; Marquis de Lafayette, *Memoirs, Correspondence, and Manuscripts,* published by his family, 4 vols. (New York, 1837), 1: p. 417.

4. Ward, *Revolution,* 2: pp. 873–74; Wickwire, *Cornwallis,* pp. 330–34.

5. Wickwire, *Cornwallis,* pp. 342–46; Scheer and Rankin, *Rebels and Redcoats,* pp. 543–45. Tarleton thought Cornwallis missed an opportunity to damage Lafayette (*Campaigns,* p. 356).

6. Clinton to Cornwallis, July 8, 1781, BHP.

7. Clinton to Phillips, Apr. 26, 1781, ibid.; see also Clinton to Phillips, Apr. 30, May 3, 1781, ibid. The plan was suggested by a Pennsylvania Loyalist, Colonel William Rankin. See George W. Kyte, "A Proposed Attack on Philadelphia, 1781," *PMHB,* 76 (1952): pp. 379–93.

8. Cornwallis to Clinton, May 26, 1781, BHP.

9. Germain to Clinton, May 2, 1781, ibid.

10. Germain to Cornwallis, June 2, 1781, ibid.

11. Cornwallis to Clinton, July 8, 1781, ibid.

12. Germain to Clinton, July 14, 1781, ibid.

13. Charles L. Lewis, *Admiral de Grasse and the American Revolution* (Annapolis, 1945), pp. 136–39; Mackesy, *War for America,* p. 419.

14. Lewis, *De Grasse,* pp. 140–41; Mackesy, *War for America,* pp. 419–20.

15. Freeman, *Washington,* 5: pp. 318–21; Clinton to Cornwallis, Aug. 31, 1781, with postscripts, Sept. 1, BHP; Willcox, *Clinton,* p. 418. Ward, *Revolution,* 2: p. 884.

16. Cornwallis to Clinton, Aug. 31, Sept. 1, 1781, BHP; Lewis, *De Grasse,* p. 142.

17. A full account of the battle of the Chesapeake Capes is in Lewis, *De Grasse,* chap. 16. See also Harold L. Larrabee, *Decision at the Chesapeake* (London, 1965), esp. chaps. 18–20.

18. Freeman, *Washington,* 5: pp. 340–41.

19. Wickwire, *Cornwallis,* pp. 360–63; Clinton to Cornwallis, Sept. 6, 1781, BHP; Tarleton, *Campaigns,* pp. 374–75.

20. Freeman, *Washington,* 5: pp. 513–15; Freeman discussed this factor in *Lee's Lieutenants: A Study in Command* (New York, 1942–45), 1: xxviii; 3: xxi. For the allied force see Ward, *Revolution,* 2: pp. 886–87 and Higginbotham, *War of Independence,* p. 382.

21. Clinton to Cornwallis, Sept. 24, 25, 30, Oct. 18, 1781, BHP.

22. Cornwallis to Clinton, Oct. 20, 1781, BHP.

23. *Quoted in Commager and Morris, eds., Spirit of 'Seventy-Six,* p. 1246, along with a commentary on the tradition surrounding the song.

24. Germain to Clinton, Mar. 3, 1781, BHP; Cornwallis to Germain, Apr. 18, 24,

1781, ibid.; Ian Christie, *The End of the North Ministry, 1780–1782* (London, 1958), pp. 263–64; *Parliamentary Register*, 3: pp. 536–42.

25. Christie, *North Ministry*, pp. 237–38.

26. Ibid., pp. 53–62.

27. Ibid., pp. 88–98.

28. Ibid., pp. 100–04.

29. Ibid., pp. 71, 190–94.

30. Mackesy, *War for America*, p. 460.

31. Christie, *North Ministry*, pp. 272–76; Mackesy, *War for America*, pp. 460–61.

32. Alan Valentine, *Lord North*, 2 vols. (Norman, Okla., 1967), 2: pp. 286–89; Fortescue, ed., *Writings of George III*, 5: no. 3485; Mackesy, *War for America*, pp. 463–66.

33. Valentine, *North*, 2: pp. 307–10; Mackesy, *War for America*, p. 469.

34. Valentine, *North*, 2: pp. 319–21; Mackesy, *War for America*, pp. 472–73.

35. Mackesy, *War for America*, pp. 474–77, 487–94.

36. Ward, *Revolution*, 2: pp. 836–37.

37. Thayer, *Greene*, p. 383; Greene to Captain Joseph Eggleston, Oct. 21, 1781, quoted in ibid., p. 384.

38. Ibid., p. 385; Gregorie, *Sumter*, p. 88.

39. Ward, *Revolution*, 2: p. 838; Thayer, *Greene*, pp. 385–88.

40. Ward, *Revolution*, 2: pp. 839–40; Thayer, *Greene*, pp. 391–92; Greene, *Greene*, 3: pp. 425–26.

41. Greene, *Greene*, 3: p. 428; George Washington, *Writings*, ed. Jared Sparks, 12 vols. (New York, 1858), 8: p. 323.

42. Thayer, *Greene*, pp. 389–93; Gregorie, *Sumter*, p. 195.

43. Greene, *Greene*, 3: pp. 434–39.

44. Thayer, *Greene*, pp. 388–89.

45. Greene, *Greene*, 3: pp. 452–54; Lee, *Memoirs*, p. 426; Thayer, *Greene*, p. 401.

46. Thayer, *Greene*, pp. 406–09.

CONCLUSION

1. *Parliamentary Register*, 3: pp. 536–42.

2. Christie, *North Ministry*, p. 269.

3. Tarleton, *Campaigns*, pp. 230–31; for a full account of British Loyalist policy, see Smith, *Loyalists and Redcoats*.

4. Greene to Sumter, Jan. 8, 1781, Greene Papers, LC.

5. Theodore White, *In Search of History: A Personal Adventure* (New York, 1978), p. 86.

✳ ✳ ✳ Essay on Sources ✳ ✳ ✳

Anyone who writes about the history of the War of Independence should have within arm's reach several nearly indispensable tools. These are Mark M. Boatner III, *Encyclopedia of the American Revolution* (1966), a comprehensive compendium of people and events, with excellent accompanying maps; Howard Peckham, editor, *The Toll of Independence: Engagements & Battle Casualties of the American Revolution* (1974), which lists virtually every clash of arms between British and American forces, large and small, with authoritative figures for American casualties, and, in many cases, for the British also; Henry Steele Commager and Richard Morris, editors, *The Spirit of 'Seventy-Six: The Story of the Revolution as Told by Participants* (1975), valuable not only for its source material but also for its excellent bibliography; George F. Scheer and Hugh F. Rankin, *Rebels and Redcoats* (1957), which also contains an excellent bibliography along with a narrative of the war. There is a great deal of printed source material, some of which first appeared during the centennial celebration in the nineteenth century as well as during the recent bicentennial. An excellent guide to this "eyewitness" history is Charles Lesser and J. Todd White, editors, *Fighters for Independence* (1977).

Research in manuscript sources leads sooner or later to the William L. Clements Library in Ann Arbor, Michigan. Here are the fine collections of the papers of Sir Henry Clinton, Lord George Germain, and General Nathanael Greene. The other principal manuscript sources used for this book were the Sir Guy Carleton Papers, more familiarly known as the British Headquarters Papers, held by Colonial Williamsburg and available on microfilm; The Cornwallis Papers, Library of Congress, which are transcripts from the British Public Record Office 30/11, also available on microfilm.

As indicated above, an enormous amount of material has found its way into print. Many of the pertinent items from the British Headquarters Papers were reproduced by Benjamin F. Stevens, editor, *The Campaign in Virginia 1781: An Exact Reprint of Six Rare Pamphlets on the Clinton-Cornwallis Controversy with very Numerous Important unpublished notes by Sir Henry Clinton, K.B . . .* (2 vols., 1890). George W. Greene, in his *Life of Nathanael Greene, General in the Army of the American Revolution* (3 vols., 1867–71), reproduced a wealth of Greene's correspondence. I have not hesitated to use this material since, in instances where I could check with the original, I found him to be scrupulously accurate, except for some changes in punctuation. Other printed sources that were especially valuable were Sir Henry Clinton, *The American Rebellion: Sir Henry Clinton's Narrative of His Campaigns, 1775–1782*, edited by William B. Willcox (1954), which reveals perhaps as much about the author as it does about the campaigns. Banastre Tarleton, *A History of the Campaigns of 1780 and 1781 in the Southern Provinces of North America* (1787), must, of course, be used with caution, but he includes many valuable documents. The same cautionary note applies to Henry (Light Horse Harry) Lee, *Memoirs of the War in the Southern Department of the United States* (1869). I have used the edition prepared by Lee's distinguished son, Robert E. Lee.

Of the many accounts by participants I found the following most valuable, principally because they struck me as being straightforward, without any of the self-serving vanity that characterized some of the eyewitnesses. These were ordinary men in the ranks, who did not especially enjoy soldiering and who admitted on occasion that they were scared to death: [James P. Collins,] *Autobiography of a Revolutionary Soldier* (1859); R[oger] Lamb (that imperturbable redcoat), *An Original and Authentic Journal of Occurrences in the Late American War* (1809); Joseph Plumb Martin, *Private Yankee Doodle, Being a Narrative of Some of the Adventures, Dangers, and Sufferings of a Revolutionary Soldier*, edited by George F. Scheer (1962); William Seymour, "Journal . . ." *Pennsylvania Magazine of History and Biography*, 7 (1783); and Thomas Young, "Memoir of Thomas Young," *Orion* (~~1843~~).

Of the general histories of the war I relied most heavily on Christopher Ward, *The War of the Revolution*, edited by John R. Alden (2 vols., 1952), and Don Higginbotham, *The War of American Independence: Military Attitudes, Policies, and Practices, 1763–1789* (1971). Piers Mackesy, *The War for America, 1775–1783* (1965), tells the story from the point of view of British policymakers who directed the war and is especially helpful in understanding the conflict in its European context, as well as describing the failure of English sea power.

The most detailed account of the war in the South is Edward McCrady, *History of South Carolina in the Revolution* (2 vols., 1902). McCrady and many of the earlier historians were sometimes guilty of florid language and seemingly lacked the objectivity of "modern" scholars, but they were painstaking in their research, and their exhaustive treatment of their subjects helped to fill many gaps.

There are biographical studies of most of the principals of the war in the South. Most useful were William Willcox, *Portrait of a General: Sir Henry Clinton in the War of Independence, 1775–1782* (1964); Franklin and Mary Wickwire, *Cornwallis: The American Adventure* (1970); Theodore Thayer, *Nathanael Greene, Strategist of the Revolution* (1960); George W. Greene, *Greene*; William Johnson, *Sketches of the Life and Correspondence of Nathanael Greene* (2 vols., 1822); Hugh F. Rankin, *Francis Marion: The Swamp Fox* (1973); Don Higginbotham, *Daniel Morgan, Frontier Rifleman* (1961); and Clyde R. Ferguson, "General Andrew Pickens" (dissertation, Duke University, 1960).

Special studies that were indispensable to an understanding of their subjects were Robert Barnwell, Jr., "Loyalism in South Carolina, 1765–1785" (dissertation, Duke University, 1941); Edward E. Curtis, *The Organization of the British Army in the American Revolution* (1926); Lyman C. Draper, *King's Mountain and Its Heroes: A History of the Battle of King's Mountain, October 7, 1780* (1871), which contains a mass of information about the war in the backcountry and includes pertinent documents; Harold L. Peterson, *The Book of the Continental Soldier, being a compleat account of the uniforms, weapons, and equipment with which he lived and*

[handwritten marginal notes:]
E208. L21
E275. M28
E207. 59 G74
The† (Nov 43]
100 – 108
.3 (oct 1843) ; 84–88 &

[handwritten note at bottom:]
p. 86 At Kg's Mt the only distinguishing marks
were patriots wore paper in their hats
loyalists wore pine knots.

fought (1968); Peterson, *Round Shot and Rammers* (1969). Paul H. Smith, *Loyalists and Redcoats* (1964), is perhaps the most insightful study of the failure of British Loyalist policy.

Finally, I would be remiss if I did not mention John Shy, *A People Numerous and Armed* (1976), which provided much food for thought and sent me down some roads that I surely would not otherwise have traveled.

✳ ✳ ✳ Index ✳ ✳ ✳

ABOUT THE AUTHOR

John S. Pancake is Professor of History, The University of Alabama. He received his B.A. from Hampden-Sydney College and his M.A. and Ph.D. from the University of Virginia. He is author of *Samuel Smith and the Politics of Business* (1972), *Jefferson and Hamilton* (1974), *Thomas Jefferson, Revolutionary Philosopher: A Selection of Writings* (1976), and *1777: The Year of the Hangman* (1977).

Check

Richard Pearis (in W.F. biogs)

accuracy of artillery
the difference between grapeshot, caseshot & canister
Were S.C. state docs discovered at Monk's Corner.

p201 (anecdote re surrender of Ft Granby)   SC *Royal Gaz* 30/5/81

an elderly gent. c. 70 yrs of age who resided in the interior part of this
province, finding his situation disagreeable, that it necessary to retire for
security into the garrison at Congaree [Ft Granby] under the command of
Major Maxwell [of PofW Vols], where he remained until it surrendered. When
the garrison was marched out & carried to some distance, as the old gent
with another prisoner was passing, one of the rebel party from behind a tree
fired his piece & killed them both. On complaint being made & some
investigation of the matter it appeares that one Wadehampton, by giving
some rum, procured the villain to commit that horrid act, for some
resentment he bore the old gent.

p 93. The Br. under Cornwallis try to form Loyalist Associations in imitation of the American model.

Jane Dysart

Quoted Axtell on ethnohistory

No good any more regarding Indians as pawns in a European chessgame. Indians had their own sensible diplomacy

No European power was concerned with welfare of Indians

Sp. missions were devices to consolidate territorial grip.

Creeks were wary of all Whites.

They preferred Eng because they knew trade goods came from

Amy Bushnell discussed the protectorate pueblos in Sp. Florida

The Indians in them eventually lost their respect for the church & their own heritage or became Latinos, forgetting or trying to forget they were Indians.

Kathryn Braund

Allen Gallay discussed Jonathan Bryan (Georgia politician)

KB Questioned his interpretations of Creek treaties 1763-1773

KB: did not regard British as threat in 1763. They did not
 ^Creeks know they were in decline. Also the Br. did not police the frontiers efficiently. The Creeks looked to Br to help them keep the crackers under control.

Bryan obtained 1773 a large tract from Creeks as a leasehold.
Gov. Wright repudiated the deal. KB suggest Gallay investigate Spalding or Kelsall's firm or so stores.

The Bryan leases were never approved by any Creek council.
Important town Coweta did not sign.

K.B. suggests that it was Bryan who was duped. Maybe the Indians who wanted trade goods knew that the leases wd be repudiated.

SHA meeting, New Orleans, 13/11/87